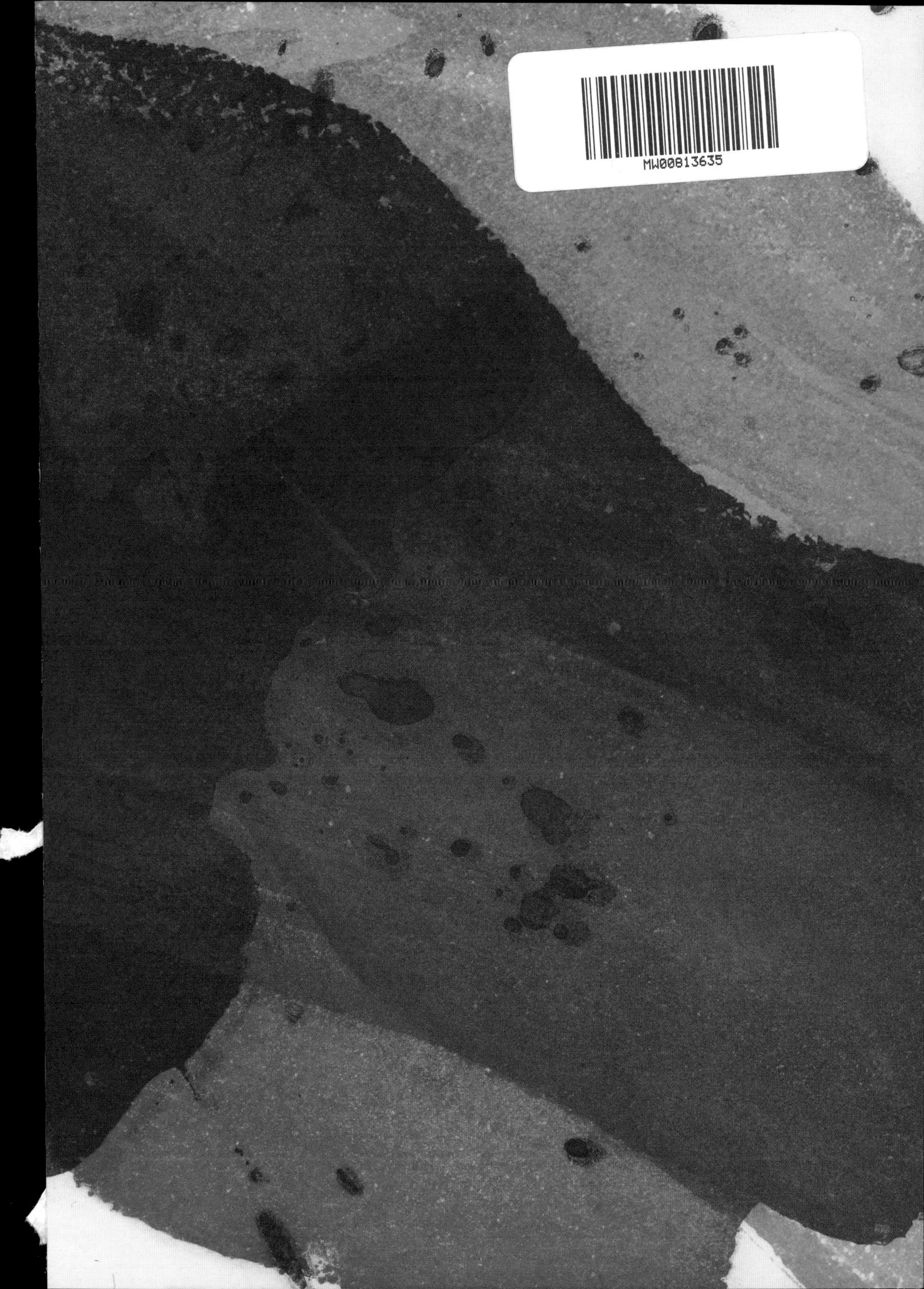

THE PRIVATE LIFE OF

LORD BYRON

THE PRIVATE LIFE OF

LORD BYRON

ANTONY PEATTIE

First published in 2019

Unbound
6th Floor Mutual House, 70 Conduit Street, London W1S 2GF
www.unbound.com

Text Design by Ellipsis

A CIP record for this book is available from the British Library

ISBN 978-1-78352-426-6 (hardback)
ISBN 978-1-78352-427-3 (ebook)

Printed in China by 1010 Printing International Ltd

In memory of Howard Hodgkin

6 August 1932 – 9 March 2017

Photograph Terence Donovan, 9 October 1990
© Terence Donovan Archive

Endpaper artwork: Howard Hodgkin, For Antony *(detail), 260 x 420 mm, 5.1.2015: an etching on three copper plates, two with sugar lift, Vert Solide/ Titanium white mix and Ruby Madder/Rubis red mix and one dry on dry, Ultramarine Blue.* For Antony *was printed in an edition of 100 with 10 Artist's Proofs, made by Andrew Smith and Jane Smith at Andrews Print Works, Dorset and published by Alan Cristea Gallery, 43 Pall Mall, London SW1Y 5JG. Sales of the print made it possible to illustrate this book. See further, www.howard-hodgkin.com.*

What would Byron have thought?
'He expressed a settled determination never to take any steps towards forming a collection of pictures, or any other works of art; he said, that all dealers in pictures, etc made a strong push to get every young man of rank and fortune, when he first entered into public life, into their snares, that they might make him their dupes & plunder him of his property.' Timothy Sheldrake, 'On Distortions of the Feet: Lord Byron's Case', Lancet, *(Vol. 10, issue 264, 20 September 1828, 779). Sheldrake, an expert on the topic, published* A Practical Essay on the Club-Foot *in 1798 and was consulted by Byron on his disability.*

By setting things in their right point of view,
Knowledge, at least, is gained
John Johnson to Don Juan, *Don Juan*, V, 23

Byron's attention to food anticipates the new formalist criticism of recent years by impelling the reader into pleasure in formal texture and applying the brakes of a historicist critique.
Jane Stabler, 'Byron's World of Zest', Timothy Morton, ed., *Cultures of Taste/ Theories of Appetite: Eating Romanticism*, 2004, 141[†]

† To see further how contemporary critical theory can be applied to Byron studies, Jane Stabler, ed., *Byron*, 1998 and *Palgrave Advances in Byron Studies*, 2007.

OPPOSITE PAGE: *Byron commissioned this silver urn from Samuel Hennell in 1811 and gave it to the poet and novelist Walter Scott in 1815. Byron had attacked Scott six years before in his furious early satire* English Bards and Scotch Reviewers: *'I had my share of flagellation among my betters,' Scott remarked tolerantly. Scott was an Elder in the Presbyterian Church, a Freemason and a founder of the Tory* Quarterly Review. *The poets became friends, in spite of differences in age, politics and religion. Scott could have been one of Byron's mentors, as he was seventeen years older and the younger poet 'invariably mentioned him with almost filial respect and reverence'. Byron called Scott 'the most wonderful writer of the day' and claimed to have read all his novels at least fifty times. They shared a Scottish background and a passionate interest in heroism. At the end of Byron's life, when he was dedicating himself heroically to the Greeks' struggle for independence, his letters refer repeatedly to Scott's novels. The writers substantiated their common interest in heroism with an act in the epic tradition: 'Like the old heroes in Homer,' Scott wrote, 'we exchanged gifts: – I gave Byron a beautiful dagger mounted with gold, which had been the property of the redoubted Elfi Bey [Muhammad Al Alfi, the heroic Mameluke Chief, who visited London in 1803].'*

Scott gives an oriental dagger to the writer of Orientalist tales; Byron gives the Gothic Scott a neo-classical funerary urn. 'We had a good deal of laughing,' Scott remembered, 'on what the public might be supposed to think or say, concerning the gloomy and ominous nature of our mutual gifts.'

Byron's strikingly munificent present was 'a large sepulchral vase of silver. It was full of dead men's bones, and had inscriptions on two sides of the base.' One ran thus: 'The bones contained in this urn were found in certain ancient sepulchers within the land walls of Athens, in the month of February, 1811.' The other face bears the lines of Juvenal:

Expende – quote libras in duce summon invenies. – Mors sola fatetur quantula hominum corpuscular. Jun. x. 39, 40

Here Byron chose to link two separate passages from Juvenal's Tenth Satire: in the first the poet asks, "Weigh Hannibal: how many pounds will you find in that supreme general?" Byron cited these words in a note to Childe Harold *II, 89, evoking Marathon, the battle where outnumbered Greeks turned back the Persian invaders in 490* BC. *For £900 Byron could have bought this archetypal site of heroic resistance. He later resorts to the quotation to express his disappointment in his fallen hero, Napoleon.*

Byron also added Juvenal's words from thirty lines later to the other side of the base: 'Death alone shows how insignificant are the puny bodies of men'. Their meaning goes to the heart of Byron's attitude to spiritual as opposed to physical reality, a discrepancy experienced by both lame poets, one of the central themes of Byron's work, his life and this book.

Image courtesy of the Faculty of Advocates,
Abbotsford Collection Trust

CONTENTS

MORE HORRORS

AUTHOR'S NOTE

All quotations from Byron's letters and journals are taken from Leslie A. Marchand, ed., *Byron's Letters and Journals*, 13 vols, 1973–94, identified in the notes by date and recipient and reproduced by kind permission of the publisher, John Murray.

All quotations from Byron's poems are taken from Jerome J. McGann, ed., *Lord Byron: The Complete Poetical Works*, 6 vols, 1980 and reproduced by permission of the publishers, Oxford University Press.†

Quotations from historical sources reproduce the spelling and grammar of the original texts.

This book builds on the foundations of many scholars. To avoid littering the text with too many names and spare the reader endless repetitions, the sources of all quotations and important references are given in the notes at the end.

† cf. Peter Cochran, 'Byron and the Politics of Editing,' Jane Stabler, ed., *Byron Studies*, 2007, 34–59.

INTRODUCTION

Byron was thirty-six when he died in 1824. Yet the autopsy recorded that his brain and his liver were those of an old man. He lived his life with such intensity that verdict seems apt. His poetry fills eight volumes; his bisexual love life encompassed a choirboy at Cambridge and a pageboy in Greece, as well as 200 women in less than two years in Venice; he committed himself actively to radical politics and died in the attempt to free Greece from Ottoman rule. How to cover all that in a biography? It took Leslie Marchand three volumes in 1957. Since then scholarly new editions of Byron's letters and journals, poetry and prose as well as dozens of specialist studies have illuminated Byron's relationships with his family, his lovers and his contemporaries; his time at school; in Greece; in London; in Geneva; in Italy; his politics; his medical history; his accounts; his relationship to Orientalism, the Gothic, Romanticism. . .

Marchand claimed in his biography that he had 'no thesis' and 'consciously avoided formulating one'. This book approaches Byron from a different angle. It aims to see Byron's world and his work through his eyes in order to understand him better. As a 'partial portrait' it explores some neglected or misunderstood, marginal aspects of his private life in order to cast new light on other, central areas, such as his heroic ideal and its relation to Napoleon. Every age rewrites the biography of Lord Byron to reflect current concerns, as Marchand pointed out in 1957. At least nine recent studies have focused on Byron's public life and afterlife, Byronism and Byromania. That's surely more than enough about celebrity.

Considering his diet, what he ate, what he didn't eat, when and why, yields insights into Byron's love life and his intentions in his masterpiece, *Don Juan*.

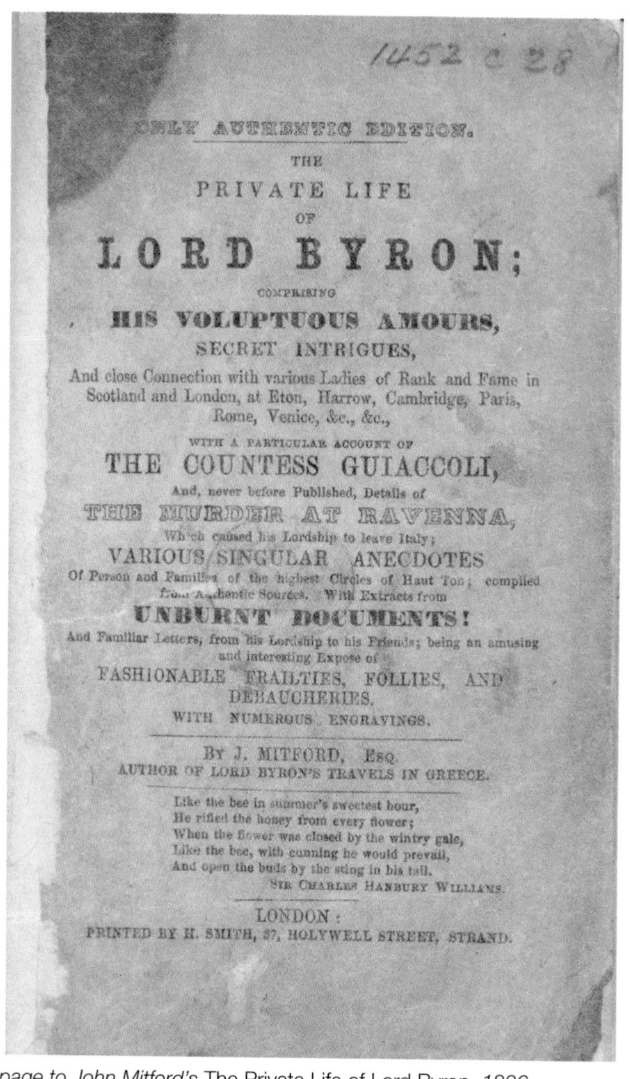

ONLY AUTHENTIC EDITION.

THE
PRIVATE LIFE
OF
LORD BYRON;
COMPRISING
HIS VOLUPTUOUS AMOURS,
SECRET INTRIGUES,
And close Connection with various Ladies of Rank and Fame in Scotland and London, at Eton, Harrow, Cambridge, Paris, Rome, Venice, &c., &c.,
WITH A PARTICULAR ACCOUNT OF
THE COUNTESS GUIACCOLI,
And, never before Published, Details of
THE MURDER AT RAVENNA,
Which caused his Lordship to leave Italy;
VARIOUS SINGULAR ANECDOTES
Of Person and Families of the highest Circles of Haut Ton; compiled from Authentic Sources. With Extracts from
UNBURNT DOCUMENTS!
And Familiar Letters, from his Lordship to his Friends; being an amusing and interesting Expose of
FASHIONABLE FRAILTIES, FOLLIES, AND DEBAUCHERIES.
WITH NUMEROUS ENGRAVINGS.

BY J. MITFORD, ESQ.
AUTHOR OF LORD BYRON'S TRAVELS IN GREECE.

Like the bee in summer's sweetest hour,
He rifled the honey from every flower;
When the flower was closed by the wintry gale,
Like the bee, with cunning he would prevail,
And open the buds by the sting in his tail.
SIR CHARLES HANBURY WILLIAMS.

LONDON:
PRINTED BY H. SMITH, 37, HOLYWELL STREET, STRAND.

The title page to John Mitford's The Private Life of Lord Byron, *1826. Mitford claimed, falsely, that he 'was long a companion of the noble lord, and if I am not able to paint his private life truly, there is no other alive that can'. His book was extravagantly inaccurate and not just about Byron's amours:* Beppo, *for example, was 'originally written in Italian and rendered into English by his lordship, at his country seat on the island of Santa Mura'; Teresa Guiccioli came with Byron to Greece, where he died in her arms, shortly after asking for chocolate, 'of which he was very fond.'*

Recently, writers on Byron's private life have tended to focus on his bisexuality. This book explores two other areas (which may be related to one another): his intermittent eating disorder and his obsession with fatherhood.

The first half of this book traces patterns of behaviour that began in childhood and recurred throughout Byron's life.

The rest of the book follows chronology from 1809 to 1824 to explore the ways in which Byron's adult affairs with women (love) and his relations with men (glory) affected both his private life and his work.

There are so many books devoted to Byron that it seems fair to let the reader know where this one says anything new. In the Contents pages I follow the example of Stella Gibbons in *Cold Comfort Farm*: she used one, two or three stars to grade her favourite passages of 'Literature'.

PART I

BISCUITS AND SODA WATER

Byron's friend Elizabeth Pigot recorded aspects of his life at Southwell, when he was nineteen, in a series of sketches, 'The Wonderful History of Lord Byron & His Dog, 1807'. Here, the page opposite the illustration records: 'He went into the Bath, to boil off his Fat/And when he was there Bo'sun worried a Cat'. Boatswain was Byron's Newfoundland dog.

Harry Ransom Center, The University of Texas at Austin

I

BYRON'S FIRST DIET, 1807

The Wish'd for Effect

George Gordon Byron, 6th Baron Byron of Rochdale, went on a diet in January 1807 when he was nearly nineteen.

He was only 5 feet 8½ inches tall (1.74 m) but early in 1807 he weighed 14 stones 6 pounds (91.63 kg).

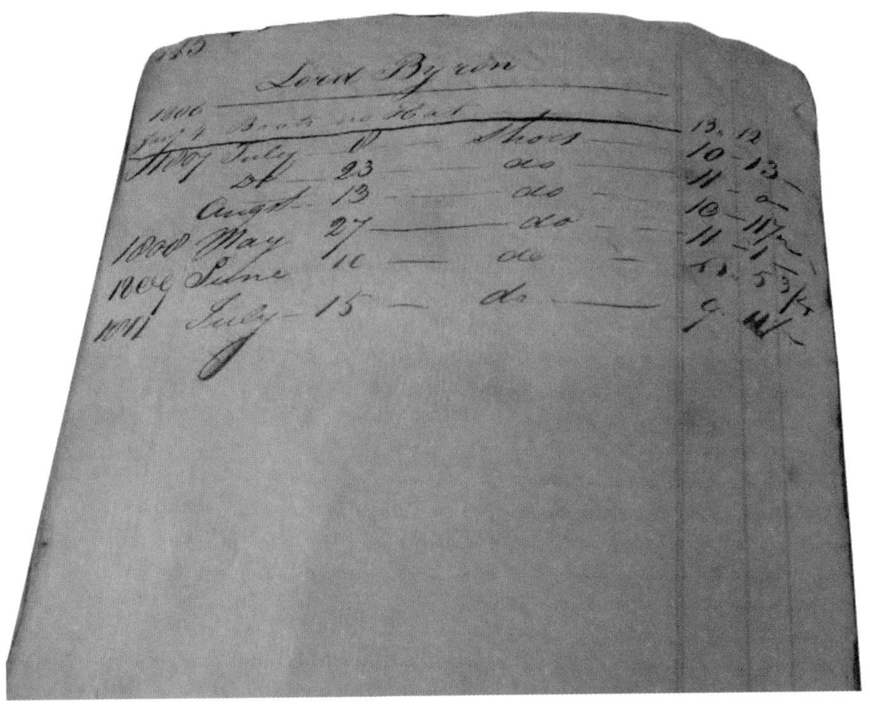

Byron's changing weight, recorded in the ledger kept by his wine merchants, Berry Bros of St James's.

Founded in 1698, Berry Bros sold coffee at 3 St James's (hence the coffee mill on their shop sign), before they became wine merchants. The large scales for weighing coffee were then used to weigh customers, such as Byron.

Photo: Matthew Burdis

Given Byron's weight and height, our modern Body Mass Index registers obesity and recommends tersely, 'should lose weight'.

Fat as a child, he grew into a plump adolescent. Mr Baillie, who knew him in Aberdeen, which Byron left when he was ten, failed to recognise him in Cambridge, because he 'had then grown so fat'. A month after he went up to Trinity College, in October 1805 at the age of seventeen, Byron grew self-conscious about his appearance. The family lawyer called him jolly, which annoyed him. Like 'ruddy', 'robust' (or the Byronic 'robustious'), 'jolly' meant fat. Byron corrected the mistake in the first letter that he wrote from Cambridge to his half-sister Augusta on 6 November 1805: 'that fool Hanson in his *vulgar Idiom*, by the word Jolly did not mean Fat, but High Spirits'. Byron had himself weighed regularly and reported that, far from 'increasing', he managed to lose one pound (0.45 kg) in a fortnight. The man who notices that he has lost one pound obviously cares about it and is concerned to change his shape. However, Byron did nothing about it for a year. On 4 January 1806, wearing boots but no hat, he weighed 13 stones 12 pounds (88 kg).

His self-consciousness reflected wider concerns about his identity.

In 1806 he prepared his first volume of poetry for (private) publication. *Fugitive Pieces* showed off exercises in borrowed forms, as Byron experimented with styles borrowed from authors he admired, such as Alexander Pope, Thomas Campbell, Thomas Moore and Scott.

He demonstrated the same delight in speaking with different voices that August, when he acted the principal roles in two plays that were staged in Southwell, the town near Nottingham where Mrs Byron rented a house, while Newstead Abbey was let to a tenant. As the hero of Richard Cumberland's *The Wheel of Fortune*, Byron played a misanthrope, Roderick Penruddock, who bears 'the mark of Cain, the stamp of cruelty' imprinted on his forehead. Penruddock's conversion to sensibility makes him less Byronic: Byron's heroes resemble Cain, but never convert to sensibility.

In John Till Allingham's comedy *The Weathercock* Byron played Tristram Fickle, who considers various careers entirely according to their costume, convinced that his inability to make up his mind demonstrates 'the versatility of my genius'. There were obvious parallels between this hero and Byron himself, such as mobility of temperament and a fascination with costumes. 'Regimentals are the best travelling dress,' he announced in the 'Additional Note, on the Turks', that he attached to *Childe Harold* II. He told his mother on 12 November 1809 that, to meet the Albanian ruler Ali Pasha, he 'dressed in a full suit of Staff uniform with a very magnificent sabre &c'.

It is striking how often Byron in his portraits wears a costume that amounts to a uniform (of his own invention). In 1813, preparing to go abroad again, he ordered 'a superfine scarlet staff uniform trimmed with rows of gold twist buttons, fifty-eight in number – embroidering the buttonholes cost £15. 19s. – twenty-five yards of gold lacing, a scarlet sash for seven guineas, a pair of "Very rich Gold Epaulettes" for £33 1s. 1d. and a great many extras and accessories', such as gold bullion knots, embroidered belts, crimson cords and gilt gorgets.

In 1806 Byron's Southwell friend Elizabeth Pigot, whom he called his 'only *rational* companion', addressed him as Tristram Fickle. Thomas

Moore, Byron's friend and first biographer, suggested that 'the gloom of Penruddock and the whim of Tristram' represented types 'of the two extremes, between which [Byron's] own character, in after-life, so singularly vibrated'. However, his most characteristic moment, that anticipates the role he adopted in his poetry as an outsider/satirist, came between the plays, when he joined the audience and watched an interlude. It commemorated General Sir Ralph Abercrombie, who died slowly of his wounds, having defeated the French at Alexandria, on 21 March 1801. The general, 'sinking into the outstretched arms of his two friends, warbled out his dying words in a style which convulsed Byron with laughter'. Byron's refusal to empathise anticipates the way his Narrator behaves in *Don Juan*.

The autumn of 1806 was a stressful period for him in that it preceded that 'hazardous experiment', which caused him '*sundry palpitations*': the publication of his first publicly available book of poems, which he called, defensively, *Hours of Idleness*.

Byron consulted his Southwell doctor Benjamin Hutchinson about his obesity in the autumn of 1806. Hutchinson's prescription of 19 November is transcribed from the doctor's manuscript in the John Murray Archive and published complete for the first time:

> Mr Hutchinson judges it to be essentially requisite that Lord Byron should arise every morning at 8 o'clock, and take a walk of three or four or *more* miles, and a repetition of Exercise in the Course of the Day would materially conduce to the production of the wish'd for effect.
>
> Abstinence from Malt liquor of *every* Description should be most scrupulously attended to.
>
> Animal food [i.e. meat] ought to be taken only once in the Day, and at Meals nothing but Imperial (Cream of) Tartar or water should be drunk, the Quantity of Animal Food to be rather in a *limited* than in an excessive degree.
>
> Two Glasses of Port may be drunk after Dinner but no white wine: nor any Supper should be taken except a biscuit and a glass of water or Imperial.

The tepid Bath may be used three times a week at the Temperature of 90 or 100 degrees of Fahr: the time of bathing about noon, Exerxise [*sic*] is recommended after the immersion. One of the powders is to be taken twice or three times a day mixed in nearly half a pint of Water.

These directions ought to be immediately attended to for the space of three months, with such Variations as may from time to time be deemed necessary.

The principal ingredient of 'Imperial' was cream of tartar, purified and crystallised bitartrate of potassium, an acid salt with diuretic and laxative properties. This was the first of many occasions when Byron resorted to such means.

One biographer has suggested that Dr Hutchinson was treating a venereal disease. But the full text of the prescription and, in particular, its promise that taking long daily walks will produce 'the wish'd for effect' makes that seem unlikely.

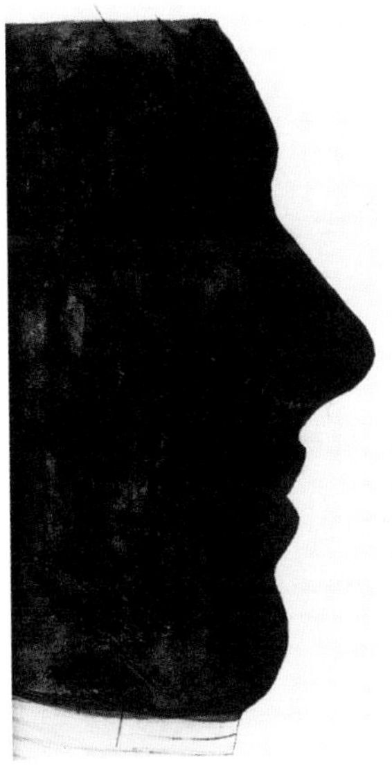

John Nicholson, a silhouette, inscribed, 'A profile of Lord Byron, drawn in the gaiety of the moment, when he was at Southwell April 1807. This is a plain likeness of a handsome man but as it is impossible to look at it without being reminded of Ld Byron it is valuable.' It was bound for Elizabeth Pigot into a volume reuniting the four cantos of Childe Harold *and was sold by Sotheby's on 14 December 1989.*
Private collection

'His form it was stout,' Byron noted eleven days later in a brief self-portrait, adding, 'and his shoulders were broad.'

Despite his concern about his weight, Byron did not start to diet until the New Year. He celebrated his birthday on the 22nd, so January always seemed a propitious time for new initiatives in his life. In 1807 he acted with rather more rigour than his doctor had advised. He boasted to Hanson on 2 April 1807 that he took 'every means' to lose weight, principally 'violent exercise, & Fasting'. He ran and played cricket while wearing '*seven* Waistcoats, & a great Coat . . . till quite exhausted by excessive perspiration'; he used 'the hot Bath daily', when normal Englishmen did not. At a time when those of his countrymen who could afford to, ate meat at most meals, he limited his intake to 'only a quarter of [a] pound [113.4 g], [of] Butchers meat in 24 hours'. He ate 'no Suppers, or Breakfast, only one meal a Day', and drank 'no malt Liquor, [only?] little wine'. And Byron did not stop after three months. In the same letter he admitted that he also took 'physic occasionally' – meaning laxatives again. Hanson warned him 'against all those violent and extreme modes of reducing your weight' – to no effect.

In three months Byron lost 18 pounds (8.16 kg). His clothes had to be 'taken in nearly *half* a *yard*', he told Hanson on 2 April 1807. Two weeks later he assured his Harrow friend Edward Noel Long that he would continue his 'System' until he weighed 12 stones (76.2 kg) and he would 'always live temperately and take much exercise'. On 14 May he revised his target, telling Long that he had determined to settle at 11 stones (69.8 kg) '& there stop . . . one month will effect this,' he presumed, 'with the assistance of a great coat, 8 Waistcoats, flannel Bandages, daily Physic, no Ale, one meal a Day, & the Hot Bath.'

At the beginning of 1807 his debts forced him to stay with his mother in Southwell, 'this *Crater* of Dullness . . . this *Abode* of *Darkness*'. The previous summer he had escaped by running away to London. But now, unable to pay his college expenses, he could not even go back to Cambridge.

He did not, indeed he could not, stop starving himself. He lost 4 stones in weight (25.4 kg). Back at Trinity College, Cambridge in June, his face

Elizabeth Pigot's sketch: 'He went out to cricket to make himself thinner/And when he came back, he found him at Dinner', dated 26 March 1807.

Harry Ransom Center, The University of Texas at Austin

and his figure were 'of such *preter-natural* Longitude' that some of his friends failed to recognise him. His choirboy lover John Edleston seemed 'thunderstruck at the alteration'.

Byron was overweight at eighteen, in fact obese, but his dieting outlived necessity. He continued to lose weight even after joining what he told Elizabeth Pigot on 13 July was London's 'perpetual vortex of dissipation'. In the summer of 1807 he found that he now weighed considerably less than 11 stones (69.85 kg). That meant he was 'at least 14 LB [6.35 kg] below the *Fashion*'. 'However I *decrease* instead of enlarging.' Dandyism was evidently not Byron's prime motivator. As he did not engage in any '*violent* exercise in London', he attributed the '*phenomenon* to our *Evening squeezes*, at public & private parties'. But his starvation diet had more to do with it. It set a pattern that endured, as contemporary witnesses over the next nine years repeatedly confirmed.

We need to look back in order to understand what brought on his eating disorder. According to his long-term mistress Teresa Guiccioli, 'Lord Byron attached great importance to childhood influences in character training.'

PART II

CHILDHOOD INFLUENCES, 1788–1807

'An engine-turned tortoiseshell snuff-box, gold-mounted, with a miniature of Byron in the lid, signed P. N. 1795', when Byron was seven.

Photo: Harrow School and the Harrow School Archive

2

TENDER PARENTS

Lord Byron interests us more and more. . . It is sad to see a naturally fine mind ruined by early ill treatment from his parents &c.

Mary Loveday to Penelope Hind, September 1811, in. Sarah Markham, ed., *A Testimony of Her Times, Based on Penelope Hind's Diaries and Correspondence 1787–1838*, 1990, 99

Byron's parents were well matched only in their family histories, pockmarked by incidents of infamy, depression and madness. On his mother's side Catherine Gordon's father and grandfather seem to have committed suicide. Byron's paternal great-uncle, the 5th Lord Byron, inherited the title at the age of fourteen together with a large fortune. He killed his Nottinghamshire neighbour and kinsman William Chaworth in 1765, in a more than usually stupid duel: they argued about the best way of preserving game. Fined, but acquitted of manslaughter, Lord Byron retired to the family seat, Newstead Abbey in Nottinghamshire. He spent lavishly on pictures and on Gothick buildings around the lake as well as on boats, including a twenty-gun schooner, which allowed him to stage naval battles. He soon ran into debt and was forced to sell a large number of paintings at Christie's in 1772 and then more valuables at an auction held in the house in 1778. He allowed Newstead Abbey to fall into a dilapidated state.

Byron's father Jack, the eldest son of the 5th Lord Byron's younger son, was educated at Westminster School. As a child he rarely saw his father, Vice-Admiral the Hon. John Byron, who served at sea for much of the time.

Sir Joshua Reynolds's portrait of Vice-Admiral the Hon. John Byron, Byron's grandfather, 1758. The stormy background may allude to his nickname, as Sir William Wraxall explains in his Historical Memoirs of My Own Time, *1815. Byron owned two copies of this book (one in French), lots 322 and 324 in the 1816 catalogue of his library. 'An intrepid and skilful, no less than experienced naval Officer, he was nevertheless deficient in the judgment, promptitude and decision of character requisite for conducting the operation of a numerous fleet. On the element of the water an evil destiny seemed invariably to accompany him from his first expedition under Commodore Anson, down to the close of his professional life. So well was this fact known in the Navy, that the sailors bestowed on him the name of "Foul Weather Jack," and esteemed themselves certain of stormy weather, whenever they sailed under his command.' Byron used details from his grandfather's memoir,* The Narrative of the Honourable John Byron, *1768, in* Don Juan *II.*

The west front of Newstead Abbey, from A Souvenir of Newstead Abbey, *1874.*
Photo: Richard Allen & Son

Jack became an officer in the Guards and saw action in the American War of Independence. On his return he sold his commission and was soon known as a rake, as 'the most profligate libertine of the age', 'a spendthrift, a gambler, and a debauchee', known as 'Mad Jack'. 'Byron's father was notorious,' Byron's friend John Cam Hobhouse remembered, 'and the correct number of his amours is no longer to be arrived at.'

Captain Byron

Before he was twenty-one Jack had seduced a married noblewoman, Amelia, the Marchioness of Carmarthen (9th Baroness Conyers and *de jure* 12th Baroness Darcy de Knayth as well as 5th Countess of Mértola in her own right). She left her husband, as well as two sons and a daughter (all under the age of five), for Captain Byron. She was tried for adultery and divorced on 26 March 1779. The lovers married on 9 June at St George's, Hanover Square, and then made their home in Paris. Amelia Byron gave birth to

The Marchioness of Carmarthen and her lover Captain Byron, an illustration from Town and Country Magazine*, 1779.*

three children, but only one survived, the Hon. Augusta, Byron's half-sister, who was born on 26 January 1784. Her mother died the following day. Captain Byron lost not only his wife but also her income of £4,000 a year, which is why he resorted to Bath, England's informal marriage market.

There he met the overweight Scottish orphan Miss Catherine Gordon, the 13th Laird of Gight and the heiress to a considerable fortune.

In the teeth of informed opposition she insisted on marrying the handsome, disreputable, penniless ex-Guards officer. Captain Byron did not tell his mother about their wedding on 13 May 1785. No one, except his bride, had any illusions about his motives. As a ballad put it:

> This youth is a rake, frae England is come,
> The Scots dinna ken his extraction ava;
> He keeps up his misses, his landlords he duns,
> That's fast drawn the lands o'Gight awa'.

Vice-Admiral 'Foul Weather Jack' Byron died later that year leaving £500 to his son, whom he called 'that scapegrace Jack who has behaved in a most shocking manner to his Mother, & goes on as usual like a Rascal'.

When he was eighteen in his poem 'Childish Recollections' Byron blamed 'Stern Death' for depriving him of his father's care. In reality, Jack Byron abandoned his wife and only son when the boy was two years and seven months old, in order to escape his creditors. He fled to France, where he survived for only another year. Captain Byron had married Catherine Gordon because she was rich; he left her when he'd spent her fortune.

Mrs Catherine Byron was, her son said, 'perhaps the proudest woman in England'. Tracing her ancestry back to King James I of Scotland made her, in Byron's words, 'as haughty as Lucifer'. The Stewart connection and descent from the 'right line, from the *old Gordons*' meant that she looked down on all other Gordons (including the Dukes of Gordon) almost as disdainfully as she looked down on her husband's family.

The Byron–Gordon marriage began under the shared burden of a notorious past, with no hope of a better future. Catherine Gordon was known for her 'Impetuousness of Temper', which was reinforced by obstinacy. The motto on her seal promised '*Je ne change qu'en mourant*' ('I shall not change until I die'). On the other hand, she read widely, entertained enlightened political views and preserved an unusual resourcefulness. She needed it.

Eighteen months after their marriage, Captain Byron's debts had absorbed nearly all his wife's assets. She wrote to her agent to ensure that what remained was 'settled in such a manner that it would be out of Mr Byron's power to spend, and out of my own power to give up to him'. To hide this

Catherine Gordon as a girl in an oval miniature, on ivory, 'said to be the only contemporary miniature known', that conjures up an unsophisticated, unselfconfident, provincial young woman.
Harrow School and the Harrow School Archive

stratagem from her husband she asked her agent to address his answer to her maid. With an annual income of only £135 she now rated as one of the poor, according to Mrs Rundell's *New System of Domestic Economy* (1810). This authority defined £150 as the minimal annual income for gentlemen.

George Gordon Byron was born into obscurity on Tuesday, 22 January 1788 in rented rooms in Holles Street, London, an only child in an impoverished and (effectively) one-parent family. Captain Byron was, characteristically, absent: he could not see his son, even if he wanted to, since debtors could be arrested on every day except Sunday. Byron's parents had been married for less than three years, mostly spent in nomadic discomfort as Captain Byron evaded his creditors.

By the summer of 1789 the family had moved to Aberdeen, presumably to save money. The city represented home territory to the Gordons: their ancestral home Gight Castle, which Catherine's family had inhabited for some 350 years, was only twenty-five miles away.

As a child Byron's local connection through his mother ranked more highly than his English father's distant connection to the barony, which is why he was known as 'George Bayron Gordon'. The spelling points to its pronunciation. But Captain Byron had sold Gight Castle in 1787 (for £17,850) to meet part of his debts. It cannot have been easy for the proud Mrs Byron to revisit the area where she had been well known before she lost all her money and compromised her position in society.

In Aberdeen the Byrons lived together briefly but they soon quarrelled and separated, staying at opposite ends of the same street. They continued to visit 'and even to drink tea with each other', as Moore says, 'but the elements of discord were strong on both sides and their separation became, at last, complete and final.

'[Captain Jack Byron] would frequently, however, accost the nurse and his son in their walks, and expressed a strong wish to have the child for a day or two, on a visit with him. To this request Mrs. Byron was, at first, not very willing to accede.' His nurse forecast that 'if he kept the boy one night, he would not do so another', so Mrs Byron agreed. 'The event proved as the nurse had predicted; on enquiring next morning after the child, she was told by Captain Byron that he had had quite enough of his young visiter [*sic*], and she might take him home again.'

Anticipated Life

Mrs Byron bullied and spoiled her only son, 'now kicking and now kissing' him, in the words of Byron's friend John Cam Hobhouse. May Gray, Byron's nursemaid in Aberdeen, abused him sexually when he was nine. But she was also 'perpetually beating him', he told John Hanson, the family lawyer, so that 'his bones sometimes ached from it'. In effect, his nursemaid reinforced Byron's early experience of punishing love.

The traumatic experience left an imprint on his adult relationships, which followed a pattern. 'Having always been governed by them [women],'

Byron's Venetian friend Countess Albrizzi explained, 'it would seem that his very self-love was pleased to take refuge in the idea of their excellence, – a sentiment which he knew how (God knows how) to reconcile with the contempt in which, shortly afterwards, almost with the appearance of satisfaction, he seemed to hold them.' She concludes: 'who does not know that the slave holds in detestation his ruler?' 'Byron has a false notion of women,' Lady Blessington observed, 'he fancies that they are all disposed to be tyrants, and that the moment they know their power they abuse it.'

Captain Byron made one 'short visit' to Aberdeen and later spent two or three months there, but only 'to extract still more money, if possible, from the unfortunate woman whom he had beggared'. Mrs Byron went further into debt for £300, which she gave to him. She also tried to borrow £30 or £40 from her sister-in-law Mrs Leigh.

At Valenciennes, where he had settled, the captain had numerous affairs with servants, actresses and a third of the town's population, or so he claimed. He boasted about his conquests in letters to his younger sister Frances, Mrs Leigh, reminding her, 'still the *Birons* are irresistible. You know that Fanny.' Letters show that he had an incestuous relationship with Frances. Byron apparently never knew this. Captain Jack's daughter Augusta later married her cousin, George, Frances's son by General Charles Leigh.

Byron's father died in squalid poverty on 2 August 1791, at the age of thirty-five. Byron was three and a half years old. He had no brothers, uncles, grandparents or other near male relations. His godparents, the Duke of Gordon and Colonel Duff, showed no interest in him. The current holder of the family title, the 5th Baron Byron, was a distant relation, the boy's great-uncle. For the first six years of Byron's life, both of the 5th Baron's direct heirs, his elder son and grandson, enjoyed good health. And the titled part of the family wanted nothing to do with the young boy or with his foolish, disgraced mother, widowed at twenty-six.

In 1806, when Byron described himself as an 'orphan', his mother was still living:

Can Rank, or ev'n a Guardian's name supply,
The Love, which glistens in a Father's eye?
For this, can Wealth, or Title's sound atone,
Made, by a Parent's early loss, my own?

He later explained in *Don Juan*:

The world is full of orphans: firstly, those
Who are so in the strict sense of the phrase;
. . . The next are such as are not doomed to lose
Their tender parents, in their budding days,
But, merely, their parental tenderness,
Which leaves them orphans of the heart, no less.

It's an idea that he considered repeatedly. Byron felt that neither of his parents behaved 'tenderly'. What counts here is his perception of how they behaved, rather than any objective truth.

One parent's early absence and the other's overwhelming presence had a joint, compound, decisive impact. We look at them separately, but their conjunction proved fatal. He might not have resented his mother so much if he had not missed his father so badly.

Byron's sense of fatherlessness haunted him all his life. As we'll see, it determined his idea of heroism, a central concern of his poetry, and it also had a major impact on the way he behaved. Love and glory, the twin themes of *Don Juan*, were the poles between which his life and his fiction oscillated.

3

THE INNOCENT FAULT

I must naturally be the last person to be pointed on defects
or maladies

Journal, 22 November 1813

A Fate or Will that Walked Astray

Byron was born with a misshapen right foot.

In 1789 Mrs Byron felt 'perfectly sure' that her son 'would walk very well if he had a proper shoe'. But she did not take him back to London for treatment, probably because she could not afford the expense. Instead on 5 May 1791 she asked her husband's sister Mrs Leigh to obtain the surgeon John Hunter's 'directions for a proper shoe to be made without seeing it again'.

Hunter assured Mrs Byron on 8 May 1791 that the boy's foot 'would be very well in time'. This might have been the case if it had been treated early and properly.

But nobody made a serious attempt to alleviate Byron's condition for another ten years. Dr Matthew Baillie, Hunter's nephew and one of the leading surgeons in London, recorded on 15 July 1799 that the boy's foot 'was inverted and contracted as it were in a heap and of course did not go fully and flatly to the ground'.

It is not easy to establish exactly what his disability entailed, though it is no longer thought to be a club-foot. Recent diagnoses include Little's disease (spastic paraplegia), infantile paralysis, injury associated with post-

Byron's leather boots which he wore under the trousers of the right leg at the age of around eleven and at eighteen. The larger one (left) has a metal plate in its sole and weighs 1 pound 6 ounces (0.62 kg). Its padding supported his defective foot and concealed the wasted muscle in his calf. Byron always wore trousers that were strapped under the soles of his boots, even while swimming.

Private collection

natal trauma, congenital dysplasia and the neurogenic foot deformities associated with spinal dysraphism.

In any case, it often hurt.

Along with the title Byron inherited the prospect of £60,000: this would come to him from the estate at Rochdale. As lords of the manor the Byrons had rights to coal mining royalties in the area. The fifth baron sold them, but the sale was in dispute. In fact, the matter was not resolved until 1828.

Mrs Byron assumed she could afford to try again to correct her son's defective foot. But from his point of view, she compounded her earlier maltreatment by making him submit to torture. The truss-maker to Nottingham's General Hospital claimed he could cure the disability. In 1801 he charged £80, more than half Mrs Byron's annual income, 'for attending, Dressing, & Instruments for Lord Byron's foot'. Having rubbed the boy's foot with oil for some time, he then twisted it forcibly and screwed it up in a wooden machine. Byron insisted on taking lessons in Latin at this time, in order to catch up with his contemporaries before he attended an English school. 'He was often, during his lessons, in violent pain from the torturing position in which his foot was kept; and his teacher Mr Rogers one day said to him, "It makes me uncomfortable, my lord, to see you sitting there in such pain as I *know* you must be suffering." "Never mind, Mr. Rogers," answered the boy; "you shall not see any signs of it in *me*".' Byron 'wore a very light and thin boot which was tightly laced just under the sole and, when a boy, he was made to wear a piece of iron with a joint at the ankle, which passed behind the leg and was tied behind the shoe.'

Byron attended Dulwich School from the age of eleven for two years, and spent most of his holidays for the next five years with his lawyer's family, the Hansons. The son, Newton, remembered that Byron 'was subject to fits of nervous agitation, when, if any one approached him, he would scream out, "Don't come near me! I have a devil." His irritability of temper, which showed in his habit of gnawing his nails, continued to explode in violent rages.'

His friend Thomas Moore dismissed Byron's 'deformity' as 'trifling' but he also referred to it as the 'embittering circumstance of his life . . . which haunted him like a curse, amidst the buoyancy of youth, and the anticipations of fame and pleasure'.

It mattered so much because of the way Byron felt that his mother treated it. He never forgot 'the feeling of horror and humiliation that came over him, when his mother, in one of her fits of passion, called him "a lame brat"'. He recorded the incident in his Memoir, which was burned after his death. As 'long as I can remember,' he told a friend, 'she has never ceased to taunt and reproach me with it [his deformity]. Even a few days before we parted, for the last time, on my leaving England [in 1809], she, in one

Engraving after John Kay's portrait of Byron, 1795, a year after the boy became heir apparent to the title of Baron Byron. Byron gave the original miniature to his nursemaid May Gray. It shows him at the age of seven holding a bow and arrow, with a target in the distance. The sport suited him, because an archer remains stationary and only needs strength in his upper body. For the same reason, Byron practised pistol-shooting all his life. Captain Gronow said he 'considered himself the best shot in London'.

Private collection

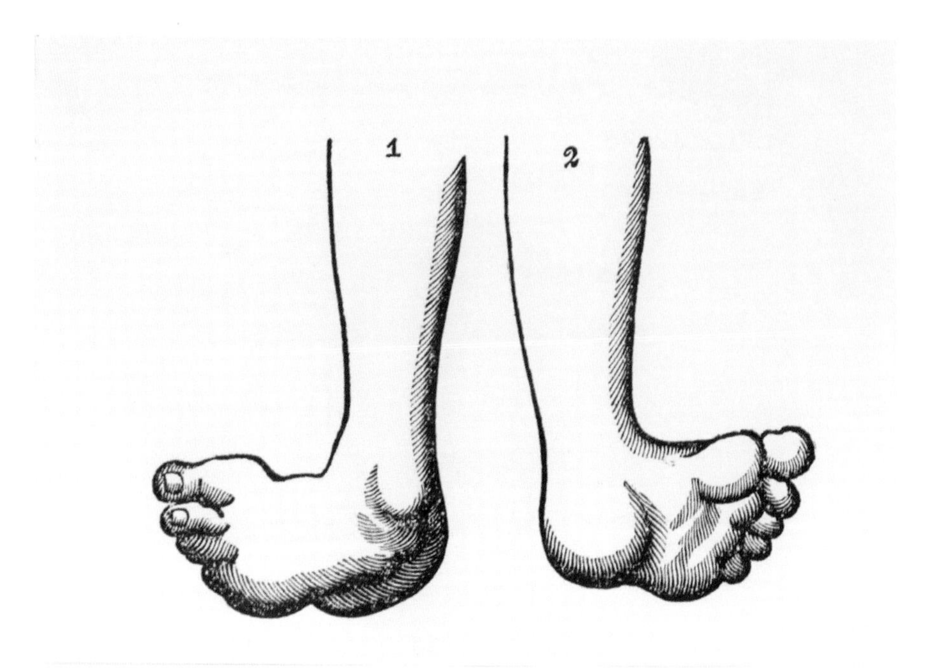

A drawing purportedly taken from a plaster cast of Byron's feet, 'one view looking at the outside, the other at the inside of his leg', published by Timothy Sheldrake in 'Distortions of the Feet: Lord Byron's Case', in the Lancet *in 1827. In* Animal Mechanics *(1832) Sheldrake complains that Byron, when a boy at Dulwich, was mistakenly put under the care of his brother William Sheldrake, the truss-maker, 'who made a mess of the case, whereas he, Timothy, would have effected a cure'.*
© The Lancet, ii, 1827, 779

of her fits of passion, uttered an imprecation upon me, praying that I might prove as ill-formed in mind as I am in body!' Byron associated the stigma of his disability with his mother. He blamed it on her 'mock delicacy' at his birth. She wore a corset and may have kept it on during her pregnancy and labour.

There is no point in querying the accuracy of Byron's memory; what matters here is what he felt he knew. 'I could have borne/It all,' he made the crippled Arnold say, in his late play *The Deformed Transformed*, 'had not my mother spurned me from her.' Mary Shelley concluded that 'No action of Lord Byron's life – scarce a line he has written – but was influenced by his personal defect.' And she wrote that on the flyleaf of her copy of *The Deformed Transformed*. It opens with a scene that seems to epitomise Byron's experience:

Illustration to The Deformed Transformed: *a mother rejects her crippled child, drawn by H. Richter, engraved by H. Cook,* The Byron Gallery, a Series of Historical Embellishments to Illustrate the Works of Lord Byron, *1833.*

BERTHA: Out, hunchback!

ARNOLD: I was born so, mother!

BERTHA: Out!

Sympathetic observers found it easy to see the disability in proportion. 'The sense which Byron always retained of the innocent fault in his foot, was unmanly and excessive,' John Galt insisted, 'for it was not greatly conspicuous, and he had a mode of walking across a room by which it was scarcely at all perceptible.' Galt spent several days on board the same ship as Byron in 1809 before he even noticed the defect: 'it was indeed so well concealed, that I was in doubt whether his lameness was the effect of temporary accident, or a malformation, until I asked Mr. Hobhouse.'

'One of his feet is shorter than the other,' an observer noticed at a country house party that Byron attended in the autumn of 1811, 'and the high clumping shoe he wears on it sounds bad.'

Byron's 'figure left nothing to be desired', according to Countess Albrizzi, who met him in Venice in 1816, 'particularly by those who found rather a grace than a defect in a certain light and gentle undulation of the person when he entered a room, and of which you hardly felt tempted to enquire the cause. Indeed it was scarcely perceptible, – the clothes he wore were so long.' She noticed, however, that he avoided being seen walking, 'so powerful in him was the desire of not showing himself to be deformed in any part of his person'.

Byron limped, he 'walked astray', as he wrote in 1816 in one of his best poems, later called the 'Epistle to Augusta'. An apt and dangerous metaphor epitomises his physical condition and its impact on his life:

> My whole life was a contest, since the day
> That gave me being, gave me that which marred
> The gift – a fate or will that walked astray . . .

4

THE FIRST WAR OF INDEPENDENCE, 1807

His Amiable Mama and Her Fat, Bashful Boy

Thomas Moore described the 'coldness with which [Byron's] mother had received his caresses in infancy, and the frequent taunts on his personal deformity with which she had wounded him'. They reflected Mrs Byron's injured feelings. Until he was six, that is to say, during the most vulnerable period in his life, the crippled boy embodied his mother's failure, the bitter fruit of her hollow marriage, that had deprived her of her inherited fortune and status; alienated her from her family and from other noble connections; and left her humiliated and unloved.

The 5th Lord Byron's direct heirs died prematurely, his son William in 1776 and his grandson William John in 1794, which meant that his great-nephew George Gordon unexpectedly became his heir at the age of six. The boy succeeded to the title as the 6th Baron Byron at the age of ten in 1798. In August that year Byron and his mother left Scotland, accompanied by May Gray and another nursemaid. They visited the dilapidated Newstead Abbey and its 3,800-acre estate in Nottinghamshire, which he had inherited (along with an 8,256-acre estate in Rochdale). Byron was now 'a fine sharp Boy not a little spoilt by Indulgence but that is scarcely to be wondered at', according to the family lawyer, Hanson.

Newstead Abbey was rented out to generate some income and Mrs Byron leased Burgage Manor in Southwell, fourteen miles away, as their home.

Thomas Stewardson, Mrs Byron, *1806, at the age of forty-two. She insisted on some forty sittings for her portrait, to satisfy 'her anxiety to have a particular turn in her elbow exhibited in the most pleasing light'. Courtesy of Nottingham City Museums and Galleries*

Her independent character shocked her more conventional English contemporaries. Soon after arriving she sent a note to a neighbour, Mrs Pigot, in which she introduced herself and asked for advice about her garden. Mrs Byron's manoeuvre clearly broke with English custom: Mrs Pigot kept the note as a curiosity because she felt so 'surprised and amused at the same time with the Scotch freedom of her peculiar style'. Mrs Byron augmented her reputation for eccentricity and independence by her political activity: she campaigned as a Whig in a Tory stronghold. An observer in 1799 described her as 'a somewhat untidy, shabbily dressed person', but she had her vanity.

In 1803, when Elizabeth Pigot first met Byron, who was then fifteen, she described him as 'a fat, bashful boy, with his hair combed straight over his forehead'. Each of those details deserves closer consideration.

His fatness suggested that Byron had inherited his mother's plumpness. A 'short and corpulent person', she 'rolled considerably in her gait'. Whether bred or nurtured, obesity signalled filial dependence.

Byron's bashfulness lasted all his life, at least in relation to women whom he did not know. It generated an '*under* look', which seemed to invite attention by seeking to evade it. As late as May 1822, at the age of thirty-four, Byron struck an American woman as 'a sensitive, gracefully bashful boy – a young Jove, hiding his thunderbolts'.

Having grown up in Aberdeen, Byron felt ill at ease in Southwell, isolated by his limp and his Scottish accent and embarrassed by his forthright mother. When Mrs Byron gave a party, her son 'was so shy that she had to send for him three times before she could persuade him to come into the drawing-room, to play with the young people at a round game'. He bit his nails, which prompted her 'sudden and violent Ejaculations of Disgust accompanied by a Box on the ear or Hands'.

On the other hand, his carefully combed hair showed the obedient child. As an adult, he let his hair flow freely. Indeed, he cultivated a rebellious disorder, so that his hair displayed a windswept look of freedom. His glossy curls owed their glossiness and curliness to artifice: he used Macassar's hair oil, which he praised in *Don Juan* as 'incomparable'. A Cambridge friend once 'found the poet in bed with his hair *en papillote* [in papers]'. Byron admitted that he was as vain of his curls 'as a girl of sixteen'.

Emancipation

While Byron was at school Mrs Byron funded her son as generously as she had his father, supplying him, Byron told Augusta on 2 November 1804, with 'more than most boys hope for or desire'. But he was, he admitted,

William Leitch's copy of a miniature portrait of Byron by George Saunders, 1831. It was sold on 2 June 2009 at Christie's, South Kensington, who supplied the photo.

'naturally extravagant'. This led to what Augusta called 'eternal Scenes of wrangling'.

His fatherless condition meant he lived under the unmitigated influence of his mother. Matters came to a head when he was eighteen, when he most needed to assert his independence and felt most frustrated.

He composed a premature epitaph on his mother around this time, as part of a game: 'Prone to take Fire, yet not of melting Stuff'. Ransacking mythology and the Bible for analogies he called her 'this female Tisiphone

. . . one of the Furies' in a letter to Augusta of 10 August 1805, and 'that *momentous Eve*' in a letter to John Pigot of 9 August 1806.

In the summer of 1805, aged seventeen, Byron prepared to leave home for university, swearing that he would never again live with 'such a vixen' as his mother. 'No Captive Negro, or Prisoner of war, ever looked forward to their *emancipation*, and return to Liberty, with more Joy, and with more lingering expectation, than I do to my escape from maternal bondage.' He resolved to be 'perfectly independent of her'. Independence represented the ideal he sought throughout his life, both for himself and for others.

Looking ahead for a moment: as an adult Byron would embark on his public career by taking his seat in the House of Lords in March 1809. 'I shall stand aloof, speak what I think, but not often, nor too soon,' he promised Hanson, the family lawyer; 'I will preserve my independence, if possible.' On the day, he was so concerned to demonstrate his independence that he managed to offend the Lord Chancellor with the coolness of his greeting.

At seventeen, as an undergraduate with '500 a year, a Servant and Horse', he told Augusta on 6 November 1805 that he felt as 'independent as a German Prince who coins his own Cash, or a Cherokee Chief who coins no Cash at all, but enjoys what is more precious, Liberty. I talk in raptures of that *Goddess* because my amiable Mama was so despotic.' But his 'independence' depended on inconstant subsidies from that despot. On the brink of his eighteenth birthday Byron referred to her '*peevish harassing* System of Torment . . . now & then interrupted by Ridiculous Indulgence'. He had not yet won his freedom.

He began to borrow large sums of money, as he expected to realise some £60,000 when the Rochdale dispute was settled. Consciously or unconsciously, Byron followed in his father's footsteps and plunged into debt. Mrs Byron's reaction demonstrates her capacity for rage, asking Hanson on 11 January 1806:

> Has he got into the hands of moneylenders? He has no feeling, no Heart. This I have long known; he has behaved as ill as possible to me for years back. This bitter truth I can no longer conceal: it is wrung from me by *heart-*

> *rending agony*. I am well rewarded. I came to Nottingham to please him and now he hates it. He knows that I am doing everything in my power to pay his Debts, and he writes to me about hiring servants!

In 1806, trapped 'in retirement' with her, in Southwell, in the 'vixen's' lair, far from his male friends in London and Cambridge, Byron felt reduced to the dependent status of an infant.

Byron established and manifested his freedom from 'maternal bondage' by altering his shape. He rejected his body – as he felt his mother had rejected him. With this momentous 'Reduction' in 1807, Byron sought to escape from the 'Trammels or rather *Fetters* of [his] domestic Tyrant Mrs Byron' as he evaded the 'bonds of clay'. In effect, he identified his mother with matter and rejected both.

It may be helpful to see Byron's behaviour in context with testimony from 'Annette', an anorexic who was treated by the renowned psychiatrist Hilde Bruch, author of *Eating Disorders: Obesity, Anorexia, and the Person Within* (1973) and *The Golden Cage* (1977):

> 'In trying to cope with the task of eating a balanced diet I have found myself most dependent on, and in rebellion against, my parents, most especially my mother . . . I feel a failure and have a need to be in control . . . and I struggle with the problem of dependence and independence.'

Starvation transformed Byron: his face seemed to lengthen, he appeared taller and his hair lightened from very dark brown to light chestnut, almost blond. The fat boy had made himself into an emaciated, pale young man, with a 'refined and spiritualized look'.

His new appearance manifested an aristocratic transcendence of the flesh. His complexion looked so pale that he was compared to 'an Alabaster vase lit up within'.

As a boy, Byron's puppy fat demonstrated his dependence on his obese mother. In separating himself from maternal obesity in such a dramatic and sustained fashion Byron mimicked the way a child establishes independence.

His transformation appeared to mark the *rite de passage* from infancy to adulthood. But adulthood is seldom achieved so neatly. In a sense it eluded him for some eleven years.

Teresa Guiccioli said that Byron was 'brought up in the midst of the aristocracy's materials and luxury, in the most aristocratic country in the world, and where material well-being is best appreciated'. This misrepresented Byron's upbringing in Aberdeen (till he was ten) and then in Southwell. But his diet was, as she said, more characteristic of a fourth-century Christian ascetic saint: it did indeed seem incongruous, in a society that was based on involuntary hunger and crowned by gross, carnal self-indulgence.

PART III

ANOREXIA BYRONICA

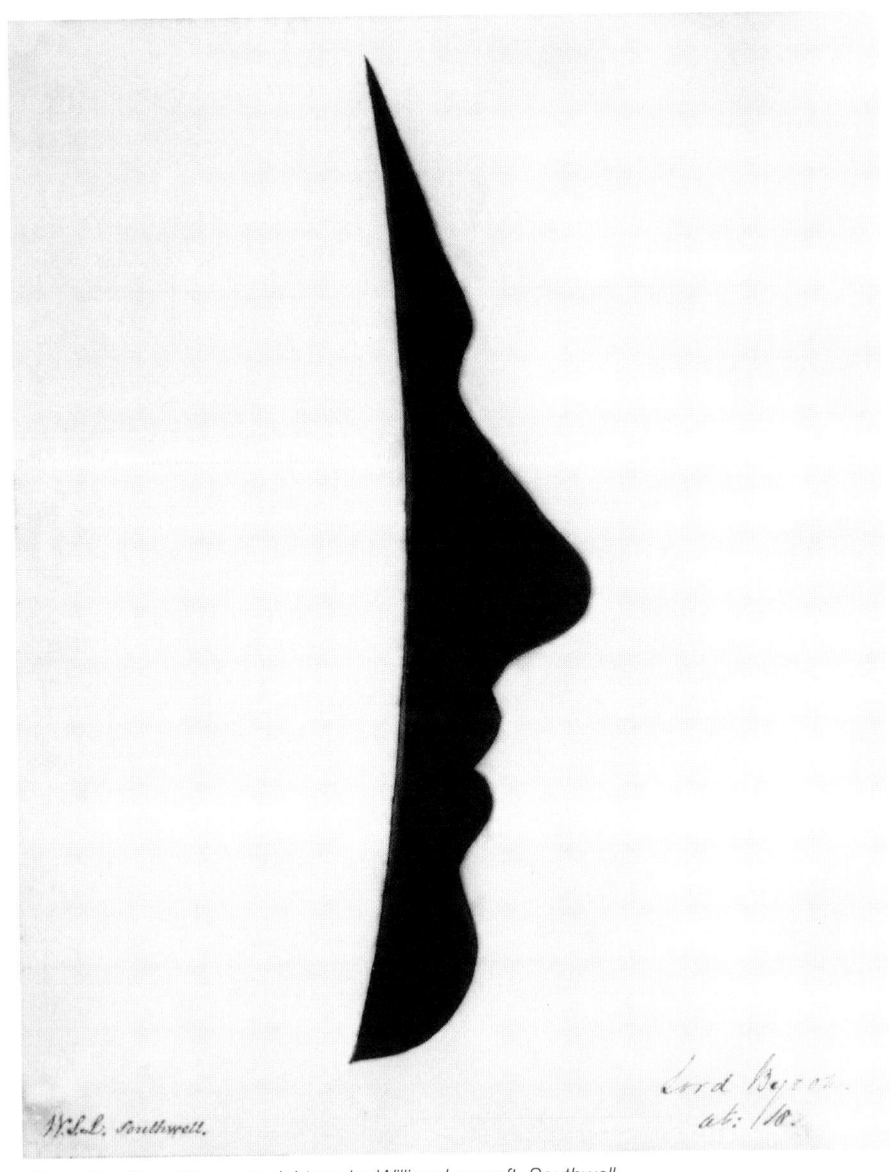

Silhouette of Lord Byron at eighteen by William Leacroft, Southwell.

Private collection

5

THE REASONABLE SOUL versus THE ANIMAL BODY

Byron's attitude to his disability was coloured by his exposure at an early age to Scottish Calvinism. He grew up in Aberdeen in the dour religion's shadow, although, as we shall see, its shadow looked very like his own shadow. His mother and his nursemaid both tried to immerse him in its doctrines. He also said that he was 'early disgusted with a Calvinist Scottish school where I was cudgelled to Church for the first ten years of my life'. Was Byron exaggerating? Critics have warned against overstating the impact of Byron's Calvinist upbringing but relying on Byron's remark in *Don Juan*, 'I was bred a moderate Presbyterian', proves counter-productive: the Narrator's unreliability means that the opposite may well be true – after all, Byron was never moderate.

In 1792 Byron attended Bowers School in Aberdeen, where one of his tutors was 'a rigid Presbyterian', a 'very serious – saturnine – but kind young man'. Byron had fond memories of another teacher: 'He was a very decent – clever – little Clergyman – named Ross – afterwards Minister of one of the Kirks (East I think)[;] under him – I made an astonishing progress – and I recollect to this day his mild manners & good-natured painstaking.'

The 'very decent – clever – little Clergyman' was James Ross whose sermons were published in 1825 along with an anonymous 'Memoir of his Life'.

Religion in Aberdeen in Byron's day was plural; rather more was available than only strict Calvinism, but Byron's respect for Ross means that it's worth looking into exactly what his master taught him.

According to Ross, Calvinism emphasised the conflict between man's flesh, predestined to damnation, and the spirit, his only hope of salvation.

> We are composed of a reasonable soul, and of an animal body; and the powers of the soul being of a superior order to the appetites of the body, it is fit, as the law of God requires, that the former should have the control and direction of the latter: and it is also necessary to our happiness, for it is impossible to be happy under the dominion of appetite and passion.

Scottish Calvinism reinforced the prejudice against his own body that Byron blamed on his mother.

Born for his Own Ruin

Its doctrines emphasised three basic tenets: predestination, man's innate depravity and his hereditary taint. As Paul Barton points out:

> This doctrine in particular is one that weighed heavily on Byron's mind, especially in light of his mother's relentless tirades against the wickedness of his father and his even more dissolute forebears. Byron as a child learned that he was a product of a long tradition of dissipation, incest, rampant promiscuity, decadence, murder and unbridled debauchery. In a conversation with his friend Thomas Medwin while in Pisa (1821–2) Byron stated that he believed he was 'predestined to evil' and, like his father, had been 'born for his own ruin' . . . Perhaps Byron truly believed that he had inherited the vices of his ancestry just as he had inherited original sin and his fallen state from his primal parents, Adam and Eve.

Calvinist doctrines preached at Byron's church, school and home served to develop his notions of original sin, hereditary taint and God's deterministic will. The combined effect of these doctrines convinced Byron that God had selected him for damnation.

Furthermore his 'deformity' may well also have served to hammer home his status as one of the damned: 'such a birth defect was believed by Scottish Presbyterians of the late eighteenth century to signify that a child was in some way cursed or blighted by God.'

Byron's wife recognised in 1816 that 'a proudly mortifying consciousness of his personal defect was associated . . . with the dark predestinarianism, which early Calvinistic impressions, and later Oriental observations, had tended to infix in his mind.' She 'regarded this [Calvinism] as the secret of her husband's character, and the source of his aberrations'. Byron may well have 'partly acted the role' of a Calvinist to annoy her, but there were elements in the creed that corresponded with his own convictions, as other witnesses testified.

When he was young, a friend tried to cheer up Byron by encouraging him to count his blessings, such as 'a mind which placed him above the rest of mankind. – "Ah, my dear friend," said Byron, mournfully, – "if *this* (laying his hand on his forehead) places me above the rest of mankind, *that* (pointing to his foot) places me far, far below them."' The antithesis formed the unquestioned basis of Byron's psyche.

Calvinism taught him that man's body compromised or betrayed his spirit. Byron's attitude to his misshapen foot sharpened the perception. The hunchback Arnold in his play *The Deformed Transformed* boasted that he did

> the best which Spirit may, to make
> Its way, with all Deformity's dull, deadly,
> Discouraging weight upon me, like a mountain,
> In feeling, on my heart as on my shoulders. . .

Arnold offers an enlightened view of disability:

> . . . deformity is daring.
> It is its essence to o'ertake mankind
> By heart and soul, and make itself the equal –
> Aye, the superior of the rest. There is

A spur in its halt movements, to become
All that the others cannot, in such things
As still are free to both, to compensate
For stepdame Nature's avarice at first.
They woo with fearless deeds the smiles of fortune,
And oft, like Timour the lame Tartar, win them.

For most of his life Byron did not feel so optimistic. Given the choice, even the heroic Arnold changes his 'deformed' shape.

Body warred with soul; Byron viewed the world through the distorting lens of a dualism inculcated by his mother's contempt and reinforced by religious indoctrination. It conditioned his thinking about society, women, art and geography. It determined his heroic ideal, exemplified by his attitude to Napoleon, and played an important role in the composition of *Don Juan*.

Like the hero of *The Black Dwarf* (published pseudonymously in 1816), Byron was 'haunted by a consciousness of his own deformity, and a suspicion of his being generally subjected to the scorn of his fellow-men'. When Byron's half-sister Augusta read the story she assumed that the credit on the title page, 'collected and arranged by Jedediah Cleishbotham', concealed Byron's identity. In fact Walter Scott wrote this and the other 'Tales of my Landlord'. Scott contracted polio at the age of eighteen months and remained lame in his right leg. Scott himself said he had been 'disfigured rather than disabled'. A disadvantage (as Scott called it), which threw a shadow over Byron's life and work, prompted Scott to exert himself physically. He never mentions feeling any pain from it. Scott grew up in a large, happy family, the third son of devoted parents. He remembered how his 'kind grandmother' lavished attention on him while his aunt also felt 'exceedingly attached' to him. His family encouraged him to follow the example of two ancestors whom lameness had spurred on to greatness. Byron's problem was not his disability, but what was made of it.

Portrait of Walter Scott in an engraving from Finden's Illustrations of the Life and Works of Lord Byron with Original & Selected Information on the Subjects of the Engravings by W. Brockenden, *2 vols., 1833. Byron called Scott a 'wonderful man!' in his Ravenna journal in 1821 and added, 'I long to get drunk with him.'*

Byron meets Scott, right, in the first-floor drawing room at their publisher John Murray's Mayfair house. Isaac D'Israeli, John Murray and Sir John Barrow are at the table; William Gifford (Byron's 'literary father') sits in the armchair; George Canning stands in the centre, beneath the portrait of Byron by Thomas Phillips, 1814. The watercolour by L. Werner dates from 1850 but it has some truth to it.

Private collection

6

DINNER WITH LORD BYRON

Obesity may have warranted Byron's first diet but that did not justify the way he continued to starve himself throughout his adult life.

His behaviour mystified his contemporaries. It continued while he was on his Grand Tour: 'The system of thinning himself, which he had begun before he left England, was continued still more rigidly,' John Galt, his companion from Gibraltar to Cagliari in August 1809, remembered. Byron then appeared 'in delicate health, and upon an abstemious regimen'. But abstemiousness and his abuse of purgatives probably caused his 'delicate health'. 'He rarely tasted wine, nor more than half a glass, mingled with water, when he did. He ate little; no animal food, but only bread and vegetables.' 'Animal food' meant meat.

Byron returned from his Grand Tour in July 1811. His mother died on 1 August, while he was on his way to see her at Newstead Abbey, the first of an almost overwhelming succession of deaths. That autumn Byron 'found himself more solitary, more unknown, more disregarded than any nameless orphan'. He knew almost nobody in London and missed his old friend from Cambridge University, John Cam Hobhouse, who was in Ireland. Ambitious as a writer, Byron lacked literary contacts of consequence. He overvalued the company of his fawning distant relative, Robert Charles Dallas, a mediocre but published author. Briefly, Byron hoped that the fifty-four-year-old Dallas, whom he considered 'a man of acknowledged Genius', would act as his mentor. Byron had invited him to move with his family to Southwell, listened to some of his comments on his writing, trusted him to see the second edition of *English Bards and Scotch Reviewers* through the press and gave him the copyright in several works. Byron showed Dallas the manuscripts of poems he had worked on abroad and then in London, the mildly satirical but effortful *Hints from Horace*, which was a sequel to *English Bards*, and *The Curse of Minerva*, a relentless, polemical attack on the Scottish plunderers of the Parthenon. But Dallas was more impressed by the manuscript of the first two cantos of Byron's travelogue *Childe Harold*. Dallas showed it to his publisher, John Murray, who agreed to publish it.

Meanwhile, Byron caught up with reactions to his comprehensively insulting *English Bards*, published anonymously in 1809, before he went abroad. To demonstrate that he was *au courant* with literary gossip, Byron had retold an old story about a supposed duel with unloaded pistols between Thomas Moore and the *Edinburgh Review*'s editor, Francis Jeffrey. As soon as the second edition's title page identified the author of *English Bards*, Moore challenged him to a duel, but Byron had already left on his Grand Tour. Now, two years later, the quarrel's impetus had dulled. Moore had since married and was now a father, and he felt more intrigued than insulted. *English Bards* may have referred to Moore as one of the 'melodious advocates of lust' but at least it cited him four times and Little (Moore's transparent pseudonym) five times.

Byron so admired Moore's light, flirtatious verse that he imitated its manner in several of his early poems. When his first publicly published book of poems, *Hours of Idleness*, went into a second edition, Byron ordered his printer to copy the size, printing and binding of Moore's poems.

On the other side, Moore was curious to meet this rhyming baron. As an Irish émigré he liked to move in London's highest social circles. His friend Samuel Rogers agreed to host a dinner in his house.

4 November 1811

On 4 November 1811 Byron met the three most important poets of the day at the house of the most senior figure, Samuel Rogers. Byron was a nobleman, the 6th Baron Byron of Rochdale, but he'd grown up in Aberdeen and then in Nottinghamshire, far from the literary circles he aspired to join.

Thomas Philips, Samuel Rogers, *1817. Rogers was a trustee of the National Gallery, to which he bequeathed Titian's* Noli Me Tangere, *the* Head of Christ Crowned with Thorns *then attributed to Guido Reni and* A Man in Armour *by an imitator of Giorgione. His portrait often hangs on loan in the private entrance to the National Gallery to inspire potentially beneficent visitors.*

He was twenty-three and known only for his juvenile satire, *English Bards and Scotch Reviewers*.

Rogers occupied a unique position in society at this time, as 'the first of living poets', in Byron's words, who was also an independently wealthy banker. Rogers's major work, *The Pleasures of Memory*, published in 1792, sold more than 22,000 copies in fourteen years. That represented a high-water mark of poetic success – at least until Byron. Byron admired Rogers's poetry because it adhered to the eighteenth-century tradition of Alexander Pope. During his initiation into the literary world Byron 'really tried to obtain' Rogers's goodwill, 'thinking him at first a good fellow'. His senior by twenty-five years, Rogers could have acted as mentor to Byron. Rogers is 'our poetical papa', Byron told Moore on 31 March 1817, adding, 'You are his lawful son, and I the illegitimate.'

Portrait of Thomas Moore by Thomas Lawrence.
Private collection

Moore and Rogers would certainly have heard of *Childe Harold* already and had probably read it in manuscript, as John Murray, an astute, ambitious and rising young publisher was in the habit of showing his new manuscripts to a select circle, including these two poets. Byron rebuked Murray on 14 September for showing *Childe Harold* to William Gifford, a leading critic and editor of the *Quarterly Review*, which Murray published.

Staying in lodgings at 8 St James's Street, Byron had only a short walk around the corner to reach Rogers's house at 22 St James's Place. A knocker in the form of a Medusa's head prepared his visitors to meet their host. The 'yellow hyena', in his friend Lady Caroline Lamb's words, was 'a mass of rancour and malevolence – gifted however with a wit so keen and deadly, that with its razor edge he cut to the heart of most of his enemies, and all of his friends'.

SAMUEL ROGERS' HOUSE, NO 22, ST. JAMES'S PLACE.

Richard Lovett's drawing of Samuel Rogers's house seen from Green Park, from London Pictures, *1890.*

The 'bard, the beau, and banker', Byron called him, meaning the word 'beau' sarcastically. Rogers was notoriously ugly, but equally celebrated for his wit, his independent wealth and his generous hospitality. The world 'courts him because he has no occasion to court it', Byron observed wistfully. As a nobleman who lacked the funds to maintain his status, Byron was already isolated within the aristocracy. Now he hoped to enter another, potentially hostile milieu, the literary world, most of whose leading figures he had attacked in *English Bards and Scotch Reviewers*.

Rogers's home made a great impression on Byron: 'If you enter his house – his drawing-room – his library – you of yourself say, this is not the dwelling of a common mind. There's not a gem, a coin, a book thrown aside on his chimney-piece, his sofa, his table, that does not bespeak an almost fastidious elegance in the possessor. But this very delicacy must be the misery of his existence.' Paintings attributed to Raphael, Titian, Giorgione, Rubens and Reynolds looked down on antique marble fragments, a collection of Greek vases and fashionably neoclassical furniture inspired by Thomas Hope,

The drawing room in Samuel Rogers's house at 22 St James's Place, in a watercolour sold by Sotheby's. An equestrian portrait of Prince Baltasar Carlos by Velasquez hangs over the fireplace. It is now in the Wallace Collection.

'The victim sad of vase-collecting spleen,/House-furnisher withal', as Byron called him.

'I thought it best that I alone should be in the drawing-room when Byron entered it,' Samuel Rogers remembered. His other guests 'accordingly withdrew'. The gesture was prompted by tact: Byron hated being watched as he came into a room.

A Poetical Group of Four

Moore then entered with another leading poet, Thomas Campbell, who had come to breakfast with Rogers and stayed all day. Byron felt an affinity with him as a fellow Scot. He had imitated Campbell's 'Exile of Erin' (1801) in 'Lachin Y Gair' and praised him in *English Bards*, under the rubric of 'Neglected Genius'.

Byron called Rogers's *The Pleasures of Memory* and Campbell's act of

'Portrait of Campbell (Author of the Pleasures of Hope,) after Lawrence, in a gilt frame' was lot 378 in the catalogue for the 1816 auction of Byron's books and possessions. It was the only portrait of a poet that he owned. It may have helped that Thomas Campbell had mentioned Byron's uncle, the vice-admiral, in The Pleasures of Hope *(1799). Finden, after Lawrence.*

homage, *The Pleasures of Hope*, 'the most beautiful didactic poems in our language, if we except Pope's *Essay on Man*' in a note to *English Bards* (801n.). As for his mistaken allusion to Moore's duel with Jeffrey, Byron corrected it in a note that he added to *English Bards*. He dated it 4 November 1811. He presumably wrote it when he came home from dinner that night.

The company that evening comprised 'a poetical group of four not easily to be matched, among contemporaries in any age or country'. As Moore commented:

> Such a meeting could not be otherwise than interesting to us all. It was the first time that Lord Byron was ever seen by any of his three companions; while he, on his side, for the first time, found himself in the society of persons, whose names had been associated with his first literary dreams, and to *two* of whom he looked up with that tributary admiration which youthful genius is ever ready to pay its precursors.

Byron was twenty-three; the others were all his seniors: Moore thirty-two, Campbell thirty-four and Rogers forty-eight. Byron wore black, since he was in mourning for his mother, who had died on 1 August and 'the colour, as well of his dress, as of his glossy, curling, and picturesque hair, gave more effect to the pure, spiritual paleness of his features.'

At dinner he refused to eat anything that he was offered.

> As we had none of us been apprised of his peculiarities with respect to food, the embarrassment of our host was not a little, on discovering that there was nothing upon the table which his noble guest could eat or drink. Neither meat, fish, nor wine, would Lord Byron touch; and of biscuits and soda-water, which he asked for, there had been, unluckily, no provision. He professed, however, to be equally pleased with potatoes and vinegar, and of these meagre materials contrived to make rather a hearty supper.

Byron's conduct astonished everyone at the table, as Rogers's own report confirms. Such behaviour would recur frequently. (Appendix 1 uses Rogers's report of this dinner to explore its contemporary context.)

7

HE WOULD RATHER NOT EXIST THAN BE LARGE

In the autumn of 1811 Byron was still insisting on starving himself, as a sympathetic witness discovered. 'I told him of the baneful effects of vinegar &c, but he tells me he would rather not exist than be large; and so he is a pale, languid-looking young man who seems as if he could not walk upright from sheer weakness.'

Persistent dieting soon damaged his health. He regularly resorted to the 'use or abuse of Acids', which forced him to seek medical attention in 1812 and again in 1813.

He suffered a stone in his kidneys in February 1812, which was treated with glystering (enemas), purging and vomiting.

Robert Charles Dallas observed him at close quarters that same year, as Byron began to make his way in the social and literary world. Dallas made a record of his relative's diet:

> It consisted of thin plain biscuits, not more than two, and often one, with a cup of tea, taken about one o'clock or noon, which he assured me was generally all the nourishment he took in the four-and-twenty hours. But he declared, that, far from sinking his spirits, he felt himself lighter and livelier for it; and that it had given him a greater command over himself in every other respect. This great abstemiousness is hardly credible, nor can I imagine it literal fact, though doubtless much less food is required to keep the body in perfect health than is usually taken. He had a habit of

perpetually chewing mastic [gum from the island of Chios], which probably assisted his determination to persevere in this meagre regime; but I have no doubt that his principal auxiliary was an utter abhorrence of corpulence, which he conceived to be equally unsightly and injurious to the intellect; and it was his opinion that great eaters were generally passionate and stupid.

In her first letter to Byron, written on 27 March 1812, Lady Caroline Lamb urged him to 'eat and drink like an Englishman'.

Another Doctor Writes

Byron was obliged to consult a Brighton doctor about recurrent pains in his kidneys in October 1812. The doctor's 'Commentary' ran as follows:

> From every Observation I have been able to make on the present state of Lord Byrons Constitution generally considerd, as well as respecting the peculiar disposition to nephritic affections, I feel convinced that a more nutritious diet gradually adopted is essential to his Health. The effect of regular tho' sparing use of animal food, is not only requisite to support a firm degree of muscular Vigor, but as being more alkalescent than any other diet will prevent the formation of that acid (especially the lyric), which is the basis of Calculous Connection & which with the adaption of appropriate remedies will gradually & certainly remove the lumbar pains. The extravagant Waste of fluid in the System, & the *habitual* excitement of the Salivary Glands, produced by his Lordships continual use of Mastick & Tobacco, not only prevents a healthy digestion & produces a consequent torpor of the Bowels (requiring an otherwise unnecessary repetition of purgatives), but in fact diminishes the aqeous Volume of the urine, & of course renders the remaining secretion more *acrid* & highly *saline* & this gives an encreased facility to the formation of calculus, & morbid irritation in the Kidneys.
>
> Lord Byron ought from this reasoning to adopt gradually an animal Diet beginning with milk, light done Eggs, then dry white Meat Veal or poultry

in small quantities & only once a day. This plan will by no means produce any disposition to *obesity*, which in point of fact is more likely to follow from large Quantities of fluid & saccharine substances, than from a diet more condensed, & animalized –

Malt liquor Cyder &c must certainly be avoided – Soda Water with a glass of white wine (Madeira or Sherry) will be the properest beverage, tho' such fluid should not be taken to excess or a false degree of thirst habitually indulged.

The Tepid Bath from 92 to 94° appears a suitable plan two or three times a Week, by brushing up a natural & regular Condition of the surface of the Body & allaying the lumbar pains. Should any return of acute pain in the region of the Kydnies be experienced the pills formerly directed shd be taken, but not continued beyond the period of relief.

The Bowels ought not to be used excessively & this I think a caution of paramount importance – The alteration of diet will of itself predispose the system to a more regular state, but shd. any Costiveness occur, the annexd pill should be taken at bed time and a couple of tea spoonsful of the Cheltenham salt the following morning.

The salt shd. be dissolved in a Wine glass of hot water, then put into a tumbler in which shd. be decanted a bottle of *Soda* Water, & drunk before the Gas has evaporated.

Lord Byron should continue to take the pills twice a day *only*, 3 each time – this quantity should *not* be encreased unless on the recurrence of pain in the region of the Kidney, or the appearance of latentious [= brick-like] Sediment [i.e. broken down calculous matter] on either of these occurrences, they may be taken *three* times – The antispasmodic mixture must be had recourse to as before in case severe pain & illness, or Nephritiic uneasiness, come on. This Medicine should not be taken more than twice in the 24 hours, as it contains a quantity of Hydrocyanus, of which an excess will produce Headache or *Stupor*, to a certain degree two pints of milk at these meals, should be taken daily with toasted Bread, or Buiscuit[.] Soda Water, as far as two Bottles may be drunk in the course of the day – & if the Bowells are at all torpid the powder containing Magnesia &c. should be

> taken occasionally at Bed time, & repeated if necessary every night while the defining of regular action continues.

For most of the time, Byron ignored this prescription of moderation. The pains continued intermittently for the next eight months. But Byron's priority was not health, but heroism.

By October 1812 another doctor was advising Byron to gain weight, to eat meat and discouraging him from 'excessive use of the bowels'. Witnesses and his own comments confirm that Byron resorted to drastic means to lose weight throughout his twenties and thirties. Repeatedly, he tried to limit his intake of food to biscuits and soda water. He continued to abuse purgatives (laxatives) all his life, telling a friend that 'his body was very weak, that all his family had bad stomachs, and he had none, that he had kept himself alive for many years entirely with medicine, and could not live a week without it'. 'Medicine' meant more laxatives.

In 1813 observers noted that he limited his daily intake to six dry biscuits and tea, and he himself recorded the same number in April 1814.

There were brief occasions throughout his time in England when Byron relaxed his diet. We'll see later how those occasions tallied with his emotional life.

While he lived in Italy, between 1816 and 1822, he stopped starving himself, and at the age of thirty he began to put on weight again. Byron himself remarked on his 'alteration', which lasted five years. In 1822, however, he reverted to his diet.

Lady Blessington met him in 1823 and reported in her journal for 1 April that he was 'extremely thin, indeed so much so that his figure has a boyish air'; 'his coat appears to have been many years made, is much too large and all his garments appear to have been purchased ready made, so ill do they fit him.' 'Byron is evidently in delicate health,' she reported, 'brought on by starvation. . . Nothing gratifies him so much as being told he is thin.'

That same year his physician in Genoa, Dr James Alexander, asked a mutual friend to speak to Byron, 'on the necessity of his accustoming himself to a more nutritious regimen; but he declared, that if he did, he should get fat and stupid, and that it was only by abstinence that he felt he had the power of exercising his mind'. Byron was rationalising his eating disorder, which was triggered by other, less accessible concerns.

He would die a year later in 1824, partly from starvation.

His private behaviour needs to be seen in context with the general, public patterns of contemporary consumption.

Costly Gluttony

'Costly gluttony' was 'one of the most distinguished extravagances of the age', Byron's friend John Cam Hobhouse pointed out in 1809. The Prince of Wales set society's tone as a sensualist who was notorious for his carnal and gastronomic appetites, regularly caricatured as a gross, pear-shaped glutton. At a dinner in the Prince Regent's Royal Pavilion in Brighton on 18 January 1817 to honour Grand Duke Nicholas of Russia, his chef Carême served thirty-six courses, including eight soups, eight Removes of Fish and forty Entrées Served around the Fish; five Platters after the Fish and eight Great Pieces.

In general, the Regency style of entertaining presupposed extravagance and licensed excess. Dinners were occasions for the display of plenty on a lavish, feudal scale. The table groaned with a plethora of savoury and sweet dishes, so that guests could help themselves to whatever they fancied. An ideal table setting might feature two kinds of soup, turbot, turkey, mutton and chicken cutlets, partridges and cod, all at once. One set of dishes was then 'relieved' by another. More than enough was the rule. Servants or other dependants would consume whatever remained uneaten.

'Suppose there are eight persons at dinner,' Louis Eustache Ude advised in *The French Cook*, a book published in 1813 that Byron owned and consulted for *Don Juan*. 'You cannot send up less than four *entrées*, a soup, and a fish. Now as a remove to the two latter, you must have two removes, *viz.* two dishes of *rôt* [joints of roast meat]. Next four *entremets*, and if you should think proper two removes of *rôt*.' 'Formerly Cook to Louis XVI, King of France, and at Present Cook to the Right Hon. Earl of Sefton',

James Gillray, A Voluptuary under the Horrors of Digestion, *2 July 1792. Gillray contrasted father and son in a memorable pair of caricatures:* Temperance Enjoying a Frugal Meal *showed King George III and his wife eating a boiled egg and salad. This, its pair, shows their son the Prince of Wales, who would become Regent (1811–20) and George IV (1820–30), picking his teeth after eating roast beef. A portrait of Alvise Cornaro (1484–1566), who taught that a long life depends on sobriety, looks down on the prince. When Leigh Hunt called the Regent 'a corpulent gentleman of fifty', in the* Examiner *for 22 March 1812 he was charged with seditious libel, along with the publisher, Hunt's brother, John. 'For he is fat,' Shelley wrote in 'The Devil's Walk: A Ballad' of 1812, 'His waistcoat gay,/When strained upon a levee day,/Scarce meets across his princely paunch,/And pantaloons are like half moons,/Upon each brawny haunch. /How vast his stock of calf when plenty/Had filled his empty head and heart,/Enough to satiate foplings twenty,/Could make his pantaloon seams start'*(71ff).

according to the title page, Ude had worked as *maître d'hôtel* for Napoleon's mother and later cooked for the Duke of York and at Crockford's gaming club in Mayfair. He was known for his moderation but he still insisted on plenty of choice.

Whenever 'there are more than four *entrées*, symmetry must always be attended to. The two flanks, for a dinner of six *entrées* must be parallel, that is to say, that if you place *petits pâtés* on one side, you must have *croquettes* on the other; if you have a *vol au vent* on one side, you must place a *pâté chaud* opposite, and so on; a judicious arrangement of dishes giving additional merit to a dinner.'

Byron chose not to attend the party held at Newstead Abbey to celebrate his twenty-fourth birthday. Susan Vaughan, a maidservant who was briefly his lover and also celebrated her birthday on 22 January, reported to him how the table was laid:

> I had a spare rib of pork at the top an apple pie at the bottom a pork pie in the middle potatoes at one corner sellery at the other mince pies and Custards at the other two Corners after that cheese and the Cloath was removed a small table set Round with glasses and punch we had forsooth Mr Murry Drank your health wishing you many happy returns of the Day – three Cheers follow'd in the next glass {little} They afterwards asked me to give a toast I immediately Thought of you paused a moment, and rose up with My fine toast it was the following) Long may me Lord live happy may he be blest with Content & From Misfortune free. – The others Sanction,d It Said The Same I did not tell you of a nice plum cake we had more singing and dancing ended this grandure.

Great Meals of Beef

Over the course of the eighteenth century Britons repeatedly defined themselves by contrast with the French. The neighbours were at war between 1702 and 1713 (the War of the Spanish Succession); 1739 and 1748 (the War of the Austrian Succession); and 1756 and 1763 (the Seven Years War) as well as between 1803 and 1815, almost uninterruptedly. National cuisines played a role in differences. To eat beef was not only behaving traditionally, it meant you were being English, even patriotic.

> For we all know that English people are
> Fed upon beef
> *Don Juan*, II, 66

Englishmen liked to celebrate their land of plenty. Traditionally they associated heroism with meat, in particular with beef. 'Give them great meals of beef,' Frenchmen commented in *Henry V* before the Battle of Agincourt, and 'they will eat like wolves and fight like devils'. William Hogarth epitomised the tradition of identifying the English with roast beef in his painting, *The Gate of Calais*, in 1749. In 1813 'the thirty yeomen on duty at St James's Palace received rations of twenty-four pounds of beef a day, along with eighteen pounds of mutton, sixteen pounds of veal, thirty-seven gallons of beer and, on Sundays, three plum puddings. Assuming that the guards ate two main meals a day, that works out as the equivalent of roughly a pound of meat per meal.'

Beef eating came to identify the typical Englishman: John Arbuthnot personified him as John Bull in 1712 in his satire *Law is a Bottomless Pit; or, the History of John Bull.* For a time he appeared as a bull, 'a fitting image in a society where ordinary people were expected to pay taxes, obey government, and have no official voice in public affairs'.

Caricaturists began to portray John Bull not as an animal, but as a stout, carnivorous middle-aged man. Occasionally, his stout, no-nonsense ordinariness merged with the stout, frugal, no-nonsense pragmatic (if rather German) figure of George III, who reigned from 1760 to 1820. As Byron's contemporary the poet Leigh Hunt said, 'the English nation were pleased to see in him a crowning specimen of themselves – a Royal John Bull'. The king even referred to himself as John Bull, explaining that he enjoyed domestic comforts and tended 'to despise what I am not accustom'd to'.

If beef and plenty were English, vegetables and hunger were foreign. Englishmen liked to contrast plump John Bull with French scrawniness and want; traditional English food (roast beef) with heterodox foreign dishes such as *soupe maigre* (thin, i.e. meatless soup) and innovations such as vegetarianism. Reality sharpened the traditional contrast in 1788, when a cruel winter followed the worst French harvest for forty years. In 1789 hunger helped to prompt revolution in France.

In *French Liberty; British Slavery*, on 21 December 1792, James Gillray opposed a ragged, starving but happy French revolutionary who chews onions, against an obese John Bull, who carves a joint of beef and complains about taxes.

John Bull Loses Weight

The long, bitter course of the Napoleonic Wars complicated simple oppositions between prosperous England and impoverished France.

France prospered during the wars, as Napoleon secured a remarkable series of victories and extended his empire over most of Europe. Food shortages in Britain reminded the poor of discrepancies in an unfair society that resolutely opposed reform. Daniel Eaton's journal of 1793, *Politics for the People: or Salmagundy for Swine*, alluded to Burke's dismissal of the (French revolutionary) people as the 'swinish multitude'. It opened with a verse motto:

> Since Times are bad, and solid food is rare,
> The Swinish Herd should learn to live on air;
> Acorns and Pease, alas! No more abound,
> A feast of Words, is in the Hog Trough found.

For the first time, John Bull shed weight. He lost the one factor common to all his different incarnations: his stoutness.

Isaac Cruikshank's *John Bull at the Sign. The Case is Altered* of 2 March 1801 showed John Bull 'lean, hungry, ragged and dejected', in front of 'his meagre fare of herring and sprats, while . . . a corpulent Frenchman, seated before a large joint of beef, says sarcastically: "Ah What Monsieur Jack Bull you going to starve me!!!"'

Hunger lurked in the background of Regency society and contributed to the expectations of Byron's contemporaries, who were bewildered by his apparently arbitrary, aberrant, abstemious behaviour at table.

James Gillray, JOHN BULL'S PROGRESS, 3 June 1794, shows how war beggars his family and reduces a fat, happy John Bull to an emaciated, threadbare cripple.

JOHN BULL Come to the Bone, *17 June 1815. The Frenchman comments on how 'Jean Bull' has diminished in size.*

Two cuts, probably by George Cruikshank, showing the Pie of State, from William Hone, 'The Political A, Apple-Pie etc'; or the 'Extraordinary Red Book', versified for the instruction and amusement of the rising generation, *1820:*

> *To the taste quite delightful, and nice to the eye*
> *'Tis the PIE of the State, made of all that is good;*
> *The ingredients all purchased by John Bull's blood*

Hone lists alphabetically all those who help themselves to the pie, such as judges, bishops, politicians, royalty, ambassadors etc., and ends:

> *Whilst poor old JOHN BULL o'er the empty dish said,*
> *'And there's none left for me nor for X nor for Z'.*

Isaac Cruikshank's caricature, *The PHANTASMAGORIA or a REVIEW of Old Times*, of 9 March 1803 shows Napoleon as First Consul conjuring up from the past a fat John Bull, in scarlet, and a thin Frenchman, who marvel at their changed descendants: the Englishman of today is 'a mere shrimp', whose clothes no longer fit, while the fat Frenchman has feasted on beef and plum pudding.

Gradually, fortunes were reversed: Britain fought back while the emperor's campaigns faltered and John Bull began to put on weight again.

The Napoleonic Wars, against an enemy known for a different cuisine, highlighted beef's patriotic associations. To celebrate the British victory at Waterloo the Romantic poets Wordsworth and Southey sang 'God save the king' and 'roasted beef and boiled plum-puddings' on Skiddaw. Vegetarianism was widely viewed with suspicion, as a dangerous, profoundly un-English innovation.

Typically, one of the most influential vegetarian tracts, John Frank Newton's *The Return to Nature; or a Defence of the Vegetable Regimen, &c*, published in 1811, advertised its political sympathies in its title, since 'Nature' then implied Jacobinism. The *British Critic* reacted to the book with unmitigated ferocity: 'Of all Quacks there is no species so dangerous as that to which this author belongs . . . To every thinking mind, to every one in the least acquainted with the functions and structure of the stomach, and the animal economy in general, this boasted "return to nature" must appear in the most glaring colours of absurdity.'

Byron avoided eating meat principally in order to lose weight, as the French novelist Stendhal observed in 1816 and 1817. But his prejudice against meat also reflected a primitive belief in 'sympathy': Byron appeared 'to have conceived a notion that animal food has some peculiar influence on the character', Thomas Moore noted; 'and I remember, one day, as I sat opposite to him, employed, I suppose, rather earnestly over a beef-steak, after watching me for a few seconds, he said, in a grave tone of enquiry, –"Moore, don't you find eating beef-steak makes you ferocious?"' Byron's behaviour may have aroused particular comment at this moment in British culture, when to be carnivorous was to be patriotic.

8

INTERPRETATIONS AND DIAGNOSES

Lord Byron's bouts of starvation, bingeing and purging constituted an eating disorder. Accounts in the medical press (and elsewhere) have confirmed that retrospective diagnosis ever since 1982, when Wilma Paterson asked in *World Medicine*, 'Was Byron anorexic?'

Though anorexia nervosa generally afflicts adolescent girls, some 10 per cent of those who starve themselves are boys and men. Several recent studies have focused on this phenomenon. Byron also suffered from the related illness bulimia nervosa, bingeing followed by starvation, purging or vomiting: 'I began early & very violently,' he told Lady Melbourne on 12 January 1813, '– and alternate extremes of excess and abstinence have utterly destroyed – oh! unsentimental word! – my *stomach*.'

Such habits may seem incompatible with an active life, and Byron was committed to sports that suited him. In particular, his swimming feats became legendary. He liked to boast that he was 'almost amphibious'. In July or early August 1807 he swam 'in the Thames from Lambeth through the 2 Bridges Westminster & Blackfriars, a distance including the different turns & tacks made on the way, of 3 miles!!' He swam across the River Tagus in Portugal from Old Lisbon to Belem Castle in a little less than two hours in July 1809 and across the Hellespont from Europe (Sestos) to Asia (Abydos) in an hour and ten minutes on 3 May 1810. In Venice he swam the length of the Grand Canal, from the Lido to near the Piazzetta, wearing trousers, in four hours and twenty minutes in June 1818. And after

Shelley's cremation on the beach in August 1822 Byron swam three miles in the sea. But there is no inconsistency: anorexics tend to display remarkable physical stamina.

Eating disorders are often precipitated by an ordinary attempt to lose weight. Once the illness has taken hold it is notoriously hard to shift: it tends to have a 20 to 25 per cent mortality rate. Byron survived to the age of thirty-six partly because he suffered only intermittently. As we'll see, the occasions when he did not diet prove more interesting, in terms of what they tell us, than the times when he starved himself.

His eating disorder began almost exactly halfway through his life, on the brink of his nineteenth birthday. For the physician the circumstances that precede the outbreak of anorexia remain strikingly consistent. They include 'open conflict between the family and the patient; a preceding history of obesity; impotence; puberty . . . at a time of attempted adjustment to the outside environment; parental pressure and a family history of neurosis or psychosis'.

Two particular factors that doctors now look for (at least in the United States) are low self-esteem, which may be evidence of sexual abuse, and father hunger. Dr Margo Maine, a specialist in treating female anorexia nervosa, coined or appropriated the phrase 'father hunger' in 1993 in her book of the same name, subtitled 'Fathers, Daughters and Food', having noted that many of her patients longed for paternal involvement. One of the prime purposes of this book is to explore the role that Byron's father hunger played in his life and work. We'll consider its implications in a later chapter.

A checklist of symptoms merely confirms the diagnosis of anorexia – rather late in the day. The diagnosis seems to lead to a dead-end. 'Poor Byron,' Arthur Crisp, Emeritus Professor of Psychological Medicine, wrote in the *British Medical Journal*, 'Poor Byron, to be reduced to our labelling.' The danger is that, as the author Cyril Connolly said of Freudian literary analysis, the key turns in the lock: such labels belong in the footnotes to a medical journal; they may seem unlikely to help in understanding Byron's work. The most banal interpretation of Byron's disorder is that, like other anorexics, he resorted to starving in order to assert control, where that was possible – over his own body.

Byron's biographers have not paid much attention to his disordered eating, which mystified witnesses, even those who knew him well, such as Thomas Moore. Those who did not know him in person have tended to misunderstand his motivation, some of them wilfully. In *The Real Lord Byron*, first published in 1883, John Cordy Jeaffreson assumed that unmanly vanity motivated the poet's diet; that he suffered from an obsession with his physical appearance. This idea so disturbed Jeaffreson that he exaggerated Byron's initial corpulence, describing his 'burdensome and disfiguring grossness' as 'a swinish state of physical depravity'. He speaks for his time, the Victorian era, when he comments that, if Byron could only have brought himself 'to sacrifice the beauty of his hands . . . with his broad shoulders, muscular neck and thewy arms, he would have been a superb oarsman'. Byron could have, and should have, rowed for Cambridge. Instead, he ended up as a degenerate, who indulged in purgatives, perhaps rather as some of Jeaffreson's contemporaries abused absinthe.

Twentieth-century writers reacted against Jeaffreson's sensationalism by adopting a tone of jaunty casualness. J. D. Symon said in 1924 that 'The impulse towards dandyism, physical and mental, made him impatient of his fat.' Leslie A. Marchand suggested it 'may be that his desire to succeed as a Lothario encouraged him to undertake his spartan regime'. In a twentieth-century anachronism, Doris Langley Moore blurred the idiosyncrasy of Byron's obsession by equating it with the modern slimming fad. If biographers discussed Byron's diet at all they attributed it to vanity.

Even after 1982, when Wilma Paterson proposed a diagnosis of anorexia in *World Medicine*, literary historians and biographers of Byron tended to ignore or minimise its importance, preferring instead to focus on his sexuality or his celebrity. Phyllis Grosskurth in 1997 made no mention of the diagnosis; Benita Eisler in 1999 consigned it to a footnote. Timothy Morton in 1999 claimed 'Byron's diet was rather thin for cosmetic reasons'. Ian Gilmour in 2002 covered it in one sentence and a useful, longer footnote. In 2003 Fiona MacCarthy speculated that his doctor advised him to go on his first diet, 'probably because Byron's weight was putting too much strain on his deformed leg'. Later she confirmed her speculation and asserted that 'Byron's avoidance of meat was not simply an ostentatious whim. On medical advice he had been eating abstemiously since the Southwell years.' In fact Dr Hutchinson's prescription, quoted above, responded to his patient's wish to lose weight. Its recommendation that Byron should take long walks demonstrates that he did not worry about placing 'too much strain on [Byron's] deformed leg'. Later medical advisers urged Byron to stop dieting. Paradoxically MacCarthy also mentioned that Byron 'kept up a more or less obsessive dependence on dieting and purgatives all through the years of his celebrity'. She did not investigate this and noted that he returned from the East in 1811 'with a delicate digestion', without exploring why. She also underplayed starvation's contribution to his final illness. In *The Cambridge Companion to Byron*, 2004, Paul Douglass remarked *en passant*, 'in addition to excess there was abstemiousness'. Harold Bloom referred to Byron as 'a perpetual dieter to check a tendency to corpulence'.

Byron's anorexia is a symptom, a disorder that expresses unresolved tensions, rather than the main issue. What matters just as much as the fact of his diet is his motivation – above all, why Byron *thought* he dieted.

Anorexia nervosa was first identified as an illness (and named), by Sir Humphrey Gull and Dr Lasègue almost fifty years after Byron's death, in 1873. Byron's illness dominated his life and work partly because neither he nor his contemporaries realised that he was suffering from a disease. He made sense of his compulsion by turning it into a philosophy. He believed he was acting on a moral conviction, that the soul had to be freed from the body. Those who knew him well accepted his rationale. Teresa Guiccioli summed it up as 'Antimatérialisme'. Her insight reflected her own need to 'disembody' Byron, which led to her recording his posthumous visitations to her in séances, but other witnesses throughout his life corroborated her views.

Byron's attitude to eating remained the same, even when his practice varied. For this reason, Teresa, who lived with him during the longest period when he was *not* dieting, between 1818 and 1822, remembered only his asceticism.

Even when he did not feel compelled to diet, Byron tended to try to starve himself, because he believed that it represented the best, the most heroic course of action.

Byron's anorexia was a complex matter. It certainly suited the Puritan, ascetic streak in his nature. He boasted to his banker and friend the Hon. Douglas Kinnaird that he 'never spent more than half an hour over a solitary supper', adding on 12 September 1822, 'my *table* don't cost four shillings a day'.

He believed that abstinence (and bathing his head in cold water) cured him of the 'dreadful and almost periodical headaches' that, he told Augusta on 12 October 1823, he suffered till he 'was fourteen – and sometimes since', as a consequence of 'a determination of blood to the head'.

His vanity also played a part. At the end of the eighteenth century it started to become 'glamorous to look sickly', as Susan Sontag said in *Illness as Metaphor* (1978). She pointed out that Byron anticipated the later cult of the consumptive appearance. 'I am well, but weakly,' he recorded in a letter to his friend Francis Hodgson on 8 December 1811, adding that yesterday a friend had told him he 'looked very ill, and sent me home happy'. Byron had a specific glamour in mind, however. Another friend found him 'weakened and thinned' by illness, in the autumn of 1810; 'standing one day before a looking-glass, [Byron] said [. . .] – "How pale I look! – I should like, I think, to die of a consumption . . . [because] the women would all say, 'See that poor Byron – how interesting he looks, in dying.'"' Byron rather liked looking ill and thin, because he thought it appealed to women, and, as we'll see, he longed to be mothered.

Finally, Byron told Moore 'that he was never altogether free from pain' in his foot. Leigh Hunt confirmed that Byron suffered from 'a real and even a sore lameness. Much walking upon it fevered and hurt it.' Putting on weight probably exacerbated it, while psychic pain contributed to generate 'the sensations of bodily uneasiness' that his wife said his deformed foot 'habitually occasioned him'. Hence, in Teresa Guiccioli's words, his 'desire and resolution to master *material man* so as to benefit *spiritual man*'.

'To hunger is to overcome the pull of gravity,' the French mystic Simone Weil wrote, 'and to liberate the spirit from the prison of its flesh.' Dieting for Byron represented a heroic endeavour, to free the spirit from the body, a battle for independence that paralleled (if it did not also reflect) his enthusiasm for other struggles for independence: his own from his mother; Italy's from Austria; and Greece's from Turkey.

To understand how he felt about his condition we should call it *Anorexia Heroica*.

We return to the scene of his first diet to consider what caused it.

PART IV

A PARTIALITY FOR SPIRIT

'Oh! that the desart were my dwelling-place,/With one fair Spirit for my Minister'. An illustration to Childe Harold, *IV, 177 in an engraving by R. Stainer after Henry Richter, from* The Byron Gallery, *1833.*

9

MIND versus MATTER

A Byronic Vocabulary

'There has not been thought to be – at least it is not readily apparent – a Byronic vocabulary as there is a Shelleyan vocabulary,' Willis W. Pratt wrote carefully in his foreword to the concordance to Byron's poetry. I suggest that there is a Byronic vocabulary. his language habitually resolves into contrasts between earthbound matter and aerial spirit. The split lies at the heart of his way of thinking and was manifested in his private language, his idiolect: 'Bound to the earth, he lifts his eye to heaven', as Byron says in *Childe Harold*. It may sound facile, reductive, an alternative to that schoolboy habit of subjecting all of literature to the procrustean dichotomy of illusion/reality, but it corresponds to the way Byron thought and felt about the world.

Appreciating the habitual nature of Byron's thought and speech helps us to understand such enigmas as why Byron would welcome a libel, because it was 'etherial'; how acting could constitute 'immaterial sensuality'; why Byron would associate Napoleon's fall with indigestion and, eventually, why he called his hero Don Juan but denied him all the major traits associated with the legend.

A list of Byron's private terms would cover these:

body, embodied	soul
clay	spirit
matter, materialism	immaterialism

form
mortal
terrestrial
perishable
earth
clod
clog
corporeal
prison
dust
mass
flesh and blood
inert, inertion
bulk
leaven
senses
sod
sink
garment
sand-pit
voluptuous
sensation
sensual
self
fall

fancy
immortal
ethereal
seraph
heaven
vapour
music
celestial
freedom
star
mind
phantom
god, goddess
glory
vision
sense
intellect
soar
deity
thought
divine
fire
ideal
lightning
fly
meteor
animate
flash
sprite
electric
spark
wing
poetry

Byron never uses these words accidentally or neutrally. Each time one of them appears it signals that, whatever the subject, his thoughts are travelling in the same groove.

I Own my Partiality for Spirit

Byron wrote about the conflict between man's mortal, material body and his immortal, immaterial soul all his life, starting with his first recorded doggerel, an 'Epigram on an Old Lady Who Had Some Curious Notions

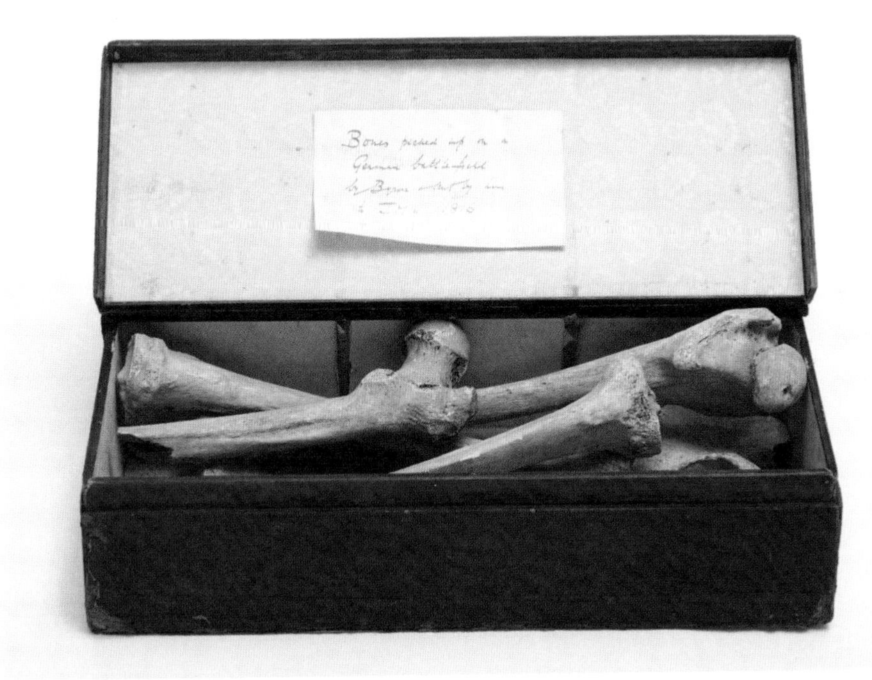

In 1816 Byron toured the battlefield of Morat, where the Swiss defeated the invading French in 1476 and thousands died. In 1798 the French invaded again and, in revenge, scattered the skeletal remains that had been gathered together in an ossuary. Byron sent Murray bones that he collected at

> *Morat! the proud, the patriot field! where man*
> *May gaze on ghastly trophies of the slain,*
> *Nor blush for those who conquered on that plain*

Byron noted that the bones he sent amounted to 'as much as may have made the quarter of a hero'. Once again Byron interrogates the nature of heroism: is there a physical basis to mental distinction? Recent research has shown that the bones are both male and female in origin.

Private collection

Respecting the Soul' in 1798. The dichotomy provides the theme of plays such as *Cain*, *Heaven and Earth* and *Sardanapalus*. But it also colours his thinking on disparate topics.

Tracing the shifting flow of the relationship between body and soul reveals the world through Byron's eyes. At first, he has no doubt at all: body and soul are a polarity; spirit *must* be freed from flesh. He defines his heroic ideal by the soul's victory over matter. So Manfred, in the play of that name, longs to be

> The viewless spirit of a lovely sound,
> A living voice, a breathing harmony,
> A bodiless enjoyment – born and dying
> With the blest tone which made me!

A Distinct Faculty or Soul

'A man's poetry is a distinct faculty or soul,' Byron reflected in a letter to Moore of 16 November 1821, 'and has no more to do with the every-day individual than the Inspiration with the Pythoness when removed from her tripod.' For most of his life he assumed poetry expressed the spirit, that it manifested the soul's freedom from matter and from the self, 'a straw, borne on by human breath . . ./A paper kite, which flies 'twixt life and death,/A shadow which the onward soul behind throws'. This illuminates why Byron reacted with such intense hostility to Keats's indulgently sensual poetry: he assumed that Keats suffered from 'inordinate self-love' and identified his poetry with masturbation.

Meanwhile sculpture and architecture were 'direct manifestations of mind – & *presuppose* poetry in their very conception'.

At first Byron's relations with women were coloured by idealism or fantasy, as he projected on to them an extreme form of non-maternal, non-threatening bodilessness.

At a point in 1813 when he had lost hope of distinguishing himself in the House of Lords, Byron saw a performance of *Antony and Cleopatra.*

It reminded him that the Roman politician Antony exerted power through his orations: 'and are not "word[s] things",' Byron asked in his Journal on 16 November 1813, 'and such "*words*" very pestilent "*things*" too?' (The source for the original formula has not yet been traced.) In theory, therefore, the theatre offered an alternative arena for oratory. Unfortunately, however, Byron still despised writers, insisting that 'no one should be a rhymer who could be any thing better'. He heard that William Windham, Secretary for War and the Colonies in the Ministry of all the Talents, 'an active participator in the events of the earth, and one of those who governed nations', regretted that he had not entirely devoted himself to literature and science. Byron could not comprehend his 'debility of mind'. The 'preference of *writers* to *agents*' struck him as 'a sign of effeminacy, degeneracy, and weakness. Who would write,' he asked in his Journal on 24 November 1813, 'who had any thing better to do?'

The idea that speaking or writing could embody action haunted Byron. It took him the next six years, his own fortuitous discovery that he could rival Napoleon's infamy, and the inspiration of Shelley to convince him. Finally, in his masterpiece *Don Juan* he asserted:

> But words are things, and a small drop of ink,
> Falling like dew, upon a thought, produces
> That which makes thousands, perhaps millions, think . . .

Such confidence was crucial to the work's success. The equation turns on the truly Byronic pivot of abstraction and action.

This movement from doubt to conviction enacts the development in Byron's work and life and is mirrored by his changing attitude to women.

The Celestial Nature of Women

In adulthood Byron 'disliked seeing women eat, or to have their company at dinner', as Captain Gronow noted, 'from a wish to believe, if possible, in their more etherial nature'. Byron could not stomach Rubens's paintings.

He called the artist 'the most glaring-flaring-staring-harlotry imposter that ever passed a trick upon the senses of mankind', which shows that most of all he hated Rubens's portrayals of shamelessly fleshy women.

Precocious as a child, Byron fell in love with a series of girls who were all older and all related to him. It looks as though those loves shared an unreal, idealised nature. 'I have a passion for the name of Mary,' he wrote in *Don Juan*, 'For once it was a magic sound to me/And still it half calls up the realm of fairy'. Before he reached the age of eight, he fell passionately in love with his distant cousin Mary Duff. He called her a 'lovely Peri' or bodiless fairy in his Journal in 1813, adding that, at the time he had not learned to write, so he had to dictate letters to her. 'I certainly had no sexual ideas for years afterwards,' he reflected, 'and yet my misery, my love for that girl were so violent, that I sometimes doubt if I have ever been really attached since.'

At the age of twelve he found refuge in another dream of idealisation. He fell in love with his cousin Margaret Parker, who was older, perhaps by a year. One 'of the most beautiful of evanescent beings', she 'died about a year or two afterwards' from consumption. Byron's novelettish description of their one-sided relationship reeks of the Gothic fiction he then enjoyed reading: 'I do not recollect scarcely any thing equal to the *transparent* beauty of my cousin . . . she looked as if she had been made out of a rainbow – all beauty and peace.'

Margaret Parker was the first woman to inspire him to write poetry. 'On the Death of a Young Lady, Cousin to the Author and Very Dear to Him', written at the age of fourteen, is also one of Byron's first poems to highlight the divorce between spirit and matter: 'Within this narrow cell reclines her clay,/That clay where once such animation beam'd'.

At fifteen Byron fell in love with his distant kinswoman and neighbour Mary Chaworth, his elder by about two years. This relationship had little chance of success – Mary was already engaged to marry John Musters. But her principal attraction may have been her unavailability. She was descended from the man whom the 5th Lord Byron killed in a duel in 1765. The Chaworths still lived at Annesley, near Newstead Abbey. Byron relished

John Hazlitt, Mary Chaworth, *1805.*

Private collection

the weight of inherited history on both sides, attracted or reassured by 'the curse of blood'. The relationship between Byron and Mary Chaworth ended when he was either told of, or overheard, her saying to her maid, 'Do you think I could care anything for that lame boy?' The remark struck him, he said, 'like a shot through his heart'. He ran out of the house and some three or four miles back to Newstead.

Annesley Hall.

Photo: Richard Allen & Son, 1874

Thomas Phillips's portrait of Mary Chaworth Musters in later life.
Courtesy of Nottingham City Museums and Galleries

Mary Chaworth's marriage later broke down. She wrote to Byron and tried to see him; he fled from her advances.

Byron could be clear-sighted about his idealisation of women: 'I have taken all my fables about the celestial nature of women from the perfection my imagination created in her – I say created, for I found her, like the rest of her sex, anything but angelic.'

Through the Air Sublime

Byron's dualism coloured the particular way he appreciated landscape. He was sent to Invercauld and Braemar, to drink goat's whey in 1795–6, 'in consequence of a threatened decline after the scarlet fever'. He swam in the River Dee and roamed the Highlands in a tartan cloak (probably in the Stewart or Gordon tartan).

Mountain summits introduced Byron to a new, transcendent experience. He climbed the mountain of Lochnagar (1,155 m; 3,789 feet) and the summit of Morven, so as 'To gaze on the torrent, that thunder'd beneath,/ Or the mist of the tempest that gather'd below'. Byron explained that 'it is by no means uncommon on attaining the top of Ben-e-vis, Ben-y-bourd, etc, to perceive, between the Summit and the Valley, clouds pouring down rain, and, occasionally, accompanied by lightning, while the Spectator, literally, looks down on the Storm, perfectly secure from its Effects.' Byron sought

Byron wearing the Gordon tartan in an unsigned portrait that was sold at Gray's Auctioneers, Cleveland, Ohio, on 28 November 2011.
Private collection

Byron in Harrow Churchyard, an *engraving after Clarkson Stanfield, from Finden. Byron sat 'for hours & hours' on a tomb in St Mary's churchyard, which is strikingly situated 'on the brow of the hill looking toward Windsor', gazing down and across at the view.*

repeatedly to enjoy this experience of aerial superiority, which relieved his earthbound condition.

His wife Annabella remembered from their honeymoon how Byron liked scrambling up 'a Crag' on the seashore near Seaham, a 'jutting out, & at high tide insulated rock . . . from which [he] looked upon a solitude shared only by myself'. He enjoyed the same sensation in the Swiss mountains when he toured the Bernese Oberland in September 1816 and in 1823 at Metaxata on Cephalonia, where a plaque commemorates 'Byron's Rock' in the village of Lakithra, now with a view of an airport.

Byron relished finding the experience in fiction, in the poems of Ossian and, above all, in Le Sage's *Le diable boiteux* ('The Limping Devil').

Byron then recreated the experience of aerial flight in his own poems, in 'Lachin y Gair' and 'Granta. A Medley' ('Oh! could Le Sage's demon's gift/ Be realized at my desire,/This night my trembling form he'd lift/To place it

The devil carries the hero through the air over a town, an illustration from an early nineteenth-century edition of one of Byron's favourite novels, Le Sage's Le diable boiteux, *1747.*

on St. Mary's spire'); in *Manfred*; in an Armenian poem that he translated ('He journeys over land to the top of a mountain'); as well as in *Cain* and, in metaphorical form, in *Childe Harold* III and in *Don Juan*.

The transcendent, aerial experience goes back to Satan tempting Jesus, in Milton's *Paradise Regained*: 'So saying, he caught him up, and, without wing/Of Hippogrif, bore through the air sublime/Over the Wilderness and o'er the Plain'.

Poetry allowed Byron to display such 'powers of mind'. *Childe Harold* III celebrates this action as early as stanza 6:

> What am I? Nothing; but not so art thou,
> Soul of my thought! with whom I traverse earth,
> Invisible but gazing, as I glow
> Mix'd with thy spirit, blended with thy birth,
> And feeling still with thee in my crush'd feelings' dearth.

Another illustration to Le Sage's Le diable boiteux, *showing the devil and the hero on a rooftop, gazing down at the town's exposed rooms.*

The devil flies the hero to the roof of a church in another illustration to Le diable boiteux, *from the Novelists' Library edition of* The Devil on Two Sticks, *illustrated by Thomas Stothard, 1801.*

The act of narrating *Don Juan* also allows Byron to revel in bodilessness, which is why he compares his activity to such triumphs over gravity as floating 'on a sea of speculation', swimming 'in the abyss of thought', ballooning and sailing.

In Canto VI the Narrator asks his readers to indulge a digression that extends over ten lines. He explains:

> (I could not shut
> It sooner for the soul of me)

When Mary Shelley made a fair copy of the manuscript for Byron's publisher, she emended Byron's idiosyncratic phrase, so that it read more conventionally, more correctly,

> (I could not shut
> It sooner for the life of me)

Byron struck out her correction and reinstated 'soul' – because that word expressed exactly what he meant. In 1812 he even wrote a poem, 'From the Portuguese', on the difference between the two words.

Byron gazing out at the view from a high rock, from a nineteenth-century French illustration.

PART V

BYRON'S HEROES

The LORD of the FAITHLESS.

PREVIOUS PAGE: *George Cruikshank portrays Byron as 'The Lord of the Faithless' attended by the devil, 'his FRIEND', in William Hone's* The Men in the Moon or the 'Devil to Pay', *1820. Byron's left leg rests its cloven hoof on a page marked 'Revelation'. Satan promises him:*

Your crew below,
Have fram'd,
A Resolution,
Swearing to overthrow
The CONSTITUTION;
REFORM's their word,
'Meaning, of course, Rebellion, Blood, and Riot.'

Byron replies that he has 'No thoughts of future life':

I learn'd to hate THE WORD OF TRUTH.
So thus I spurn THE BOOK OF GOD,
And only heed thy MASTER'S nod.

William Hone brought a copy of his satire to Byron's friend Hobhouse, who was then in Newgate Prison, on 7 January 1820.

10

FATHER HUNGER

So you be
Your father's son, 'tis quite enough for me
Don Juan, VI, 93

Byron's hyper-awareness of the conflict between body and spirit helped to generate and justify his eating disorder. It reflected his sense of maternal oppression, which was exacerbated by his feeling that he lacked a father.

By 1806, when he blamed death for depriving him of his father's care, he had already sought out and found several older men to fulfil the role of guardian, patron, mentor, preceptor, instructor, master and pastor, to use his terms. The most obvious candidates for the role, however, the first older males whom he knew well, the family solicitor John Hanson and Byron's guardian, the 5th Earl of Carlisle, proved disappointing.

Byron could never respect his dilatory lawyer, that 'Chattering puppy', as a mentor.

Because he was under age when he inherited the title Byron was made a ward of chancery and the 5th Earl of Carlisle, whose maternal uncle was Byron's grandfather, the vice-admiral, agreed to become his guardian. As a nobleman, a distinguished politician and a published poet, Carlisle could have acted as a role model. He was 'the only relation he [Byron] has who possesses the *Will* and *power* to be of use to him', Augusta pointed out to Hanson on 18 November 1804.

Dulwich School's headmaster Dr Glennie discovered, as Moore put it, 'that the parent was a much more difficult subject to deal with than the child'. Mrs Byron became involved with a French dancing master and wanted to take Byron to live with them in France. Dr Glennie asked Lord Carlisle to use his influence, but the nobleman refused, saying, 'I can have nothing more to do with Mrs. Byron – you must now manage her as you can.'

Instead of attending Westminster, as his father had, Byron went to Harrow School – Carlisle's choice. When he began to write poetry in 1805 Byron followed in his guardian's wake. He dedicated *Poems Original and Translated* (1808), the second edition of *Hours of Idleness*, to Carlisle, as 'His Obliged Ward, and Affectionate Kinsman'. But Carlisle kept his distance warily, since the homicidal 5th Baron and his notorious nephew Captain Byron had disgraced the family name. Bruising encounters with the fearsome, self-willed, democratically minded Mrs Byron soon reinforced that prejudice.

My Grand Patron

> I was a most unpopular boy, but *led* latterly
>
> 'An Extract from a Journal', 1821

At Harrow School, Byron felt isolated by his limp, by his Scottish accent and by his comparative poverty. 'There goes Byron,' the headmaster's wife remembered, 'straggling up the hill, like a ship in a storm without rudder or compass.' But Byron found his first important mentor in Dr Joseph Drury, the school's headmaster from 1784 to 1805. When the boy entered Harrow at the advanced age of thirteen and a half, he appeared a 'wild mountain colt', but Drury perceived that there was 'mind in his eye'. Byron would have liked that phrase.

Drury became Byron's 'grand patron', the 'dear preceptor of my early days', the first in a long series of such figures. 'Doctor Drury,' he remembered years later, 'whom I plagued sufficiently too, was the best, the kindest (and yet strict, too) friend I ever had – and I look upon him still as a father.'

Elizabeth Pigot, a miniature portrait of Byron's right eye, dated 26 April 1807.

Private collection

Lord Carlisle told Dr Drury that Byron could not expect to inherit much property when he came of age and enquired about his abilities. 'The headmaster replied, "He has talents, my Lord, which will *add lustre to his rank*." "Indeed!!!" said his Lordship, with a degree of surprise, that, according to my feeling, did not express in it all the satisfaction I expected.' Dr Drury encouraged Byron to translate the classics into English verse, inspired him to practise declamation and oratory and gave him a gold pen when Byron went abroad in 1809.

Napoleon: the Resonance of the Father Found

Byron's longest lasting, most important hero was Napoleon Bonaparte.

While still at school Byron felt further isolated by his political sympathies. He defended his bust of Napoleon 'against the rascally time-servers, when war [with France] broke out in 1803'. The 'time-servers' were reacting to a real threat: Napoleon gathered together some 200,000

The Fourth Form Room at Harrow, showing Byron's name engraved on the wall. By the time Moore visited Harrow in order to research his book, 'BYRON' had been carved into the walls three times.
Harrow School and the Harrow School Archive

soldiers near Boulogne in order to invade England. Britain was flooded with propaganda against the emperor, much of it government sponsored. Napoleon seemed a particularly appropriate hero for Byron at this stage, however, as a rank outsider, a controversial, self-made man, who came from Corsica, a region at the margin of civilisation – it only became part of France a few months before Napoleon's birth – but who now defied the whole world.

At first Byron knew little about politics and cared even less, as he admitted. His Grand Tour, starting in Lisbon, opened his eyes, and his experience of the impact of Napoleon's invasion of the Iberian peninsula transformed his attitude. Byron first referred to Napoleon as 'Gaul's Eagle'. Then, taking the point of view of the Spanish and Portuguese, he changed the bird to 'Vulture'. In time, however, he digested this, along with other disagreeable aspects to his hero's behaviour.

While Napoleon enjoyed unlimited success, Byron backed oppressed

Design for a medal commemorating the fleet Napoleon assembled at Boulogne for the planned invasion of Britain: the naked figure of Portumnus, the god of ports, holds a dolphin in one hand and a trident in the other. The legend, Classes in Anglos Instructae *means Ships Directed against the English. From Aubin-Louis Millin de Grandmaison and James Millengen,* Medallic History of Napoleon, a Collection of All the Medals, Coins and Jettons, Relating to his Actions and Reign from the Year 1796 to 1815, *1819.*

freedom fighters – the Tyroleans, Spanish and Portuguese. On the other hand, when he told Lady Melbourne on 23 December 1812 that he would 'back Buonaparte against the field still', Napoleon was, in Hobhouse's words, 'the man against whom all Europe was rising, and as the single individual to dethrone whom, or rather to destroy, a million of men were

Olympic Games or John Bull Introducing his new Ambassador to the Grand Consul, *Isaac Cruikshank, 16 June 1803: John Bull, representing Britain, urges a muscular pugilist to be 'as gentle with him [Napoleon] as you can', while the diminutive emperor punches the Russian ambassador and threatens,* 'I'll thrash all the World D— me I'll, I'll, I'll be King of the Universe'. *The French were preparing to invade Britain.*

Image courtesy of Dreweatts & Bloomsbury Auctions

rising to arms from the banks of the Tanais to the Thames'. Napoleon's fight against overwhelming numbers re-staged the 'fight' of that 'oppressed' outsider, Captain Byron.

Byron was not alone. The emperor's British admirers included a striking number of individuals whose fathers had been ostracised by British society on the grounds of religion, class or criminality. Writers such as William Hazlitt, William Godwin and Leigh Hunt and Byron's friend Hobhouse were the sons of Dissenting ministers; the playwright Mrs Inchbald's father was a Catholic, Samuel Whitbread's a brewer and Charles James Fox's a corrupt politician. Foreign tyrants seem peculiarly attractive to those whose fathers have been rejected by their country. In the last century, for example, Hitler and Stalin appealed particularly strongly to literally or metaphorically 'fatherless' Britons – among them

Charles Williams's print After the Invasion – The Levée en Masse – or Britons Strike Home *of 6 August 1803 anticipated how patriots would react, if Napoleon dared to invade Britain.*

Private collection

the politician Lloyd George, the writer Kingsley Martin and the spy Kim Philby. When Cyril Connolly discussed the spy Donald Maclean's bond with Stalin he referred to this phenomenon as 'the resonance of the "Father Found"'.

But Napoleon did not live up to Byron's expectations. Gradually, the poet detached the idea of Napoleon from historical reality. He also learned to act out the heroic/Napoleonic ideal himself in fiction and in his life. Admiration outlasted all criticism. In his 'Detached Thoughts' of 1821, long after Napoleon's reign ended, in the year of his death, Byron referred to 'his *greatest* man – (I mean his favourite – his Buonaparte – his this – that, or tother)'. Two years later he explained to another admirer, Lady Blessington, 'I find fault, and quarrel with Napoleon, as a lover does with the trifling faults of his mistress, from excessive liking.' In a similar way, perhaps,

Goethe reacted forcefully, when others rebuked the fallen Napoleon, 'Leave my emperor in peace!'

Byron's fatherlessness manifests itself in his pursuit of father figures but also in his cult of delinquency, as he sought to enjoy the bad name that his father had earned.

11

FROM SELF-LIBEL TO SATANISM

Cette injustice fut réellement selon moi, son véritable défaut

Teresa Guiccioli, *Lord Byron jugé par les Témoins de sa vie*, 1868, I, 13

Byron 'always had the weakness of wishing to be thought much worse than he really was'. Thomas Moore confirmed Samuel Rogers's insight, referring to the 'perverse fancy [Byron] had for falsifying his own character', as did Lady Blessington and Walter Scott. In his juvenile satire *English Bards and Scotch Reviewers* Byron offered this highly critical self-portrait:

Even I – least thinking of a thoughtless throng,
Just skilled to know the right and chuse the wrong,
Freed at that age when Reason's shield is lost
To fight my course through Passion's countless host,
Whom every path of Pleasure's flowery way
Has lured in turn, and all have led astray—

Byron became notorious for his cult of infamy, for his 'tendency to malign himself', for his 'love of an ill-name'. His schoolfellow William Harness called it 'hypocrisy reversed'. Before she married Byron, Annabella Milbanke called it 'the homage of Virtue to Vice'. It appalled his wife, mystified his friends and armed his enemies.

This perverse habit may have begun as Byron's way of anticipating (and protecting himself from) his mother's attacks. But what Harness called 'a morbid love of a bad reputation' also reflects Byron's loyalty to his father. Libelling himself, Byron came into his paternal inheritance. At the age of nineteen, in 1807, he portrayed a young villain:

> In mind a slave to every vicious joy,
> From every sense of shame and virtue wean'd,
> In lies an adept, in deceit a fiend;
> Vers'd in hypocrisy, while yet a child,
> Fickle as wind, of inclinations wild;
> Woman his dupe, his heedless friend a tool,
> Old in the world, though scarcely broke from school;
> Damaetas ran through all the maze of sin,
> And found the goal, when others just begin.

Privately, hopefully, Byron labelled this fragment 'My Character'. He wished. But it bore a striking resemblance to his infamous father.

Byron's Son: As Bad as Your Father

As a child Byron defended himself with his paternity: when he accidentally wounded a girl with a stone and her nurse rebuked him, he replied, 'Do you know I'm Byron's son?'

On several occasions Byron straightforwardly imitated his father's behaviour. Shortly before he went abroad in 1809, he dined with Mary Chaworth, his 'old love of all loves' and her husband. Afterwards, he hinted that he might have eloped with her, rather as his father eloped with the Marchioness of Carmarthen. In *Childe Harold*, the poem Byron started to write while he travelled abroad, he imagined reliving Captain Byron's financial rape of Catherine Gordon and his parents' short-lived, quarrelsome marriage: Harold's 'kiss/Had . . . spoil'd her goodly lands to gild his waste,/Nor calm domestic peace had ever deigned to taste'.

Byron's attempts to follow his father's demonic example generally failed to convince other people, especially when they knew him well.

In the 'Epistle to a Friend', which Byron dated 11 October 1811, when he was twenty-three years old, he portrayed himself as 'one whose deepening crimes/Suit with the sablest of the times'. His friend Francis Hodgson wrote in the margin: 'N.B. The poor dear soul meant nothing of this. F.H.'

Byron's mother mourned her husband, when he died, but she soon turned against his memory. Captain Jack left his sister £400 in his will; he did not even mention his wife. He appointed his son heir of his 'real and personal estate', which meant that the boy had to pay his father's 'debts, legacies, and funeral expenses'. Throughout his childhood Byron heard more than enough about his father for that figure to make a great impression on him. She 'rakes up the ashes of my *father*,' Byron complained to Augusta on 11 November 1804, 'abuses him [and] says I shall be a true Byrrone, which is the worst epithet she can invent'. His mother assured her son that the name of Byron was his worst punishment, as he told Lady Holland. Whenever the boy misbehaved, his mother blamed it on the bad Byron blood in his veins. She 'used to say, "Ah, you little dog, you are a Byron all over; you are as bad as your father!"' She attacked Captain Byron so often and so fiercely that Byron could never free himself from a longing for the father whom he had scarcely known – even though he claimed to Medwin that he remembered his father 'perfectly'.

Given his claustrophobic relationship with his mother, it was perhaps inevitable that Byron would idealise his father. He longed to follow his soldiering father's example, so his 'earliest dreams were martial'. But since Captain Jack had rejected his own country and gone into exile, Byron would have to lead against the established norms.

This is surely why he identified with outsiders like Lara (in his eponymous tale), 'Cut off by some mysterious fate from those/Whom birth and nature meant not for his foes', or Alp in *The Siege of Corinth*, a Venetian Christian who has turned Muslim. He is, as the cancelled line 72 put it, 'selfexiled', in fact, another 'giaour' – a Turkish word meaning infidel or renegade. Mazeppa and that 'goodly rebel', the Duc de Bourbon, in *The Deformed Transformed*, correspond to this heroic type, which 'the apostate angel', Milton's Satan in *Paradise Lost*, modelled definitively.

Milton's Satan became of crucial importance to Byron and to his generation and the phenomenon needs to be seen in context.

Who the devil is the Devil?

Shelley asked in a note on St Luke's Gospel, 'Who the devil is the Devil?'

Aberdonian Calvinism predisposed Byron to take Satan seriously. It 'becomes an indispensable duty to enquire what we ought to believe and know concerning the existence and agency of Satan and his angels', James Ross said in his Sermon XVI, 'On Sobriety and Vigilance against Temptation'.

All 'men know/The make of Angels & Archangels', Byron remarked in *The Vision of Judgment* (1821), since

> There's scarce a scribbler has not one to show,
> From the fiends' leader to the angels' Prince;
> There also are some Altar-pieces, though
> I really can't say they much evince
> One's inner notions of immortal Spirits,
> But let the Connoisseurs explain *their* merits.

The altarpiece that Byron, as an undergraduate, saw every day in Trinity College Chapel showed 'the fiends' leader' vanquished by 'the angels' Prince', Satan writhing under the triumphant St Michael. Here is a beastly, snake-tailed devil, just the sort of conventional formula that Byron would explode in his portrait of 'the Other' in 'his finest finished poem' *The Vision of Judgment*.

In poetry Milton's *Paradise Lost* (1667) had broken with the medieval tradition of primitive devilry. It pioneered a more subtle, if not equivocal way of portraying Satan/Lucifer, erstwhile Son of the Morning.

Soon, writers such as Joseph Addison, Jonathan Richardson (father and son) and Edmund Burke taught readers to relish sensations of 'delightful horror' in the form of Milton's devil-hero, reassured by its sublimity. But illustrators to *Paradise Lost* were slow to trust such critics.

Benjamin West's painting, St Michael Binding Satan, *which he exhibited at the Royal Academy in 1777, still hangs above the altar in Trinity College Chapel, Cambridge, where Byron would have seen it every morning that he was in residence. Byron later dismissed the painter as 'the flattering, feeble dotard West,/Europe's worst dauber, and poor Britain's best'.*

Photo courtesy of the Master and Fellows of Trinity College, Cambridge

Satan Rousing the Rebel Angels, *probably by Henry Aldrich, in the first illustrated edition of* Paradise Lost, *1688, portrays a beastly Satan, but at least his heroic stance recalls both his antagonist St Michael and also St George, when he confronts the dragon.*

The poet William Hayley complained to the painter George Romney in 1778 that while artists favoured Milton's St Michael, 'drawn divinely bright,/In all the splendour of angelic Might',

> how poor the prostrate SATAN lies,
> With bestial form debas'd and goatish eyes!
> How chang'd from him who leads the dire debate,
> Fearless tho' fall'n, and in Ruin great!

In a note Hayley added, 'It is remarkable that the greatest painters have failed in this particular. Raphael, Guido, and West are all deficient in the figure of Satan.'

Hayley may well have been referring to Benjamin West's recently exhibited painting. Hayley called on Romney:

> Let thy bold Pencil more sublimely true,
> Present his Arch Apostate to our view,
> In worthier Semblance of infernal Pow'r,
> And proudly standing like a stately tow'r,
> While his infernal mandate bids awake
> His Legions, slumbering on the burning Lake.

This may help to explain why eighteenth-century readers found it hard to engage with *Paradise Lost*. 'The want of human interest is always felt,' Dr Johnson complained in his life of Milton. He called it 'one of the books which the reader admires and lays down and forgets to take up again' and probably assumed correctly that he was speaking for the majority in 1780: 'None ever wished it longer than it is. Its perusal is a duty rather than a pleasure. We read Milton for instruction, retire harassed and overburdened, and look elsewhere for recreation; we desert our master, and seek for companions.'

'I DO NOT', the artist Henry Fuseli wrote at this point in the margin of his copy.

The Swiss/British painter was probably the first to portray Milton's Satan as heroic. He first sketched him as the Apollo Belvedere with wings in a Roman drawing from 1776. His pioneering approach proved influential and helped secure the new popularity of *Paradise Lost* in the Romantic era. It annoyed Gillray, who showed Satan as heroic in his caricature *Satan, Death and the Devil* in 1792 but used the epigraph to attack the new flood of illustrated editions of *Paradise Lost*: 'NB: The above performance containing Portraits of the Devil & his Relatives, drawn from the Life, is recommended to Messrs Boydell, Fuselli and the rest of the Proprietors of the Three Hundred & Sixty Five Editions of Milton now publishing, as necessary to be adopted, in the classic Embellishments.'

There were other independent figures who declared their admiration early on: 'Give me a spirit like my favourite hero, Milton's Satan,' Robert Burns wrote on 11 June 1787, '. . . one who brings/A mind not to be chang'd by place or time!'

Fuseli offers an interesting parallel to Byron, whom he knew. He first encountered *Paradise Lost* in the German translation made by his teacher, mentor and friend Johann Jakob Bodmer.

Johann Heinrich Füssli (as he then was; when he moved to England in 1763 he changed his name to Henry Fuseli) became fascinated by Milton and obsessed with the figure of Satan.

Only ten years after Johnson's dismissal, Fuseli heralded and defined the way the British attitude to Milton's Satan changed, as 'respect' warmed into enthusiasm and even into need. The energy that Fuseli invested in his representation of Satan infuses other images.

Satan makes the same bravura leap in other Miltonic works by Fuseli, such as *Satan Calling Up His Legions*. But the pose also recurs in his painting *William Tell's Leap from the Boat*, of 1788–90.

Bodmer's translation of Milton's epic, *Das verlorene Paradies*, also inspired a young German poet, Johann Friedrich von Schiller, who was to have a major impact and influence on British Romantics. Trapped in an oppressive military school, he avenged himself on patriarchal autocracy by glorifying the rebel Karl Moor in his play *Die Räuber* (*The Robbers*) of

Fuseli's Self Portrait in conversation with Johann Jakob Bodmer *manifests the artist's debt to his mentor, who addresses him in front of a bust of Homer. Finished in 1724, censorship delayed publication of Bodmer's translation until 1732. Eight years later Bodmer still had to defend Milton against charges of blasphemy of* Paradise Lost *in another book (Bodmer, 1740).*

Kunsthaus Zürich, Donated by Heinrich Escher-Escher zum Wollenhof, 1847

1781. Moor himself praises Milton's Satan as an 'extraordinary genius' in a phrase that was omitted from the first edition, but Schiller repeatedly haloes his anti-hero with a Satanic aura.

In his *Selbstrecension der Räuber* (1781) Schiller pointed out that Milton, the 'Panegyricist of Hell', turns even the most devout of readers,

In 1780 (two years after Hayley tried to inspire Romney) Fuseli showed a heroic Satan Starting from the Touch of Ithuriel's Lance *at the Royal Academy. Representing the naked male body was one of the highest aims of art, according to Sir Joshua Reynolds, first President of the Royal Academy. But here, beauty is invested in evil; reversing conventional eschatology, good angels drift down, while Satan soars upward, which emphasises his heroic energy.*

Photograph © Staatsgalerie Stuttgart

for a few moments, into a fallen angel. Schiller's cult of heroic, Romantic Satanism had a great impact on Byron, but its influence was also felt more widely. On 21 April 1788 Henry Mackenzie lectured on Schiller's play to the Royal Society in Edinburgh. His talk inspired Walter Scott to start learning German and probably prompted Alexander Fraser Tytler, Lord Woodhouselee, to translate the play into English. Published in 1792, his version of *The Robbers* astonished William Hazlitt ('It stunned me like a blow, and I have not recovered'), Samuel Taylor Coleridge and William Wordsworth. But by that time Satanism had become topical.

Fuseli's drawing, Satan Departing from the Court of Chaos, *1781–2:*

> *He [Chaos] ceased; and Satan stayed not to reply,*
> *But glad that now his sea should find a shore,*
> *With fresh alacrity and force renewed*
> *Springs upward like a pyramid of fire*

The Pierpont Morgan Library, New York. 1975.43. Gift of Miss Louise Crane in memory of her mother, Mrs. W. Murray Crane.

Photographic credit: the Pierpont Morgan Library, New York

Satanism was a conventional trait of the Gothic villain, in Gothic novels by Ann Radcliffe (Schedoni in *The Mysteries of Udolpho*, 1794, and Montoni in *The Italian*, 1797) and Matthew Lewis (Ambrosio in *The Monk*, 1794). But Byron seems to have been the first writer to colour his heroes with that trait. Byron's corsair Conrad, that quintessential Romantic hero/villain, may owe much of his Satanic heroism to Schiller's Karl Moor. Byron boasted in March 1807 that Mackenzie and Tytler had written to congratulate him on his early privately printed poems, but he only admitted reading *The Robbers* in a diary entry for 20 February 1814 – eighteen days

William Tell, transporté par le Génie de la liberté, *an engraving after Fuseli, by Carl Gottlieb or Gottfried Guttenberg. The Swiss freedom fighter became a hero for those who sympathised with the ideals of the French Revolution – long before Schiller's eponymous play of 1804. In fact, as the Gothic exhibition at Tate Britain in 2006 showed, Fuseli's heroes tend to share the same thrusting posture, large stature, six-pack abs and tight buttocks, whether the hero is called Odysseus, Siegfried, Prometheus, Saul, Cain, Thor or Macbeth.*

Karl and Franz Moor in early nineteenth-century illustrations to Schiller's Die Räuber.

after *The Corsair* was published. It is surely not a coincidence that, three weeks before he began to compose that portrait, Byron asserted his own extreme, Satanic, heroic ambitions with the motto, '*Aut Caesar, aut nihil*' ('either Caesar or nothing'). It was borrowed from Cesare Borgia, but it's surely significant that it's cited by another of Schiller's robbers.

The dark glamour of numerous loosely 'Byronic' heroes reflects back the shadow cast by Milton's complex portrait of heroic villainy in *Paradise Lost*. But why did the poem and the character seem so much more compelling, some ten to twenty years after Dr Johnson dismissed it?

12

SATAN AND REALITY

Did literary fashion alone make *Paradise Lost* so popular at the end of the eighteenth century? This chapter follows a narrow path through the vast topic of Romantic Satanism towards a better understanding of Byron. It focuses on Coleridge, rather than Blake, Wordsworth, Hazlitt or Shelley, whose relations to Milton have been ably discussed elsewhere. Coleridge's writing about Satan would have an important impact on Byron and on *Don Juan*.

Paradise Lost, Rebellion and Revolution

Surely reality made first Milton and then Miltonic Satanism newly topical. The centenary of Britain's Glorious Revolution in 1788 reawakened interest in seventeenth-century literature. A year later the French Revolution broke out. Its aftermath renewed Milton's relevance: he was 'the poet of our republic', as the poet Walter Savage Landor said in 1798. 'Milton! thou should'st be living at this hour,' Wordsworth wrote in 'London, 1802': 'England hath need of thee.'

It looked at first as though the French Revolution would fulfil the promise of reform that the British revolution had never delivered. Freedom of worship did not exist, for example, as Dissenters, indeed, all non-Anglicans were forbidden to hold public office. Bills to repeal the Test and Corporation Acts, which enacted these prohibitions, were introduced and defeated in 1787, 1789, 1790 and 1791.

But after the first, libertarian stages of the Revolution, events in France soon eroded sympathy among all but fanatics. In 1790 the French abolished nobility, gave the clergy a civil constitution and confiscated their property. In 1793, they scrapped the Christian calendar, executed Louis XVI and declared war on Britain and Holland. The Terror erupted in 1794. It looked as though the French were trying to achieve glorious ends (liberty, equality, fraternity) through wicked means (anarchy, arbitrary imprisonment, massacre). Events retold the story of a Fall. *Paradise Lost* came to be read as a multivalent manual for rebellion.

Milton had epitomised the discrepancy between ideals and reality in his portrait of Lucifer-who-became-Satan. He may have been inspired by his own disappointment in Oliver Cromwell, as William Hayley suggested as early as 1796 in his *Life of Milton*: 'Though in the temperate judgment of posterity, Cromwell appears only a bold bad man, yet he dazzled and deceived his contemporaries with such a strong and continued blaze of real and visionary splendor, that almost all the power and all the talents on earth seemed eager to pay him unsolicited homage.'

The phrase 'bold bad man' harks back to Edmund Spenser's *Fairy Queen*, and it became a popular expression, appearing in plays by Shakespeare and Massinger.

Paradise Lost remained topical throughout the vicissitudes of political life between 1789 and 1815, because the 'noble picture' of Satan never lost its contemporary relevance: readers could interpret it in so many different ways. As Hazlitt realised: 'when any interest of a practical kind takes a shape that can be at all turned into this, (and there is little doubt that Milton had some such in his eye when writing it,) each party converts it to its own purpose [and] feels the absolute identity of these abstracted and high speculations.'

Supporters and opponents of the French Revolution found the analogy with Milton's Satan equally appropriate. Edmund Burke effectively initiated the debate. An Irish Catholic M.P., who could have represented the oppressed margins of society, he spoke out for conservatism and enlisted Milton in support. 'The beginnings of confusion with us in England are at present feeble enough,' he warned in his prophetic *Reflections on the Revolution in France*, which he addressed to a Frenchman and published as early as 1 November 1790, 'but with you, we have seen an infancy still more feeble, growing by moments into a strength to heap mountains upon mountains, and to wage war with Heaven itself.' He returned to the Satanic analogy elsewhere in the *Reflections*, as well as in *A Letter to a Noble Lord* of 1796. Cartoonists such as Cruikshank also popularised the analogy.

Those who opposed Burke's politics neatly re-evaluated Lucifer's act of rebellion: they read it as a just, heroic struggle against an omnipotent tyrant: 'The Devil was the first Jacobin, for which he was hurled neck and heels out of heaven,' according to the radical *Politics for the People* of 1793.

Fuseli reacted enthusiastically to the dawn of the French Revolution. Three months after the fall of the Bastille he commented that this was 'an age pregnant with the most gigantic efforts of character, shaken with the convulsions of old, and the emergence of new empires. Whilst an unexampled vigour seemed to vibrate from pole to pole through the human mind, and to challenge the general sympathy.'

Fuseli's portraits of Satan reflected his political sympathies.

That year Fuseli determined to create a Milton Gallery single-handedly, inspired by Boydell's Shakespeare Gallery, a group effort in 1789. He assembled the works over nine years, rejecting offers from Thomas Lawrence and John Opie to contribute paintings. At least fourteen of twenty-seven pictures inspired by *Paradise Lost* featured Satan. Fuseli began with an enormous work, 13 by 10 feet (396 by 305 cm), *SATAN encount'ring DEATH, SIN interposing*, which survives only as a sketch in the British Museum and shows a handsome, wholly un-fiendish Satan. In *The Triumphant Messiah* Fuseli altered Milton, so as to ensure that Satan took pictorial precedence, heroic even as he falls.

Fuseli's Milton Gallery in Pall Mall ran from 20 May to the end of July 1799. The next year he added seven more pictures, including *SATAN's first Address to Eve*. The influential but commercially unsuccessful exhibition ran from 21 March to 18 July 1800.

Fuseli's Satan glories in the energy or 'unexampled vigour' admired by William Blake, his friend, who engraved his paintings. Blake wrote that 'The reason Milton wrote in fetters when he wrote of Angels and God,

Fuseli's Head of Satan, *engraved by Henry Barlow for Johan Kaspar Lavater's* Essays on Physiognomy, *translated by Thomas Holcroft (1789), eschews bestial deformity. Instead, the heroic, tragic Archangel's bulging musculature, low forehead and thick neck give him the attractive air of a bruised pugilist. Lavater was a Zurich friend of Fuseli, who also studied with Bodmer.*

Photo: Look and Learn

and at liberty when of Devils and Hell, is because he was a true Poet, and of the Devil's party without knowing it.' Blake's poem was engraved in 1793, the same year that William Godwin's *Political Justice* first appeared. The author was another member of the circle around the radical publisher Joseph Johnson, and they may have exchanged ideas about Satan, as well as much else. William Godwin emerged as a committed enthusiast for the French Revolution, when it seemed likely to realise rationalist, philosophical ideals. 'Can intellectual energy exist without a strong sense of justice?' he asked in his *Enquiry into Political Justice*. Turning to *Paradise Lost* for the answer, he explained that Satan rebelled, 'because he saw no sufficient reason for that extreme inequality of rank and power which the creator assumed'. Godwin went on, 'He was not discouraged by the apparent inequality of the contest: because a sense of reason and justice was stronger in his mind, than a sense of brute force.' Godwin's representation of Satan as a Promethean rebel would have a major effect on the writings of his daughter, Mary Wollstonecraft Godwin, and her lover, Shelley (see p. 282).

The Fall of Robespierre

The first wave of the French Revolution threw up the energetic intellectual Maximilien de Robespierre. In Britain he was widely identified with Satan since, as leader, he 'wielded the sceptre of the Atheist crew', as Wordsworth wrote in *The Prelude*, referring to *Paradise Lost*. Robespierre became infamous for his qualities of mind and his lack of humanity, for his intellect

Maximilien Robespierre on the day of his execution, 28 July 1794: a drawing by Jacques-Louis David. 'His jaw was shattered by a pistol ball;' Mme de Staël recorded, 'he could not even speak in his own defense.'

The Morgan Library & Museum. MA 1059.6. Purchased, 1928

and his arrogance. Godwin may have been thinking of Robespierre when he portrayed Satan as an intellectual, 'manly radical', though Godwin is just as likely to have been in Godwin's mind.

Robespierre's villainous heroism made him quintessentially Satanic, as Coleridge and Southey hinted in the title of *The Fall of Robespierre*, the play they wrote in 1794, and confirmed in the opening speech. In the dedicatory epistle Coleridge commented that Robespierre's 'great bad actions cast a disastrous lustre on his name'. He called him 'worse than Cromwell/The austere, the self denying Robespierre'. Cromwell was 'one of the great bad men of the old stamp', as Edmund Burke put it, echoing Clarendon. Coleridge and Wordsworth may have discovered in Robespierre an alarming, distorted version of themselves.

'*Robespierre* had a mind too great to be debauched by any thing but ambition,' the radical John Thelwall wrote in the *Tribune* on 23 May 1795. He attacked Robespierre as 'the ambitious Dictator' and 'usurper', but he also paid tribute to him: he had 'a soul capacious, an imagination various, a judgment commanding, penetrating, severe', while the 'energy of his mind commanded success'. Implicit in this was a comparison with Oliver Cromwell, another 'ambitious usurper', who had 'a mind not only bold and enterprising, but capacious, versatile, and penetrating'.

Thelwall's friend William Godwin explored many of the same Satanic/Robespierre traits in his novel *Caleb Williams*, published in 1794. Vindictively, neatly, Godwin may have portrayed Burke in his fiendish persecutor, the chivalry-obsessed Falkland, who combines sublime intellectual powers and god-like ambition. Robespierre also inspired such fiendish hypocrites as the Veiled Prophet of Khorassan in Thomas Moore's *Lalla Rookh* (1817).

In reality, however, Robespierre soon drowned in blood any potential claim to sublimity or intellectual lustre. He degenerated into merely another fiend, as Byron saw: '"Robespierre," observed his Lordship, "of all monsters, was the *ne plus ultra*: not contented with the common mode of execution, he tortured his victims like a Demon."' Robespierre's reign did not last long but, as Byron pointed out, it set a precedent, which

Napoleon soon followed. Byron's Harrow school protégé William Harness remembered the couplet that Byron improvised: 'Bold Robert Speer was Bony's bad precursor,/Bob was a bloody dog, but Bonaparte a worser'.

Napoleon, Satan and Coleridge

All the countries that encountered Napoleon identified him with the devil.

British observers who disagreed about politics, such as Shelley, Wordsworth and Southey, agreed to damn Napoleon as a devil, even when they refused to allow him any Miltonic distinction.

Southey and Byron differed on this point, as Southey told a friend on 29 April 1814: 'The last time I saw him [Byron] asked me if I did not think Bonaparte a great man in his villainy. I told him, no, – that he was a mean-minded villain.' In general, however, Napoleon was recognised as the quintessential 'bad great man'. 'What do you think of my supernatural

The Corsican with his Bloodhounds at the Window of the Thuilleries Looking over Paris, *16 April 1815. Private collection*

An anonymous caricature of The Corsican's last trip under the guidance of his Good Angel, *18 April 1815. Ashton, II, 223*

friend, the emperor?' Moore asked a correspondent as late as 1815. 'If ever tyrant deserved to be worshipped, it is he: Milton's Satan is nothing to him for portentous magnificence – for sublimity of mischief!'

Napoleon rose and fell – again and again. His Satanism became Miltonic when he inspired a volatile commixture of admiration and contempt. For some, the *coup d'état* of 18 Brumaire 1799 proved the watershed, the moment that the hero dwindled into a tyrant, if not 'the Devil incarnate, the Appolyon mentioned in Scripture', as Hester Thrale Piozzi called him. She believed his Corsican name was N'Apollione, 'the Destroyer'. Other observers persisted in admiring Napoleon: even after his 'butcheries' in Spain; after he had the Duc d'Enghien assassinated; after he invaded Switzerland; after he had the sick poisoned in Egypt; and after he crowned himself emperor. Southey's admiration appeared to last long: for him, Waterloo represented 'nothing less than the historical equivalent of the fall'.

Some observers, like the poet Heinrich Heine, managed neatly to detach Napoleon's admirable genius from his despicable actions. Even at the height

An English caricature of Napoleon dwarfed by his coronation robes.
Ashton, II, 26

of the invasion panic, British observers could still admit that their enemy's villainy was a complex, ambivalent matter. *Sly Reynard*, a popular ballad 'still heard on the streets' in 1803 referred to 'The Corsican Nero/That Terrible Hero'.

Coleridge remained loyal for a long time: 'Mercy on the man!' he exclaimed defensively in the *Morning Post* on 17 February 1800, adding on 11 March: 'What a bundle of incompatible villainies have they strung together, and christened by his name!'[40] In March 1800 he called Bonaparte 'a man of various talent, of commanding genius, of splendid exploit'. The next month he was still 'without a rival in renown' and Coleridge distinguished nicely between 'the detestable means' by which Bonaparte obtained power and 'the wise and moderate use he has made of it'. Coleridge had already made that distinction in 1795: 'The Patriots of France either hastened into the dangerous and gigantic Error of making certain Evil the means of contingent Good, or were sacrificed by thc Mob.' It will prove important later with regard to Coleridge's relationship with Byron.

Peter Vandyke's portrait of the young, visionary, enthusiastic, wide-eyed, open-mouthed Samuel Taylor Coleridge, 1795.
© National Portrait Gallery, London

For a time, Coleridge evidently identified with Napoleon and envied his power. News reached Britain in May 1802 that the Corsican had been elected consul for ten years, a term soon extended to life. He now had the right to name his successor. Coleridge was inspired by a vision of what *he* could do with such power: 'Poet Bonaparte', he wrote in a notebook in 1802, '– Layer out of a World-garden –'. The pseudonym that Coleridge now adopted, Estese, Greek for 'He has stood', puns on the initial letters of his name, STC, but it also refers to the Archimedean plea, 'Give me somewhere to stand' ('. . . that I may move the world') and, perhaps, to Milton's Satan.

Eventually, belatedly, Coleridge turned against Napoleon. Since he had at first been so impressed and then, by 21 September 1802, so 'miserably disappointed', the analogy with Milton's Satan seemed increasingly apt. He alludes to it repeatedly, in the *Courier* of 21 December 1809, 26 July 1811 and 28 December 1812. When he wrote a full-scale, comparative analysis of villainy in 1809 Coleridge never named Napoleon. But he uses Milton's Satan to enquire into the causes and sources of the emperor's power:

> So doing we shall quickly discover that it is not Vice, as Vice, which is thus mighty; but *systematic* Vice! Vice self-consistent and entire; Crime corresponding to Crime; Villainy entrenched and barricaded by Villainy; this is the condition and main consistuent [*sic*] of its power. The abandonment of all *Principle* of Right enables the Soul to chuse and act upon a *Principle* of Wrong, and to subordinate to this one principle all the various Vices of Human nature . . . But [he] who has once said with his whole heart, Evil be

John Martin's mezzotint of Satan enthroned, or in council, *1827, probably alludes to Ingres's coronation portrait of Napoleon, 1806, and to his* Jove and Thetis, *1811.*

> thou my Good! has removed a world of Obstacles by the very decision, that he will have no Obstacles but those of force and brute matter.

Napoleon's power lasted so long that it threatened to represent 'a perpetual lesson of immorality', as Madame de Staël suggested, when she asked, 'If he had always succeeded, what should we have been able to say to our

Jean-Auguste-Dominique Ingres, Napoleon 1er sur le trône impérial.
Photo © Paris – Musée de l'Armée,
Dist. RMN-Grand Palais/Emilie Cambier

Ingres, Jupiter et Thétis.

Photo © RMN-Grand Palais/Jean Popovitch

Richard Westall's illustration to Boydell's edition of Paradise Lost, *1794:* Satan rouses his followers to wage war against God. *The heroic image follows others by James Barry, reflecting fashion rather than politics.*

© The British Library Board, 76.i.10 volume 1 book 4, opposite p. 107

children?' *Paradise Lost* offered a comforting mirror to political reality, since Milton's portrait of an intellectually distinguished, heroic, rebellious 'villain' showed that he would, eventually, suffer defeat. The literary analogy reassured observers exhausted by the long war with France and troubled by what Coleridge on 13 January 1809 called the emperor's 'strange fortunes and continual felicity'.

Fuseli politicised Satan, but there were others who treated the heroic Satan as merely a fashion item, a creature of the Zeitgeist.

Thomas Lawrence thought that *Satan Summoning his Legions*, the vast painting he showed at the Royal Academy in 1799, was his masterpiece, though it was dismissed as 'a mad German sugar-baker dancing naked in a conflagration of his own treacle'. As a boy Lawrence loved to recite Milton's verses, confessing that he preferred '"Satan's Address to the Sun"; but that his father would not permit him to give it. [Those present] insisted and promised to obtain his father's forgiveness. He then turned to the forbidden passage, and a written slip of paper dropped from it; a gentleman picked it up and read it aloud. "Tom mind you don't touch Satan."' As an adult, now that he could 'touch Satan' Lawrence could not resist hamming it up.

OPPOSITE: *Thomas Lawrence,* Satan Summoning His Legions, *1799. The painting reflects the artist's longing for the stage, as theatrical lighting confines the spectator to the stalls and suggests he's on his knees. It says less about politics than fashion: it's a self-serving assault on the 'Grand Style' by an artist celebrated for society portraits. Its 'wild posture', like its heroism, is factitious – copied from Fuseli, as he stood on a high rock overlooking the bay of Bristol. The head was modelled by the actor John Philip Kemble and Kemble's sister, the actress Mrs Siddons, inspired a demon in the pit at Satan's feet (no longer clearly visible), while the boxing champion 'Gentleman' Jackson modelled for the body of Satan, twice life-size.*

Lawrence portrayed Satanic heroism and he collected images of it – he bought Fuseli's Satan risen from the Flood *and* Satan encount'ring Death *at the sale after the artist's death, but he was not a partisan. When he read Byron's play about the Devil's temptation of Cain, Lawrence identified Byron with Satan: 'I think it is likely to do much harm,' he told Mrs Wolff on 26 December 1821, 'and with exactly that Class of Persons whom we should most wish to preserve from it. On those of more intelligence it will fall hurtless, who will see in it the writhings of a proud and rebuk'd Spirit, driven to that last fatal climax of Human Error, in which, as we togethcr agree'd, goaded by the just reproaches of Society it turns upon it with Demoniac Hate, and says, "Evil! be thou my good"'.*

© Royal Academy of Arts, London; photographer: Marcus Leith

13

DIABOLISM

'If Byron were not a great poet, the charlatanism of affecting to be a Satanic character, in this our matter-of-fact nineteenth century, would be very amusing.'

Lady Blessington's Conversations of Lord Byron, (1834), ed. Ernest J. Lovell, Jr., 1969, 170

During his years of fame in London Byron habitually wore black, the Satanic colour, ostensibly in mourning for his mother. 'I will, some day or other . . . raise a troop,' Byron predicted as a boy, '– the men of which shall be dressed in black, and ride on black horses. They shall be called "Byron's Blacks," and you will hear of their performing prodigies of valour.' The motif recurs in his fiction: the Giaour rides a 'jet black steed' and a 'sable plume' tops the Corsair's helmet. It was said of Ulric, another rebel, and Werner's son in Byron's late play of that name:

> That in the wild exuberance of his nature,
> He had join'd the black bands, who lay waste Lusatia,
> The mountains of Bohemia and Silesia,
> Since the last years of war had dwindled into
> A kind of general condottiero system
> Of bandit warfare; each troop with its chief,
> And all against mankind.

Those 'black bands' return as 'Bourbon's black banditti' in *The Deformed*

Transformed. The Stranger in that play, a 'tall black man' who turns out to be Lucifer, admits that he has 'a penchant/For black' and explains, '– it is so honest, and besides/Can neither blush with shame nor pale with fear'.

Byron spent his 'whole life', as he said, 'in open opposition to received opinions'. His oblique stance generated his fundamental attitude to politics, his sympathy for those who were oppressed.

Byron's 'moral masquerade', his identification with his wicked father, went so far that he relished being associated with Satan. His Calvinist upbringing exacerbated a sense of family loyalty, while his limp seemed to predestine him to be damned, as it identified him with the devil. Arnold, the hero of *The Deformed Transformed*, is a hunchback, but his double, the Stranger, still refers to 'this/Cloven foot of thine'.

Byron's wife reported that his 'deepest feeling' was that he was damned, that 'his transgressions [were] beyond forgiveness' and 'It was in vain to seek to turn his thoughts for long from that *idée fixe* with which he connected his physical peculiarity as a stamp.' At another point, when she discussed the 'morbidly tenacious feeling he [Byron] had as to his lameness', she concluded, 'There was a connection in his Imagination between that & his Predestination to Evil, or his being an Exiled Angel . . . These ideas were not suggested to his mind by chance-circumstances, but appeared to be deeply rooted there.' That is surely why his wife called Calvinism that 'creed of despair'.

A year after Byron and his wife separated, she stressed this remarkable idea in one of many notes that she made on her husband: 'His imagination dwelt so much upon the idea that he was *a fallen angel* that I thought it amounted nearly to derangement.' It would be easy to dismiss that as another of her libels, but it may indeed be possible that, as Crabb Robinson reported, 'Byron had an impression he was the offspring of a demon.'

'Diabolism' (Byron uses the word in a letter to Leigh Hunt of 9 February 1814) proved that he lived up to his inheritance from his absent, demonised father. On the other hand, as the Prophet Isaiah said, Satan became the first rebel. The model would therefore, theoretically allow Byron to rebel against (paternal) authority, as well as follow in his father's wake.

The demonic analogy came frequently to mind.

When *Hours of Idleness* was published in 1807 his distant kinsman, Robert Charles Dallas, wrote to congratulate him. Byron knew that Dallas wrote moralistic fiction so, when he replied on 20 January 1808 he exaggerated his own notoriety: 'I have been already held up as the votary of Licentiousness, and the Disciple of Infidelity. – How far Justice may have dictated this accusation, I cannot pretend to say, but like the *Gentleman* [the devil], to whom my religious friends in the warmth of their Charity have already [compared?] me, I am made worse, than I really am.' Byron ended: 'my hand is almost as bad, as my Character.' And the next day

A Noble Poet – Scratching up his Ideas, *an anonymous caricature of Byron in Venice, sitting under an image of Cain killing Abel, attended, or inspired by the Devil, 1823.*

© Trustees of the British Museum

he subscribed himself as '*wicked* George Ld. B'. As he wrote this the day before he turned twenty, his worst crime was wishful thinking.

Characteristically, when he accepted an invitation to stay with James Wedderburn Webster and his wife on 31 August 1811, Byron compared himself to Lucifer, looking at Adam and Eve.

Coleridge and Southey's 'The Devil's Thoughts' was published anonymously in the *Morning Post* on 6 September 1799. In 1812 it inspired Byron to begin a politically minded, satirical poem, 'The Devil's Drive', in which he described himself as 'a friend' of the Devil. After the fall, Lucifer, 'the bearer of light' and most beautiful of the archangels, lost his distinction and became Satan, the adversary. Byron gave Satan the benefit of his former title as 'a *quondam* Aristocrat', the gesture representing another attempt to appropriate Satanism to his own uses.

Later, to mark the distance between his region of literature and Thomas Moore's, Byron identified Moore with St Michael and himself with Satan. In the same spirit Byron joked that the author of 'some gratuitously impertinent remarks . . . had better have written to the Devil a criticism upon Hell-fire'.

Byron seemed just as keen on making a bad first impression in 1822, when he was introduced to a friend of Shelley, Edward E. Williams. Byron immediately handed him a book, explaining that it 'takes infinite pains to prove that I am the Devil'. 'What Mortal would not play the Devil?' Byron asked on 6 May 1823. 'Most persons assume a virtuous character,' Colonel Stanhope noticed a year later. 'Lord Byron's ambition, on the contrary, was to make the world imagine that he was a sort of "Satan".'

Byron went out of his way to endow his heroes with Satanic associations borrowed from Milton's epic, among them Childe Harold, Conrad the Corsair, Lara and Manfred.

As a result, the poet was regularly, indeed conventionally, identified with the devil – by those who knew him, such as Lady Caroline Lamb and Harriet Wilson, as well as by those who knew only his work or his reputation. According to Mrs Opie, Byron's 'voice was such a voice as the devil tempted Eve with; you feared its fascination the moment you heard it'.

Byron became infamous merely for looking Satanic. 'I have been asked by some, if his appearance and manner did not convey the idea of a fiend incarnate,' Dr Charles Kennedy wrote, having got to know Byron in Greece in 1822 and 1823. 'On the contrary,' the physician reported carefully, 'his appearance and manner gave the idea of a kind-hearted, benevolent, and feeling man, with an amiable and pleasing countenance.'

Byron toyed with other devils, such as Belphegor (from the Bible), Cazotte's *diable amoureux* and Le Sage's *diable boiteux*. He signs the Preface to *The Vision of Judgment* as Quevedo Redivivus, meaning Francisco de Quevedo, resurrected. Quevedo was known as the 'Lame Devil', and portrayed as 'El Diablo Cojuelo', in Luis Velez de Guevara's novel of same name, published in 1641 but better known in Lesage's French version, *Le diable boiteux* of 1770. Milton remained, however, for Byron, as for Coleridge, 'that most interesting of the Devil's Biographers'. That phrase comes from a note to Coleridge and Southey's 'The Devil's Thoughts'. And Milton's Satanism would constitute a lasting, significant link between Coleridge and Byron.

PART VI

BOYS AND MEN: DOUBLES AND ROLE MODELS

PREVIOUS PAGE: *George Sanders,* Lord Byron Attended by his Page, *c.1805–7. Before leaving England Byron commissioned this portrait to hang at Newstead and paid 250 guineas for it. Mrs Byron assured him on 9 September 1809 that 'the countenance is angelic and the finest I ever saw and it is very like.' Byron chose to immortalise himself as an intrepid explorer, stepping ashore to claim an uninhabited, wild coast. The setting reflects his headmaster's advice that 'the most improving way' Byron could spend his summer vacation was to tour the Highlands, visit the Hebrides and maybe sail to Iceland.*

A breeze tousles Byron's hair, so that his loosely tied neck-cloth echoes the movement of the British standard in the background. Byron steps from a dinghy steadied by a page, presumably Robert Rushton, who stands, or rather stoops in the water. The maritime setting and Byron's nautically inspired costume were natural to the artist, George Sanders; to the time, in the wake of Nelson's victories and death; to the family, given Byron's enthusiasm for his naval grandfather; and to the poet, who loved the sea's freedom from earthbound being. Byron interfered on several occasions in the making of his portraits and he included his page partly to substantiate his noble status. The two male bodies' symmetrical curves suggest the complementary nature of their relationship: the head against the mountain is balanced by the head against the sail. Meanwhile the blues of Byron's costume and the red of the boy's uniform are united by the standard flying between them. An engraving of the painting was the only illustration in Moore's biography of 1832. It therefore 'made an important visual contribution to the Romantic Movement'.

14

PARENTAL FEELINGS

Dear is the helpless creature we defend
Against the world . . .

Don Juan, I, 126

Byron's chronic lack of a father not only led him to look for heroes, whom he could look up to as father figures or mentors, it also inspired him to behave like an ideal father towards other, younger males.

Loneliness at Harrow made Byron value his friends particularly. He kept the notes and letters that his principal school favourites sent him. And he reflected:

> Ah! sure some stronger impulse vibrates here,
> Which whispers friendship will be doubly dear
> To one, who thus for kindred hearts must roam,
> And seek abroad, the love denied at home.

Harrow allowed Byron to act as the leader of a gang. 'Here, first remembered be the joyous band,/Who hail'd me chief, obedient to command'. He would later seek out or recreate this relationship, in his domestic life, in his poetry and in politics.

As we saw, Byron found a mentor in Harrow's headmaster but the boy soon learned to recreate the father–son relationship that he had scarcely known, by acting as a 'patron' towards others. He began when still a schoolboy, 'unblest by social ties', and the habit continued all his life.

Paternalism mattered more than sex, but it did not rule it out. Biographers have explored his bisexuality in some depth, but have paid less attention to the ways in which Byron compensated for his fatherlessness by fostering relationships with dependent creatures.

At school he had passionate friendships with his social equals and with boys of an even more elevated status, such as the Earl of Clare, Earl Delawarr and the Duke of Dorset. But in general, as Moore pointed out, Byron 'chose his intimates . . . from a rank beneath his own . . . the chief charm that recommended to him his younger favourites was their inferiority in age and strength, which enabled him to indulge his generous pride by taking upon himself, when necessary, the office of their protector.' Byron's superior rank endowed him with a potentially paternal status.

Benevolent, loving and pedagogic relationships between older and younger male partners formed a constituent part of society in ancient Greece, as every schoolboy knew. The structure resurfaced in the English public school system where, as Byron explained, 'the junior boys are completely subservient to the upper forms, till they obtain a seat in the higher Classes. From this state of probation, very properly, no rank is exempt; but after a certain period, they command in turn, those who succeed.' Byron himself later demonstrated the versatility of this role-playing: in 1808 he asked a master at Eton, Henry Drury, to look after a new boy there, called John Cowell. He also wrote to the boy paternalistically 'to bid him mind his prosody'. Four years later, on 12 February 1812, Byron wrote to Cowell, asking him to look after another friend's son, 'a little boy of eleven years', who would be joining the same school.

His First Double

Byron was only fourteen when he took on 'the office of protector'. 'If any fellow bullies you, tell me; and I'll thrash him if I can.' Byron intervened to defend a twelve-year-old boy, William Harness, who had just entered Harrow and was being bullied by a much older and stronger boy. Lame from an early accident, Harness also looked pale and thin after a recent illness. He himself recognised that 'This dilapidated condition of mine – perhaps my lameness more than anything else – seems to have touched Byron's sympathies.' Lameness made Harness another Byron: the older boy could look after him – as Captain Jack should have looked after his son. It was, as a contemporary observer later commented, 'extraordinary . . . and contrary, I believe, to the conduct of the generality of lame persons, that [Byron] pitied, sympathised, and befriended those who laboured under similar defects'.

Harness was Byron's double – as we will see, the first of many such relationships in Byron's life. The pattern proved important and fruitful: infused

William Harness and Byron became inseparable at Harrow, in spite of the significant age difference of two years. Byron told Harness on 6 December 1811 that he could fix 'no date to our Intimacy for it commenced before I began to date at all'. He addressed the first poetry he wrote at Harrow to Harness. Byron called him 'Child' in several letters infused with poignantly paternal concern: 'what art thou doing? reading I trust,' he wrote on 8 December. 'I want to see you take a degree, remember this is the most important period of your life, & don't disappoint your Papa & your Aunts & all your kin, besides myself'. Harness became a clergyman. Byron would have dedicated Childe Harold *I and II to him, 'but was prevented . . . "for fear it should injure him in his profession"'.*

George Lance's portrait of William Harness from the 1820s. © Victoria and Albert Museum, London.

with the same impulse that boxing satisfied, it inspired an intimate, increasingly troubled friendship with another poet, Shelley; contributed to the central theme of a novel, *Frankenstein*, and to several plays and poems, among them Shelley's *Julian and Maddalo* and Byron's masterpiece, *Don Juan*.

I Dreamt of my Father

> I dreamt of my father –
> And now my dream is out!
>
> Frederick, *Werner*, V, i, 385f.

Byron looked for role models and parallels to his paternal feelings in fiction and found a passage from Virgil's *Aeneid*, Book IX, which he translated. Nisus is all man, 'Well skill'd, in fight, the quiv'ring Lance to wield'; whereas his 'glowing friend', beautiful, beardless Euryalus is 'As yet a novice in the martial strife'. Byron commemorated his school friend Lord Delawarr as 'Euryalus': 'A form unmatch'd, in Nature's partial mould'. He also imported the same theme into an imitation of Ossian: 'No maid was the sigh of [Calmar's] soul; his thoughts were given to friendship! to dark-hair'd Orla; destroyer of heroes!' Orla's dead father, incidentally, 'will rejoice in his boy'.

John Moore's *Zeluco* (1789) became one of Byron's favourite books, perhaps partly because the eponymous, villainous hero lost his father at an early age. Around the age of fourteen Byron discovered a novella exploring the theme of inheritance that had 'a strange effect' on him. Harriet Lee's story 'The German's Tale. Kruitzner' appeared in 1801 in volume 4 of *The Canterbury Tales* (which she wrote with her sister Sophia). The story 'has haunted me ever since,' Byron told his sister on 12 December 1822, '– from a singular conformity between it & my ideas.' It played an important role as his marriage broke down, when Byron was in his twenties, and again in his thirties, when it inspired his play *Werner*.

'The German's Tale. Kruitzner' abounds in mirror images of sons who rebel against their fathers and yet repeat their errors. It also gave Byron his type of villainous heroic ideal. As an adolescent, he identified with Conrad, the rebel leader of a gang of outlaws, another Karl Moor, an 'extraordinary and mysterious being', 'the very master-daemon and moving spring of all', with 'the feelings of a gladiator and the eye of an assassin'. Conrad briefly mistakes his father Siegendorf for the same sort of hero and therefore admires him as 'some bold and daring transgressor who stands aloof from society, and despises its obligations: – it was the leader of the banditti that seemed to start up before him under the name of father; and every faculty of his soul had been roused to attention.' In effect, the son projects his own demonic nature on to that of his father. Byron later named his Corsair Conrad.

At Newstead Byron seems to have formed a romantic attachment to the son of one of his tenants, who died young. In a memorial poem that Byron dated 1803 and published in his first book, he usurped the paternal role: 'What though thy sire lament his failing line,/A father's sorrows cannot equal mine!'

Lord Grey de Ruthyn rented Newstead Abbey from March 1803 until Byron reached the age of twenty-one. Byron became friends with the twenty-three-year-old noble tenant, but then turned against him and refused to see him. Byron certainly resented the fact that Lord Grey encouraged Mrs Byron's amorous attentions. In effect, the boy was competing with his mother for Grey. Byron hinted that the older man had made some sort of sexual advance towards him. Perhaps Byron reacted so badly because Lord Grey usurped the manly role of Nisus, leaving Byron to play the unfamiliar role of the 'novice' Euryalus?

Patrons and Protégés

Byron took up residence as an undergraduate at Trinity College, Cambridge, in October 1805, feeling 'about as unsocial as a wolf taken from the troop', since he missed the 'family' he had nurtured at Harrow. His closest friends had gone to Christ Church, Oxford, which had been his first choice. At Cambridge he tended to mix with other Harrovians, drinking soda water with Edward Noel Long, and listening to his flute playing.

Byron planted an oak tree on one of his first visits to Newstead Abbey. When at the age of nineteen he revisited the park he found the tree smothered by ivy, for which he blamed his noble tenant.

In his poem, 'To an Oak at Newstead', Byron treated the tree like a son:

Ah, droop not, my Oak! lift thy head for a while;
Ere twice round yon Glory this planet shall run,
The hand of thy Master will teach thee to smile,
When Infancy's years of probation are done.

He foresaw that he would be buried in its shade and that his descendant, 'The Chief who survives' would visit it 'with his boys'. The oak flourished, as this photo from 1874 shows, but it has since died and is now represented by a large stump.

Richard Allen, A Souvenir of Newstead Abbey, Formerly the Home of Lord Byron, Illustrated, *1874, opp. p.10*

George Sanders's miniature of Byron, 1812. He wears the fur-trimmed pelisse that is also visible in Sanders's portrait of his then mentor, William Bankes (next page), which Byron probably commissioned.
Private collection

As at Harrow, Byron found a mentor at Trinity College but also acted as a mentor to another, younger male. He looked up to William Bankes, his senior by two years, a rich, independent, confident and witty aesthete, who had been educated at Westminster School (like Byron's father and Hobhouse). Byron later described himself to Bankes as 'the humblest of your servants'. Bankes was, Byron told Murray on 31 August 1820, 'a wonderful fellow', 'the father of all mischief'. Bankes told Harriet Arbuthnot that Byron 'used to confide all his iniquities to him'.

George Sanders's miniature portrait of William John Bankes, 1812. It may have been commissioned by Byron, who collected portraits of his friends. Bankes seems to draw attention to his fur-trimmed pelisse. Bankes later distinguished himself as an intrepid, 'stupendous traveller', pioneering Egyptologist and passionate, informed connoisseur. He came to stay with Byron in Venice and Ravenna. After Byron's death he was twice arrested for sex with soldiers, a private in the Coldstream Guards in 1833 and another guardsman in 1841, at a time when the 'nameless crime' was regularly punished with death; in 1806 there were more executions for sodomy than murder. Bankes was acquitted on the first occasion and exiled himself to Venice on the second.

© National Trust / Simon Harris

At Cambridge, Byron remembered, Bankes 'was good-naturedly tolerant of my ferocities'. He had so much respect for his older friend that he dreaded hearing what Bankes thought of *Poems on Various Occasions*: 'He has too much of the *Man*,' he told Edward Noel Young on 23 February

Bankes owned these neo-Gothic paintings on vellum from 1804. They portray him kneeling in prayer beneath an angel and his family coat of arms in his rooms at Trinity College, Cambridge. On 12 November that year Bankes's great-uncle Sir William Wynne promised to send him 'as many Gothick ornaments as can well be employed in the intended improvements of your rooms'. A contemporary reported that Bankes 'fitted up some of his rooms in imitation of a Catholic Chapel & used to have the Singing boys in dress suitable to the occasion, to come and sing there for him and that it was constantly asked "What the devil does Mr. Bankes do with those singing boys?"' He burnt incense at his altar every day. Bankes introduced Byron to the mock-archaic poetry of Walter Scott and may have inspired him with a temporary taste for the Gothic, evidenced in the affected, archaic idiom of much of Byron's 'Romaunt', Childe Harold *('whilome. . .wight' etc). The National Trust bought the paintings from Lowell Libson for £22,000, with help from the Art Fund. They now hang in Kingston Lacy, Bankes's country house in Dorset.*

© Lowell Libson Ltd

1807, 'ever to approve the flights of a *Boy*.' On 19 November 1820 Byron called Bankes his 'collegiate pastor, and master, and patron'. He used all three terms to evoke his relationship with his boxing trainer and friend, 'Gentleman' John Jackson.

Meanwhile Byron soon realised his own, ideal Nisus and Euryalus relationship. He fell in love with John Edleston, a Cambridge choirboy, in October 1805. There are conflicting accounts of how they met. In one, Byron may have saved the boy from drowning; while in another he was first drawn to Edleston by hearing him sing. Edleston became Byron's '*almost constant* associate'. He told Elizabeth Pigot on 5 July 1807, in a letter bristling with breathy italics:

> I certainly *love* him more than any other human being, & neither *time* or Distance have had the least effect on my (in general) changeable Disposition . . . He certainly is perhaps more *attached* to *me*, than even I am in *return*, during the whole of my residence at *Cambridge*, we met every day summer & Winter, without passing *one tiresome moment*, & separated *each time* with increasing Reluctance. I hope you will *one day* see *us* together, he is the only *being* I *esteem*, though I *like many*.

The cornelian ring that Edleston gave Byron, who wrote in 'The Cornelian', dated December 1806:

He offered it with a downcast look,
As fearful that I might refuse it;
I told him when the gift I took,
My only fear should be to lose it.

Cornelian is an inexpensive stone, while, ironically, 'Edelstein' in German means 'noble stone'. Byron gave the ring to Elizabeth Pigot. Five years later, after Edleston's death, he wrote to ask her mother to return it.
Private collection

Moore rightly noted that the 'disparity in their stations' played a major role in their relationship, 'founding the tie between them on the mutually dependent relations of protection on the one side, and gratitude and devotion on the other'.

Byron called himself Edleston's '*Patron*' and described the boy as his '*protegé*'. At Harrow William Harness's lameness made him particularly apt as a protégé/double; Edleston wasn't lame but he was in other respects another, younger Byron – 'exactly to an hour, 2 years younger than myself'; 'nearly my height, very thin, very fair complexion, dark eyes, & light locks'. By then, in June 1807, Byron was starving himself and so turning himself

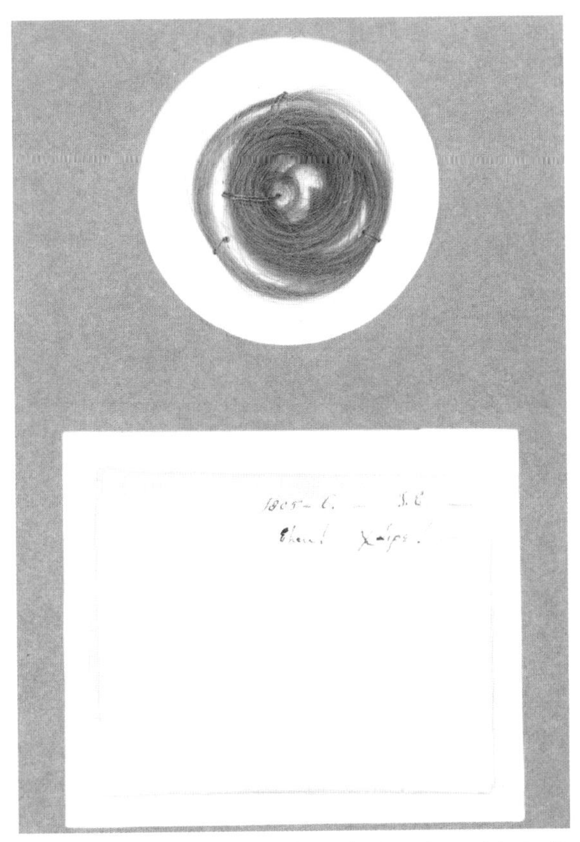

A lock of Edleston's hair that Byron kept and annotated with the date, 1805–6, the initials J. E. and the words, 'Alas!' in Latin and 'Goodbye' in ancient Greek.

Private collection

into another Edleston: 'I appear taller, & somewhat *slim*,' he told his friend Long on 14 May, '& "mirabile dictu!!" [a miracle] my Hair once black or rather very dark brown, is turned (I know not how but I presume by perpetual perspiration) to a *light Chesnut*, nearly approaching *yellow*.'

Incidentally, Byron also shared his birthday with another lover, Susan Vaughan (see above, p. 59).

Edleston later thanked Byron for his 'parental kindness'.

After leaving Cambridge in October 1807, Byron found the young man work in a mercantile house in London, intending to offer him the choice between a partnership in the business or simply living with Byron. But on his return to England from his Grand Tour, after more than a year's absence, Byron clearly made little attempt to reach the young man, since he did not hear of his death for three months. 'I almost rejoice when one I love dies young,' he admitted to Hodgson on 16 February 1812, after learning that Edleston had died prematurely from consumption, 'for I could never bear to see them old or altered.'

15

LET A PERSON DEPEND ON YOU

'I have observed one thing in you which I like,' his erstwhile mistress Claire Clairmont told Byron on 12 January 1818, the day that their daughter Allegra celebrated her first birthday:

> it is this: let a person depend on you, let them be utterly weak and defenceless, having no protector but yourself and you infallibly grow fond of that person. How kind and gentle you are to children! How good-tempered and considerate towards your servants, how accommodating even to your dogs! And all this because you are sole master and lord; because there is no disputing your power you become merciful & just.

How did Byron behave towards these three kinds of dependent beings, children, pets and servants?

Children: Our Little Selves

He addressed a poem 'To my Son!' in 1807. This was not his son by one of the Newstead maids, however, who was born in 1809. Byron may have been addressing one of two illegitimate children that he later told his wife he meant to provide for. But the poem's feeble, formulaic language suggests it was an exercise in wish fulfilment: 'Fair cherub, pledge of youth and joy –/A father guards thy birth, my Boy!'

Byron's only legitimate child was his daughter Augusta Ada, born on 10 December 1815. Her mother Lady Byron left with her five weeks later, and Byron did not see either of them again. He regretted this, of course. But he was thrilled when he heard that a miniature of Ada at the age of seven showed that she was 'in mind and feature the very image of her father'. An observer said he never saw 'man feel more pleasure than Lord Byron' did; 'his eyes lightened with ecstasy'. His daughter reflected back a mirror image of himself.

In 1819 Byron moved from Venice to Bologna to be with his mistress, Teresa Guiccioli, leaving Allegra, his illegitimate daughter by Claire Clairmont, with Richard Belgrave Hoppner, who was British Consul in

Byron embraces a child in a nineteenth-century illustration by John Arliss, 'celebrated as one of the most elegant printers of his time. Mr. Arliss likewise possessed considerable taste in embellishing juvenile works with wood engravings.'

Private collection

Venice, and his Swiss wife. Byron only brought Allegra to live with him two months later, after his mistress had left town and he fell prey to lonely gloom, 'ill health & worse nerves'. Once he needed company, he liked his daughter, telling his half-sister Augusta on 23 September 1819 that Allegra 'has a good deal of the Byron – can't articulate the letter *r* at all – frowns and pouts quite in our way – blue eyes – light hair growing *darker* daily – and a dimple in the chin – a scowl on the brow – white skin – sweet voice – and a particular liking of Music – and of her own way in every thing – is not that B. all over?'

And yet Teresa Guiccioli remembered that Byron 'used to turn away in disgust' whenever Allegra 'came into her father's presence', because she looked too much like her mother. He left his daughter £5,000 in a will dated 17 November 1818, to be paid on her twenty-first birthday or on her marriage, but only 'on condition that she does not marry a native of Great Britain'. He longed to impose the same intrusive, selfish inhibition on his daughter Ada.

While he lived in Ravenna Allegra stayed in a convent twelve miles away at Bagnacavallo. Byron tended to delegate the task of visiting her to his secretary. Shelley went and found her in good shape, though nourished upon 'improper food' (probably meat) and indoctrinated with the 'trash' of Catholic dogma. It seemed obvious to him (as it did to her mother Claire) that when Byron moved from Ravenna to Pisa, a distance of some 130 miles, Allegra should be brought nearer to her father, but she was left behind in the convent. The child's future was another of the issues on which the friends 'differed': Byron never considered taking Allegra to live with him. He heard that she was ill during the week of 13 April 1822 but he did not go to see her and she died of typhoid fever a week later. Two messengers accompanied her embalmed body to Pisa, but Byron refused to receive them and sent the body to England for burial in Harrow churchyard. He probably did suffer from remorse, knowing, as Mary Shelley told Maria Gisbourne on 2 June 1822, that 'he had acted against everybody's counsels and wishes'.

'Have you any notion – but I suppose *you* have – of what they call the parental feeling?' Byron once asked Moore. 'For myself, I have not the least.' Moore calls this an 'artificial speech': when Allegra died, Byron 'was so overwhelmed by the event, that those who were about him at the time actually trembled for his reason'.

It looks as though Byron behaved better towards other people's children than towards his own. He did experience 'the parental feeling', but perhaps more in metaphor than in reality. He loved watching beautiful children at play and repeatedly fell in love with little girls. 'I should love [her] for ever,' he told Lady Melbourne of Lady Charlotte Harley on 5 April 1813, 'if she could always be only eleven years old.' He once joked that he would 'like nephews better than sons'.

While he was on his Grand Tour, and once the inhibiting Hobhouse had returned to London on 17 July 1810, Byron went native, giving free rein to his pederastic impulses. They often involved parental feelings as well as lust. He became 'very much enamoured' of a boy called Eustathius Georgiou, until he became too demanding and had epileptic fits. Byron sent him home after a 'grand quarrel' and told Hobhouse twelve days later, 'I think I never in my life took so much pains to please any one, or succeeded so ill.' The remark highlights a feature of such relationships (whether with boys or pets): Byron's unavailing attempt to please.

In Athens he stayed in a monastery with six resident pupils. There he formed another of what Moore called 'those extraordinary friendships, – if attachment to persons so inferior to himself can be called by that name . . . in which the pride of being a protector, and the pleasure of exciting gratitude, seem to have constituted to his mind the chief, pervading charm'. Using the Italian that one of the pupils, Nicolo Giraud, taught him, Byron told Hobhouse on 29 July 1810 that he became the boy's '"Padrone" and his "amico," and the Lord knows what else besides'. Nicolo nursed Byron when he fell sick, before he succumbed to the same fever. On 26 November 1810 Byron told Hobhouse that Nicolo was acting as his 'Dragoman and Major Domo'. When he left Athens on 22 April 1811, he took Nicolo with him and in Malta he paid for the boy to attend school. Nicolo later wrote to Byron: he promised that he would study hard and hoped to be 'like your son and Your Excellency like my kindly father' – just as Edleston had. In his will of 12 August 1811 Byron left Nicolo £7,000, to be paid when he reached twenty-one years of age. Later wills omitted that bequest.

> The Moslem orphan went with her protector,
> For she was homeless, houseless, helpless.
>
> *Don Juan*, VIII, 141

Byron loved the idea of fatherhood. Don Juan saves a ten-year-old Turkish girl from slaughter. He calls her his 'protegee' and resolves not to surrender 'This child, who is parentless and therefore mine'. The Narrator comments:

> And thus they formed a rather curious pair;
> A guardian green in years, a ward connected
> In neither clime, time, blood, with her defender;
> And yet this want of ties made their's more tender.

For Byron children represented an extension, or a mirror of their parents' identities: 'they/In whom our brightest days we would retrace/Our little selves re-formed in finer clay', as he wrote in *Don Juan*. They seemed to function as doubles.

And yet, Byron could be brutally honest: after Shelley died, his estranged father offered Mary Shelley an income, on condition that she gave up her three-year-old son to a guardian's care. Percy Florence was the only survivor of her four children by Shelley. Byron urged Mary to give up the boy and take the money. She refused: 'I literally withered under the idea that one so near me should advise me to a mode of conduct which appeared little short of madness and nothing short of death.'

Among the refugees in Greece in 1823 Byron found a pretty ten-year-old Turkish girl, whose two brothers had been killed in the revolution. Her mother wanted to return to Prevesa but, given 'the present state of the Country', she preferred to leave her daughter in an Englishman's care.

Don Juan saves the child from the Cossacks, from George Cruikshank's Forty Illustrations of Lord Byron, *10 December 1824*

Byron mentioned Hatadje or Hato to his mistress Teresa Guiccioli in one of his brief postscripts to her brother's letters, promising that he would 'write shortly at greater length'. He added that he meant to send Hatadje to Teresa 'by and bye – she is beautiful as the Sun – and very lively – you can educate her'. Byron gave the girl costly dresses and a necklace of sequins. He would send for her twice a week, 'take the little girl on his knees, and caress her with all the fondness of a father'. He also considered sending her to Augusta, or even to Lady Byron 'as a Companion' for Ada. Hatadje referred to Byron, after his death, as her '*adopted father*'.

In November 1823 the fifteen-year-old Luka Chalandritsanos became Byron's page, and by the end of December Byron was buying him grammar books, so that he could act as his secretary. Byron fell in love with Luka, a boy 'of a most prepossessing appearance', as the bluff William Parry

Count D'Orsay's portrait of Count Pietro Gamba, Cini-Gamba collection, destroyed during the Second World War. Pietro, Teresa Guiccioli's younger brother, considered Byron as his 'friend and father'. When Pierino (he was known by his diminutive) disappointed him, Byron commented to G. Stevens on 19 January 1823 that 'this comes of letting boys play the man'. Pietro agreed to accept any punishment willingly, 'not so much from a superior officer, as from one who is to me a father'.

remembered, and lavished money and gifts on him. Luka attended Byron, sporting 'very handsomely chased arms in his girdle'. But Byron was disappointed with the way the boy responded and recorded his frowns in two poems. On the other hand, Luka displayed the untamed, untameable spirit that Byron appreciated.

Byron marked his thirty-sixth birthday with a poem addressed to Luka:

'Tis time this heart should be unmoved,
Since others it hath ceased to move;
Yet though I cannot be beloved,
Still let me love!

Two weeks later he rebuked Luka for drinking tea, as Byron did; tea was not a Greek drink. Luka may have abused his (equivocal) status. Certainly, Byron swung from indulgence to coldness. There is a note of pique in Byron's order that Luka would be paid 'five dollars a month . . . like the others of the household. He will eat with the Suliots – or where he pleases.' On the other hand Byron gave the boy a company of thirty irregular soldiers to command and referred to him as Luke, adding, '(not the Evangelist, but a disciple of mine)'. Byron addressed a second, untitled poem to Luka, which is now known as 'Love and Death'. It records his love for the boy, while acknowledging that Luka was not obliged to love him in return. In battle, in shipwreck, when Missolonghi suffered an earthquake, Byron's first concern was for Luka: if the boy died, Byron felt he would never recover.

Pets: Tame (but Not Tamed)

To his dog, every man is Napoleon;
hence the constant popularity of dogs.

Aldous Huxley, *Readers Digest*, 1934

Claire Clairmont's observation illuminates Byron's particular fondness for unlikely pets. Animals can function as surrogate children, but Byron's relationships with them reflected his partiality for unusual, difficult and even savage dependents.

Nelson, the 'beautifully formed, very ferocious, bull-mastiff' he had at Southwell in 1805, always wore a muzzle, but escaped 'and going into the

Lord Byron and his Dog, *by Elizabeth Pigot.*
Harry Ransom Center, The University of Texas at Austin

stable-yard fastened upon the throat of a horse, from which he could not be disengaged'. He had to be shot. 'Ferocious' is important here. Another dog '(half a *wolf* by the she side) . . . doted on me at ten years old, and very nearly ate me at twenty'. This was probably Lyon, whose portrait Byron commissioned from the local artist Clifton Thomson.

Byron kept Boatswain his Newfoundland dog, for five years, nursed him through an attack of rabies and commissioned a magnificent tomb for him.

Notoriously, when Byron wasn't allowed to bring his bulldog Smut to Trinity College, Cambridge, he kept a bear in his rooms, and in 1809 the bear came to live at Newstead. Byron commissioned their portraits. In his taste for exotic animals he may have been following a family tradition: the 5th Lord Byron imported a wolf from Spa in 1765.

As soon as he moved into Albany in Piccadilly in 1814 Byron bought a macaw and a parrot, which bit him, he told Moore on 20 April 1814. The composer Isaac Nathan noted that Byron had rendered one of his parrots 'so attached to him, that though entirely at war with strangers, it evinced the greatest anxiety to be always with him. If his Lordship seemed to notice any person particularly, this bird would express its indignation and jealousy

Lyon, a portrait by Clifton Thomson, 1808.
Courtesy of Nottingham City Museums and Galleries

Byron's Newfoundland, Boatswain, responded so well to training that he imitated his master's patronage of his protégés. He 'protected' Mrs Byron's quarrelsome terrier Gilpin 'against the insults of other dogs . . . and, if he but heard Gilpin's voice in distress, would fly instantly to his rescue'.
Courtesy of Nottingham City Museums and Galleries

In 1808 Byron chose to site the monument to his Newfoundland Boatswain on the spot where, he believed, the high altar of Newstead Abbey once stood. The 'Inscription on the Monument of a Favourite Dog' reads in part: 'But the poor dog, in life the firmest friend,/The first to welcome, foremost to defend,/ Whose honest heart is still his master's own,/Who labours, fights, lives, breathes for him alone'. In 1811 Byron planned to recreate his favourite father/son embrace in eternity by being buried there, together with Boatswain and his oldest servant Joe Murray.

Photo: David Wrightsman, from Rosalys Coope and Pete Smith, Newstead Abbey, A Nottinghamshire Country House: Its Owners and Architectural History, 1540–1931, *2014* in the most amusing manner, and would immediately attack his Lordship, until he bestowed his caresses on it.' One day it lacerated Byron's foot, 'till the blood flowed copiously; instead of being excited by the pain produced, his Lordship was only lost in admiration at the strong attachment of the bird'. He explained that the wound was intended for Nathan, but that the bird 'in her jealous fit mistook her aim'.

In Switzerland in September 1816 Byron told Augusta (who owned a hideous dog called Tip) that he had bought 'a very ugly dog – but "*tres mechant*" – this was "his great recommendation in the owner's eyes & mine"'. Byron taught the dog, called Mutz, to shut the door when he was told. Geoffrey Bond speculates that he may have been 'one of the large, tough, Swiss dairymen's or butchers' dogs used for herding cattle ... from which the modern Rottweiler breed has been developed'. Byron later boasted that the dog, who stole several legs of mutton when left to his own devices, was 'learning to obey the word of command with a piece of bread on his nose until permission is accorded to eat it'.

Byron kept 'two monkeys, a fox – and two new mastiffs' on the ground floor of Palazzo Mocenigo in Venice. A monkey played about his room in Ravenna as he wrote. In a letter to Augusta he mentioned his daughter Allegra in the same breath as his menagerie, 'all scratching – screaming and fighting – in the highest health and Spirits'.

As soon as Byron's mistress left him in Palazzo Mocenigo in Venice in May 1819 he wrote to his sister, for the first time in eight months. Four days later he asked Murray to send him two bulldogs, a terrier and a Newfoundland dog. He said that Italian bulldogs, 'though good and ready to fly at anything – yet have not the tenacity of tooth and stoicism in endurance' of British ones. He did not send for his daughter until the end of August. He took on a civet cat in spring 1820, which he called admiringly, 'the fiercest beast I ever saw'. He told Moore on 24 May 1820 that it ran away after scratching the monkey's cheek. His 'flourishing family' of 'two Cats – six dogs – a badger – a falcon, a tame Crow – and a Monkey' cooperated, apart from 'an occasional civil war about provisions'. He later referred to 'the tame (but *not tamed*) crow', which he had to beat 'for stealing the falcon's victuals'.

Byron's room in Palazzo Mocenigo, from Interiors and exteriors in Venice by Lake Price. Lithographed by Joseph Nash from the original drawings, *[London?] 1843.*
Ravenna, Biblioteca Classense. Photograph by Gabriele Pezzi

Even after the loss of a cat, two monkeys and a crow he assured Augusta on 22 June 1821 that his 'menagerie' was 'still a flourishing and somewhat obstreperous establishment'. Shelley told Peacock in August 1821 that he counted 'ten horses, eight enormous dogs, three monkeys, five cats, an eagle, a crow, and a falcon; and all these, except the horses, walk about the house, which every now and then resounds with their unarbitrated quarrels, as if they were the masters of it'. He added that he had 'just met on the grand staircase five peacocks, two guinea hens, and an Egyptian crane'.

In Pisa, Byron's accounts show that the pets, namely '2 monkeys, 2 to 3 dogs, and a few birds, 3 of which were geese, were in general provided for more liberally than their master'. As he was about to sail for Greece in 1822, Byron asked his banker to look after three geese, 'for which, he told me, he had a sort of affection'.

The following year Byron was given another Newfoundland dog, which accompanied him to Greece. In Missolonghi William Parry noticed that 'Beyond the walls of his own apartment, where he seemed to derive amusement from his books, and from his dog, Lion; and pleasure from the attachment of his servants, particularly from the attentions of Tita, [Byron] had neither security or repose.'

Frontispiece, William Parry, The Last Days of Lord Byron with His Lordship's Opinions on Various Subjects, Particularly on the State and Prospects of Greece, *1825: inside Byron's house in Missolonghi. Suliotes play cards in the background and weapons hang on the wall. He used to 'commune very much, and very often' with Lion, 'who was perhaps his dearest and most affectionate friend . . . His most usual phrase was, "Lyon, you are no rogue, Lyon;" or "Lyon," his Lordship would say, "thou art an honest fellow, Lyon." The dog's eyes sparkled, and his tail swept the floor, as he sat with his haunches on the ground. "Thou art more faithful than men, Lyon; I trust thee more." Lyon sprang up, and barked and bounded round his master, as much as to say, "You may trust me, I will watch actively on every side." "Lyon, I love thee, thou art my faithful dog" and Lyon jumped and kissed his master's hand, as an acknowledgment of his homage.'*

Image courtesy of the American School of Classical Studies at Athens, Gennadius Library

In training his dogs Byron recreated the band of inferiors 'obedient to command', that he longed to lead.

> (Let deeper sages the true cause determine)
> He had a kind of inclination or
> Weakness, for what most people deem mere vermin—

Savage, for his bulldog puppy; Lyon, Tiger for later dogs: Byron's names betray his partiality for fierce animals. Turning them into pets may have enabled Byron to relive and rewrite the terms of his earliest experiences of hostile, hazardous love. Bulldogs were bred to attack in the popular sport of bull baiting. 'The bulldog is scarcely capable of any education and is fitted for nothing except ferocity and combat.' Naturally Byron identified with their nature. 'You do not have that name of *Bulldog* for nothing,' his friend Elizabeth Pigot told him. He compared himself to the species when he was defending himself against the critics of *Don Juan* in 1819.

Incidentally, Byron shared his love for savage pets, for very ferocious, '*tres mechant*', 'tame (but *not tamed*)', fierce, obstreperous beasts, with several other 'fatherless' Napoleonists, such as Lord Erskine, William Godwin, Leigh Hunt, William Whitbread and Charles James Fox. Cultivating wild animals allowed them to act out an ideal father's role. *The Napoleonists, A Study in Political Disaffection* by Edward Tangye Lean (1970) also lists several twentieth-century sympathisers with foreign tyrants who cultivated wild animals, such as the left-wing journalist Kingsley Martin, who found that boa constrictors, 'if not too large, make admirable pets' and the spy Kim Philby, with his raccoons, birds, fish, pet vixen, mouse, half-breed Alsatian, canary, budgerigar and parakeet: 'In Beirut he allowed the fox cub to drink whisky and suck his pipe.'

Servants: The Inmates of his Family

'The inmates of his family were all extremely attached to' Byron, Moore reported, 'and would have endured any thing on his account. He was indeed culpably lenient to them; for even when instances occurred of their neglecting their duty, or taking an undue advantage of his good-nature, he rather bantered than spoke seriously to them upon it, and could not bring himself to discharge them, even when he had threatened to do so.'

When his mother discovered that Frank Boyce, a manservant attending Byron at Cambridge, 'had obtained money from a Nottingham tailor on false pretences, she wrote advising his discharge'. Byron rebuked her.

A portrait of Joe Murray by T. Barker, which Byron commissioned. The 5th Lord Byron employed Joseph Murray in 1755 as 'the sailor boy' to attend on the twenty-gun ship that he kept with other vessels on the lake at Newstead Abbey. Murray was over sixty when he became Byron's butler and he later travelled abroad with him. At the age of fourteen, on 22 March 1804, Byron swore to Augusta, 'whilc I live [Murray] shall never be abandoned In his old Age.' Murray's income remained constant, even when Byron himself was penniless.

Courtesy of Nottingham City Museums and Galleries

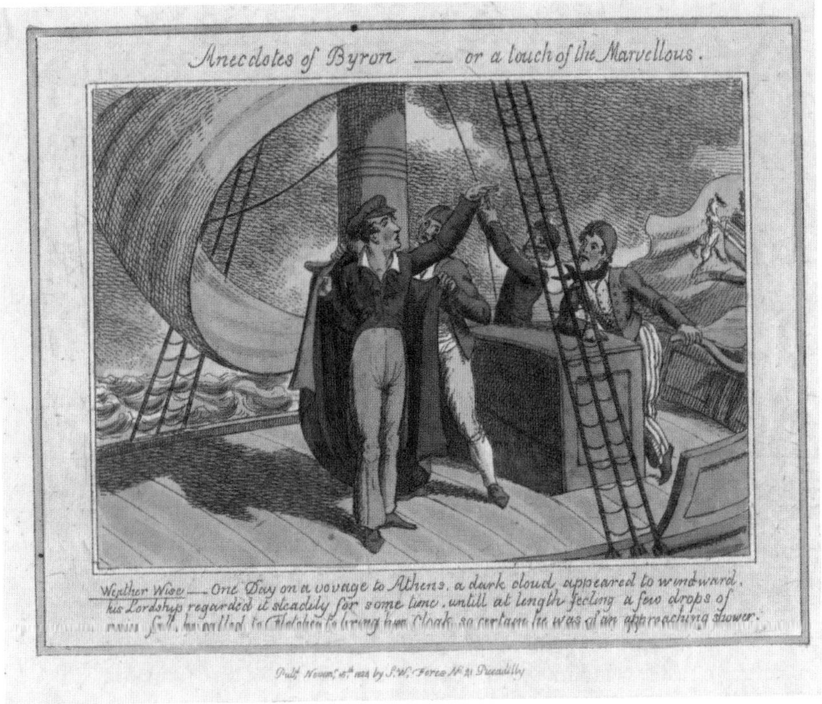

Weather Wise: *a satirical print issued after Alexander Kilgour published the anonymous* Anecdotes of Lord Byron *in 1825.*

Private Collection

Ultimately the valet had to be prosecuted for theft and was transported for seven years, despite Byron's pleas for mercy.

As he entered adulthood, Lord Byron reinforced his feudal status by taking on a page, Robert Rushton, the son of a tenant at Newstead. Byron told his mother on 22 June 1809 that he liked him 'because like myself he seems a friendless animal'. Younger than Byron and his social inferior, Robert was an ideal protégé. They formed the first of many important master–servant relationships in Byron's life and work. Byron wrote about his page in a stanza that he then cut from *Childe Harold* I:

Of all his train there was a (guilty) henchman page
A (dark-eyed) peasant boy, who (loved) served his master well
And often would his pranksome prate engage
Childe (Burun's) Harold's ear, when his proud heart did swell –

With sable thoughts that he disdained to tell
Then would he smile on him (and) as (Robin / Rupert) Alwin smiled
When aught that from his young lips archly fell
The gloomy film (of) from (Burun's) Harold's eye beguiled
(And pleased the Childe appeared nor eer the boy reviled)

Byron had the boy vaccinated against cowpox and, when he stayed at Newstead Abbey, Robert slept in a truckle bed adjacent to the red bedroom. Byron paid for Rushton to attend boarding school in Newark for three years. When he moved to London, Robert stayed with him in Jermyn Street – until Byron's groom/valet William Fletcher took him to a prostitute. Byron reacted with disgust and fury. Why did he care so much about his page's loss of innocence? Perhaps because he needed Robert to stay a child? In the will Byron signed on 14 June 1809 he left the boy an annual income of £50, 'and a further sum of one thousand pounds on attaining the age of twenty-five years'. He repeated that provision in his will of 12 August 1811. On both occasions he magisterially delayed the boy's adulthood by four years.

Byron intended to train Robert Rushton to become his steward, but the boy could be difficult. At the beginning of 1812 Robert refused to carry letters from one of the maidservants at Newstead Abbey, who was, briefly, Byron's lover. Byron addressed the boy in paternal fashion: 'I am truly sorry to have any subject of complaint against *you*; I have too good an opinion of you to think I shall have occasion to repeat it, after the care I have taken of you, and my favourable intentions in your behalf.' A second letter of 25 January 1812 shows Byron trusted his page more than his lover and demonstrated infinite patience: 'I am sure *you* would not deceive me,' he told the boy, 'though *she* would. Whatever it is, *you* shall be forgiven.'

Byron employed a 'gaunt and witch-like' housemaid, whom his visitors disliked but he kept her with him from his time at 4 Bennet Street, St James's, through Albany and into married quarters at 13 Piccadilly, because 'The poor old devil was so kind to me.'

Byron 'was More to me then [*sic*] a father', his valet William Fletcher told Murray after his master's death.

His 'tolerance towards his domestics turned into an almost fatherly solicitude if the slightest misfortune befell them', Teresa remembered. Byron's groom Tita Falcieri said that 'in Lord Byron he had lost a father rather than a master; and expatiated upon the indulgence with which he had always treated his domestics, and the care he expressed for their comfort and welfare.' Tita called him 'my good master and second father'.

Daniel Maclise's portrait of Tita Falcieri, Byron's groom, the former Venetian gondolier, after Disraeli took him on as house steward at Hughenden Manor, dated 31 May 1836. Byron delighted in the way that Tita hid a soft nature under a fierce, moustachioed and deliberately oriental, Kleftic exterior, the heroic combination he admired in Ali Pacha and recreated in his pirate, Lambro, in Don Juan.

16

'BOXER BYRON'*

* John Clare, note, dated Easter Sunday, 1841, Jonathan Bate, *John Clare: A Biography*, 2003, 437

Byron arrived at Newstead Abbey after his mother had died, early in August 1811. A procession left from Newstead Abbey, accompanying her coffin on its way to the family vault. Byron watched it go but stayed behind. His reaction pays an eloquent, unspoken tribute to the combative element in his relationship with his mother, which could never have seemed as potentially fatal, as after her death. Then, 'turning to young Rushton, who was the only person left beside himself, he desired him to fetch the sparring-gloves, and proceeded to his usual exercise with the boy. He was silent and abstracted all the time, and, as if from an effort to get the better of his feelings, threw more violence, Rushton thought, into his blows than was his habit; but, at last, – the struggle seeming too much for him, – he flung away the gloves, and retired to his room.'

Byron's 'usual exercise' with his pageboy highlights the sport's attraction for Byron. Every bout enacts a potentially ambivalent partnership, for boxing matches confront a hero with his double, his doppelgänger. As Joyce Carol Oates pointed out:

> The boxer meets an opponent who is a dream-distortion of himself in the sense that his weaknesses, his capacity to fail and to be seriously hurt, his intellectual miscalculations – all can be interpreted as strengths belonging

> to the Other; the parameters of his private being are nothing less than boundless assertions of the Other's self. This is dream, or nightmare: my strengths are not fully my own, but my opponent's weaknesses; my failure is not fully my own, but my opponent's triumphs. He is my shadow-self, not my (mere) shadow.

Byron boxed with those who were older and better than he was – but also with those who were younger. The sport enacted his favourite relationship – that between patron and protégé – while its versatility as sport and as metaphor allowed for the exchange of roles: Byron could act both parts. His fiction frequently recreates this ideal, necessary versatility. In *Werner* and in *Cain*, for example, the hero is both father and son. That allowed Byron to recreate the comfort that he embraced when he travelled in 1809 and again in 1819 with 'my boy Robert, and the old man Murray'. *Don Juan* would prove to be the most successful vehicle for this literary feat of driving two-in-hand. In the second canto's shipwreck the boyish hero briefly shows himself a man while his tutor (in Latin, *magister*), merely weeps:

> It seem'd as if they had exchanged their care,
> For Juan wore the magisterial face
> Which courage gives

Boxing was fundamental to Byron's way of thinking and writing. Its private meaning for him needs to be seen in context with its public significance in Regency England.

Boxing became central to British society in the early nineteenth century, as it never has been before or since. At war with France almost uninterruptedly from 1739 to 1815 and under repeated threat of invasion, heroism was called for. 'The dexterous use of the fist is a truly *British* exercise' Edmund Hoyle wrote in 1754; 'and the sturdy *English* have been as much renowned for their boxing as their beef; neither of which are by any means suited to the watery stomachs and weak sinews of their enemies the *French*.'

James Gillray, Fighting for the Dunghill or Jack Tar settling Buonaparte, *20 November 1798.*
© National Portrait Gallery, London

Boxing's popularity also reflected fashion, the contemporary neo-classical cult of the heroic, naked male body. It was expressed in Canova's three-metre-tall nude statue of Napoleon (1811, now in Apsley House) and the Wellington Monument (1822, in Hyde Park). In June and July 1807 artists, intellectuals and gentlemen watched as naked pugilists adopted attitudes and sparred amid ancient Greek statuary, including recent shipments from Lord Elgin. The boxer, Tring, modelled as Hercules, and his body can be seen in paintings by Sir Joshua Reynolds, John Hoppner and Sir William Beechey.

'Public exhibitions of boxing . . . certainly keep up a bold and manly spirit,' Sir John Sinclair wrote in his comprehensive *Code of Health and Longevity*, 'not only amongst those who are trained for that purpose, but even among the spectators, who seeing what their countrymen can bear without flinching, must aspire to similar strength of person, and firmness of mind.' Byron owned two copies of this work, first published in 1807, perhaps partly because Sir John paid tribute to Byron's boxing coach, 'Gentleman' John Jackson in the body of the book and also in an appendix,

The Wellington Monument at Hyde Park takes the form of a naked Achilles. Richard Westmacott sculpted it and cast it from captured French cannon, 1822.

Photo: Matthew Burdis

'A Collection of Papers, on the Subject of Athletic Exercises, &c.', where he printed an extended conversation with Jackson (reproduced as Appendix 2).

The Sportsman's Delight: Blood, Bone, Action and Game

Boxing displayed John Bull in heroic, fighting mode. It represented 'The Good Old English Custom of Deciding a Quarrel', as the medal pictured overleaf proclaimed.

The title page of another book on boxing, *Pancratia*, published anonymously in 1812, offered 'an Argumentative Proof, that Pugilism, considered as a Gymnic Exercise, demands the Admiration, and Patronage of every free State, being calculated to inspire Manly Courage, and a Spirit of Independence – enabling us to resist Slavery at Home and Enemies from Abroad'.

Prize fights attracted the nobility as well as the populace, though they were not strictly legal. The Prince of Wales attended Jackson's first fight on 9 June 1788. Having witnessed a death in the ring later that year he never

This medal was issued to commemorate the boxing match between Bill Neat, a butcher, and Tom Hickman, 'The Gas Man', on 11 December 1821. It lasted eighteen rounds, before Neat knocked Hickman out. Hazlitt reported on this, his first experience of a boxing match in his essay 'The Fight'. Its other side displayed the motto, 'Blood, Bone, Action and Game'.

Private collection

attended one again, but he invited prize fighters to 'preserve order' at his coronation in 1821. Several of his brothers continued to patronise the sport.

In June 1814 London welcomed representatives of the allied forces who defeated Napoleon.

> Lord Lowther invited the Emperor of Russia, Generals Platoff and Blucher, to an elegant *dejeuné* [*sic*], when the national sport of Boxing . . . was introduced for their approbation . . . Those distinguished visitors were so much gratified with this generous mode of settling quarrels, and the scientific mode of attack and defence exhibited, they earnestly requested of Lord Lowther that another *trial of skill* might take place . . . when . . . [they were joined by] the King of Prussia, the Prince Royal of Prussia, Princes Frederick, and William of Prussia,

> the Prince of Mecklenburgh, General D'York, &c. &c... The ... *sparring* of JACKSON was particularly admired. The elegance of his positions, the celerity of his attack, the fortitude of his manner, and the superior mode he developed of guarding his frame from the attacks of his adversaries, created a lively interest among the royal warriors. His symmetry of figure and fine muscular powers, also, did not pass unnoticed.

John Jackson himself taught Byron to box at Harrow. The school's fencing master, Henry Angelo (whose father, Domenico, wrote the definitive book on the sport, *École des Armes* (1763)) probably introduced Byron to him. Henry Angelo's brother-in-law was the Revd Mark Drury, Byron's housemaster and the son of the headmaster. Angelo and Jackson, boxing Champion of England 1795–1803, the 'masters of the polite and vulgar arts', opened a club at 13 Bond Street and used the premises on alternate days. During one of the school holidays Byron lived in London, supposedly to study French, but spent most of his time fencing and boxing 'to the no small disturbance of the reverend teacher and his establishment'.

Fencing and boxing may seem unlikely sports for Byron, who had difficulty in walking, but boxers then needed to move rather less than they do now. Indeed, dodging or retiring showed bad form. 'Activity, or *milling on the retreat*,' Pierce Egan noted of boxing in 1818, 'is, at the present period, a greater requisite toward victory than it was formerly considered. Some have censured *shifting* as an unmanly custom, but without reason.' The tradition suited Byron, however, who 'remained stationary' in fencing and in sparring '& merely used his arms'.

'I fought my way very fairly,' Byron remembered of his boxing at Harrow. 'I think I lost but one battle out of seven' and then only because of 'the unfair treatment of his [opponent's] own boarding-house, where we boxed – I had not even a second'. He was a 'hard hitter'.

Byron called himself 'not a bad boxer – when I could keep my temper – which was difficult – but which I strove to do ever since I knocked down Mr. Purling and put his knee-pan out (with the gloves on) in Angelo's and Jackson's rooms in 1806 during the sparring'.

Art of Self Defence: *Tom and Jerry receiving Instructions from Mr Jackson at his Rooms in Bond Street, from Pierce Egan's* Life in London*, 1822, illustrated by I. Robert and George Cruikshank.*

Silent Rages

As we have seen, Mrs Byron's bitterness cast a dark shadow over the first six years of Byron's childhood in Aberdeen. The shadow only lifted when, unexpectedly, he became heir apparent to his great-uncle's title. As late as 1891, Aberdonians remembered Byron's 'violent and improper conduct in his youthful days'. He thought he inherited his 'violence and bad temper' from his mother. Certainly, his 'violent paroxysms of rage' began in frustration at the claustrophobia of his home. They represent the ground soil, which would generate his anorexia. Thomas Moore interviewed those who knew Byron in Aberdeen and reported that as a child his 'temper was violent, or rather sullenly passionate'.

> Even when in petticoats, he showed the same uncontrollable spirit with his nurse, which he afterwards exhibited when an author, with his critics. Being

> angrily reprimanded by her, one day, for having soiled or torn a new frock in which he had just been dressed, he got into one of his 'silent rages' (as he himself has described them), seized the frock with both his hands, rent it from top to bottom, and stood in sullen stillness, setting both his censurer and her wrath at defiance.

The 'old china saucer, out of which he had bitten a large piece, in a fit of passion' was kept as a relic in Aberdeen. In 'my sullen moods', Byron himself remembered in his Journal for 27 November 1813, 'I was always a Devil. They once (in one of my silent rages) wrenched a knife from me, which I had snatched from table at Mrs Byron's dinner (I always dined earlier) and applied to my breast.' He was known as 'that little deevil, Geordie Byron'.

Byron also expressed his anger in fighting. One of his schoolfellows remembered that Byron was 'always more ready to give a blow than take one'. As a boy, he fought to survive. He was constantly reproached for his pride but it was 'originally *defensive*', he assured Annabella Milbanke, later his wife, on 26 September 1813 '– for at that time my hand like Ishmael's was against every one's & every one's against mine'. Byron had to defend himself from 'mortification', bullying on account of his 'physical inferiority'. For that reason he carried 'at all times, small loaded pistols in his waistcoat pockets'. Boxing served to reaffirm Byron's masculine identity, which seemed threatened by his oppressive relationship with his mother, and it offered a release for his anger.

'Gentleman' Jackson: He Alone Knows the Sort

Byron saluted Jackson in *Don Juan* as his 'corporeal pastor and master'. Byron put himself into Jackson's care, as a professional boxer entrusts himself to his trainer. When Leigh Hunt first saw Byron, probably in 1809, Byron was swimming in the River Thames 'under the auspices of Mr Jackson the prize-fighter . . . a respectable-looking manly person . . . I forget what his tutor said of him; but he spoke in terms of praise.'

Charles Turner's mezzotint engraving after the oil painting by Ben Marshall. John Jackson rests his top hat on the plinth of a classical sculpture of a boxer. His stylish, sober costume and elegant posture put the ancient, naked pugilist into the shade. Having boxed in only three fights Jackson retired from the ring and taught gentlemen to spar. He also represented an ideal in masculine deportment. According to Pierce Egan, 'It was impossible to look on his fine ample chest, his noble shoulders, his waist (if anything too small), his large, but not too large hips . . . his limbs, his balustrade calf and beautifully turned, but not over delicate ankle, his firm foot, and peculiarly small hand, without thinking that nature had sent him on earth as a model.' Jackson 'was designated the Commissary-general of the milling-tribe, his rooms in Old Bond-street were the resort of the most distinguished characters in the kingdom . . . In the above rooms might be daily witnessed some of our most celebrated lawyers, enlightened statesmen, impartial judges, immense landowners, &c. &c. unbending from their various vocations in society, putting on the gloves one with another, giving hit for hit, imbibing additional courage from every blow.' According to Thomas Moore, 'This gentleman (as he well deserves to be called, from the correctness of his conduct and the peculiar urbanity of his manners) forms that useful link between the amateurs and the professors of pugilism which, when broken, it will be difficult, if not wholly impossible, to replace.'

Private collection

Jackson introduced Byron to the manly world of the 'fancy'. In 1807, at the age of nineteen, Byron played a major role as a patron of boxing, and he arranged and attended at least two major boxing matches in 1808. Contemporary reports demonstrate that they were occasions for the display of courage, 'science' and bottom – the ability to endure inordinate amounts of pain.

The bouts Byron sponsored at the Rubbing House on Epsom Downs on 14 April 1808 opposed the 'most elegant' boxer Tom Belcher and the Irish champion Dan Dogherty, who was 'as game a pugilist as ever stripped a shirt over a head' and 'a pleasing and scientific boxer'. The odds were six to four on Belcher. Characteristically, Byron backed Dogherty, who lost. By round fifteen his face looked 'hideously disfigured' and 'The battle was now considered decidedly Belcher's' and yet it still dragged on into the thirty-third round. The whole of the match report for this fight and for the other bout Byron sponsored, in May 1808, between John Gully and Bob Gregson can be read in *Pugilistica*, and on the internet.

Moore noted that in 1814 when Byron talked at dinner with Jackson, his 'early instructor in pugilism, all his boyish tastes seemed to revive; – and it was not a little amusing to observe how perfectly familiar with the annals of "The Ring," and with all the more recondite phraseology of "the Fancy," was the sublime poet of Childe Harold'. Byron filled stanza 19 of *Don Juan*'s Canto XI full of boxing slang, as used by 'the select mobility and their patrons' and in a note referred the reader 'so ignorant as to require a traduction . . . to . . . John Jackson, Esq., Professor of Pugilism; who, I trust, still retains the strength and symmetry of his model of a form, together with his good humour, and athletic as well as mental accomplishments'.

There was a little more to their relationship. Like his headmaster, Drury, and Napoleon, 'Gentleman' John Jackson played some aspects of a mentor's role in his life. Byron relied on him to collect medicine from Lamb's Conduit Street and choose him greyhounds; to act for him in a dispute over an unsound pony; to dispose of bidets that he had installed; and to arrange lodgings for his mistress in Brompton and in Brighton, where he paid Jackson to visit him during summer 1808. Byron addressed him as 'Dear Jack' and 'My dear Jack' and invited him to stay at Newstead over Christmas.

Byron continued to see the boxer when an undergraduate at Trinity College, Cambridge. When his tutor 'remonstrated with him on being seen in company so much beneath his rank, he replied, "Really, sir, I cannot understand you. With the single exception of yourself, I can assure you that Mr. Jackson's manners are infinitely superior to those of the Fellows of the College whom I meet at the high table."' Byron gave the boxer a gold watch 'engraved on the case of it, as a strong token of his opinion – "Manners, not strength"'. The words highlight an important trait: Byron loved the discrepancy between surface manner and the potential for violence. He would be drawn to it again later when he encountered the 'Mohammedan Buonaparte', Ali Pacha. It also formed part of Napoleon's own character, as far as Byron knew his nature. And he would celebrate it in *Don Juan* – explicitly in his portraits of heroes like the pirate Lambro, and implicitly in the poem itself. Byron highlighted an affinity between the boxer and Napoleon, in terms of their roles in his imaginative life, when he referred to Jackson as 'the Emperor of Pugilism'. His portrait engraving hung in Byron's bedroom at Newstead Abbey, along with a portrait of Napoleon. When Byron dropped his swordstick into Lake Leman in 1816, he insisted to Hobhouse on 23 June that Jackson should procure him a new one – 'he alone knows the sort'.

Hobhouse was so struck by Byron's association with the boxer that he wrote a lampoon about it, which has since disappeared. Hobhouse felt jealous of Jackson, as Byron's wife noticed. Hobhouse 'frequently dictated measures to him as to a child – "Now Byron you must do so & so" – or phrases of that kind – nor do I ever recollect that he disobeyed, or delayed to comply'. As Byron's 'guide philosopher & friend' Hobhouse relished the paternal role he played in his friend's life. He was Byron's 'bulldog' and he therefore resented even Byron's favourite dog Boatswain – which he admitted.

Byron continued to fence and to use the broadsword after he left Harrow. But Jackson and boxing mattered to him in a way that fencing never did. Jackson himself insisted that

> Boxing is the best exercise of any, from exercising all the members of the body. Fencing occupies only one side. Most people are right-handed, and

Portrait of John Cam Hobhouse, drawn and etched by Richard Dighton, 1819. Hobhouse, 'this genial but stunted invert', was Byron's friend from their days at Cambridge, a fellow admirer of Napoleon, his companion on his Grand Tour, the best man at his wedding. Byron dedicated Childe Harold IV *to him, saying he was 'wakeful o'er my sickness and kind in my sorrow, glad in my prosperity and firm in my adversity, true in counsel and trusty in peril'. But Hobhouse's inhibited possessiveness meant that he resented Byron's friendships with others, such as Thomas Moore; did not approve of* Don Juan*; and took the most active role in burning the manuscript of the Memoirs after Byron's death, meaning to protect his friend's reputation.*

Private collection

John Jackson in a popular print
Private collection

> the exercise is partial, but boxing calls both arms into action; and both hands must be equally employed both in hitting and parrying. In this species of exercise, the mind also must necessarily be more occupied.
>
> . . . By training, the mental faculties are also improved. The attention is more ready and the perceptions more acute, probably owing to the clearness of the stomach and the better digestion.

'I have been sparring with Jackson for exercise this morning,' Byron recorded in his diary in March 1814:

> and mean to continue and renew my acquaintance with the muffles. My chest, and arms, and wind are in very good plight, and I am not in flesh . . .

> At any rate, exercise is good and this the severest of all, fencing and the broad sword never fatigued me half so much . . . Today I have been very sulky – but one hour's exercise with Mr Jackson of pugilistic memory has given me spirits & fatigued me into that state of languid laziness which I prefer to all others.

Boxing supplemented dieting in Byron's recipe for heroism in that it too enabled the spirit to dominate the flesh. It also offered him an arena in which to practise his skills as an aggressive male, under the tuition of a superior, older man.

Another Sort of Sparring

Boxing showed Byron how to behave in other fields of endeavour. On 17 March 1814 he made the analogy between fighting and writing: having spent the morning boxing with Jackson he commented that Isaac D'Israeli's *Quarrels of Authors* (1814) was 'another sort of sparring'.

In *Don Juan* he compared contestants for the title of the 'greatest living poet' to 'the champion in the fisty ring'.

From the beginning, Byron took writing very seriously. His first two books of poems, *Fugitive Pieces* (1806) and its expurgated successor, *Poems on Various Occasions* (January 1807), were printed 'for the perusal of a friendly circle'. *Hours of Idleness*, his first book of poems to be actually published, went on sale at the end of June 1807. Much was at stake and his ambitiousness emerged as defensiveness. With the book's title he tried to 'arrest the arm of censure', while its title page qualified the author as 'A Minor'. He claimed in the Preface, as he would often claim, that this would be his 'last attempt'. He had 'hazarded [his] reputation and feelings in publishing this volume'; he persisted, because '"to do greatly", we must "dare greatly".' In the Preface to his *Hints from Horace* he later claimed that his 'literary pursuits were not very aspiring', but the Preface to *Hours of Idleness* shows that, from the beginning, writing always meant 'doing greatly'. 'I have passed the Rubicon,' Byron

Byron acquired this screen some time between 1812 and 1816. One side is devoted to actors, the other to boxers. Portraits and illustrations of boxing matches are interspersed with newspaper clippings and texts, principally from volume I of Pierce Egan's Boxiana *(July 1812 edition). The portraits go back as far as James Figg, champion 1719–1730. The screen records two of Jackson's three fights. One account is hand-written. The full-length portraits are of Tom Belcher, Dan Mendoza, Tom Cribb, Molyneaux, Thomas Futrell and John Jackson. The screen includes a Rowlandsonesque print of a fight with female seconds and a drawing of 'Female Pugilism'. Pierce Egan referred to it as 'ANGELO'S SCREEN' in volume II of* Boxiana *(1818) and noted that 'It originally cost his Lordship £250'. John Murray bought the screen at the sale of Byron's books in 1816, when it cost him £16 5s 6d. According to an advertisement in Piece Egan's* Life in London and Sporting Guide, *another boxing screen of eight panels was offered for sale, 'originally made for the amusement of the late Lord Byron, at a great expense, under the immediate direction of Mr Angelo'.*

Private collection

declared, 'and must stand or fall by the "cast of the die".' Like a trumpet fanfare, the first poem in this first volume (and his next three books), 'On Leaving Newstead Abbey', dated 1803, summons up Byron's ancestors, his 'fathers', the 'Shades of heroes'. His career enacts his search for heroic renown, rather than profit, since his aristocratic antipathy to trade would not allow him to accept payment for his work – until after he left England in 1816.

Byron anticipated that *Hours of Idleness* would be attacked: 'If so,' he told Elisabeth Pigot on 2 August 1807, 'have at 'em.' Combative from the start, he was ready to challenge a reviewer to a duel and then die. When he left Cambridge after Christmas 1807 and stayed in London he owed some £5,000 to moneylenders, Mrs Byron and others. Within a year his debts had risen to 'perhaps twelve thousand pounds'. He felt lonely and vulnerable. The all-important *Edinburgh Review*

Byron's pistol.

Harrow School and Harrow School Archive

published a hard-hitting, even cruel, notice in its January 1808 issue, which Byron resented bitterly, partly because he shared the magazine's Scottish character and its Whig principles.

So Byron resorted to tactics he had learned from Jackson: he explored boxing's heroic potential in his poetry, with words replacing fists. 'I remembered only the maxim of my boxing-master, which, in my youth, was found useful in general riots, – "Whoever is not for you is against you – *mill* away right and left," and so I did.' He had already begun a mild, Horatian satire in October 1807, which he then called 'The British Bards'. He now broadened its focus, took its savage tone from another, very different Roman poet, Juvenal, sprayed insults indiscriminately and changed its name to *English Bards and Scotch Reviewers*. 'And though I hope not hence unscathed to go', he warned his critics, 'Who conquers me, shall find a stubborn foe'.

Byron explained to Leigh Hunt on 22 October 1815 that he wrote that 'ferocious rhapsody' *English Bards* because 'I was angry – & determined to be witty – & fighting in a crowd dealt about my blows against all alike without distinction or discernment.' Disappointed by Carlisle's perfunctory guardianship, Byron retaliated in *English Bards and Scotch Reviewers*, dismissing his relative's poetry as 'paralytic puling'. Maliciously, he revealed that the earl's 'works, most resplendently bound, form a conspicuous ornament to his book-shelves'.

Seven years later, when Shelley told him that Keats had been killed off by a bad review, Byron replied on 26 April 1821 that he himself had reacted to a savage critique with 'rage, and resistance, and redress'. He added that 'especially in the career of writing, a man should calculate upon his powers of *resistance* before he goes into the arena.' The word 'arena' implied a boxing ring.

In Italy, where he lived from 1816 to 1822, Byron eventually accepted that he had wasted his energy, time and money in fostering the cause of Italy's independence from Austrian and papal tyranny. It remained a distant ideal, 'the very *poetry* of politics'. Instead, he turned to the politics of poetry. This campaign took the form of a paper war fought between those who attacked Alexander Pope (such as his latest editor, William Bowles)

A detail from Byron's boxing screen: 'I am not again to be trifled with,' Richard Humphreys told Daniel Mendoza on 15 November 1788. Humphreys appears here in an engraving by John Young after the painting by John Hoppner, now in the Metropolitan Museum, New York.

Private collection

and those who defended him. The 'battle', as Byron called it, satisfied his frustrated martial or 'fistic' instinct. That is why he could not help digressing into anecdotes from his days as patron of the boxing ring when he wrote a very long essay on the controversy ('Observations upon "Observations"'). Indeed, he compared the controversy itself to 'a boxing-bout'. In defending Pope, incidentally, Byron was again standing up for a father figure: 'A detracting Editor,' such as Bowles, 'is a parricide.'

MONUMENT TO JOHN JACKSON IN BROMPTON CEMETERY.

THOMAS BUTLER, *Sculpsit*, 1847.

W. Thomas's engraving, Monument to John Jackson in Brompton Cemetery, *sculpted by Thomas Butler, 1847. The monument now lacks its naked gladiator front.*

PART VII

WOMEN AND EATING I, 1809–16

Lady Caroline Lamb, sketch of Lord and Lady Byron, 1815.
© John Murray Archive, National Library of Scotland

17

FATTENING, 1809–13

The next two parts of this book cover Byron's 'years of fame', the remaining seven years that he lived in England. They chart the impulses behind his private life, which was governed by women, and the private reasons for his public actions, which were inspired by men.

Focusing on his diet highlights a consistent pattern to his love life: when he finds women to mother him he reverts to infantile behaviour, stops dieting and starts to put on weight – until claustrophobia returns, and panic born of embattled dependence disorders his eating.

As in his early passions, Byron's first strategy for dealing with women in fiction was to idealise them. Most of his fictional heroines also lack body. As early as 1830 his acquaintance and biographer John Galt drew attention to 'the icy metaphysical glitter of Byron's amorous allusions' and complained of the poet's 'bodiless admiration of beauty, and objectless enthusiasm of love'. The pattern endured for much, but certainly not all, of Byron's work. His fictional female characters put on flesh, once he meets Italian women.

Byron expected his Grand Tour from 1809 to 1811 would provide sexual release, but he was thinking of homosexual relations. Abroad, women tended to remain distant, ethereal creatures, if they weren't prostitutes. In Lisbon he was lionised and he 'became the idol of the women', but it seems likely that nothing much happened.

In Malta he fell in love with an older, married woman, Mrs Constance Spencer Smith, who was 'perfectly mistress of herself & every art of intrigue personal or political, not at all in love'. They had an affair of a Platonic kind, since he said he escaped adultery.

Title page and frontispiece to John Galt's Life of Lord Byron, *1830.*

On Christmas Day 1809 Byron met his 'Maid of Athens'. He celebrated his adoration for her in several poems, but Theresa Macri was only twelve. Such relationships probably were, as his biographer Galt said, 'equally innocent and poetical'. On the other hand Byron boasted to Hobhouse on 15 May 1811 that he 'had a number of Greek and Turkish women' and that he had been '*clapped*'.

On his return to England, Byron grew 'foolishly fond' of Susan Vaughan early in 1812. She was one of the servants at Newstead Abbey, who was unfaithful to him. On 16 February he forbade his friend Francis Hodgson to mention a woman or even allude to the existence of the sex. He also refused to read a word of the feminine gender. 'Unaccustomed to female society', Dallas observed, Byron 'at once dreaded and abhorred it; and spoke of women, such I mean as he neither dreaded nor abhorred, more as playthings than companions'. But he longed for love. 'I cannot exist without some

Scrope Davies, caricature of 'Ld B. as an Amatory Writer', c.*1815.*
© John Murray Archive, National Library of Scotland

object of love,' he told Lady Melbourne on 9 November 1812, repeating himself to her almost exactly a year later, on 13 October and again on 29 November (to Annabella Milbanke). By 30 April 1814 he had simplified his neediness: 'one must like something,' he told Lady Melbourne.

The Maniac and the Mathematician: Hot Suppers and Cold Collations

The first two cantos of *Childe Harold* were published at the beginning of March 1812, when the expensive, quarto edition of 500 copies sold out in three days. Byron woke and found himself famous. He was still so isolated, however, that, when he received an early fan letter, he assumed it came from a relative. The poem portrayed its hero/author as wicked but redeemable; a weary pathos fused sin with sensibility. Its sophisticated reek of sulphur and tears attracted two formidable women, among many others: Lady Caroline Lamb, the twenty-seven-year-old mother of two children, and the virginal, twenty-year-old Annabella Milbanke. Byron had a passionate affair with one of them and married the other. They were cousins by marriage and apparently opposites, in terms of character and experience. But, at a time when, as Lady Morgan observed, 'The women suffocated him,' they distinguished themselves by not pursuing the author.

Lady Caroline Lamb, the wilful, beautiful daughter of the 3rd Earl of Bessborough and niece of the famous Georgiana, Duchess of Devonshire, had married William Lamb MP seven years before. Lady Caroline insisted on meeting the author of *Childe Harold*, even though Samuel Rogers warned her that he had a clubfoot and bit his nails. 'I was one night at Lady Westmoreland's,' she remembered later; 'the women were all throwing their heads at him. Lady Westmoreland led me up to him. I looked earnestly at him, and turned on my heel. My opinion in my journal was, "mad – bad – and dangerous to know".' Lacking self-knowledge, highly strung if not, at times, almost deranged, she projected her problems on to Byron. If thwarted she could be malicious – 'rumbustial when misunderstood'. She understated the matter. When Byron eventually dared to declare independence from her tyranny, she dedicated herself to destroying him.

Lady Holland presented Lady Caroline to Lord Byron on 24 March 1812. He visited her the next day at Melbourne House, in Whitehall, now the Scottish Office, where she and her husband lived in his parents' home. There, another young lady, who was more simply dressed than the rest of the assembly, kept her distance from Byron. Anne Isabella Milbanke, known as Annabella, was an only child, born fifteen years into her parents' marriage, after a long and difficult labour, when her mother was already forty. Her parents spoiled her. Her father was Lady Melbourne's brother, so Lady Caroline's husband William Lamb was her cousin.

Byron fell in love with Lady Caroline Lamb, calling her 'the cleverest most agreeable, absurd, amiable, perplexing, dangerous fascinating little being that lives now or ought to have lived 2000 years ago'. For the first time he was involved with a woman of his rank and intellectual reach. She was also the first of the wild women he loved, as 'dangerous fascinating' as

Thomas Phillips, Lady Caroline Lamb dressed as a pageboy, c.*1813, probably alludes to Sanders's miniature portrait of Byron, 1812, which Byron gave Lady Caroline, with an inscription quoting from Jacques Cazotte's* Le diable amoureux, *1772. Lady Caroline Lamb had herself painted as Biondetta, heroine of the same novel: the devil takes the identity of a young woman dressed as a page 'carrying a platter of fruit' in order to seduce a young man. Lady Caroline called herself Biondetta in a letter to Byron of 9 August 1812. She was known for her frolicsomeness: among her nicknames were Puck and Ariel. She had a boyish figure and liked breaking the conventions of her gender and class. She disguised herself as a man to witness her husband make his maiden speech in the House of Commons in 1806, which appalled her mother-in-law Lady Melbourne. Lady Caroline also occasionally dressed as one of her pages, wearing a uniform that she had devised.*

the savage animals that he favoured as pets. Her character was, she boasted, 'so like an untamed tigress'. She told Byron in 1814: 'I lov'd you like a Beast who sees no crime in loving & following its Master – you became such a one to me – Master of my soul more than of anything else.'

Byron once complained that he had been more ravished than anybody since the Trojan War. But the scenario recurred so often as to suggest that he may have sought it out, that he felt excited *and* threatened by a potential fiendishness in the women he loved. When Lady Caroline continued to hound him, Byron commented that 'The Devil, & Medea, & her Dragons to boot, are possessed of that little maniac.' But he later admitted that he would 'have preferred Medea to any woman that ever breathed'. Medea killed her children and their father, Jason, when he left her for another woman. Byron's fascinated ambivalence may reflect the paradoxically 'tender and peremptory' treatment he received from his mother and his nurse. 'And femininely meaneth furiously', his Assyrian self-portrait Sardanapalus remarks, 'Because all passions in excess are female'. The model was set by the first woman in his life, his mother, 'Mrs Byron *furiosa*'.

Lady Caroline sent Byron some poems written by her husband's cousin, Annabella. They included 'Lines to be spoken at the Grave of Derwoody', a poet who drank himself to madness and death in 1802. Annabella called him 'An outcast from mankind, one whose hard fate/Indignant virtue should forbid to weep'. Those words seemed bound to catch Byron's eye. He praised the poems carefully, but added that he had 'no desire to be acquainted with Miss Milbank [*sic*], she is too good for a fallen spirit to know or wish to know, & I should like her more if she were less perfect'. Byron presented himself in familiar, self-libelling, Satanic guise, but his hint at Annabella's smugness seems prescient. Years later, his friend the Revd Francis Hodgson remarked that, while Byron 'considered his salvation hopeless; she *knew* that she was saved'.

Byron fascinated Annabella, his person ('without exception . . . more agreeable in conversation than any person I ever knew') and his sinister glamour of a familiar, Satanic kind: 'he is a very bad, very good man,' she told Lady Milbanke on 16 April 1812. Sensing a rival in her young cousin,

Lady Caroline advised Annabella on 22 May to 'shun friendships with those whose practice ill accords with your principles'. Between the rivals stood Lady Melbourne, Lady Caroline's mother-in-law, Annabella's aunt.

Lady Caroline's 'total want of common conduct' threatened to involve her and Byron in scandal. He would be blamed for having ruined her, for the man was always responsible. If it came to a divorce, he would then be

Thomas Lawrence, portrait of Lady Melbourne. She relished her pivotal position as Byron's 'Good Genius', his 'director' and his confidante in an extensive, revealing correspondence. She was over sixty and, Lady Caroline complained, 'too wholly without sentiment & romance' – a great attraction for Byron, particularly since Lady Caroline herself had, as she boasted, 'too much of it'. He loved Lady Melbourne, '(filial) or (fraternally) better than any being on earth'. She 'might have been my mother', he told a friend after her death.

obliged to 'save' her by marrying her. But he knew they could never be happy together. The affair had to 'be broken off at once'. He had 'to take some step which will make her hate me effectually, for she must always be in extremes'.

That autumn Byron had a brief affair with an Italian artiste of the opera, perhaps in the hope that it would derail Lady Caroline's passion. 'I only wish she did not swallow so much supper,' he complained, 'chicken wings – sweetbreads, – custards – peaches & *Port* wine.' He gallantly relaxed the terms of his ban on women eating in his presence, however, to insist, 'a woman should never be seen eating or drinking, unless it be *lobster sallad* & *Champagne*, the only truly feminine and becoming viands.'

Lady Caroline was not to be diverted, however. It looked as though he had to marry someone in order to escape and he thought of Annabella Milbanke.

Byron said he never saw a woman whom he '*esteemed* so much'. If she proved unobtainable, he told Lady Melbourne that he would accept the very first woman who did not look as if she would spit in his face. Annabella declined Byron's first proposal, transmitted by her aunt. Rejection helped him to see matters objectively. Annabella was an intellectual, a cold virgin, an 'amiable Mathematician' and 'Princess of Parallelograms'. 'Her proceedings are quite rectangular,' he commented with chilling accuracy, 'or rather we are two parallel lines prolonged to infinity side by side but never to meet.' A month later, he had no regrets: 'That would have been but a *cold collation*, & I prefer hot suppers.'

Lady Oxford: Bread and Butter

Byron stayed with Lady Oxford and her tolerant husband at Eywood, their estate in Herefordshire, for four weeks from 24 October and again over Christmas. He felt comfortable with them and called Eywood the palace of Circe, after the enchantress who turned her lovers into animals – in his case, into an infant. He relished his first experience of happy family life; read, laughed and played at blind man's buff with the children, while 'a month slipped away in this & such like recreations'. He spent his time 'scrambling

Engraving after George Hayter's portrait of Annabella Milbanke, 1812. An unsympathetic contemporary witness reported that 'her manner was stiff and formal, and gave one the idea of her being self-willed and self-opinionated. She was almost the only young, pretty, well-dressed girl we ever saw who carried no cheerfulness along with her . . . it is certain that the impression which she produced on the imagination of her acquaintance was unfavourable: they looked on her as a reserved and frigid sort of being whom one would rather cross the room to avoid than be brought into conversation with unnecessarily.'

Jane Elizabeth, Countess of Oxford, 1797, John Hoppner (1758–1810) That autumn of 1812 Byron found solace and sustenance in the arms of Lady Oxford, a wise, experienced, married woman of thirty-eight with numerous children by different lovers. In a sense she was another, younger version of Lady Melbourne. Lady Oxford used to say 'seriously' that 'a broken heart means nothing but bad digestion'.

and splashing about with the children'. Inevitably he grew 'much *fatter*'; he could not even think of starving himself down. Given 'the necessity of conforming to a less Eremitical regimen' than he observed on his own in London, he 'lived on tea & bread & butter'. In June 1813, having stayed with Lady Oxford once again, he reported that he was 'in the most robust health – have been eating & drinking – & fatten upon ill fortune'.

Bread and butter was associated with breakfast, the meal taken in the day's infancy. It represented the archetypal children's food. 'The Nursery still lisps out in all they utter' Byron objected of shy, awkward British girls in *Beppo*, 'Besides, they always smell of Bread and Butter'.

Lady Caroline's 'persecution' forced Byron to consider quitting England. If he didn't travel, he would take orders. When Lord and Lady Oxford left London for the Continent at the end of June, Byron intended to follow them but, instead, he stayed in town to see his half-sister Augusta.

Augusta and Baby B

'My heart always alights on the nearest perch,' Byron told Lady Melbourne on 30 April 1814, adding 'if it is withdrawn it goes God knows where.'

Byron and Augusta became lovers. She replaced the absent Lady Oxford with striking neatness, offering him the same kind of unquestioning, maternal support, while he continued to be 'haunted with hysterics'. Piqued by his indifference to her dancing at a party on 5 July, Lady Caroline cut herself twice – accidentally with a glass, and deliberately with a pair of scissors – and bled all over her dress.

A sense of humour, as well as lineage, linked Byron to Augusta. When she hoped that he would reform, he replied on 19 December 1816: 'we laugh too much for hopes,' referring to a Methodist preacher who rebuked his congregation, '*No hopes for them as laughs.*' In the summer of 1813, before she knew what was going on, Annabella observed his 'playful and affectionate manner' towards his sister and approved of it.

Augusta looked 'very much older' than Byron, probably because, as Lady Shelley noted in December, she did 'not make the most of herself.

George Hayter's portrait of the Honourable Augusta Leigh, Byron's half-sister. Six years after their affair started in 1813 he looked back to assure her, 'I have never ceased nor can cease to feel for a moment that perfect & boundless attachment which bound & binds me to you – which renders me utterly incapable of real love for any other human being – what could they be to me after you?' Byron celebrated their blood link, inscribing a copy of Childe Harold *to 'my dearest sister, and my best friend, who has ever loved me much better than I deserved', from her 'father's son and most affectionate brother'. I don't think he ever referred to her as his half-sister. Incest may have been a sin, rather than a crime, but it certainly offered grounds for a scandal and divorce. Augusta apparently suffered no remorse, until their affair became public knowledge. It later infuriated Lady Byron that Augusta 'did not appear to think these transgressions of consequence'. But the relationship's sinfulness and its dangers excited Byron; they substantiated his conviction that he was predestined to damnation.*

© The Trustees of the British Museum

She is dowdy in her dress, and seems to be quite indifferent to personal appearances.' In this she resembled Byron's mother. Augusta also treated Byron as her child: 'Mrs Leigh has evidently great moral influence over her brother, who listens to her occasional admonitions with a sort of playful acquiescence,' Lady Shelley noted. 'Her manner towards him is decidedly maternal; it is as though she were reproving a thoughtless child.' Augusta's nickname for him was 'baby' Byron. Byron called her 'Goose', perhaps from the middle syllable of her name, pronounced in the northern manner – she grew up in Derbyshire. It also evoked her motherliness and foolishness.

Each could act as the other's parent: he addressed her as 'Child'. She boasted to Annabella on 11 January 1815 that she was 'thoroughly *his* enfant gaté [spoiled child]'.

Once again, in the arms of a motherly lover, Byron's anorexia yielded to infantile indulgence. 'Everything in this life depends upon the weather & the state of one's digestion,' Byron wrote to Lady Melbourne on 20 August 1815, '. . . – I have been eating & drinking – which I always do when watched for then I grow fat & don't show it – & now that I am in very good plight & Spirits – I can't leave off the custom though I have no further occasion for it.' Lady Holland remarked on his '*fattening*'.

That September Byron once again sought to follow in his father's rakish footsteps. He accepted an invitation to visit James Wedderburn Webster at his home, Aston Hall, Rotherham, piqued by his (mistaken) belief that his father had committed adultery there with Augusta's mother. Byron asked his host to invite Augusta.

When she refused to join him, he went to Aston Hall determined on '*transferring* [his] regards to another'. Stimulated by the thought that his father had committed adultery in the same house, Byron flirted with his host's wife, Lady Frances Webster, and tried hard to fall in love with her. But 'the feeling that it was an effort spoiled all again'.

On 1 November 1813 he started to write *The Bride of Abydos*. Selim's love for Zuleika celebrates the theme of incest, since they believe they are brother and sister. Byron was persuaded to change the plot, before the

Richard Westall's illustration to Childe Harold *IV, 148–51:* Childe Harold, *whose profile resembles Byron in portraits by Westall and Richard Phillip, gazes at a depiction of Roman Charity: a daughter saves her imprisoned father from starvation by breastfeeding him. The ancient Roman story exemplified filial piety. Artists often show the daughter averting her gaze. Here the couple gaze into one another's eyes, which highlights the story's erotic, incestuous implications.*

Private collection

Lady Frances Webster, from an engraving by Robert Cooper after the painting by A. W. Devis, January 1812.
© National Portrait Gallery, London

poem was published, so that the lovers were not related by blood. He also explored his ambivalence towards the father who abandoned him. Selim faces rejection by the man he assumes is his father, the Pacha Giaffir; he's 'reared, not with tender help,/But like the nephew of a Cain'. 'Proscribed at home,/And taunted to a wish to roam', Selim rebels and becomes the leader of a pirate horde. Learning that his real father was murdered by Giaffir he declares, 'My father's blood in every vein is boiling'.

Zuleika at the feet of Selim, an illustration from The Bride of Abydos, The Byron Gallery, *1844.*

18

WARS OF INDEPENDENCE, 1813–16

The Corsair's Diet

In November 1813 Augusta told Byron that she was pregnant. He believed he was the father. He spent Christmas with her and her family at Six Mile Bottom, which was 'far too small even for the company it contained'. There, with Augusta more than five months pregnant, he succumbed again to his eating disorder. 'Baby B' needed to re-establish his independence from Augusta, as he would, eventually, from any woman who was his lover but acted as if she were his mother. By 10 December he had reverted to his diet: he fasted for two days and wished he 'could leave off eating altogether'.

In effect he relived the claustrophobia he felt in 1806–7, trapped at home with his mother, which prompted his first diet. Meanwhile he wrote *The Corsair*. It was, Samuel Smiles reported, 'literally "struck off at a heat," at the rate of about two hundred lines a day, – "a circumstance," says Moore, "that is, perhaps, wholly without a parallel in the history of genius." "The Corsair" was begun on the 18th, and finished on the 31st of December, 1813.' Edward E. Williams remembered Byron telling him later 'that during the composition of his "Corsair"' he was in 'a very low state of mind, turning night into day, the sight of which he could not endure. He lived upon biscuits and soda water, and completed the poem in ten nights – and almost without correcting a line.' Byron's wife remembered him saying that, during this period 'he sat up drinking brandy & water till four or five in the morning, and the last night was reduced to such a state of nervous debility that he cried like a child.'

Medora waits passively for Conrad the Corsair to return, illustration from Finden.

In this light *The Corsair*'s Gothic colouring hardly veils the brutally realistic way it documents an Oedipal dilemma, which generates anorexia. The hero Conrad flees from blue-eyed Medora, a nurturing mother figure, who offers him food, which he cannot eat. The ascetic pirate only 'feels of all his former self possest' when he has left her. He 'mans himself' once he's back on board his ship, where he can revert to his habitual, teetotal, vegetarian, if not vegan regimen.

Ne'er for his lip the purpling cup they fill,
That goblet passes him untasted still –
And for his fare – the rudest of his crew
Would that, in turn have pass'd untasted too;
Earth's coarsest bread, the garden's homeliest roots,
And scarce the summer luxury of fruits,
His short repast in humbleness supply
With all a hermit's board would scarce deny.

Later his disguise as a dervish enables Conrad to shun the sumptuous fare he's offered at a banquet, without alienating his host. He is imprisoned by the older, paternal Pacha, but when he escapes the Corsair cannot bring himself to murder the Pacha in his sleep, so the Tale's other woman, the black-eyed, auburn-haired siren 'Gulnare the homicide' does the deed.

Gulnare 'the homicide' in a contemporary illustration to The Corsair.

Private collection

Illustration to The Corsair, *showing Conrad weeping at Medora's death.*

Medora dies, conveniently. Conrad's 'wild eyes' weep 'like an infant's', as Byron wept when he finished the poem.

Once he had re-established his independence Byron could afford to be mothered and fed by Augusta, who occasionally persuaded her brother to relax his rule of abstinence (vegetarianism): when he stayed with her during Lent in 1814 he ate a 'collar of brawn one evening for supper (after an enormous dinner [= lunch] too)'.

On 15 April 1814 Augusta gave birth to her fourth child, Elizabeth Medora. It 'is *not* an "Ape"', Byron reassured Lady Melbourne on 25 April, 'and if it is – that must be my fault'. He refers to the superstition that a child born of incest would be deformed. Later he liked to point out to his wife, in front of Augusta, that George Leigh was not around when Medora was conceived. Byron became the girl's godfather. He never enquired after the child's health, but that was how he tended to behave as a father. Byron now felt tempted to leave England and elope with Augusta. Lady Melbourne urged him not to take such a drastic step, 'for the sake of Augusta', words she then crossed out.

At this crisis point Byron heard from Annabella, who wrote on 13 April to relay her father's invitation to visit them at Seaham. Byron agreed to come, knowing perfectly well that a visit would imply a matrimonial motive. But he delayed his arrival for six weeks.

Byron remained committed to Augusta; his heart was not available to Annabella: he was 'perplexed about 2 – and would rather have both', he admitted to Lady Melbourne on 16 May, as he did not 'see any use in one without a chance at least of the other'. He wanted to marry, but principally so as to ward off Lady Caroline and to shield his affair with Augusta under the cover of Annabella's famous virtue – she was 'the most prudish & correct person' whom Byron knew. Sin veiled by marriage constituted the Regency recipe for decorum. Lady Melbourne owed her son William Lamb, and Lady Oxford several of her children, to extramarital affairs.

Yet out of loyalty to his father Byron fought against conventional discretion. He flirted with damnation, never more so than in his affair with his sister Augusta. Once rumours circulated, thanks to the treacherous Lady Caroline, Byron did not try to discredit them. Instead, he went out of his way to remind his public of the topic of incest. It's hard now to imagine how shocking it must have been for his contemporaries to encounter scarcely veiled versions of Byron's relationship with the Honourable Augusta Leigh in his fiction, pre-eminently in *The Bride of Abydos*. In the end he did not publish the 'Opening Lines to *Lara*', which he began in May 1814, alluding repeatedly to a love that cannot be named, and featuring the name 'Azora dearest'. But the story still turns on a secret that cannot be betrayed.

Byron bought this elaborately enamelled, gold musical snuffbox from Love & Kelty, jewellers, on 12 July 1813 for £105. Inside an automata group shows two female musicians, one playing a harp, the other playing a piano, with seated and standing male singers, all in contemporary dress. Its movement features eight white hammers striking on eight white bells. Byron kept it until he went to Greece in 1822, when he left it in the hands of the British Consul in Genoa, along with eight other snuffboxes. Christie's sold it on 19 November 1997 in Geneva, where the box was originally made.

'Thou lovedst me', *Manfred*'s hero tells his sister Astarte,

> Too much, as I loved thee: we were not made
> To torture thus each other, though it were
> The deadliest sin to love as we have loved.

In *Cain*, the hero celebrates his love for his 'sister-bride' Adah (when Byron's child by Annabella was called Augusta Ada); 'Great is their love', Cain's granddaughter Anah insists in *Heaven and Earth*, 'who love in sin and fear'.

Lady Byron: As a Mother to Her Child

Annabella rejected Byron's second proposal on 10 August 1814. On 9 September he enquired whether there was 'any line or change of conduct which could possibly remove' her objections to marrying him. He merely wished 'to learn a possibility', he wrote carefully. She did not answer his question. Instead, characteristically, Annabella seized on Byron's enquiry, interpreted it as his third proposal of marriage, and promptly accepted it.

But when at last Byron visited his fiancee's family, he was disappointed that Annabella did not behave in the way that he most needed. 'I fear she won't govern me –', he wrote to Lady Melbourne on 4 November, '& if she don't it will not do at all.' It reflected what he called his 'weak side – viz. – a

Bark from a tree in the Newstead Abbey park. Byron and Augusta carved their names and the date into it on 20 September 1814, the day before they left: Byron was due to visit his fiancée's family for the first time.

Courtesy of Nottingham City Museums and Galleries

propensity to be governed'. The remark illuminates the paradox at the heart of his relationships with women: he wanted to feel governed and so he sought out commanding, mother/Medea types – until he could not bear to feel 'unmanned', dependent. He used the same word 'governed' when he reverted to anorexia in 1823. He expressed his aversion to Lady Caroline in the dry phrase, 'I do sometimes like to choose for myself.'

Annabella tried to learn, when Byron told her that his sister always treated him like a child, and that she herself reminded him of Augusta – when she was 'playful'. But for most of the time she presented herself as a 'grave, didactic, deplorable person' (in her words). His valet Fletcher commented of Byron's marriage: 'I never yet knew a lady that could not manage my Lord, *except* my Lady.'

Despite his misgivings, Byron married Annabella on 2 January 1815.

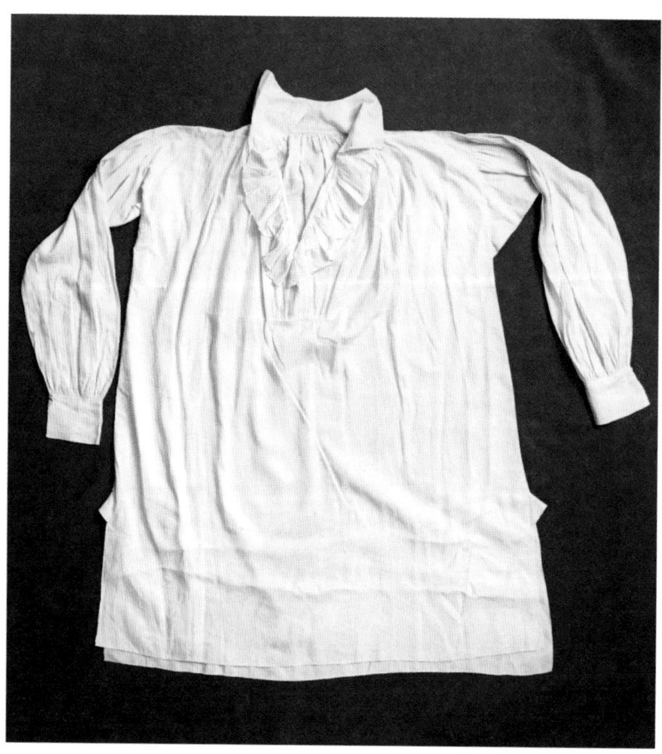

A shirt Byron wore while he lived in England, given by Lady Byron to George Lovejoy, and acquired from his son-in-law in 1924.
Private collection

A fragment of the crimson damask hangings that surrounded the Byrons' honeymoon bed. That night, according to Rogers, who read about it in the Memoirs that were burned after Byron's death, Byron woke from a nightmare. Seeing the ruddy glare from a candle flame through the bed's red curtains, he called out, 'Good God, I am surely in Hell!'

Private collection

He regretted what he later called 'our funeral marriage', even before the ceremony. As they drove to Halnaby Hall for their 'treaclemoon' he rebuked his wife savagely for not having accepted his earlier proposal: she might have saved him once; now it was too late.

But Byron's relationships with women always had two sides. Husband and wife sometimes succeeded in recreating the temporary bower of infantile bliss that he had already found in the arms of Lady Oxford and Augusta.

Lord and Lady Byron stayed with her parents between 21 January and 9 March. The Milbankes spoiled their only child Annabella, who tended to indulge her appetite for food, in particular for what she called 'divine mutton'. Even her partial biographer, Ethel Colburn Mayne, admits that 'she was inclined to be greedy'. Annabella once ordered so many mutton chops that, in her own words, she 'frightened the waiters'. There is some evidence to suggest that food later became 'an emotional compensation', and that she may have developed her own eating disorder. Byron noted that the Milbankes themselves were fond of 'hot luncheons'. He occasionally insisted on eating on his own, i.e. probably not eating – his mother-in-law tactfully 'never taking it amiss', when he did so. But he began to eat more regularly. Annabella said that her mother 'would go to the bottom of the sea herself to find fish for B.'s dinner'. Augusta was impressed: 'I am so glad he allows himself to dine,' she wrote to Annabella on 8 February, '– *improvement* the first!' A week later she was 'quite convinced that if he would condescend to eat & drink & sleep *like other people* he would feel ye good effects – but you know his way is to fast till he is famished & then *devour* more than his stomach in that *weak* state can bear – & *so on* – but I really do hope your wise & judicious endeavors will bring about a reformation on those points.'

Briefly, Byron reverted to childhood again. He became 'a wild mirthful boy when climbing the rocks & defying me to follow him in scrambling'. At some point in the marriage Byron told his wife, 'I believe you feel towards me as a mother to her child, happy when it is out of mischief.' She later remembered that he occasionally reverted to his 'child-side', resembling a guileless playful child – it was more than acting. 'He would then speak of himself, as little children do, in the third person, as "B," and forget entirely all that belonged to later years.'

Husband and wife played a parlour game of 'bout-rimés', composing alternate lines of verse. In her contributions, printed in italics, Annabella made a great effort to be playful. But, while she gleefully notes Byron's consumption of nursery food, he regrets that they ever married:

Perplexed in the extreme to find a line
A different destiny is yours and mine.

If rhymes be omens what a fate is ours –
And bread and butter eagerly devours.

My husband is the greatest goose alive
I feel that I have been a fool to wive.

Lady Byron, profile sketches of Byron, 1815.

Private collection

The moment marks a watershed. From then on, instead of indulging in bread and butter, Byron increasingly limited himself to biscuits and soda water.

In March he was 'grieved and tortured' to discover that, after his marriage, Augusta refused to sleep with him. Even Annabella never doubted this. From Byron's point of view his marriage had lost its main purpose. But husband and wife could still be happy together, when they lived on their own in London. Annabella discovered that she was pregnant and remembered that Byron 'was kind again – kinder for about ten days . . . than I had almost ever seen him'. Augusta came to stay, however, and so created a frustrating, claustrophobic *ménage à trois*. Byron's 'black agitation' returned, exacerbated by increasing financial worries.

Once Augusta left, at the end of June, Lord and Lady Byron again lived happily together, their domesticity marked by gluttony. Annabella was 'afflicted with a raging appetite and rapid power of digestion'. But she was not alone. She told her mother that a goose-pie was 'highly approved and gratefully acknowledged by B.'s voracious stomach'. Augusta assured

Hobhouse that Byron ate 'very heartily of *meat*, bread, and biscuit, allows himself half-a-pint of claret at dinner, when at home (and he seldom dines out), has abjured brandy and other spirituous liquors'. On 7 July Byron admitted to Thomas Moore that, since his marriage, he had 'lost much of my paleness, and, – "horresco referens" (for I hate even *moderate* fat) – that happy slenderness, to which when I first knew you, I had attained'.

The sensual idyll did not last. The later stages of his wife's pregnancy exacerbated Byron's antipathy to seeing women eat. 'For 4 or 5 months before my Confinement,' Lady Byron remembered, 'he objected unkindly to dine with me, though I was willing to conform to his hours, and once when his dinner was accidentally served at the same table with mine, he desired his dish to be taken into another room (in my presence, & the servants attending) with an expression of rage.' They entered what she called '*a labyrinth of difficulties*'. The crisis came at the end of August, when Annabella's pregnancy had reached almost exactly the same stage as Augusta's had in December 1813. For four days Byron was 'perfectly ferocious towards' his wife, she later remembered, and as for 'the nights he ordered a bed apart'. Byron denied that he had ever treated his wife badly, but he admitted that he had a 'Vile temper & that he is told his head is not right which he believes may be the case says his Stomach is in a Bad way'. Annabella blamed her husband's depression and his love of tormenting on his 'vitiated stomach'. That suggests Byron had resumed his extreme form of diet.

Phrenzy

When his wife was in the last stages of her pregnancy, Byron experienced a sort of nervous breakdown. His description of dogs in *The Siege of Corinth*, which he wrote at this time, 'Gorging and growling o'er carcase and limb', extended over twenty-four lines, may reflect his state of mind.

Some months later, he accepted that 'he may have been *bereaved of reason* during his paroxysms with his wife'. As always, he tried to horrify her with 'such intimations as to the nature of his own character, as must leave a rankling anxiety. In particular,' Annabella remembered, 'he brought me the

German's tale to peruse [Harriet Lee's 'The German's Story. Kruitzner'], with a reference to Conrad's character as his own, and identifying most pointedly the keystone of the narrative. He constantly alluded to that Tale.' That autumn of 1816 he started to turn it into a play, *Werner*, which he abandoned after 283 lines of the second scene in Act I. In Harriet Lee's original story the hero Frederick was 'habitually morose and abstracted'. Byron projects his own trauma on to Werner, whose 'late deep distemperature of mind & fortunes/. . . since have almost driven him into phrenzy'. Six years later, when he returned to the play, Byron omitted that trait.

Looking back, in *Childe Harold* III he described how his 'brain became,/ In its own eddy boiling and o'erwrought,/A whirling gulf of phantasy and flame'. The phenomenon is not unique: husbands sometimes do 'go mad', when their wives first become pregnant. There's even a popular guide to the topic, James Douglas Barron's *She's Having a Baby – and I'm Having a Nervous Breakdown*, 1998 and its sequel, *She's Had a Baby and I'm Having a Meltdown*, 1999. In becoming a mother, Lady Byron was leaving an already fragile partnership to create a new bond with 'her' child. Byron had reacted badly to the last stages of Augusta's pregnancy in 1813. He was probably reminded of his claustrophobic, bitter relationship with his mother; perhaps he also felt threatened by the prospect of his child (he assumed it would be a son) as a rival. He announced that he would go abroad as soon as the child was born, 'because a woman always loves her child better than her husband'.

During her labour Lady Byron thought that her husband was throwing soda-water bottles at the ceiling of the room below, 'in order to deprive her of sleep'. Hobhouse inspected the ceiling and reported that it 'retained no mark of blows'. He explained that Byron's 'habit of drinking soda-water in consequence of taking magnesia in quantities, and of knocking off the heads of the bottles with a poker, sufficiently accounted for the noise'. Byron resorted to magnesia because he had destroyed his digestion with purgatives and starvation.

On 15 January 1816 Lady Byron left London to stay with her parents, taking her daughter with her. Byron never saw either of them again.

PART VIII

THE HEROIC SPIRIT, 1809–16

Detail from Isaac Robert Cruikshank, Lobby Loungers, taken from the Salon of the Drury Lane Theatre, *1816. It shows a fashionably dressed Byron and implies that he used his position on the theatre's committee of management to meet actresses, which he probably did. Beau Brummell pioneered the wearing of trousers, rather than breeches, and Byron made the habit his own. He wears the star of the Legion of Honour medal, which Lady Caroline Lamb sent him from Waterloo.* The Examiner *published Byron's poem 'On the Star of the Legion of Honour' on 7 April 1816. According to Iris Origo, when Louis XVIII read it he sent Byron a message, granting him the right to wear the medal, which 'can now be seen in the Museo Correr in Venice'. The museum now denies this.*

19

HOW TO BE A HERO, 1809–14

Politics and Poetry

Byron initially assumed that he would make his mark in politics. However, unquestioning loyalty to his absent, 'renegade' father meant he could not identify with the British establishment: he was, as he said in *Don Juan*, 'born for opposition', specifying nicely that it was 'mostly on the weaker side'. Mostly, but not always: he also felt drawn to strong, even tyrannical father figures. Napoleon incarnated his ideal hero, once Byron had managed to detach the mythical figure from the fallible historical entity.

Byron encountered a Napoleonic ruler, who was also a father figure, while he travelled abroad on his Grand Tour. He was intending to visit Asia and began to take lessons in Arabic while he was staying on Malta. But on an impulse he and Hobhouse accepted an offer to sail to Albania, a country then unknown to most Europeans. This is where their journey became an adventure. Albania constituted a largely self-contained world, ruled by Ali Pacha. It has been suggested that Byron 'allowed himself unwittingly to be used as a toyboy in the interests of English diplomatic and naval diplomacy, by travelling north for the pleasure of Ali Pacha, so as to compensate him for the fact that he could not have the Ionian Islands'.

Nominally a vizier in the service of the Ottoman Empire, Ali Pacha acted as his own master. Napoleon had offered to make him King of Albania, and to support his fight for independence from the Turks. When Byron and Hobhouse arrived in Joannina they were told that Ali Pacha 'was sorry to be obliged to leave his capital, to finish a little war in which he was engaged, but that he begged we would follow him'. He uses impressively worldly understatement (*une petite guerre*) to evoke absolute authority. Litotes would become one of Byron's favourite weapons in his armoury of linguistic heroism.

Finden's engraving after F. Stone's portrait of Ali Pacha. The sixty-nine-year-old Pacha and the twenty-one-year-old poet met at Tepelene on 19 October 1809. Ali Pacha 'has the appearance of any thing but his real character', Byron told his mother on 12 November, 'for he is a remorseless tyrant, guilty of the most horrible cruelties, very brave, & so good a general, that they call him the Mohammedan Buonaparte'. Ali Pacha invited Byron 'to consider him as a father whilst I was in Turkey, & said he looked on me as his son.– Indeed he treated me like a child, sending me almonds & sugared sherbet, fruit & sweetmeats, 20 times a day . . . To me he was indeed a father, giving me letters, guards, & every possible accommodation.'

Byron paid homage to the Albanian tyrant's Napoleonic character. Ali Pacha showed his guests a splendid gun, which the French emperor had given him. Its stock was 'inlaid with silver, and studded with diamonds and brilliants, and [it] looked like a handsome present'. Ali Pacha himself had added all the jewels, Hobhouse noted drily, 'to make it look more like a royal gift'. Characteristically, Byron followed in Napoleon's footsteps when he sent Ali Pacha a 'curious pistol' on 25 June 1815.

Byron started to adopt Napoleon as a role model even before he returned from his Grand Tour. In June 1811, while still on board the frigate moored off Dover, he intervened in the management of the Newstead Abbey estate, which he called his 'little *empire*', conscious that he was behaving 'like Buonaparte'. Byron told his mother on 25 June 1811 that he had decided to diminish the '*kingdom*' of a philandering farmer so as to erect 'part of it into a *principality*', to reward his groom, 'Field Marshal Fletcher who has served me faithfully'.

In the same letter he prepared his mother for his homecoming. For 'a long time I have been restricted to an entire vegetable diet', he warned her, 'neither fish or flesh coming within my regimen, so I expect a powerful stock of potatoes, greens, & biscuit, I drink no wine'.

However Mrs Byron died on 1 August, before her son reached Newstead. At the abbey, Byron told Hobhouse on 30 August 1811, he passed his time 'boxing in a Turkish pelise [*sic*] to prevent obesity'.

Now that he was 'in tolerable leanness' Byron chewed tobacco to ward off hunger. To Augusta on 9 September 1811 he claimed that the habit was the only thing he had acquired abroad, apart from 'a smattering of two languages'. His even-handed new diet book by William Wadd reported that one authority recommended chewing tobacco as a means to lose weight, though another objected to it, as it might lead to consumption.

Byron's path to glory in Britain seemed clear: his headmaster and his mother both assumed he would be a great orator, at a time when oratory was still 'politically important'. For a peer, the obvious arena was the House of Lords. Byron conscientiously attended debates there six times during January 1812 before he made his maiden speech on 27 February.

Cursory

REMARKS

ON

CORPULENCE:

BY

A MEMBER OF THE ROYAL COLLEGE OF SURGEONS.

William Wadd

Think not, ye candidates for health,
That ought can gain the wish'd-for prize;
(Or pill or potion, power or wealth,)
But temperance and exercise.

London:

PRINTED FOR J. CALLOW, MEDICAL BOOKSELLER,
CROWN COURT, PRINCES STREET, SOHO;
BY J. AND W. SMITH, KING STREET, SEVEN DIALS.
1810.

Price Two Shillings.

Title page of William Wadd's Cursory Remarks on Corpulence, or Obesity Considered as a Disease: with a Critical Examination of Ancient and Modern Opinions, Relative to its Causes and Cure, *1810, which Byron bought on returning to London from his Grand Tour in 1811. Corpulence was 'an object to an intellectual being, on account of its enfeebling the mental energy'. The prospect of returning to live with his mother may have intensified Byron's anorexic longing to free himself from flesh.*

Henry Meyers's engraving after George Sanders's portrait, which Byron hated. He wanted the proofs burnt and the plate broken. He wears the sable-trimmed pelisse.

LORD BYRON SPARRING WITH JOHN JACKSON *A. Forbes Sieveking, Esq., F.S.A.*
From a Photograph of a Print

The frontispiece to Pierce Egan Junior's edition of his father's Every Gentleman's Manual: A Lecture on the Art of Self-Defence *(1845): Byron wears his pelisse while he spars with 'Gentleman' John Jackson. Their poses and the background of the club at 13 Bond Street (with fencing as well as boxing equipment) are borrowed from an illustration to Pierce Egan's* Life in London, *1821 (reproduced earlier in Chapter 10). Byron bought three pelisses at the extortionate price of £26 4s each in January 1812, September 1812 and February 1813, which mystified the costume historian and Byronist Doris Langley Moore. The bill describes the garment as 'An Extra Superfine Corbo Pelisse full trimmed with braid, & Sleeves body & Skirt lined with Silk £18. Rich Sable Fur collar & trimming £8. 4s.' Byron's use of the garment for sweaty exercise may explain why he got through them so quickly. But perhaps he also gave one to William Bankes (see his portrait on p.140)?*

He chose to intervene in the debate on a bill to punish frame-breaking with death. Advances in technology diminished Nottinghamshire weavers' income or made them redundant. They began to protest and to break the new, mechanical frames. Between 14 November and 9 December 1811, 900 cavalry and 1,000 infantry were sent to Nottingham to quell the disturbances. Two additional regiments arrived on 8 January 1812. Staying at Newstead in the autumn of 1811 made Byron aware of the weavers' suffering.

He rehearsed his debut performance in the House of Lords carefully. He 'altered the natural tone of his voice, which was sweet and round, into a formal drawl', Dallas observed, 'and he prepared his features for a part – it was a youth declaiming a task'. 'I have traversed the seat of war in the peninsula,' he informed the peers on 27 February 1812. 'I have been in some of the most oppressed provinces of Turkey; but never, under the most despotic of infidel governments, did I behold such squalid wretchedness as I have seen since my return, in the very heart of a Christian country.' His delivery was 'loud & fluent enough, perhaps a little theatrical', he admitted; he 'spoke very violent sentences with a sort of modest impudence'. The seriously playful style of his oratory anticipates his mature poetic manner in *Don Juan*, which he used, in part, as a campaigning platform.

At almost exactly the same moment Byron ventured into an alternative arena for political activism, newspaper poetry. One week after making his debut in the House of Lords he sent the *Morning Chronicle* an 'Ode to the Framers of the Frame Bill', which it published anonymously on 2 March. He attacked the government's heartless reaction to the weavers' protests with savage humour. No one paid any attention to his ode, however. He followed it up with two political poems, 'Impromptu on a Recent Incident' and 'Lines to a Lady Weeping', which appeared anonymously in the *Morning Chronicle* on 6 and 7 March. The Prince of Wales had consistently and publicly sided with liberal opposition to his father George III's conservatism. But as soon as he became regent on 5 February, standing in for the indisposed king, he abandoned his youthful principles. His daughter's tears appeared to manifest her grief at his behaviour. Byron's poems, two in a flood of rebukes to the prince, again attracted no attention. It looked as though poetry would not serve Byron's political ambitions.

He made a second speech in the House of Lords, on 21 April 1812, on behalf of another persecuted minority, in the debate on the Catholic Claims Bill. But his delivery was thought 'mouthing and theatrical'. He made the peers laugh, which did not help his arguments being taken seriously or, indeed, his parliamentary career.

Meanwhile, after thirteen years the tide of the Napoleonic Wars was beginning to turn. It built up momentum in Spain but, after he left the country in 1809, Byron made no comment on the Peninsular War. He never shared Britain's adulation of Wellington, who stormed Ciudad Rodrigo in January 1812, sacked Badajoz, took Salamanca and entered Madrid on 12 August. Wellington was made an earl in April and then a marquess and given £100,000 to sustain the honour. French eagles, trophies from Salamanca, reached London in August 1812. The capital was illuminated at the regent's command and the Archbishop of Canterbury prepared a prayer of thanks, read in every church in the three kingdoms.

Byron's unresolved sympathy for his proscribed father left him hostile to patriotic success. He had no respect for Wellington: 'You did great things,' he told him in *Don Juan*; 'but not being great in mind,/Have left undone the greatest – and mankind'. Instead, over the next four years Byron celebrated the cult of the anti-hero/good-bad villain or renegade in a series of Gothic romances. His heroes functioned as a series of screens, on to which he projected sins that he had not (yet) committed. The Byronic hero may have been partly inspired by the Suliotes, tribesmen whom he encountered in Greece in November 1809, and their cult of the bandit-hero or kleft, which they celebrated in songs.

John Murray published the first two cantos of *Childe Harold* in March 1812. The poem, in which the hero was originally called Childe Burun, begins Byron's 'self-libelling' in verse. Harold resembles the Wandering Jew; but he is also 'Pleasure's palled Victim! life-abhorring Gloom/Wrote on his faded brow curst Cain's unresting doom'. Ironically, for a work celebrating

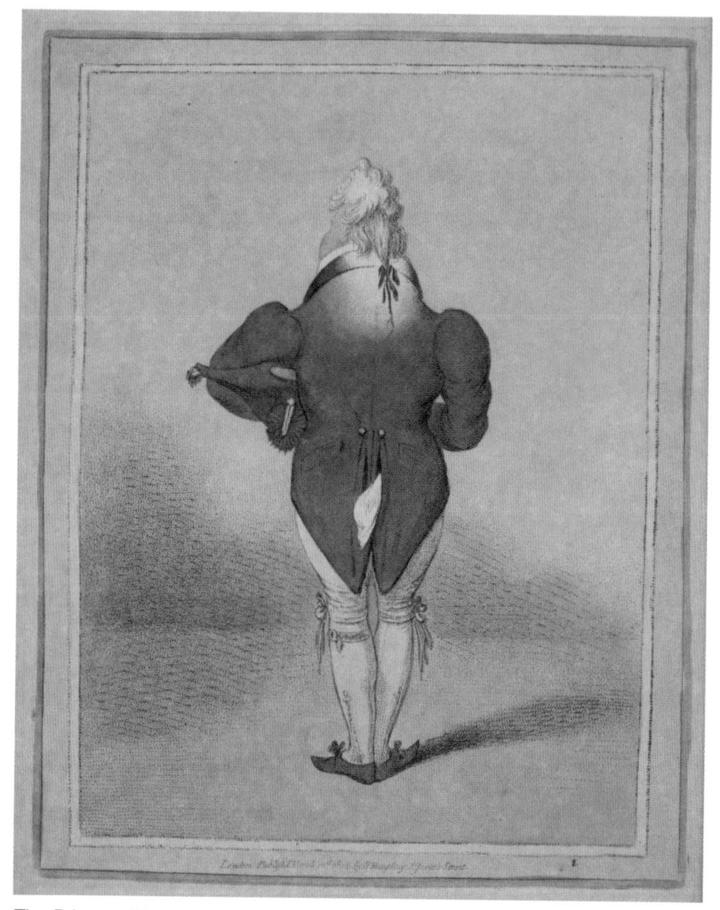

The Prince of Wales seen from behind, a caricature from July 1808.

Howe'er the mighty locust, Desolation,
Strip your green fields, and to your harvests cling,
Gaunt Famine never shall approach the throne –
Though Ireland starve, great George weighs twenty stone.

Private collection

an outsider, the poem propelled Byron's rise to social distinction. It reached a peak in June, when he was presented to the admiring Prince Regent.

News reached Britain in the middle of July 1812 that Napoleon had invaded Russia. But he continued to prove fallible. At the Battle of Borodino in September he failed to achieve a crushing victory and he was unable to conceal his difficulties even in his bulletins. In the middle of October Napoleon began to retreat from Moscow, beaten by winter. He abandoned

NAP nearly NAB'D or a Retreating Jump Just In Time, *cartoon by Thomas Tegg, June 1813, referring to Napoleon's retreat from Russia.*

Private collection

his army on 5 December and when he tried to raise a new one in France he met significant resistance to the draft. Further ignominy followed in 1813: the Germans' recapture of Hamburg in March; ambiguous victories such as Bautzen in May; Wellington's invasion of France on 7 October, having driven the French out of Spain; and, pre-eminently, the Battle of Leipzig, on 16–19 October, 'when Napoleon was deserted by his Saxon allies and defeated by the combined Austrians, Prussians, and Russians'. Having driven the French out of Spain, Wellington was made a Knight of the Garter in March.

Far from enthusiastic about Britain's victories, Byron reflected in his Journal on 8 March 1813 that, twenty years earlier, he would have become an English version of Lord Edward Fitzgerald, a renegade Irish nobleman who joined an Indian tribe and then the United Irishmen before allying himself with the French, so as to help them invade Britain.

Byron spoke in the House of Lords for the third and last time on 1 June 1813. He supported a protest against the civil and military forces

Richard Westall painted this portrait of Byron at his most Byronic in 1813, shortly after John Murray invited him to illustrate the first two cantos of Childe Harold. *Lady Oxford may have commissioned the portrait, whose theatrical, even posturing quality is heightened by the contrast between the pallor of the face and the dark 'Renaissance' velvet costume, with a ruff-like collar, a visible sword hilt and the fur-trimmed pelisse that has slipped off his left shoulder. 'His mouth continually betrays the acrimony of his spirit', Annabella Milbanke noted in her journal for 25 March 1812, 'I should judge him sincere and independent –* sincere *at least in society as far as he can be, whilst dissimulating the violence of his scorn . . . it appeared to me that he tried to control his natural sarcasm and vehemence as best he could, in order not to offend, but at times his lips thickened with disdain, and his eyes rolled impatiently.'*
© National Trust Images

that interrupted the circulation of a petition which argued for the reform of representation in Parliament. He opposed the entire House, with only the Earl of Stanhope on his side. But he confessed in his Journal for 1 December that he was 'not "i'th'vein"' for this business, a reference to Shakespeare's *Richard III*.

Seven days later Byron asked John Galt for information about the history of 'Soliman the Renegade' and in the autumn of that year he began to write the first of his oriental tales, *The Giaour*. Byron ransacks the Gothic armoire for picturesque attributes, such as monkishness from Ann Radcliffe's Schedoni in *The Italian* (1796). But the Giaour becomes truly Byronic when 'he mocks at Misery'. Gothic writers sometimes borrowed Satanic traits from Milton for their villains, to achieve a short cut to 'horrid' sublimity. Byron rescued that trait and gave it to his heroes. His Giaour looks like an 'evil angel' and passes 'like a demon of the night'. His face breathes a 'dark spirit' of death and on his brow is written 'of Cain the curse and crime'. The poem adds that he will be sent back from

Le giaour *by Ari Scheffer.*
© Musée de la Vie Romantique/Roger-Viollet/Topfoto

hell to earth as a vampire to haunt his native place and suck the blood of all his race. His youngest child will bless him 'with a *father's* name'. The nameless hero is twice a renegade: a Christian among Muslims; a pagan or a disbeliever inside a monastery.

One Should Be Something

Journal, 14 November 1813

It seemed increasingly obvious that Napoleon's lustre had dimmed, as he failed to win a decisive victory and his soldiers began to defect or desert in significant numbers. For Byron, Napoleon 'ran away from himself' – that is, he failed to live up to Byron's idea of him: Napoleon was a '"Héros de Roman" [literary, or imaginary hero] of mine – on the continent; I don't want him here'. Public failure had private consequences. Napoleon's decline represented a failure of spirit, which threatened Byron's own mental health. Byron dined 'regularly' (i.e. normally) only once a week. 'All the rest, tea and dry biscuits – six *per diem*', he recorded in his Journal for 17 November 1813, adding:

> I wish to God I had not dined now! – It kills me with heaviness, stupor, and horrible dreams; – and yet it was but a pint of bucellas [a Portuguese white wine not unlike his favourite Hock], and fish. Meat I never touch, – nor much vegetable diet. I wish I were in the country, to take exercise, – instead of being obliged to *cool* by abstinence, in lieu of it. I should not so much mind a little accession of flesh, – my bones can well bear it. But the worst is, the devil always came with it, – till I starve him out, – and I will *not* be the slave of *any* appetite. If I do err, it shall be my heart, at least, that heralds the way. Oh my head – how it aches? – the horrors of digestion! I wonder how Buonaparte's dinner agrees with him?

The question reflects Byron's assumption that Napoleon's gradual loss of mental power over his body of men must produce an internal reverse: his body will overpower his spirit – hence indigestion or madness, a fate Byron predicted in his 'Ode'.

Thomas Phillips's portrait of Byron, 1813, shows him in another theatrical guise, wearing an Albanian costume that he bought in 1809. The original painting is generally on view in the British Embassy, Athens while Phillips's copy hangs in the National Portrait Gallery, London. The original costume can be seen at Bowood House, Wiltshire.

© National Portrait Gallery, London

British politics seemed another dead-end; Byron felt sick 'of parliamentary mummeries' and looked for an alternative arena for oratory.

And yet, even as he denied it, Byron was hinting and even demonstrating that his writing could, potentially, represent a political act: 'I have no throne,' he reflected in his Journal for 6 December 1813, while he waited to hear how readers would react to *The Bride of Abydos*, 'nor wish to have one *now.*'

The Corsair as a New Napoleon

But who that CHIEF?

The Corsair, I, 61

Napoleon losing his grip on the minds and hearts of his followers prompted Byron to create a new, improved hero. His pirate Conrad excels just where Napoleon failed: the Corsair has such power over his exhausted followers that – unlike Napoleon's forces, they rally as soon as he calls them:

They make obeisance, and retire in haste,
Too soon to seek again the watery waste:
Yet they repine not – so that Conrad guides,
And who dare question aught that he decides?

He
Still sways their souls with that commanding art
That dazzles, leads, yet chills the vulgar heart.
What is that spell . . . that thus their faith can bind?
The power of Thought – the magic of the Mind!
Linked with success, assumed and kept with skill,
That moulds another's weakness to its will . . .

Byron makes it clear that Conrad owes his mental strength, his heroic capacity to lead, to his ascetic, strictly teetotal and vegetarian diet (detailed on p.443):

But while he shuns the grosser joys of sense,
His mind seems nourished by that abstinence.
'Steer to that shore!' – they sail. 'Do this!' – 'tis done.
'Now form and follow me!' – the spoil is won.

The title page illustration from William Hone's Lord Byron's Corsair, Conrad, The Corsair; or, The Pirates' Isle, A Tale by Lord Byron Adapted as a Romance, *1817. 'The burst of light blazed on the assembly; the seeming Dervise startd up, and dashing off his cap, and tearing away his saintly robe, stood forward the mailed Corsair, with glittering casque, and eye that shone still more terribly.'*

Dieting yields the spirit authority over the body, which corresponds to or, indeed, generates leadership over the body politic. Byron held to this rationalisation for his compulsive behaviour all his life. Doubtless, as he explains of another pirate, Lambro in *Don Juan*, 'he who can command himself/Is good to govern'. The word 'govern' highlights the way that Byron's life and work pivot on dependence/independence.

The Corsair doesn't just succeed where Napoleon failed, in harnessing his followers: he trumps the wider failure of nerves that Byron observed on the contemporary, political scene. Britain and its allies conspired to return Europe to a pre-revolutionary state, restoring the old Bourbon dynasty to thrones that Napoleon and his satellites had briefly occupied. Byron called this state of affairs 'a damned insipid medium'. 'Long have I led them,'

Conrad boasts of his hold over his men, '– not to vainly bleed:/No medium now – we perish or succeed!' His extremism echoed Napoleon's character, just as it reflected Byron's own ambition to be either Caesar or nothing. A year later Byron was delighted when the new science of phrenology confirmed that his faculties and dispositions were 'strongly marked – but very antithetical'.

The eponymous hero Lara in Byron's 'sequel' to *The Corsair* shares this trait: '– he ransack'd all below,/And found his recompence in joy or woe,/ No tame, trite medium'; 'In him inexplicably mix'd appeared/Much to be loved and hated, sought and feared'.

Napoleon, Conrad and Byron share another, crucial leadership trait: they lack bonhomie. Conrad's authority *depends* on his lack of fellow feeling: he mixes with his followers only 'to command'. To those few who 'enquire his will . . . brief answer and contemptuous eye/Convey reproof, nor further deign reply'. His 'power of Thought – the magic of the Mind' would be weakened by compromise with his 'body' of men.

Hobhouse spent eight months on the Continent during the Hundred Days. He returned to London on 8 February and told Byron 'ten thousand anecdotes of Napoleon, all good and true' and 'all in favour of his intellect and courage' – which clearly established his mental strength, 'but against his *bonhommie*', which, for Byron, guaranteed the hero that necessary distance from his 'body of men'. 'No wonder,' Byron noted in his Journal for 18 February 1814, '– how should he, who knows mankind well, do other than despise and abhor them?' This distance or lack of bonhomie would play an important role in *Don Juan*. Hobhouse recorded in his diary for 11 August 1814 that he had dined with Baron Arnhem, who had spoken several times to Napoleon and reported that the emperor's 'most striking feature . . . was a disgust and contempt of the human race'. This was a generally accepted truth; Madame de Staël agreed: 'What, then, was the destructive principle which haunted his triumphal steps? What was it? the contempt of mankind.' The French author Stendhal wrote *A Life of Napoleon* in 1817–18 (but first published in 1929) in order to refute Madame de Staël's attacks on Napoleon. He insisted that what was charming about him was his language, his frankness, 'sa bonhomie'. But even he referred to Napoleon's 'supreme contempt of mankind'.

Earlier, in December, Byron remembered how Madame de Staël once asked him whether he 'had really any *bonhommie*' (*sic*). His comment highlights the issue's heroic implications: 'She might as well have asked that question before she told C.L. [Caroline Lamb] "c'est un démon." True enough,' he added in his Journal for 10 December 1813, 'but rather premature, for *she* could not have found it out.'

Madame de Staël counted as something of an expert on the devil. In her book *De l'Allemagne*, which John Murray published in 1813 in French and in English (translated by Byron's old friend Francis Hodgson and edited by William Lamb), she presented Goethe's witty, critical, 'civilised devil' Mephistopheles as an alternative to the sublime Miltonic tradition.

> The Devil [Mephistopheles] is the hero of this piece [*Faust*], the author has not conceived him like a hideous phantom, such as he is usually represented to children; he has made him, if we may so express ourselves, the evil Being *par excellence*... Goethe wished to display in this character ... the bitterest pleasantry that contempt can inspire, and at the same time an audacious gaiety that amuses. There is an infernal irony in the discourses of Mephistopheles, which extends itself to the whole creation, and criticizes the universe like a bad book of which the Devil has made himself the censor.

Mephistophelean and Satanic associations repeatedly halo Conrad the Corsair: there was 'a laughing Devil in his sneer'; the Pacha's slaves would as soon seize Zatanai (Satan) as him ; he displays an 'evil pride'.

Mme de Staël was implicitly aligning Mephistopheles with Napoleon. So when Byron portrayed his Corsair as a Satanic hero, was he covertly portraying Napoleon? The Russian author Alexander Pushkin considered this idea:

> *The Corsair* was indebted for its incredible success to the character of the hero, hauntingly reminiscent of the man whose fatal will at that time ruled

Portrait of Madame de Staël, the frontispiece to Madame Necker de Saussure, Sketch of the Life and Writings of Baroness De Staël-Holstein, *1820.*

over one half of Europe and threatened the other.

At any rate the English critics assumed Byron to have had this intention, but it is more likely that the poet here too presented the character who appeared in all his works, and one which he finally assumed himself in the person of Childe Harold. Be that as it may, the poet never clarified his intention, the comparison with Napoleon being pleasing to his self-esteem.

Pushkin's insight came in 1827, haloed by specious hindsight and geographical distance. When *The Corsair* was published in 1814 no critic remarked on the hero's Napoleonic character. On the contrary, Francis Jeffrey explained in the *Edinburgh Review* that the poem's strong emotions appealed because the times were now so settled: 'When the pleasures of security are no longer new, and the dangers of excessive or intemperate vehemence cease to be thought of in the upper ranks of society, it is natural that the utility of the precautions which had been taken against them should be brought into question, and their severity in a great measure relaxed.'

By 1814 Napoleon had already been discredited as a hero. *The Corsair* represents Byron's first attempt to fill the vacuum, to create 'Some new Napoleon'. Byron's fascination survived the emperor's fall, once the poet learned how to imitate and even to succeed him, to appropriate the *idea* to his own ends. His triumph in *Don Juan* would mean that he could become more Napoleonic than Napoleon himself. The way there led through Byron's discovery that he could usurp Napoleon's notoriety.

20

NAPOLEON FALLS, 1814–16

Where is the hero now?

Courier, Friday 7 January 1814

Byron had little respect for writing, compared to action in the world, until February 1814. He then discovered that writing could offer an ideal platform for heroic, public and even for specifically Napoleonic action.

Byron already knew that, like Conrad the Corsair, he enjoyed one crucial advantage over the emperor: independence from his followers, from his public. 'I am not – never was – nor can be popular –' he insisted to Lady Melbourne on 10 January 1814, 'and you will own I do not deserve nor indeed strive to be so – I never *won* the world – & what it has awarded me has always been [wrung?] from it's [*sic*] caprice –.'

Observing the emperor's slow fall, Byron began to 'pity poor Napoleon', asking Lady Melbourne two days later: '– and are these your heroes? – this man's spirit seems broken – it is but a bastard devil at last – . . . a thorough mind would either rise from the rebound or at least go out "with harness on it's [*sic*] back".' Napoleon's failure means that he has lost spiritual or mental power (his 'mind' is not 'thorough'); he therefore forfeits his claim to Satanic status ('a bastard devil').

The poet learned from the emperor's failure. Eight days later, on 22 January 1814, the day, not by chance, that he celebrated his twenty-sixth birthday, Byron instructed John Murray to republish 'To a Lady Weeping' in his new volume of verse headed by *The Corsair*.

Charles Williams's caricature of 1814: Boney Forsaken by his Guardian Genius. *The devil deprives Napoleon of his crown and explains, 'you cannot expect to reign for ever, besides I want you at home to teach some of the young imps wickedness.'*

POEMS.

To a Lady weeping.

WEEP, daughter of a royal line,
  A Sire's disgrace, a realm's decay;
Ah, happy! if each tear of thine
  Could wash a father's fault away!

Weep—for thy tears are Virtue's tears—
  Auspicious to these suffering isles;
And be each drop in future years
  Repaid thee by thy people's smiles!

March, 1812.

In 1812 Byron published a short poem, 'To a Lady Weeping', that attacked the Prince Regent anonymously. It sank without trace and in 1814 it was out of date. But when he republished it as 'Sympathetic Address to a Young Lady' (its new title) in the second issue of the first edition of The Corsair *– once Lord Byron boasted that he was behind the rebuke to royalty – it caused a scandal, just as he hoped it would. Murray dropped it from the third edition but Byron made him reinstate it in the fourth edition.*

Byron highlights the über-Napoleonic nature of his initiative in insisting on republishing his forgotten poem when he boasts to Murray on 22 January that his letter had to 'advance through more Snows than ever opposed the Emperor's retreat'. He repeated the same point to Hobhouse two days later. He was writing from Newstead Abbey, where the 1815 sale catalogue of the contents reveals that Byron had surrounded himself with imperial references: the abbey dining room held 'a superb carved eagle, richly gilt and standing upon a scarlet and gold stand and gold balls'. The state room's 'elegant French window Curtain of scarlet morine' was topped by a japanned and gilt battle-axe cornice. This was en-suite with the splendid 'lofty' bed with japanned and gilt pillars, a 'domed top surmounted by a coronet' and 'rich crimson furniture . . . and scarlet draperies supported by eagles, richly gilt'. Meanwhile the breakfast parlour had 'a sopha . . . the frame enriched with four carvings of eagles', as well as 'a pair of bronze eagles supporting single lights mounted in ormulu'. Napoleon followed ancient Roman practice when he gave bronze imperial eagles to his regiments. They were carried into battle and were defended to the death. When in 1816 Byron and his physician Dr William Polidori visited the chateau outside Brussels where Napoleon had stayed they bowed to the eagles that remained on the chairs. 'Sigh to behold the eagle's lofty rage,' Byron said of Napoleon on St Helena, 'Reduced to nibble at his narrow cage'.

Shelley used the same analogy to highlight a Napoleonic trait in Maddalo (Byron):

> The sense that he was greater than his kind
> Had struck, methinks, his eagle spirit blind
> By gazing on its own exceeding light.

For the Sake of Another Outcry

The Corsair sold 10,000 copies on the day of publication, 'a thing perfectly unprecedented', Murray assured Byron on 3 February. For the moment, on the next day, Byron confirmed that it was his 'finale'; he would not publish anything ever again, 'not from any affectation – but a thorough conviction that it is ye. best policy – & is at least respectful to my readers – as it shews that I would not willingly run ye. risk of forfeiting their favour in future'. His wistful postscript in a letter to John Murray of 4 February 1814 again signals the metaphorical implications of publishing and reveals the model he has in mind: 'Don't you think *Bonaparte's* next *publication* will be rather expensive to the Allies?'

But why would Byron want to seem 'respectful' to his readers? Any humbleness evaporated overnight. The next day, 5 February, he reflected that his present and past success appeared 'very singular – since it was in the teeth of so many prejudices – I almost think people like to be *contradicted.*' Inspired by his hopes for '*Bonaparte*'s next *publication*', Byron now sent Murray a much more scandalous poem, 'Lines inscribed upon a Cup formed from a Skull', which he had written six years before. 'If you like,' he now told Murray on 5 February, '– add them ['Lines inscribed'] to C[hilde] H[arold] if only for the sake of another outcry.'

Why did Byron think of reprinting this obscure poem now? Probably because the *Courier* of 1 February reminded him of it. When it attacked

Byron's skull cup. When he discovered a skull in the grounds of Newstead Abbey in 1808 Byron had it set in silver (at a cost of seventeen guineas), and used it as a drinking cup. It was reburied in the grounds of Newstead Abbey in the 1860s by John Murray III and Mr. and Mrs. Webb, the then owners of Newstead Abbey.

Private collection

him for republishing 'To a Lady Weeping' it also printed a new poem, 'On reading the Lines written by Lord BYRON, and engraven on the Silver Mounting of a Human Skull, formerly used as a Goblet at his residence Newstead Abbey':

> Why hast thou bound around with silver rim
> This once gay peopled 'palace of the soul?'
> Look on it now – deserted, bleach'd and grim –
> Is this, thou feverish Man, thy festal bowl?

The poem was attributed to St, which presumably stood for Strada, a pseudonymous writer who had already identified Byron with Satan in the *Champion*'s 'Portraits of Authors'. An editorial disclaimer preceded that portrait and no other in the series.

Byron's decision to republish his original skull cup lines could hardly have appeared less 'respectful to [his] readers'. It manifested an attitude to his audience/subjects that he would later praise in Napoleon as 'glorious contempt'. It also demonstrated Byron's affinity with his renegade father.

In Byron's next oriental tale, *Parisina*, the hero Hugo falls in love with his stepmother and blames his fate on his lack of 'paternal care'.

But Hugo is proud of what he has inherited from his father, Azo, who seduced his mother and then abandoned her. Byron could have addressed Captain Jack in the words Hugo uses to his father:

> From thee – this tamelessness of heart –
> . . . From thee in all their vigour came
> My arm of strength, my soul of flame –
> Thou didst not give me life alone,
> But all that made me more thine own.
> See what thy guilty love hath done!
> Repaid thee with too like a son!
> I am no bastard in my soul,
> For that, like thine, abhorred control.

In October 2017 a skull cup was sold at Charterhouse Auctions in Sherborne, Dorset. It belonged to a brain surgeon and its silver rim (which the auctioneer dated to the end of the nineteenth century) proclaimed it belonged to Byron. It has since been sold by Finch & Co. for £7,500. It would make sense that, when it was buried in the 1860s, the skull lost its silver rim and stand, both engraved with the mermaid from Byron's crest. But it could equally well be another skull. Byron ornamented his study at Newstead Abbey 'with a number of skulls highly polished, and placed on light stands round the room'.
Photograph courtesy of Finch and Co.

Even when Hugo waits for his father to punish him he tells him, 'I feel thou art my father still.' Exultant, Hugo tells Azo, 'As erred the sire, so erred the son'.

Back in London Byron delighted to find 'all the newspapers in hysterics, and town in an uproar . . . some of the abuse good, all of it hearty'. He relished it all, even the scurrilous attacks on his supposed atheism and his deformity, since, as he told Lady Melbourne on 10 January 1814, they proved that he was not, 'nor can be popular'. The 'outcry' confirmed Byron's Satanic status, at a moment when Napoleon had lost his right to it: another paper 'very downrightly says I am the *Devil* (*boiteux* they might have added) and a rebel and what not'.

Byron learned that, 'to complete the farce', his republication of the poem would be raised in Parliament. Instead of speaking in the House of Lords he would now be discussed there, 'probably about the same period

W. Chevalier's engraving after H. Richter, an illustration to Parisina, *as Hugo begs his father to delay his exile, from* The Byron Gallery, *1833.*

with the treaty of Peace. – I really begin to think myself a most important personage.' This struck him as 'a little too ludicrous to be true', but there is nothing funny about his heroic attitude. He glories in what he calls his 'Diabolism', assuring Lady Melbourne on 11 February 1814, '–"the Demon whom I still have served – has not yet cowed my better part of Man – ["] and whatever I may & have or shall feel – I have that within me that bounds against opposition.' Here Byron conflates two separate quotations

Portrait of Byron in 1815 by G. H. Harlow. Leigh Hunt claimed he had asked Byron 'if he knew what Mrs Hunt had said one day to the Shelleys of his picture by Harlow? (It is the fastidious, scornful portrait of him, affectedly looking down.) He said he did not, and was curious to know. An engraving of it, I told him, was shown her, and her opinion asked; upon which she 'observed that "it resembled a great school-boy, who had had a plain bun given him, instead of a plum one." I did not add that our friends shook with laughter at this idea of the noble original, because it was "so like him." He looked as blank as possible, and never again criticised the personal appearance of those whom I regarded.' Medwin commented that the portrait was 'as unlike as possible, and yet it furnishes the frontispiece to most of the foreign Editions of his Works'.

Private collection

from *Macbeth,* but he changes Shakespeare's 'angel' into 'Demon', in order to *strengthen* his identification with the devil.

The conservative Murray did not want to publish the anti-royal 'Sympathetic Address'. On 12 February Byron forced his hand with bravado worthy of his Corsair: 'I *do not* & *will* not be supposed to shrink – although myself & every thing belonging to me were to perish with my memory – .'

Republishing the two poems demonstrated an outrageously cool lack of bonhomie, the coldness that Byron (thanks to Hobhouse) identified as Napoleonic, and knew to be demonic too, from that authority on Napoleon, Madame de Staël (whom he mentions in that same journal entry).

Rafael Morghen's engraving after Stefano Tofanelli's painting shows Napoleon in his coronation robes. This portrait, a 'very fine impression, in a gilt frame' was listed as lot 376 in the 1816 auction of Byron's possessions. Byron commented that 'the Emperor becomes his robes as if he had been hatched in them.' This engraving hung in Byron's bedroom in Newstead Abbey, along with his other icon of male authority, the mezzotint of John Jackson (reproduced above, p. 172). Naturally, when 'the Academy of N.Y.' asked for Byron's portrait in September 1822, he insisted that Morghen engrave William Edward West's painting, adding, 'at his own price – and at my expence'. Morghen said he would take three years and charge $4,000, so Byron gave up the idea. 'However I shall not think of any other engraver – he is the only one.'

© National Portrait Gallery, London

Byron partly felt so close to Napoleon because of Bonaparte's Satanic aura. It represented common ground between the 'dark & diabolical' emperor and the poet who longed to invade that territory.

Once the emperor fell, his throne and mantle became available to a new claimant. When Mr J. Tournier brought Napoleon's coronation robes to London in 1816, Byron implied that he was interested in buying them.

If Napoleonic generally meant Satanic, Satanism could become Napoleonic. Thinking of one inevitably brought the other to mind, as Hazlitt commented in his essay 'On Means and Ends'. In the wake of Napoleon's failure, Byron was delighted to discover that Satanic could mean Byronic. From now on his fictional hero-villains become increasingly Satanic.

Raphael Morghen engraved Luigi Bartolini's bust of Byron in 1822, but Byron 'would have given any thing to have suppressed it altogether'.
Private collection

'The worst they could do would be to exclude me from society,' Byron told Samuel Rogers on 16 February. He had never courted it, nor enjoyed it '– and "there is a world elsewhere!"' That quotation from *Coriolanus* comes in handy, once again. His language reflects his search for alternative forms of heroism and at this time, more than ever, Byron resorts to Shakespeare, his source book for the language of heroics. In one journal entry alone, on 27 February 1814, he refers to Shakespeare five times. Byron found a new hero in the theatre, now his favourite place of resort.

Kean: The Triumph of Mind over Matter

The actor Edmund Kean was distinguished by memorably piercing, large, dark eyes and by his small stature – 5 foot 6¾ inches (1.7 metres). Kean was only 1¾ inches (4.45 cm) shorter than Byron. His height restricted him to comic roles, until he learned to exploit the (Byronic) discrepancy between his great spirit and his 'mean-looking' appearance. When he played Alexander the Great in Sheerness in 1807, someone heckled him: 'Alexander the Great, indeed! It should be Alexander the Little.' Kean quelled the audience's laughter with a look and said, 'Yes – with a GREAT SOUL.'

As Byron probably knew, Drury Lane Theatre engaged Kean on the recommendation of Dr Joseph Drury, Byron's headmaster, who had inspired his original taste for oratory. A distant family connection linked the theatre and the Drury family.

Kean made his debut at the Drury Lane Theatre on 26 January 1814 as Shylock. William Hazlitt reviewed his performance for the *Morning Chronicle* and the conjunction between actor and critic made the reputation of both men. Leigh Hunt, the doyen of theatre critics, was still in prison for libel, when Kean made his debut.

Hazlitt, a passionate Napoleonist (like Samuel Whitbread, who chaired the committee for the rebuilding of the theatre, and others associated with Drury Lane), made a campaign out of his backing for Kean, who 'destroyed the Kemble religion'. John Philip Kemble at Covent Garden Theatre represented the grand, traditional status quo: his acting tended to be 'swayed by a single impulse'; he played Hamlet 'like a man in armour'. Kemble was 'an icicle upon the bust of Tragedy'. Kean's acting embodied a new, Romantic spirit: he excelled in versatility, displaying 'a lightness and vigour in his tread, a buoyancy and elasticity of spirit, a fire and animation'.

Byron interpreted Kean's genius in terms of his private ideal of intellectual heroism, as the spirit's triumph over the body. 'By Jove, he is a soul!' he exclaimed on seeing Kean's Richard III. Kean 'is the triumph of mind over matter', he told Annabella Milbanke on 19 October 1814, 'for he has nothing but countenance and expression – his figure is very

Byron's screen celebrated boxing on one side (reproduced above, p. 178) and, on the other, the English theatre. Portrait engravings of Sarah Siddons as the Tragic Muse (after Joshua Reynolds) and her brother John Philip Kemble as Richard III (after William Hamilton) dominate the central panels. The left-hand panel features Shakespeare, Garrick and the monument to Garrick in Westminster Abbey. Four mezzotints after paintings by Zoffany fill the bottom panels, illustrating Samuel Foote in his play The Mayor of Garratt*; Samuel Foote and Tom Weston in the former's play* The Devil upon Two Sticks *(a version of Byron's favourite novel* Le diable boiteux*); a scene from Richard Cumburland's* The West *and Parsons, Bransby and Watkins in Garrick's* Lethe*, and the fourth panel features Edmund Kean as Shylock at the top left.*

Private collection

little & even mean'. The review in the *Champion* gives an impression of how Kean achieved this: 'Throughout the whole play he was careful to preserve the appearance of thought following thought, through the immediate operation of the mind, – instead of shewing by his delivery of the first line of a passage, that he accurately knew the tenor of the last. This kept his expressive countenance in a perpetual and picturesque animation, chequered according to the nature of each new idea.'

When Kean played Iago, Byron stayed '*close* to him (in the orchestra)' and judged that he was 'perfection . . . particularly the last look. I . . . never saw an English countenance half so expressive. I am acquainted with no *im*material sensuality so delightful as good acting.'

Byron implicitly parallels the actor's career with that of the beleaguered emperor in a letter of 19 February and his thoughts go directly from Kean to Napoleon when he wrote to James Wedderburn Webster the next day. Observers often noted affinities between the actor and the emperor. 'Kean gives me the idea of Buonaparte in a furor,' Lord Granville Leveson Gower commented. Kean as Othello reminded Lady Caroline Lamb of Byron in 1814; Hobhouse recorded that Kean and Byron exhibited Napoleon's 'habit of chewing'. Byron himself referred to the analogy in one of his 'Detached Thoughts', on 15 October 1821. In 1825 the *Roscius*, a theatrical magazine stated: 'As the man, blind from birth, likened scarlet to the sound of a trumpet, so in modern time, in action we have a Napoleon, in poetry a Buonaparte, in music a Weber, and (it is not too much to say) in histrionic adventure a Kean . . . He would seem born only to recite the poetry of Byron.'

Byron took a box for Kean's benefit on 25 May and sent the actor the enormous sum of fifty guineas. He was 'enchanted with Edmund', Kean's sister-in-law noted, 'and is like a little dog behind the scenes, following him everywhere'. He gave the actor a costly Turkish sword, probably to equip him for a heroic stage role, and a handsome snuffbox. Kean inspired Byron to involve himself with the management of the Drury Lane Theatre and, like Keats, Coleridge and Shelley, to write plays with roles to suit the actor's strengths.

George Clint's painting of Edmund Kean as Sir Giles Overreach, who is driven into insanity, in Massinger's A New Way to Pay Old Debts. *Byron told Murray on 12 August 1819 that Kean's acting in this role so affected him that he had convulsions.*

© Victoria and Albert Museum, London

Kean's innovative style had an important effect on Byron's later writings, inspiring aspects of the characters of Ulric in *Werner* and Sardanapalus. A 'terrible jocundity' characterised Kean's Richard III. Hobhouse, who attended with Byron, called it 'a sportive ferocity'. Another witness in 1815 mentioned 'a predominant feature of his [Kean's] acting – a certain, sarcastic, epigrammatic turn, which gives peculiar force and meaning to particular passages'. These stylistic features recur in *Don Juan*.

21

BYRON RISES, 1814–16

To Keep up the Ethereal Part of Me

On 8 April 1814 Byron recorded in his Journal that his 'poor little pagod, Napoleon' had been 'pushed off his pedestal; – the thieves are in Paris. It is his own fault.' The news of his abdication crushed Byron, who did not leave his rooms for some four days. He felt 'utterly bewildered and confounded. I don't know – but I think *I*, even *I* (an insect compared with this creature), have set my life on casts not a millionth part of this man's.'

Napoleon's ignominious fall threatened the sanity of many of his British admirers. Hazlitt, for example, 'seemed prostrated in mind and body: he walked about unwashed, unshaved, hardly sober by day, and always intoxicated by night, literally, without exaggeration, for weeks.' Byron acted promptly to ensure that his mind would survive. On 10 April 1814, the day after he heard that Napoleon had abdicated, he wrote in his Journal:

> I have sparred for exercise (windows open) with Jackson an hour daily, to attenuate and keep up the ethereal part of me. The more violent the fatigue, the better my spirits for the rest of the day; and then, my evenings have that calm nothingness of languor, which I most delight in. To-day I have boxed one hour – written an ode to Napoleon Buonaparte – copied it – eaten six biscuits – drank four bottles of soda water – redde away the rest of my time.

Byron's entry records how he reinforced his claim to heroic status ('to attenuate and keep up the ethereal part of me'). Boxing, like dieting, helped to secure his spirit's independence from the flesh. His first reaction is to follow suit: on the same day that Byron recorded Napoleon's abdication, he himself abdicated (once again), telling Moore that he would write no more poetry. His 'great comfort' (which also represented his unspoken superiority to Napoleon), was

> that the temporary celebrity I have wrung from the world has been in the very teeth of all opinions and prejudices. I have flattered no ruling powers; I have never concealed a single thought that tempted me. They can't say I have truckled to the times, nor to popular topics . . . and whatever I have gained has been at the expenditure of as much *personal* favour as possible; for I do believe never was a bard more unpopular, *quoad homo*, than myself . . . Every body may be d----d, as they seem fond of it, and resolved to stickle lustily for endless brimstone.

'Oh – by the by,' he added in the same letter to Moore of 9 April, the colloquial phrase betraying an unspontaneous 'non-non sequitur', 'I had nearly forgot. There is a long Poem, an "Anti-Byron," coming out, to prove that I have formed a conspiracy to overthrow, by *rhyme*, all religion and government, and have already made great progress! It is not very scurrilous, but serious and ethereal. I never felt myself important, till I saw and heard of my being such a little Voltaire as to induce such a production.' Sadly, Murray refused to publish it, 'for which he was a fool, and so I told him'. Byron longed to see the *Anti-Byron* published, because it would demonstrate that as a leader/writer he displayed a 'glorious contempt of the rascals', his subjects (i.e. his readers). He admired the attitude of the Roman dictator Sulla (138–78 BC), who, unlike Napoleon, 'dared depart in utter scorn/Of men that such a yoke had borne'. That is what made the *Anti-Byron* 'ethereal', a word that otherwise makes no sense.

Byron's resolve to abdicate as a poet weakened, once he saw that he could act out his idiosyncratic notion of heroism in poetry. The next day, 10 April, he resolved to 'think higher of rhyme and reason and very humbly of your heroic people' and he sent Murray his *Ode to Napoleon Buonaparte*.

The magnificent silver cup that Byron bought from Samuel Hennell in 1809 or 1810 and gave to his publisher John Murray in 1815. It contained 'a phial of hemlock gathered under the walls of Athens' in February 1811, that Byron brought back from Greece. The phial has since disappeared.

Private collection

To ensure that Murray (a Tory) would publish it, Byron bribed him with a gift of the copyright.

In the *Ode* Byron attacks Napoleon for compromising his independence from his followers, by clinging too long to power: by the time Napoleon abdicated, the allies had entered Paris. The emperor has lost the Corsair's distinction, his 'magic of the Mind': 'That spell upon the minds of men/ Breaks never to unite again'. Napoleon is therefore an 'Ill-minded man'. That is why Byron told Annabella Milbanke on 20 April 1814 that the emperor's fall implied 'the utter wreck of a mind which I thought superior even to Fortune'. Byron assumed that public failure would have private consequences: Napoleon 'must eat [his] heart away!'; he must go mad and die. The emperor has again lost his Satanic distinction: 'miscall'd the Morning Star' (Lucifer), he is now 'a nameless thing'. For the moment, Byron can see no alternative to Napoleon's failure: a successor is unimaginable, for 'who would soar the solar height,/To set in such a starless night?' The words 'soar' and 'starless' betray the special, Byronic nature of the heroism that is no longer possible (see Chapter 9's section on 'A Byronic Vocabulary').

Byron wrote the *Ode* as part of his own campaign to 'soar', along with starving and sparring: all helped him 'to attenuate and keep up' his 'ethereal part'. He used the same word, 'ethereal', to evoke both the printed attack and the way exercise affected him: like his diet, they reinforced the primacy of his mind or soul over his body.

The emperor offered to abdicate in his son's favour. Wellington refused to allow the Bonaparte dynasty to continue, so on 15 July Napoleon surrendered. Byron reacted to his hero's defeat with poems written from different viewpoints. 'Napoleon's Farewell' imitates the emperor's voice. 'From the French' speaks for a devoted officer and 'On the Star of "The Legion of Honour"' articulates the disappointment felt by those whom Napoleon once inspired: 'When thy bright promise fades away,/Our life is but a load of clay'.

Some of Napoleon's most devoted British admirers had invested him with the attributes of the father whom they lacked. They therefore experienced a second loss at his fall, which frequently had a traumatic effect. A son's relationship with his father dominates the three works that Byron now tackled, *The Siege of Corinth*, *Parisina* and the first act of his play *Werner*.

After Lady Byron left her husband, Augusta tried to mediate between them. Four days later Augusta tried to reassure her sister-in-law that Byron was getting better: 'now he is gone to eat mutton broth for dinner', she reported on 19 January 1816. 'I have seen him but a moment today,' she added two days later (the eve of his birthday), 'when he was eating a stewed knuckle of Veal with broth & rice.' The fact that she details what he ate may indicate that, in general, he had stopped eating. Augusta had

The medal of the Legion of Honour, instituted by Napoleon and awarded on merit alone.

determined to look on the bright side but she became convinced that her brother was mentally ill when she heard him boast on his birthday to his cousin George Anson Byron, 'that he considered himself *the greatest man existing*. G. said laughing, "Except Buonaparte." Ye answer was, "God! I don't know that I do except even him!"'

Annabella began to talk to her parents about some aspects of her life with her husband. Appalled, her father wrote to Byron asking for a

A caricature by George Cruikshank, Fashionables of 1816, Taking the Air in Hyde Park! *Dressed in a floor-length coat, that parts to reveal voluminous trousers, Byron appears between two women.*
Courtesy of the Lewis Walpole Library, Yale University

separation. He refused and asked his wife to explain her behaviour, which she never did. She became obsessed with the idea that Byron would get custody of their daughter – and hand her over to Augusta. Rumours infested the smoking ruins of the marriage. Lady Byron fomented them with private hints, loud, public silence and by distancing herself from her sister-in-law. From the summer of 1816 onwards Lady Byron pointedly dropped her daughter's first name, Augusta, and insisted on calling her by her second name, Ada. Appendix 4 explores Byron's private reasons for choosing that name. Had Lady Byron known, she might have preferred to call her daughter Augusta.

Gossip hinted that Byron had implicated himself in unspeakable, criminal activity, such as murder, incest and worse. While incest could be named, his other supposed crime, sodomy, was merely referred to as '—'. Byron's rank, his literary fame, his personal notoriety and the sinister glamour of his villainous heroes conspired to create a vicious, explosive phenomenon. He was 'accused of every monstrous vice by public rumour, – and private rancour', as he later reflected; 'my name which had been a knightly or a noble one since My fathers helped to

George Cruikshank's caricature, A Scene at the London Museum, Piccadilly, *1816. William Bullock displayed Napoleon's coach, which was attended by the emperor's coachman, Jean Hornn. Byron's copy of the carriage required four to six horses to pull it and broke down repeatedly. It served spiritual, rather than practical ends, since it offered Byron ideal, rather than merely vehicular, transport. 'Besides a lit de repos, it contained a library, a plate-chest, and every aparatus for dining in it.'Byron's replica cost £500 and it took him many years to pay the bill.*

Private collection

conquer the kingdom for William the Norman, was tainted.' Byron now trumped his villainous father's criminal reputation; he even surpassed Napoleon's fall from grace.

Byron thought of writing a 'romance in prose' in 1816, 'intended to shadow out his own matrimonial fate'. To seal his notoriety with diabolic glory, he would call it the 'Marriage of Belphegor'. Belphegor was another 'satanic personage' from the Bible.

As he prepared to go into exile, Byron may have felt he was reliving his father's flight. He certainly ensured that Napoleonic associations haloed his journey. He wrote to Miss Mercer Elphinstone on 10 April, bidding farewell to the heiress (whom he felt he should have married) and pointing out that the paper he used came from Malmaison: its watermarks featured the wreathed head of Napoleon and the imperial eagle. He also commissioned an extravagant new carriage, an exact copy of the one used by Napoleon, which was captured on the battlefield at Waterloo.

In His Wake

Byron left England with Hobhouse on 25 April 1816, eight months after Napoleon sailed for exile on St Helena on 7 August 1815.

Byron's route took him on a pilgrimage of sites invested with Napoleonic glamour. Visiting Brussels, so that his impractical carriage could be repaired, he toured the site of the Battle of Waterloo.

In Flanders he was impressed by the evidence of Napoleon's interventions, such as the fortified basins at Antwerp, 'very superb', he told Augusta on 1 May, 'as all his undertakings were'. On 5 October Byron and Hobhouse left Switzerland and crossed into Italy through the Simplon Pass.

According to Lady Blessington Byron remarked, 'To pass through Italy without thinking of Napoleon . . . is like visiting Naples without looking at Vesuvius.' On Isola Bella Byron saw the laurel tree with 'Battaglia' (battle) carved in it, supposedly etched by Napoleon, shortly before his victory at Marengo. Byron entered Milan in October 1816, fourteen years after Bonaparte, admiring an unfinished triumphal arch that Napoleon commissioned, 'so beautiful as to make one regret its non-completion'.

In *Childe Harold* III, which he began to write as soon as he left England, Byron reflects at length on Napoleon. In retrospect, the Hundred Days, the brief period when Napoleon escaped from Elba and resumed power in France, makes Byron less critical of his hero. He now allows the emperor the distinction that he had recently denied him:

> Extreme in all things! hadst thou been betwixt,
> Thy throne had still been thine, or never been;
> For daring made thy rise as fall.

George Cruikshank's caricature of Byron's marital troubles as he prepared to leave Britain, dated in the original caption, April 1816. It identifies the actress, 'beauteous Mrs Mardyn' on his arm. In her left hand she grips his medal of the Legion of Honour.

www.CartoonStock.com

But there is an important development in the way the poet looks at the hero. In 1814 Byron explored the Napoleonic aspects of his own behaviour; now he celebrates the Byronic nature of Napoleon's achievement. The emperor's resilience mirrors Byron's stoicism in the face of persecution: 'When Fortune fled her spoil'd and favourite child,/He stood unbow'd beneath the ills upon him piled'. He now blames Napoleon's defeat on his (Byronic) lack of bonhomie, 'That just habitual scorn which could contemn/Men and their thoughts':

> If, like a tower upon a headlong rock,
> Thou hadst been made to stand or fall alone,
> Such scorn of men had help'd to brave the shock;
> But men's thoughts were the steps which pav'd thy throne,
> *Their* admiration thy best weapon shone.

Richard Westall's illustration to Childe Harold *III, 30: the hero, modelled on Byron, reflects on the death of his cousin Frederick Howard at the Battle of Waterloo:*

> *But when I stood beneath the fresh green tree,*
> *Which, living waves where thou didst cease to live,*
> *And saw around me the wild field revive*
> *With fruits and fertile promise, and the Spring*
> *Come forth her work of gladness to contrive,*
> *With all her reckless birds upon the wing,*
> *I turn'd from all she brought to those she could not bring.*

Private collection

The Simplon Pass was one of Napoleon's most impressive 'grands projets', *which demonstrated, as Madame de Staël put it, 'that nature obeyed Bonaparte with almost as much docility as men'. Built between 1800 and 1807, it covers over 12½ miles, crosses 6,000 bridges and goes through many rock-pierced tunnels. Thomas Moore said it 'baffles all description. A road, carried up into the very clouds, over torrents and precipices; nothing was ever like it.'The image comes from a* Medallic History of Napoleon 1820. *A woman rests her left arm on a wheel and points to a Latin inscription, 'Dedicated to the great and invincible Consul Napoleon, for having commissioned the Simplon route'.*

A medal to commemorate Napoleon's triumphal entry into Milan on 20 May 1796 from Stefano Egidio Petroni, La Napoleonide, *1813, 43*

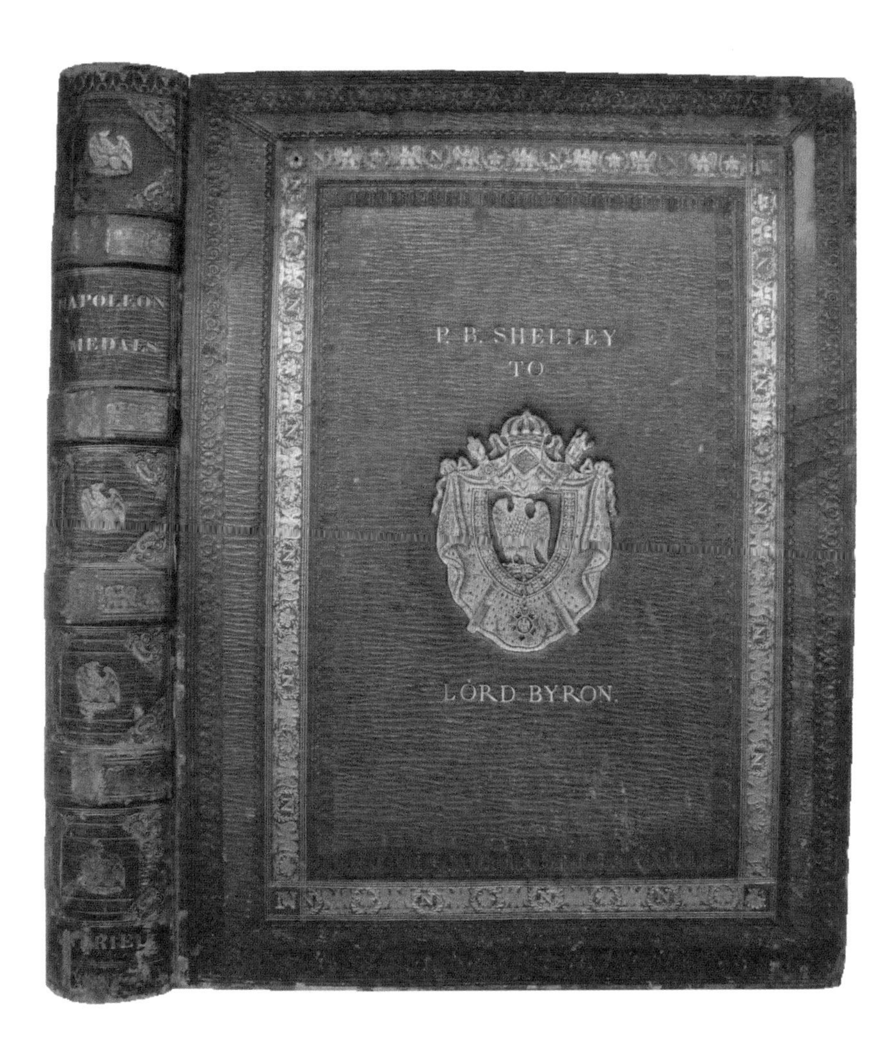

The gilt morocco cover of the book on Napoleonic medals that Shelley gave Byron. This could be the French original [Aubin Louis Eleuthérophile Millin de Grandmaison and James Millingen], Histoire Métallique de Napoléon, ou Recueil des Médailles et des Monnaies qui ont été frappées depuis la première campagne de l'armée d'Italie jusqu'a son abdication en 1815*, 1819, or the* Histoire Médallique de Napoléon, *or the* Medallic History of Napoleon Bonaparte, translated by Miss Ann Mudie Scargill from the original manuscript intended to have been published by the late government of France*, 1820. Only the cover survives.*

Photo: Harrow School and the Harrow School Archive

The Consultation, *a French caricature on Napoleon's loss of power during the Hundred Days. As his crown falls from his head he consults his cousin about his 'state'. Cambacérès assures him, 'It cannot last long: your Majesty's constitution is too bad'.*

Private collection

The tower standing alone evokes Milton's Satan, who 'above the rest,/In shape and gesture proudly eminent/Stood like a tower'. It may also recall *Paradise Regained*, where the devil flies Jesus above the temple in Jerusalem: 'There stand, if thou wilt stand; to stand upright/Will ask thee skill'. 'Tempt not Lord thy God. He said, and stood'. With this image Byron celebrates his own independence, and his superiority to Napoleon: 'I stood and stand alone, – remembered or forgot'.

Tourism is made to serve this game of comparative heroics. The 'chiefless castles' along the Rhine remind Byron of his own heroic isolation: 'And there they stand, as stands a lofty mind,/Worn but unstooping to the baser crowd'. The analogy becomes explicit; the verb 'stood' and the heroic enjambement hint at his Satanic model:

> in the crowd
> They could not deem me one of such; I stood
> Among them, but not of them; in a shroud
> Of thoughts which were not their thoughts.

But, for the moment, *Childe Harold* III records how Byron *fails* to act out Napoleonic heroism in writing. The poet deprecates 'these words, thus woven into song', which 'may be . . . a harmless wile'. Indeed, he deprecates all poetry. In November 1813, after seeing a performance of *Antony and Cleopatra*, Byron saluted the ideal of writing as action, the idea that 'words' could be 'things'. Now he almost asserts his faith in this notion but then falters: 'I do believe,/Though I have found them not, that there may be/Words which are things'. He believes – but only in the way that other unlikely phenomena 'may be', such as 'hopes which will not deceive,/And virtues which are merciful'. For now, Byron accepts his impotence.

The situation would change, but only when Shelley persuaded Byron to believe that poetry could play a major role in the world.

PART IX

BYRON VERSUS SHELLEY, 1816–23

Marianne Hunt's silhouette of Byron after his daily ride, the frontispiece to Leigh Hunt, Lord Byron and some of his contemporaries; with recollections of the author's life: and of his visit to Italy, *1828.*

22

TÊTE-À-TÊTE, 1816–18

I think with you
In some respects, you know
Maddalo to Julian, *Julian and Maddalo*, 240f.

Byron and Shelley; Shelley and Byron: it sounds like a meeting of equals. Given how the relationship ended in fracture it's worth looking for flaws from the start. Each already knew of the other's work before they met, but their relationship began with a debt: Shelley stole two lines from Byron's verse and incorporated them into his own – without acknowledging the theft. Byron and Shelley first met on the shore of Lake Geneva on 27 May 1816. Shelley seemed 'bashful, shy, consumptive', Byron's physician Polidori noted in his diary. Byron formed his most important masculine friendship with Shelley: intense, productive and conflicted, it generated a series of literary works whose private resonances chart the course of their relationship.

Shelley and his lover Mary Wollstonecraft Godwin were travelling with Mary's stepsister Claire Clairmont, who persuaded them to wait for Byron at a hotel in Sécheron, a suburb of Geneva. The eighteen-year-old Claire had offered herself to Byron in London the previous month. He took advantage of her offer but he never loved her. Claire may have wanted to trump Mary, who had fallen in love at the age of sixteen and eloped with her (rather less celebrated) poet. Claire left notes for Byron at the Swiss hotel; he ignored them.

In Some Respects

Byron offered Shelley dinner. Like Byron at his less extreme moments, Shelley was a vegetarian. An eccentric diet signalled common ground between the two poets, but it also concealed major differences. Shelley 'abstained' from meat because he objected to 'the unnatural craving for flesh', as he explained in *A Vindication of Natural Diet*, published anonymously in 1813. He also translated two essays by Plutarch on vegetarianism that have since disappeared. Shelley's temperament reinforced his principles: with no interest in food he sustained himself happily on bread and water and 'never drank' wine. Sitting opposite him at dinner on 20 January 1817, the painter Benjamin Robert Haydon observed a 'hectic, spare, weakly, yet intellectual-looking creature . . . carving a bit of broccoli or cabbage on his

The unsigned portrait of Shelley that serves as the frontispiece to Edward John Trelawny's Records of Shelley, Byron, and the Author, *1878.*

plate, as if it had been the substantial wing of a chicken'. Forgetful of such mundane matters, Shelley would occasionally ask, in his 'cracked soprano', 'Mary, have I dined?'

Byron's 'system of diet' in Switzerland 'was regulated by an abstinence almost incredible', Moore reported, probably from Mary Shelley's observations. 'A thin slice of bread, with tea, at breakfast – a light, vegetable dinner, with a bottle or two of Seltzer water, tinged with vin de Grave, and in the evening, a cup of green tea, without milk or sugar, formed the whole of his sustenance. The pangs of hunger he appeased by privately chewing tobacco and smoking cigars.' Byron often starved himself, but he certainly cared about what he ate, and had a particular fondness for petits pois and asparagus. He could never have forgotten whether he had dined.

Amelia Curran's unfinished portrait of Shelley, Rome, May 1819, which Shelley hated and wished to destroy.
© National Portrait Gallery, London

The poets' differences as vegetarians held true for their relationship, in that they had so much in common and yet, increasingly, differed so widely.

Byron and Shelley became friends and they spent three months together in Switzerland. After parting in August 1816 they did not meet again until 22 August 1818, when they spent two months together in Venice. Nearly three years passed before Shelley visited Byron in Ravenna on 6 August 1821 and stayed for fifteen days. Byron joined Shelley in Pisa that November, and they again lived in close proximity for six months. During the last two months of Shelley's life, they saw each other infrequently.

Like his alter ego Julian, in *Julian and Maddalo*, Shelley was 'of good family'. His father, Timothy Shelley MP, the heir to a baronetcy, assumed that his son would follow him into Parliament. But Shelley rebelled against everything his father stood for and demonised him as intensely as Byron idealised his demonic father. After Eton Shelley was sent down from Oxford for refusing to disown an anonymous pamphlet that advocated atheism. His father cut him off, when he eloped with the sixteen-year-old Harriet Westbrook, who briefly became his first wife. Both poets left England after their marriages broke down and their relatives threatened to imprison them for insanity.

Byron's parallel education at Harrow and Cambridge could not erase the stains left by his notorious, criminal, paternal inheritance and by his impoverished upbringing in Aberdeen. Assuming that he belonged on the margins of society, he felt torn between infamy and respectability. Obsessively aware of his disability, he was fastidious about his clothes and his teeth and he never lost his self-consciousness in society. Shelley never shared Byron's bourgeois fear of 'indecorum'.

Shelley described himself in a Swiss hotel register (in Greek) as 'Democratic, philanthropist and atheist'. When Byron saw the entry he tried to erase it. Shelley stooped, he didn't clean his boots, his clothes didn't fit and his teeth were bad. Indifferent to his own appearance, he could even forget the effect of his nudity on visitors. Shelley preached and practised guiltless free love, Byron revelled in guilt and sin. Byron's liberal attitudes on major political issues never interfered with his aristocratic assumptions.

He remained, as Scott noted, 'a patrician on principle', backing reform in England, where Shelley dreamed of revolution. In Italy Byron took major risks as a political activist (hiding the Italian insurgents' guns in his house), while Shelley's interest remained theoretical.

But Byron respected Shelley's mind. 'Byron . . . never talked seriously and confidentially with any person but Shelley,' according to Trelawny. 'Shelley was disconnected from all Byron's set, and from everyone else that he knew, besides being a far superior scholar.' Calling himself 'the Elfin Knight' and 'Ariel', Shelley 'seemed rather Spirit than man', Teresa Guiccioli said, calling him 'the epitome of intellect . . . who lived in the world like a spirit who had fallen into it against his will, rather than as a being clothed in human nature'. Shelley's appearance in those days, a friend remembered, was 'wild, intellectual, unearthly; like a spirit that has just descended from the sky; like a demon risen at that moment out of the ground'. 'As to real flesh & blood,' Shelley himself once remarked, 'you know that I do not deal in these articles, – you might as well go to a ginshop for a leg of mutton, as expect anything human or earthly from me.' Shelley incarnated Byron's disembodied ideal.

Before they met, Shelley knew Byron's work. He liked *English Bards* and, having listened to Mary reading from Byron's poems, Shelley commented, in an entry to her journal for August 1814: 'I was not before so clearly aware how much of the colouring our own feelings throw upon the liveliest delineations of other minds.' It's a revealing remark: briefly, he recognised how much his feelings could distort reality. The poets' relationship pivoted precariously between 'our own feelings' and 'other minds'. Shelley sent Byron *Queen Mab*, first published in 1813, and called *Lara* 'the finest of Lord Byron's poems'. He also sent Byron another of his own poems, before they ever met. It was probably the sonnet 'Feelings of a Republican on the Fall of Bonaparte'. Byron never responded, perhaps because Shelley dismissed Bonaparte as 'a most unambitious slave', while Byron's recent ode had compared him to Prometheus.

At twenty-eight Byron was only four years older than Shelley but Byron's rank gave weight to that minor seniority, which was reinforced by his greater fame as a poet. Shelley repeatedly sought out older mentors, such

Byron's coat of arms in a panel of stained glass that once hung in Newstead Abbey. The family motto is 'Crede Byron' (Trust Byron).

Private collection

as Dr Lind at Eton, Coleridge, Southey and Godwin, and then broke with them, as he had broken with his father. That pattern may help explain why Shelley eventually turned against Byron with such bitter, irrational intensity.

Shelley described Byron as 'an exceedingly interesting person' in a letter to Thomas Love Peacock of 17 July 1816, six weeks after they met. But he also asked, 'as such is it not to be regretted that he is a slave to the vilest and most vulgar prejudices, and as mad as the winds?' Shelley could not sustain his defensive condescension. He felt such respect for Byron's work and envy for its success that they stifled his creativity. 'If I esteemed you less,' he wrote in a 'Sonnet to Byron', one day after reading *The Corsair*, 'Envy would kill/Pleasure'. Shelley compares himself to a worm (twice) and Byron to a god. Six months after they parted, Shelley told Byron on 17 January 1817 that he still felt 'the burden of my own significance and impotence'. Typically, he worried that his poem *The Revolt of Islam* represented an 'involuntary imitation' of Byron's *Corsair*, but equally felt that to highlight his allusion to it 'might justly be considered presumptuous', so he cancelled the note.

Byron never expressed negative feelings about Shelley. He told Douglas Kinnaird, a friend who acted as his financial adviser while he was abroad, on 29 September 1816, that Shelley was 'a very good very clever – but a very singular man – [who] was a great comfort to me here by his intelligence & good nature'.

The 'very singular man' inspired Byron with a fascination for the theme of the double. It also characterised their relationship with one another.

Shelley's Doubles

Doubles enter European consciousness first in German literature, with doppelgängers featuring in works by Schiller, Heine, Goethe and others. Most famously, the theme played a central role in *Faust*. Byron read Madame de Staël's essay on Goethe (and generous extracts from the play) in *De l'Allemagne* in 1813. De Staël claimed that in Christianity, 'the soul's bad impulses are personified as demons'. She was following Goethe's lead. When Margaret hears Mephistopheles whispering to her in church she recognises 'the thoughts that are born in my soul and rise up against me'. When the novelist Matthew Lewis visited Byron between 14 and 19 August 1816 he translated parts of *Faust* to the assembled company. *Faust*'s intellectually questing hero and his Satanic double Mephistopheles inspired Shelley, Mary Shelley's *Frankenstein* and Byron's *Manfred*, the play he worked on that summer.

Matthew Lewis, engraving after G. H. Harlow, Finden.

The double haunts Gothic fiction. 'I was thy slave,' the demonic stranger calls out in Shelley's fragmentary romance of 1814, *The Assassins*; 'I am thine equal and thy foe.'

Shelley's narcissistic vision of life and love relied heavily on the idea of the double. On 23 November 1811 he called his lover Elizabeth Hitchener his 'second self'. 'They were two cousins,' he said of himself and Harriet Grove, 'almost like to twins.' He mistook his first wife for his own 'purer mind' and equated love with 'The discovery of its anti-type', when we 'seek to awaken in all things that are a community with what we experience within ourselves'. The theme recurred obsessively: it emerged strongly in

Alastor (1815), in *Prometheus Unbound* (when Zoroaster 'Met his own apparition walking in the garden'), and drove Shelley's interest in the Spanish dramatist Calderón de la Barca. According to Teresa Guiccioli, Shelley's 'fantasy often caused him to hallucinate; he saw spectres – visions that were now lovely, now disgusting.' Occasionally, he saw visions of himself and he exerted so much influence on his friends that others, including Byron, did so too. Duality and doubles increasingly infest Byron's work, from *The Dream* (written some six weeks after he met Shelley in July 1816 and beginning, 'Our life is two fold'), through *Manfred*, *The Lament of Tasso* and onwards.

Incest is, naturally, the doppelgänger's delight, for Byron, as for Shelley. Manfred's sister Astarte is his double: 'She was like me in lineaments – her eyes,/Her hair, her features, all, to the very tone/Even of her voice, they said were like to mine' Manfred's love reflects Byron's relationship with Augusta, but it also echoes the hero's love for the Veiled Maid in Shelley's *Alastor* ('Her voice was like the voice of my own soul').

While they toured Lake Geneva and its sites of literary pilgrimage, between 23 and 30 June, Shelley 'dosed' Byron 'with Wordsworth physic even to nausea'. He also inspired Byron with his optimistic idealism, which surfaces in *Childe Harold* III and the 'Sonnet on Chillon'. But to Shelley's frustration, Byron soon reverted to fatalistic empiricism in *Manfred*, in *Childe Harold* IV and elsewhere. Shelley lectured him in letters, such as one written on 29 September 1816; he dropped oblique hints in the Preface to the *Revolt of Islam*, in a narrative ('The Coliseum') and in allusive poems (*Lines Written Among the Euganean Hills*; *The Two Spirits: An Allegory*; *Prometheus Unbound*; *Hellas*). Nothing had any effect on Byron.

On the other hand, Shelley would eventually transform Byron's attitude to poetry: Byron's friends in London included several poets but he had never met anyone from his social class who took poetry seriously, who invested it with a moral and political purpose. Shelley valued poetry as the 'most unfailing herald, companion, and follower of the awakening of a great people to work a beneficial change in opinion or institution'. For years Byron refused to accept payment for his writing. Shelley saw himself

Manfred conjures up Astarte, engraved by J. Romney after H. Corbould, The Byron Gallery, *1833.*

as a professional author; he expected to be paid for his work and badgered his publisher about promoting it.

Byron started to rethink his previously dismissive attitude to writing, as opposed to action, when Napoleon lost power in 1814. In Switzerland, two years later, Shelley's fervour and the example of such locally resident 'mighty minds' as 'Rousseau – Voltaire – our Gibbon – and de Staël' convinced Byron to believe in literary heroism.

He began to write his second drama, *Manfred*, before he met Shelley, but the younger man left his mark on the play. For this study, what matters is the moment when the Promethean hero confronts his Satanic double, his 'Genius'. The eponymous hero's intellect and extremism establish him as another 'new Napoleon'. He loathes matter in its literal form, the body, and also in metaphor, as the body politic: he 'had no sympathy with breathing flesh'; in the company of ordinary mortals he felt himself 'degraded back to them,/And was all clay again'. He cannot conceal his disdain for mankind, the 'habitual scorn which could contemn/Men and their thoughts' that Byron called 'just', so he abandons politics – the ambition 'To make my own the mind of other men,/The enlightener of nations'. Byron now felt that Napoleon lost power because he had to rely on his subjects' favour. By turning to the abstract world of science or magic Manfred realises his ambition in a 'tyrant-spell'. But concentrating on the mental world leaves him marooned in isolated self-sufficiency – rather like Napoleon, 'The Captive Usurper', on St Helena.

Fifteen lines after citing Satan, 'The mind is its own place/And makes a heaven of another's hell', Manfred dies spontaneously, without apparent cause. Shelley quotes the same lines in the *Defence of Poetry* he wrote in 1821, but there he insists that 'poetry defeats the curse which binds us to be subjected to the accident of surrounding impressions'; it 'creates for us a being within our being'. Shelley has not yet convinced Byron to share his messianic faith in poetry. Manfred's tragedy, then, is that he cannot respect, let alone write poetry. Bleakly he insists that 'words are breath'.

Thanks to Shelley, Byron would eventually believe in the heroic potential of poetry, so that he could insist in *Don Juan* that 'words are things'.

He first expressed such confidence in his 'Monody' in memory of Richard Brinsley Sheridan, the playwright and Whig politician, who died on 7 July 1816. Byron turned him into a distinctively Byronic/Shelleyan hero, celebrating Sheridan's 'mighty Spirit', 'bright Intelligence', 'immortal mind' and 'Powers of Mind almost of boundless range'. As a parliamentarian Sheridan was 'the delegated voice of God'; as a dramatist, his characters, 'These wondrous beings of his fancy wrought/To fullness by the fiat of his Thought', reflect his 'Promethean heat'. That may also betray Shelley's tutelary impact: he read Byron his translation of Aeschylus's play *Prometheus Bound* in 1816.

Prometheus Reborn

That summer of 1816 Byron, Shelley and Mary Wollstonecraft Godwin adopted Prometheus as their model, as the 'Champion . . . of mankind', in Shelley's words. Prometheus stole fire from the gods of ancient Greece and gave it to men. Punished by Jove, the ruler or father of the gods, he remained chained to a rock, 'where a vulture continually devoured his liver, that grew to meet its hunger', through all eternity.

The figure of Prometheus fascinated both poets, long before they met. In 1812 Shelley had interpreted the myth in dietary terms, to support his argument in favour of vegetarianism: fire enabled man to eat meat, but as a result he suffered indigestion (the vulture attacking his liver). As a schoolboy, Byron told John Murray on 12 October 1817, he was 'passionately fond' of Aeschylus's play on the subject. He translated a chorus into English verse

Henry Fuseli, Prometheus, *1770–71. Kunstmuseum Basel, Kupferstichkabinett. Photo: Kunstmuseum Basel, Martin P. Bühler*

as the first exercise that his headmaster set him. Though it 'was received by him but coolly', Byron included it in all his early volumes of verse, dated 1 December 1804. In 1814 Byron rebuked Napoleon for not living up to Prometheus's heroic example. In *The Age of Bronze*, however, written in 1822–3, Byron allows Napoleon to be Prometheus.

In the spring of 1817 Byron wrote that the sculpture of Apollo Belvedere, that 'poetic marble', showed its creator had 'repaid' the fire 'Prometheus stole from Heaven'. In 1819 in *The Prophecy of Dante* the poet is 'the new Prometheus of new men/Bestowing fire from heaven'. Aeschylus's play had an obvious influence on *Manfred*, as Byron admitted to Murray in that same letter of 12 October 1817. In his new poem 'Prometheus' (which Shelley carried to England at the end of the summer), Byron interpreted the gift of fire to suit his obsession with man's dualism: 'Thy Godlike crime was to be kind,/. . . And strengthen Man with his own mind'. His Prometheus sounds rather like Shelley.

Mary Shelley could not share Byron and Shelley's optimism. Her *Modern Prometheus*, as she subtitled *Frankenstein*, is the only version to interpret the myth negatively: Frankenstein regrets giving his creation life but dies before he can kill him. She began it that 'wet, ungenial summer', as they 'crowded around a blazing wood fire', prompted by Byron's suggestion that they should each try to write a ghost story. Byron abandoned 'Augustus Darvel', but it starts to outline a classic, Byronic double relationship, which pivots on the familiar patron/protégé axis, between an initiate and a novice. Polidori 'vamped [it] up' and published it as *The Vampyre* in 1819.

All that survives of Shelley's attempt is eight lines of verse, 'Fragment of a Ghost Story' and some lines in 'Hymn to Intellectual Beauty'. But his *Prometheus Unbound* (published August 1820) seems to answer *Manfred*, in that it resolves the parental tension underlying the poets' intimacy, predicting that Jove, the father of the gods, will be overthrown by his son. Byron and Shelley's literary output looks like a sparring match between doubles. Each work reflects a different dynamic in that shifting relationship. We focus in this book on Byron's side. But a third person wrote the first work to see the light.

Illustration to The Vampire, *probably reflecting its London staging, November 1820.*
Private collection

Round I: *Frankenstein*

We are unfashioned creatures, but half made up, if one wiser, better, dearer than ourselves – such [as] a friend ought to be – do not lend his aid to perfectionate our weak and faulty natures.

R. Walton to Mrs Saville, 13 August 17–,
Frankenstein, Vol. One, Letter IV, 27f.

Theodore Von Holst, frontispiece to Frankenstein, *1831, showing the double nature of creator and creature.*

William Godwin's wife died in giving birth to Mary. Afterwards he always kept his distance from his daughter. Fatherhood obsessed her. She even acknowledged her 'excessive & romantic attachment' to Godwin. She gave his first name to her son, who was born on 24 January 1816, dedicated *Frankenstein* to her father and reused his name for the child that the creature murders.

Her first two stories, *Frankenstein* and *Mathilda*, portray the perils of parenting, as though on opposed panels of a diptych. Frankenstein rejects the being he has created, before that creature does anything at all, stigmatising him as 'the wretch – the miserable monster', merely because he is 'hideous' and 'ugly'. Frankenstein fails to recognise his creation as a 'spirit of good', his 'guiding spirit', who repeatedly saves his life. The creature rightly blames his 'father' for turning him into 'a fiend'. And yet a close parental bond, a father who lives alone with his daughter, or with his wife who is young enough to be his daughter, recurs six times in *Frankenstein*.

In her next story, which Mary Shelley wrote in 1819, Mathilda persuades her father to confess his incestuous love for her. Mary sent the manuscript to Godwin. He never returned it. *Mathilda* remained unpublished until 1959.

Portrait identified as Mary Shelley, attributed to Richard Rothwell. The Bodleian Libraries, University of Oxford, Shelley relics 39

Byron fascinated Mary. He became her protector in reality (after Shelley's death) but also in her fiction: he appears as Lord Raymond, Protector of England, in her novel *The Last Man* (1826). She recorded her 'unsuccessful attempt to find in Shelley a father-substitute in *Mathilda*'s exquisitely beautiful but limp poet Woodville'. In her later novels Shelley repeatedly emerges as 'frail, effeminate, boyish or ineffectual . . . twice pictured as a woman' and as an inadequate foil to the 'thoroughly masculine Byron, the father, foster father, lover or husband of Mary'. And that was written in 1951, eight years before *Mathilda* was published.

Given the pattern of her later writings, I suggest that *Frankenstein* preserves Mary Shelley's early, inchoate, but prophetic insights into the tensions behind the two poets' intimacy. It's not a *roman à clef*, however; there are no simple equivalences.

Readers have long recognised that Victor Frankenstein incorporates aspects of Shelley, who used the name Victor and described researching into decaying corpses, as Frankenstein does. Frankenstein learns about electricity and galvanism from a 'most violent and terrible thunderstorm'. Shelley was fascinated by lightning and electricity. As a child he bought a generator and conducted literally hair-raising experiments on himself, his sisters, the servants and the local tom-cat, which he attached to an 'electrical kite' and flew, during a thunderstorm.

Frankenstein's monster had a 'loud and fiendish laugh'. It 'rang on my ears long and heavily', Victor Frankenstein remarks, '. . . and I felt as if all hell surrounded me with mockery and laughter'. Shelley's laugh was notorious. He greeted the news of his expulsion from Oxford with a 'loud, half-hysteric laugh'. On his first honeymoon, in Edinburgh in 1811, passers-by reprimanded him when he 'laughed aloud, with a fiendish laugh' out in the street – on the Sabbath. He even 'burst into a shrieking laugh' when he attended a Presbyterian Catechism class. In October 1819, having read a long, well-informed and vindictive attack on him, 'Shelley burst into a convulsive laughter, closed the book with an hysteric laugh, and hastily left the room, his Ha! Ha's ringing down the stairs.' Shelley 'laughed like a giant, as he used to say', which exposed his bad teeth. His 'intolerably shrill, harsh, and discordant' voice heightened its impact. He had no sense of humour, his friend James Hogg and Teresa Guiccioli agreed.

On the other hand, *Frankenstein* may also pay tribute to Byron's celebrated laugh. 'Of all the peculiarities of B.,' Hobhouse reflected, 'his laugh is that of which I have the most distinct recollection.' Leigh Hunt evoked Byron's 'kind of goblin laugh, breathing and grinning, as if, instead of his handsome mouth, he had one like an ogre, from ear to ear'.

'Treat a person ill, and he will become wicked.' Shelley identified that as *Frankenstein*'s 'direct moral', when he reviewed it anonymously: '. . . divide him, a social being from society, and you impose upon him the irresistible obligations – malevolence and selfishness. It is thus that, too often in society, those who are best qualified to be its benefactors and its ornaments, are branded by some accident with scorn, and changed, by neglect and solitude of heart, into a scourge and a curse.'

Was Shelley referring to himself, as a recent biographer has suggested? But the doubt-free, un-self-critical Shelley could never think of himself as wicked, malevolent, selfish; as a scourge or curse? No, he was surely alluding to Byron. Rejected by his mother, and vilified by the British press, Byron certainly felt divided from society and complained that he was 'treated ill'. As a peer, he alone was 'best qualified to be' its benefactor and ornament; he was also far more egregiously 'branded . . . with scorn, and changed, by neglect and solitude of heart, into a scourge and a curse'. Shelley had read Byron's curse in *Childe Harold* IV and the scourging 'Incantation', which Byron published in *The Prisoner of Chillon and Other Poems* (and imported into *Manfred*).

Frankenstein's 'direct moral' seemed familiar: Milton's Satan was the great exemplar of a victim treated badly who went to the bad, as William Godwin pointed out in 1793 in his *Enquiry Concerning Political Justice*. *Paradise Lost* supplies the epigraph to *Frankenstein* and is one of only three books that the creature reads. In 1816 only Byron was widely identified with Satan. Lady Caroline Lamb's *roman à clef Glenarvon* (1816) reached Switzerland that summer. Byron appears in the title role as 'that arch fiend', 'the fallen angel'. In dying he restages Lucifer's fall almost word for word. Shelley was still too obscure a poet to warrant demonisation.

In any case, Mary Shelley consistently refers to Milton's Satan to identify the Byronic character in her later novels. By 1836 her novels had featured so many glamorous, Satanic noblemen that Claire Clairmont dreaded reading about 'another beautified Byron'. Mary Shelley was already toying with an ideal, doting, paternal Byron in her second story, *Mathilda*. As soon as the heroine's father declares his passion for his daughter, that 'man of rank' feels that he has become a Satanic 'Monster' and is as 'changed in mien as the fallen archangel'.

In *Frankenstein* both the creator and his creature identify themselves with Milton's Satan. The doubling reinforces its portrait of an intimate, destructive relationship. Readers reflect this aspect when they carelessly refer to Frankenstein and mean the 'monster'. The novel blends traits from Byron and Shelley in both figures: Victor loves his sister and has Byron's low voice; the monster shares Shelley's political naiveté. When Frankenstein considers 'the being . . . nearly in the light of my own vampire, my own spirit let loose from the grave, and forced to destroy all that was dear to me', it may suggest that he has read *The Giaour*.

Mary Shelley traced the origins of *Frankenstein* to the poets' conversations about 'the nature of the principle of life'. I suggest that the dialogue itself, as much as its subject, inspired her. 'Many and long were the conversations between Lord Byron and Shelley,' she recorded, 'to which I was a devout but nearly silent listener.' 'Since incapacity and timidity always prevented my mingling in the nightly conversations of Diodati, they were, as it were, entirely tête-à-tête between my Shelley and Albe [LB = Lord Byron].' Shelley, 'an eager, bold and unwearied disputant' (as Hogg said), described Maddalo's (Byron's) 'more serious conversation' as 'a sort of intoxication; men are held by it as by a spell'. According to Leigh Hunt, 'there is reason to believe, that Lord Byron never talked with any man to so much purpose' as he did with Shelley. In Mary Shelley's *The Last Man*, Adrian (Shelley) 'had the superiority in learning and eloquence; but Raymond [Byron] possessed a quick penetration, and a practical knowledge of life, which usually displayed itself in opposition to Adrian, and thus kept up the ball of discussion.'

From this point of view, then, *Frankenstein* represents the first major double portrait in a series of conversations, dialogues and oppositions, round one in the poets' sparring match, since only Byron's fragment 'Augustus Darvel' and parts of *Manfred* preceded it. In its wake followed Shelley's *Julian and Maddalo*; Byron's *Don Juan*; Shelley's *Prometheus Unbound* and his translation of two scenes from *Faust*; Byron's *Cain*, *The Deformed Transformed* and *The Island*, as well as comparatively minor poems such as *The Prisoner of Chillon* and *The Lament of Tasso*, and the later novels of Mary Shelley.

Most are haunted by Milton's Satan, who was (as Shelley said in the Preface to *Prometheus Unbound*), 'the only imaginary being resembling in any degree Prometheus'.

After Shelley left on 29 August 1816 the poets did not meet for two

George Cruikshank's illustration to The Prisoner of Chillon, *10 July 1824, from* Forty Illustrations of Lord Byron, *1824.*

years. But Shelley told Byron on 11 September that he felt 'a deep interest in everything' that concerned him. Distance sanctioned generosity: he encouraged Byron's ambitions from England on 29 September: 'I hope for no more than that you should . . . feel that you are chosen out from all other men to some greater enterprise of thought; and that all your studies should, from that moment, tend towards that enterprise alone.'

Claire Clairmont gave birth to Byron's illegitimate daughter on 12 January 1817, in Bath, which had consequences for the poets' relationship. The Shelleys looked after the unmarried mother and her baby, but their anomalous presence threatened the Shelleys' tenuous hold on respectability. After Shelley's first wife Harriet committed suicide on 9 November 1816 the Lord Chancellor deprived him of his rights to their children, because of his atheistical writings, his views on marriage and his conduct. On the same basis, Shelley and Mary could lose custody of *their* children, William and Clara Everina. On 23 April 1817 Shelley invited Byron to return to England and acknowledge his paternity. Byron ignored this proposal. But he decided to 'acknowledge & breed' his child in Italy. Claire agreed to give up her daughter, so as not to 'deprive her of a brilliant position in life'. Shelley and Mary resolved to accompany Claire and her baby to Italy and then live there.

Claire believed Byron had promised that he himself would look after their daughter, at least until the child reached the age of seven. Hearing that he had broken his word she persuaded Shelley to accompany her to Venice. When they met, Byron took Shelley to the Lido to ride along the sand and they did not part until five the next morning. Shelley told Mary on 23 August that their conversation consisted of 'histories of his wounded feelings & questions as to my affairs, & great professions of friendship & regard for me'. Since they last met, Shelley had published several major works, such as 'Hymn to Intellectual Beauty', *Laon and Cythna* (written in the Spenserian stanza form that *Childe Harold* had already inspired Shelley to use in 'On leaving England for Wales'), 'Ozymandias' and two prose pamphlets. None attracted as much attention as his wife's first novel *Frankenstein*.

Amelia Curran's portrait of Claire Clairmont, 1819. Byron called Claire 'that odd-headed girl – who introduced herself to me . . . I never loved her or pretended to love her – but a man is a man.' Shelley remarked on her 'insensibility & incapacity for the slightest degree of friendship'.
Courtesy of Nottingham City Museums and Galleries

Round II: *Julian and Maddalo*

Shelley was probably wrestling with his feelings about Byron in the fragmentary *Prince Athanase*, which he worked on in 1817. He was surely referring to Byron when he evoked, 'a child of fortune and of power,/Of an ancestral name the orphan chief', associated him with the Alps and compared him to an eagle.

In 1818 Shelley wove aspects of his relationship with Byron into a labyrinthine poem, *Julian and Maddalo: A Conversation*. It begins as a jaunty, anecdotal record of the poets' evening rides, ringing with 'aerial merriment

... laughter ... glee'. The only ominous note is struck by the remark that their talk, 'forlorn/Yet pleasing' about 'God, freewill and destiny', was such as once 'The devils held within the dales of Hell' – an inflammatory allusion to *Paradise Lost*. Convivial conversation returns at the end of the poem: Julian longs to stay in Venice, 'where I might sit/In Maddalo's great palace, and his wit/And subtle talk would cheer the winter night/And make me know myself'. But the poem's central section covers the friends' visit to a mad man and his long, wild monologue. Civilised dialogues frame and contrast with his outburst. It is tempting to focus on the frame and pass over the centre. But that is to ignore 34 per cent of the poem.

Julian and Maddalo represents Shelley's answer to Byron, above all to the *Lament of Tasso* (written in a day; published in July 1817), which made the younger poet weep. He named his Byronic Maddalo after a friend of Tasso (who betrayed him) and he reused verses from his own (unfinished) drama on Tasso's incarceration. The poem's broken sections, separated by crosses, repeat the *Giaour*'s fragmentation. *Julian and Maddalo* reads like Byron's *Lara*, which Shelley greatly admired, as another eloquent exercise in *not* revealing the truth. The maniac's intrusion unbalances the poem. But it authenticates its portrait of the poets' uneasy intimacy. Does the maniac represent Shelley (another disappointed, radical idealist), Byron himself or, perhaps, a composite: the Byronic hero who was a Shelleyan idealist? Perhaps he is what is left out from civilised, witty discourse, the shadow cast by the conjunction of Byron and Shelley?

Shelley's ambivalence towards Byron surfaced soon after they parted. He celebrated Byron's 'Mighty Spirit' in 'Lines written among the Euganean Hills', comparing his residence in Venice to Petrarch's at Arqua and Shakespeare's at Stratford. But 'Stanzas Written in Dejection – December 1818, Near Naples' highlights the poets' differences. It refers implicitly to Byron as one of those people who live surrounded by fame, power, love and leisure: 'Smiling they live and call life pleasure' – unlike, we may assume, Shelley. On 22 December Shelley told Thomas Love Peacock that he blamed the weaknesses and excessive gloom of *Childe Harold* IV on Byron's promiscuous association with Italian women, 'perhaps the

Shelley, from a draft of Julian and Maddalo:

> *We descanted; and I (for ever still*
> *Is it not wise to make the best of ill?)*
> *Argued against despondency, but pride*
> *Made my companion take the darker side.*
> *The sense that he was greater than his kind*
> *Had struck, methinks, his eagle spirit blind*
> *By gazing on its own exceeding light.*
> *Meanwhile the sun paused ere it should alight,*
> *Over the horizon of the mountains. Oh,*
> *How beautiful is sunset, when the glow*
> *Of Heaven descends upon a land like thee,*
> *Thou Paradise of exiles, Italy!*

The Bodleian Libraries, University of Oxford, MS. Shelley adds. e. 11, p. 65 most contemptible of all who exist under the moon; the most ignorant, the most disgusting, the most bigoted, the most filthy'. What motivated this outburst? Could it be jealousy of Byron's dogged promiscuity? As for Byron's male companions, they were 'wretches who seem almost to have lost the gait and physiognomy of man, & who do not scruple to avow practices which are not only not named but I believe seldom even conceived in England. He says he disapproves, but he endures. He is not yet an Italian & is heartily & deeply discontented with himself, & contemplating in the distorted mirror of his own thoughts, the nature & destiny of man, what can he behold but objects of contempt & despair?' Shelley's revulsion points to the 'distorted mirror of his own thoughts'. It echoes his short-lived discovery 'how much of the colouring our own feelings throw upon the liveliest delineations of other minds'. He may also have been motivated by 'unconscious homosexuality'.

That autumn of 1818 Byron began to compose *Don Juan*, a 'conversation' like *Julian and Maddalo*, one that glories in the 'greater enterprise of thought' that Shelley urged on him. It also embodies another round in the poets' sparring: Byron incorporates aspects of Shelley into his portrait of Juan as a young idealist, in opposition to his own performance as the worldly-wise Narrator.

23

THE SUN versus THE GLOW-WORM, 1821–3

After three years apart, when he was feeling lonely in Ravenna, Byron invited Shelley on 26 April 1821 to 'take a run here *alone*'. Shelley responded on 16 July but he warily used the word 'invading' and asked, 'Are you sure a visit would not annoy you?' He sent Byron his new poem *Adonais*, in which he portrayed himself as a persecuted victim, whose 'branded and ensanguined brow . . . was like Christ's or Cain's'. That same day, 16 July, Byron started to write *Cain*, the play he had been contemplating since 28 January. The coincidence seemed to manifest the poets' closeness.

Byron and Shelley continued to explore the theme of the double in works that reflect increasing tensions in their intimacy, intense rivalry as well as respect. Both men dramatise their reactions; only Shelley expresses his dissatisfaction in letters.

Robert Southey attacked Byron as a leader of the 'Satanic school' of poetry in the Preface to *The Vision of Judgement*, published in April 1821. Byron was, perhaps surprisingly, annoyed – after all, Southey had a point – and, less surprisingly, undeterred: his new play *Cain* portrayed Lucifer as an impressive intellectual with a deft line in cogent reasoning. It looked as though Byron gloried in Southey's charge. Satanism became common ground for Shelley and Byron, a fit arena for their sparring. They shared an interest in the devil, before they met: Shelley was inspired by Coleridge and Southey's satire 'The Devil's Thoughts' (first published in 1799), to compose 'The Devil's Walk' in 1812. Having heard that the poor in Devon were rioting from hunger Shelley rushed there, intending to distribute his satire in bottles and by balloons. It is not known whether that helped. Byron was inspired by the same poem to write a 'wild, rambling unfinished rhapsody', 'The Devil's Drive' on 8 December 1813.

The Demon of Mistrust & of Pride

Shelley and Byron met in Ravenna on 6 August 1821 and again talked through the night. Byron's moral improvement impressed Shelley and, he told Teresa Guiccioli on 22 August, he attributed it to her, as Byron's 'good Angel', as well as to his commitment to the Italians' fight for independence (my translation). But by the next morning the friends had 'as usual . . . differed', Shelley told Mary on 7 August, adding ' & I think more than ever.'

Byron read Shelley Canto V from *Don Juan*, which Shelley welcomed, partly because it showed Byron had listened to him: 'It fulfils, in a certain degree, what I have long preached of producing,' Shelley told Byron on 21 October 1821, '– something wholly new and relative to the age, and yet surpassingly beautiful.' Shelley's enthusiasm for *Don Juan* distinguished him from nearly all Byron's friends. But it took its toll: 'I despair of rivalling Lord Byron, as well I may,' he confessed to Mary on 10 August: 'and there is no other with whom it is worth contending.'

Shelley felt almost beaten down by 'the severe reproof of public neglect'. From under the shadow of Byron's presence, he confessed to his friend Thomas Love Peacock around 10 August, 'I write nothing, and probably shall write no more. It offends me to see my name classed among those who have no name.' Byron, of course, had a great name: Murray paid Moore '*two thousand pounds*' (Shelley's italics) to publish Byron's memoirs.

Shelley recognised that 'The demon of mistrust & of pride lurks between two persons in our situation poisoning the freedom of their intercourse.' He was right about the lurking demon but obtuse: 'I think the fault is not on my side,' he told Mary on 10 August; 'nor is it likely, I being the weaker.'

Shelley stayed two weeks. Byron never mentioned Shelley's *Adonais* (published July 1821); he did not admire its subject, Keats, and doubted

Murray commissioned this signet ring with a cornelian engraved with a profile of Byron and used it to seal letters to the author, who complained that it showed 'a Saracen's head'. Murray admitted it was 'vile' in a reply of 30 January 1821.

Private collection

that the *Quarterly*'s bad review had caused his early death. Byron censured Shelley's play *The Cenci* (published 1819) but he praised *Prometheus Unbound* (published August 1820). Two weeks after Shelley left, Byron completed *Cain*, his drama about the intercourse of two persons, one of whom is the devil. As he worked on it Byron may well have remembered how Shelley identified his Prometheus with Satan and with Christ.

Round III: *Cain*

> Are these people more impious than Milton's Satan? –
> or the Prometheus of Æeschylus?
>
> Byron defending *Cain*, to John Murray, 3 November 1821

Byron rarely talked about his relationship with Shelley. But *Cain* seems to embody his private feelings about the strengths and dangers of their intimacy. Byron's Lucifer is not Shelley's 'demon of mistrust & of pride', but he sounds unlike any other Byronic character. He has affinities with Shelley's Ahasuerus in *Queen Mab* – and, indeed, with Shelley himself.

Adam's son Cain feels that his family does not understand 'The *mind* which overwhelms' him; he would rather 'consort with *spirits*'; it is his '*soul*' that makes him 'fit . . ./For . . . companionship' with Lucifer. This devil personifies Cain's mind, which makes him his double or doppelgänger. 'Nothing can/Quench the mind,' Lucifer tells Cain, 'if the mind will be itself/ And centre of surrounding things – 'tis made/To sway'. The critic Francis Jeffrey in the *Edinburgh Review* recognised this at once, calling Lucifer 'little more than the personified demon of his [Cain's] imagination'. Lucifer opens Cain's eyes to dualism, the way that man's 'high thought' is 'Link'd to a servile mass of matter'. So he's like Lara, who 'charged all faults upon the fleshly form/. . . Till he at last confounded good and ill'. In effect, the devil preaches Calvinist dogma, while he urges man to use his '*reason*: – let it not be over-sway'd/By tyrannous threats to force you into faith/'Gainst all external sense and inward feeling'.

Cain practises what Lucifer preaches when he questions the dictates of God, the cruel, incomprehensible 'Parent of all things'. Cain tests the presumption (central to Christianity) that man is redeemed by sacrifice. He invites God to choose Abel's sacrifice of lambs – 'If thou lov'st blood'. Cain himself offers up fruit, 'a shrine without victim,/And altar without gore'.God's response is, for Him, unusually easy to read: '*The fire upon the altar of ABEL kindles into a column of the brightest flame, and ascends to heaven; while a whirlwind throws down the altar of CAIN, and scatters the fruits abroad upon the earth.*'

Cain is appalled to see 'How heav'n licks up the flames, when thick with blood!' He repeats the word 'blood' five more times before he tries to destroy Abel's altar and, prevented, instead kills his brother. He is not motivated by envy; in effect, he follows the example set by a bloodthirsty, even a carnivorous God.

This is clearly not what Calvinism taught.

Presbyterians in eighteenth-century Scotland (including Byron) were taught that Cain's harvest sacrifice dissatisfied God 'not because of its crudeness but rather because of its deceitfulness': 'his sacrifice is not genuine; Cain does not give of himself and thus his gesture toward God is empty of meaning.'

Cain certainly reflects Shelley's influence – as Moore and others recognised at once, in the way that it promotes vegetarianism; alludes to scientific issues; conceives of a phantasmic doubling of the world; and alternates between blank verse and prose. Lucifer's aerial tour of the Abyss of Space echoes the journey of Ianthe's spirit in *Queen Mab*. Byron evidently worried that his debt to Shelley seemed obvious. He felt obliged to specify that Shelley's 'opinions and mine differ materially upon the metaphysical portion' of *Queen Mab*. He wrote that in a note he attached to the appendix to his (un-Shelleyan) play *The Two Foscari*. And perhaps that suggests why he insisted on publishing that play with *Cain*.

In *Cain*'s Preface Byron follows Genesis in arguing that a serpent tempted Eve, not a demon. Lucifer repeats that 'The snake was the snake –/ No more' and goes on about it for over fifty lines. Goethe's Mephistopheles mentions 'my cousin the serpent'. But Byron's devil is surely referring to Shelley's remarkable essay, 'On the Devil and Devils' (probably written in November 1819), which blames Christianity for inventing Satan. Byron was returning a compliment: that essay cites *Manfred* and refers to Byron as 'a great modern poet'.

Shelley's essay wasn't published until 1880, but Byron must have read it in manuscript as he alluded to it in one of his 'Detached Thoughts', which he started to compile in Ravenna in October 1820.

Cain's journey through space owes much to Shelley's résumé of recent scientific speculation 'respecting the bounds of the Universe' in that essay 'On the Devil and Devils'.

Is there even more of Shelley in *Cain*? Does Byron perhaps portray his friend as Lucifer? Shelley's exceptionally 'acute intellect' convinced his friend the lawyer Thomas Hogg that he would have been 'a great benefactor to the world', if only he had studied law, 'instead of writing nonsensical rhapsodies'. As for Lucifer's contempt for matter, Shelley's 'brain absorbed him', Trelawny remembered; 'he put his whole strength into his mind.

Abel prepares to sacrifice a lamb in a detail from the sixth-century mosaics in San Vitale, in Ravenna. Abel's striking, crimson cloak hints at his patriarchal status and at his sacrificial fate. The theme of sacrifice dominates the mosaics around the altar. Byron arrived in Ravenna on 24 December 1820 and began to think about the subject of Cain and Abel on 4 January 1821.

Illustration, from George Cruikshank, Forty Illustrations of Lord Byron, *14 January, 1825.*

The body he looked upon as a self-acting piece of mechanism . . . his intellectual faculties completely mastered his material nature.'

Byron certainly represented himself as the questioning, independently minded outsider Cain – married to his twin sister Adah; dazzled and carried through the air by the demon, as the hero was transported in the story Byron loved and imitated, Le Sage's *Le diable boiteux*.

Cain and Lucifer surely recreate aspects of the poets' impassioned dialogues and friendship. Trelawny, who observed them together, said that Shelley 'never laid aside his book and magic mantle; he waved his

Frontispiece to Byron's Cain, from a rare pirated edition of 1821, not in Thomas J. Wise's bibliography or the British Library catalogue. Lucifer flies Cain into the Abyss of Space, from where he can see the Earth. Byron recreates his favourite sensation of bodiless flight, which he first encountered in Le diable boiteux*.*
Private collection

wand, and Byron, after a faint show of defiance, stood mute; . . . Shelley's earnestness and just criticism held him captive.' Medwin observed that 'Shelley was what Byron could not be, a close, logical, and subtle reasoner.' Byron 'listened to [Shelley] with pleasure', according to Teresa Guiccioli, 'not only on account of Shelley's good faith and sincerity of meaning, but also because he argued upon false data with such talent and originality that he was both interested and amused'.

Few people read *Cain* now, without the incentive of study or teaching. Knowing that Byron wrote Shelley into *Cain*, does it make the play any better? No, Lucifer disappears from view at the end of Act II, leaving Cain alone amid alien, orthodox characters.

Cain roused Shelley to rapture in a letter to John Gisborne of 12 January 1822: 'Space wondered less at the swift and fair creations of God, when he grew weary of vacancy, than I at the late works of this spirit of an angel in the mortal paradise of a decaying body.' Byron was now an 'angel', as he had been a 'God' (in 'If I esteemed thee less'). Shelley's language betrays his immersion in *Cain*. On 26 January he insisted that Byron's latest volume (which included *Cain*) 'contains finer poetry than has appeared in England since the publication of Paradise Regained. – Cain is apocalyptic – it is a revelation not before communicated to man.'

In Ravenna that summer of 1821 Byron and Shelley decided to collaborate on a new journal and agreed that Leigh Hunt would edit it. Ominously, however, when Shelley proposed the idea to Hunt on 26 August he refused to share in the journal's profits and 'still less in the borrowed splendour, of such a partnership'.

After Shelley had left for Pisa, Byron wrote a 'mere buffoonery', *The Blues*, in which he laughed at fashionable literature. Lady Bluebottle (Lady Holland) announces over luncheon (cold tongue and Madeira): 'I/Now feel such a rapture, I'm ready to fly'. Inkel (Byron) makes a joke of it, telling Tracy (Moore) to 'open the window', but Botherby encourages her:

BOTHERBY: 'tis an impulse which lifts
Our spirits from earth – the sublimest of gifts;
For which poor Prometheus was chained to his mountain.
'Tis the source of all sentiment – feeling's true fountain;
'Tis the Vision of Heaven upon Earth: 'tis the gas
Of the soul: 'tis the seizing of shades as they pass,
And making them substance: 'tis something divine:–
INKEL: Shall I help you, my friend, to a little more wine?

Botherby is always taken to mean William Sotheby, but Byron was surely also laughing covertly at Shelley, at his transcendentalism, his scientific interests and his enthusiastic Platonism. The reference to Prometheus shows how Byron could be facetious at his own expense. Shelley would not have seen the joke.

Byron left for Pisa on 29 October to join Teresa Guiccioli, her brother and her father, liberals who had been banished from papal territory. In Pisa Shelley was at the centre of a bohemian community of British and

Bust of Byron by Lorenzo Bartolini, 1822: 'The bust does not turn out a very good one,' Byron told Murray on 23 September 1822, '– though it may be like for aught I know – as it exactly resembles a superannuated Jesuit,' adding, 'I can not be long for this world – for it overlooks seventy.'
© National Portrait Gallery, London

Irish expatriates – until Byron usurped his place. Five weeks after Byron arrived, Shelley complained to Claire that he felt ill at ease 'in so large a society'. His nerves were 'generally shaken to pieces' at Byron's dinners, he told Horace Smith on 25 January 1822, 'sitting up contemplating the rest making themselves vats of claret, etc., till three o'clock in the morning'. Shelley's friend Edward Williams recorded the change three weeks later in his journal: 'Lord Byron is the very spirit of this place.' Their lives now ran to a Byronic schedule: late rising, pistol shooting or, if it rained, reading or billiards, followed by late dinners (for the men alone).

A silver Tuscan coin with a bullet embedded: 'This bullet was fired by Byron into the Tuscan silver dollar from a distance of 21 yards in the garden of the Casa Lanfranchi, his house in Pisa . . . Given by Byron to John Cam Hobhouse; bequeathed to his nephew Stuart Hobhouse; given by him to H. Panmure Gordon.' Byron recorded 'it was my luck to split walking-sticks, wafers, half-crowns, shillings, and even the eye of a walking-stick, at twelve paces, with a single bullet – and all by eye and calculation; for my hand is not steady, and apt to change with the very weather.'

Photo: Harrow School and the Harrow School Archive

Shelley certainly resented being sidelined by Byron's genius and his egotism. He told Leigh Hunt on 2 March 1822 that 'particular dispositions in Lord B's character, render the close and exclusive intimacy with him in which I find myself, intolerable to me.' He blamed Byron when he could make no headway with projects such as his new play: 'Pride, that ruined Satan, will kill *Charles the First*,' Shelley told his publisher Charles Ollier on 25 September 1821, 'for his midwife would be only less than him whom thunder has made greater.' His knotted syntax betrays his congested emotions. Once again Shelley casts Byron as God. He uses *Paradise Lost* to identify himself with Satan, following Byron's initiative in *Cain*.

Round IV: *Faust*

That autumn of 1821 Shelley studied Goethe's *Faust* in German and translated the two boldest scenes into English, the potentially blasphemous 'Prologue in Heaven' and the 'Witches' Sabbath'. Shelley made Mephistopheles sound rather like Byron and may have portrayed himself as Faust.

Early in December Byron returned the demonic compliment. As Shelley read aloud from his translation he came to Mephistopheles' reference to the snake that tempted Eve. He had dealt with it in his essay; Byron had discussed it in *Cain*. Now, as 'a buffoonery', Byron insisted that Shelley was 'nothing but one of her Nephews – walking about on the tip of his tail'. And from then on, Trelawny recorded, Byron called Shelley 'the Snake; his bright eyes, slim figure, and noiseless movements, strengthened, if they did not suggest, the comparison'.

Shelley even adopted Byron's nickname in his letter to Byron of 13 December 1821 and in his poetry ('The serpent is shut out from Paradise'). At least the snake improved on his previous image for himself as a worm (in his sonnet 'To Byron' and in the 'Letter to Maria Gisborne', dated 1 July 1820). But in any case the worm died: 'I do not write,' he told Horace Smith around 21 May 1822, '– I have lived too long near Lord Byron & the sun has extinguished the glowworm.'

At Byron's request Murray sent him *Retzsch's Series of Twenty-Six*

Outlines Illustrative of Goethe's Tragedy of Faust, Engraved from the Originals by Henry Moses. And an Analysis of the Tragedy, 1820. It had arrived by 12 January 1822, when Shelley mentioned it – just before he enthused about Byron's Faustian/Shelleyan drama *Cain*.

The anonymous 'Analysis' that accompanied Retzsch's illustrations highlighted the play's doubling: it recommended the reader 'to consider Faust and Mephistopheles as *one* person, represented symbolically, only in a two-fold shape'.

While he translated scenes from Goethe's play Shelley explored *Faust*'s relation to doppelgänger themes in plays by Calderón, including *El Magico Prodigioso*, which, he told John Gisborne on 10 April 1822, depicted 'a relationship between demon and hero similar to that between Mephistopheles and Faust'.

The theme of the double also dominates Byron's last two plays. On 21 December 1821 he started once again to dramatise the story that he had been thinking about for almost twenty years, Harriet Lee's 'The German's Tale, or Kruitzner'. He finished the play, *Werner*, on 20 January 1822, two days before his thirty-fourth birthday.

Lee's original story already featured a double, in Conrad's intense relationship with a devoted, swarthy Hungarian. Byron brings the doubling into the family: Werner's son Ulric is a 'busy devil!' who is also his father's 'guardian angel!'

Lee's Frederick discovers that his son Conrad murdered Stralenheim, his rival for the succession to his father's title. Conrad admits the crime but blames his father: '*who* aided the mischief-stirring spirit within me, by showing me a specious probity, secured only by an infirmity of nerves . . . is it so wonderful that *I* should dare to act what *you* dared to think?' This is unfair: Frederick never considered killing Stralenheim.

In Byron's play Werner wishes he had murdered (rather than merely robbed) Stralenheim. And he must face the fact that his son acted out the wish, which he repressed. 'Is it strange,' Ulric asks his father, 'That I should *act* what you could *think*?' Father and son recreate *Cain*'s double relationship between a man and his spirit.

Moritz Retzsch's illustration of 1820 shows Faust embracing Margaret in the summer house, watched by Mephistopheles and Martha. Shelley was 'never satiated with looking at' Retzsch's illustrations but he only dared to glance once at this picture: he told John Gisborne on 10 April 1822 that just touching the back of the page on which it appeared made his 'brains swim round'. He read Faust *'over & over again, & always with the same sensations which no other composition excites. It deepens the gloom & augments the rapidity of the ideas, & would therefore seem to be an unfit study for any person who is a prey to the reproaches of memory, & the delusions of an imagination not to be restrained.' Memory may have reproached Shelley with his 'Margaret': his first wife Harriet was pregnant when he left her. Harriet then committed suicide.*

Private collection

Round V: *The Don Juan*

In January 1822 Shelley and Edward Williams decided to commission the building of a boat. They took advice from Edward John Trelawny, a corsair, adventurer and fantasist who came to Pisa to meet his idol, Byron. 'He sleeps with the poem [*The Corsair*] under his pillow,' Byron told Teresa,

EDWARD JOHN TRELAWNY
From a sketch by Seymour Kirkup

'and all his past adventures and present manners aim at this personification.' Disillusioned by Byron's ironic reality, Trelawny then devoted himself to Shelley, who happily incarnated 'the ideal of what a poet should be'.

Shelley and Williams ordered a 30-foot yacht. Characteristically, Byron then commissioned a rather larger schooner.

Shelley bought Williams out of their boat. Byron ordered that DON JUAN was 'painted on the mainsail, and she arrived thus disfigured'. Shelley would have preferred to call the boat *Ariel*. Eventually DON JUAN was cut out and replaced with a new piece of canvas. It was named after the poem, as Mary Shelley realised and not, as Shelley assumed, after the character. A boat 'transports' its passengers, freeing them from gravity, as

Shelley's drawing of his boat the Don Juan *that he and Edward Williams commissioned and Byron's rather larger response, the* Bolivar.

The Bodleian Libraries, University of Oxford, MS. Shelley adds. c. 12, fol. 26 a spirit-hero liberates his body of men. That is why Byron commissioned his Napoleonic carriage and why he called his own boat *Bolivar*, after the liberator of Venezuela.

The incident epitomised Shelley's need to escape from his friend's shadow. Writing to John Gisborne on 26 January 1822 he praised *Cain* extravagantly but added, after a paragraph, 'I write nothing but by fits.'

Leigh Hunt agreed to come and edit a new magazine, the *Liberal*, in Pisa. Byron promised to lend him £250 with '*tolerable willingness*' (Shelley's words and italics). He pretended in a letter of 17 February 1822 that Byron did not want Hunt to know that Shelley had guaranteed the loan. 'Lord B is a rich, a still richer man,' Shelley added in a postscript, referring to Byron's prospect of inheritance after the death of his mother-in-law Lady Noel.

Round VI: *The Deformed Transformed*

Byron never mentioned Shelley's increasingly paranoid objections to their intimacy. But his last play, *The Deformed Transformed*, revolves around another destructive, diabolic, double relationship. Byron started to write it in January 1822 and worked on it sporadically. By 14 November he had completed the first part and, two months later, 'a few scenes more', which he sent to Mary for her to transcribe.

The Shelleys moved out of Pisa to a seaside villa at La Spezia at the end of April. On 18 June Shelley announced to John Gisborne that, even when Hunt arrived, he would 'see little of Lord Byron, nor shall I permit Hunt to form the intermediate link between him and me. I detest all society – almost all, at least – and Lord Byron is the nucleus of all that is hateful and tiresome in it.'

On 8 July the *Don Juan/Ariel* was shipwrecked. Shelley and Edward Williams died, along with their cabin boy, Charles Vivian. Byron was devastated. 'If you can't swim,' Maddalo warned Julian in Shelley's poem, 'beware of Providence.' According to Medwin, Byron read *Julian and Maddalo* in manuscript. It was first published in 1824.

About ten days before his friend's death Byron thought he saw Shelley 'walking into a little wood at Lerici, when it was discovered afterwards that Shelley was at that time in quite another direction'. On another occasion Byron told Lady Blessington that 'Mr Shelley's spectre had appeared to a lady, walking in a garden', 'and he seemed to lay great stress on this'. Shelley had 'conversations with his familiar', Byron remembered: 'Did he not apprize me, that he had been informed by his familiar, that he would end his life by drowning; and did I not, a short time after, perform, on the sea beach, his funeral rites?' It was enough to convince Byron that 'incorporeal beings' existed.

The Deformed Transformed continues the discussion of the doppelgänger that Byron associated with Shelley, who also inspired the play's alternation of blank verse and rhyme.

When Arnold's mother rejects her son as a 'Deformed' hunchback, he resolves to commit suicide. He sees his reflection looking 'like a demon'. A handsome Stranger materialises from the water, identifies himself as the devil, gives Arnold a conventionally heroic shape – that of Achilles – while he himself adopts Arnold's former, deformed carcass. Byron may have had Shelley in mind, whether he had read the latter's *Hellas* by now, or not, so that the play becomes 'Byron's fantasy of exchanging his own identity (the composite made up of Arnold and the Stranger/Devil), not quite for that of Shelley, but, rather, for the embodiment of the Shelleyan *ideal*'.

The devil now calls himself Caesar and promises to haunt Arnold as his doppelgänger: 'you shall see/Yourself for ever by you, as your shadow'. Byron filled the play with mirror images, instancing such mutually destructive doubles as Romulus and Remus; Gory and Glory; Lucifer and Venus; Eros and Anteros; and Huon and Memnon.

How Shelley 'would have laughed – had he lived', Byron remarked in December 1822, six months after Shelley's death. As he worked on this play, irritation with the cockney Hunt, Hunt's bourgeois, censorious wife Marianne and their six uncontrollable children, reminded Byron that he missed Shelley: 'how we used to laugh now & then – at various things – which are grave in the Suburbs.'

Caesar sneers at all 'romantic' ideals or pretensions. When Arnold defends a woman from the soldiers' assault, Caesar comments, '[*aside and*

The Deformed transformed.

The hunchback Arnold meets the handsome Stranger, or devil, in Byron's unfinished play The Deformed Transformed, *and exchanges shapes with him; an illustration, by George Cruikshank, from* Forty Illustrations of Lord Byron, *1825.*

laughing]. Ha! ha! Here's equity! The dogs/Have as much right as he'.

At the end of Part I Caesar considers the 'jest' of bringing a star down to the level of the Earth and mankind, so as to set fire to 'their ant hill . . . Ha! ha!' Later, when he hears a Wounded Man's heroic last words, 'I have died for Rome,' Caesar laughs, 'Oh these immortal men! and their great motives!'

Shelley once remarked that he was 'amused now and then with news from England of the ridiculous violence of the prejudices which are conceived against me – and as I am interested in the sight of a thunderstorm as a grand tragic ballet of the Heavens; so, at safe distance, I laugh at this comic pantomime which the good people in London exhibit, with my shadow for their Harlequin.'

Caesar uses the same phrase when he observes a Priest and a Soldier fighting: 'I have not/Seen a more comic pantomime since Titus/Took Jewry.'

In the wake of Shelley's death Byron seems to have looked back and recalled the circumstances in which the two poets first met. Arnold and Caesar define their relationship:

ARNOLD: Dog!
CAESAR: Man!
ARNOLD: Devil!
CAESAR: Your obedient, humble servant.
ARNOLD: Say *Master* rather.

Such dialogue recalls another double pair, the Satanic Frankenstein and his equally Satanic creature, who call one another 'Man' and 'Devil', 'Slave' and 'Master', and who were inspired by Mary Shelley's observation of the first stages of Byron and Shelley's relationship in Switzerland in 1816.

Byron versus Byron

There's Byron too, who once did better
From Byron's verse letter to John Murray of 21 August 1817

Byron's hero Arnold is a stereotyped Romantic poseur, sporting many of the second-hand Gothic accessories that Byron's earliest heroes wore, but without their 'power of Thought'. He's a cliché of the same species as Charles Maturin's hero Bertram, whom we'll meet later. When Arnold spouts sentimental clichés, Byron parodies Byronism.

Two years previously, when Byron sent his publisher such serious work as his translations from Italian and *The Prophecy of Dante*, Murray asked him for a 'very small volume of facetious nonsense'. During 1822 and 1823 Byron haunted Byron: his new work proved unpopular, while the public pined for more of his earlier kind of poetry. He blamed himself for writing 'exaggerated nonsense which has corrupted the public taste'. Shelley admired *Don Juan* but, as he told John Gisborne on 17 June 1822, he had

A detail of Bertel Thorvaldsen's marble statue of Byron, 1830–4, now in the library of Trinity College, Cambridge, intended to show 'the ideal picture of a gifted poet, as antiquity would present the very muse of poetry'.

Photo courtesy of Master and Fellows of Trinity College, Cambridge no time for the 'coarse music' of Byron's early poetry. During dinner on 8 March 1822 Shelley 'repeated some of the finest lines of Childe Harold, and Lord B. after listening to a stanza – cried "Heavens! Shelley, what infinite nonsense are you quoting?"' Byron admitted to Shelley on 5 May that 'no man has contributed more than me in my earlier compositions to produce that exaggerated & false taste'.

A week later Byron rebuked Murray: 'As to "a poem in the old way to interest the women" – as you call it; I shall attempt of that kind nothing further. – I follow the bias of my own mind without considering whether women or men are or are not to be pleased.' He explained to his friend Douglas Kinnaird on 2 May, 'I shall not be deterred by any outcry – they hate me – and I detest them – I mean your present Public – but they shall not interrupt the march of my mind – nor prevent me from telling the tyrants who are attempting to trample upon all thought – that their thrones will yet be rocked to their foundation.' Madame de Staël uses that phrase 'la marche de la pensée'. The 'march of my mind' occurs in the Scottish song, 'My heart is in Scotland; my heart is not here', which Allan Cunningham had recently published in *Sir Marmaduke Maxwell: a dramatic poem, The mermaid of Galloway, The legend of Richard Faulder, and Twenty Scottish songs* (1822).

Byron told Kinnaird on 21 November that all his affairs '– literary – personal – or pecuniary – appear to be out of luck'. Happy as ever to exaggerate bad news about himself, Byron embraced his status as 'the most unpopular man in England' and insisted that, 'if a whistle would call me to the pinnacle of English Fame – I would not alter it'. He stopped reading British literary magazines.

Byron confronted this issue in *Don Juan*, which deals with glory and its absence, just as much as it deals with love.

PART X

WOMEN AND EATING II, 1816–23

A joint portrait of Byron and Teresa Gamba Guiccioli. He wears his favourite 'regimental' uniform, with gold epaulettes, much gold frogging and a gorget. She was so unhappy about her portrait that she obliterated the face.

Ravenna, Biblioteca Classense. Photograph by Gabriele Pezzi

24

CORPULENCE, 1816–22

Byron grew fat in Italy over a period of five years, beginning in 1816. It happened gradually and did not last. By the time he left for Greece in July 1823 he had lost so much weight that his clothes no longer fitted and he looked as skeletal as he ever had.

The pattern persists: Byron temporarily abandons his habitual diet when he finds happiness in the arms of a series of women.

He arrived in Venice on 10 November 1816 and fell in love within 'the first week', for the first time since he left London in April. Marianna Segati, his landlord's wife, suited his particular needs: she did not 'plague' him, 'which is a wonder', he told Augusta on 18 December, and he explained that for the past month he had been 'very tranquil – very loving'. Marianna was 'amiable' and had 'a tact which is not always the portion of the fair creation', he wrote to Murray on 2 January 1817, his wedding anniversary. Venetian custom allowed Byron to play the conventional role of the wife's lover, *cavalier servente*, as a stable, ancillary supplement to a marriage. The arrangement freed him from the pressure of domestic intimacy. Signor Segati, the complaisant husband, followed the precedent set by William Lamb, Lord Oxford and George Leigh.

When Venice's hectic Carnival ended on 18 February 1817, Byron fell ill. He lost weight briefly but soon gained a 'monstrous appetite', he told Hobhouse on 31 March. On 9 May he asked Murray to tell Augusta, always concerned about his thinness, '(the truth) that I am better than ever – & in importunate health – growing (if not grown) large & ruddy – & congratulated by impertinent persons on my robustious appearance – when I ought to be pale and interesting.'

Girolamo Prepiani's watercolour on ivory miniature of Byron in his uniform in 1817. Prepiani painted two portraits of Byron in 1817, when he was thin, having been 'seriously ill', 'one the view of the face – which you like – & the other different – but both in my usual dress'. One showed him 'in pretty good health – the other is thin enough to be sure – & so was I – & in the ebb of a fever when I sate for it', he told Augusta on 3 or 4 June 1817. He wears a gorget, suspended from a button hole. Originally intended to protect the throat, as part of a man's armour, it gradually became of symbolic rather than practical importance: made of silver gilt or silver and bearing the royal coat of arms or cipher it signified variously, nobility, the rank of an officer, or that he was on duty.

Courtesy of Nottingham City Museums and Gallery

He may have continued to starve himself sporadically. According to Moore, 'his daily bill of fare, when the Margarita was his companion', from August 1817, consisted, 'of but four beccaficchi [songbirds], of which the Fornarina eat three, leaving even him hungry'.

Enormously Fat

It is worth assembling the evidence to demonstrate just how much Byron's figure changed. His 'beauty is gone, quite gone', Mary Montgomery reported gleefully to Lady Byron on 8 May 1818. 'He is enormously fat, his face bloated and complection pasty. Nothing remains of that fine antique outline so peculiar to his head.' Her brother Colonel Montgomery, a partisan of Lady Byron's, assured the apple-cheeked 'Pippin', 'His face is much more like a full moon than ever *yours* was.'

Shelley saw Byron that August and told Peacock on 8 October 1818, 'really we hardly knew him again; he is changed into the liveliest and happiest looking man I ever met.' It's significant that the Shelleys 'hardly knew him again'. John Murray's half-brother Archibald met Byron that autumn and reported on 16 September: 'He is rather stout than thin,' adding that, 'his countenance is not on the Grecian or Roman model of elegance. It is round and full and might be less agreeable in a different person.'

On 13 October 1818 Lord Glenbervie recorded that Mrs and Miss Leycester 'confirm the multiplied anecdotes of Lord Byron's metamorphoses into a fat, fat-headed, middle-aged man, slovenly to the extreme, unkempt'.

Newton Hanson, Byron's lawyer's son, came to Venice that November and reported that Byron 'could not have been more than 30, but he looked 40. His face had become pale, bloated, and sallow. He had grown very fat, his shoulders broad and round, and the knuckles of his hands were lost in fat.'

Hobhouse teased Byron about his indolence in November 1820. Annoyed, Byron replied on 9 November: 'I can go without my dinner without scolding – or eat it without finding fault with the cooking or quality.' To Murray the same day he went further and boasted at length of his ascetic, active life. But all his instances concerned the past: 'I have fed at times for two months together on *sheer* biscuit & water (without metaphor) I can get over seventy or eighty miles a day *riding* post and *swim five* at a Stretch taking a *piece* before & after as at Venice in 1818 or at least I *could do* & have done *once* & I never was ten minutes in my life over a *solitary*

George Harlow's portrait sketch of Byron in Venice, which Byron dated 6 August 1818, in Italian. It shows Byron in a casual, private moment, rather than as he generally wished to be seen – posing in Albanian mode, as a soldier, an explorer or a poet. In 1818 he was not observing his habitual, strict diet. Thomas Moore observed that Byron had not only put on weight in Venice, but grown whiskers, because someone had said that he now had the bloated face of a castrato ('faccia di musico'*). A friend of Byron's estranged wife reported that 'he now wore his hair in 'long, untied locks that hang down on his shoulders, shabbily dressed'.*

Private collection

dinner.' He used the past tense again in his Ravenna Journal on 6 January 1821, when he wondered why he had always been, 'more or less *ennuyé*' (bored) and reflected that 'Temperance and exercise, which I have practiced at times, and for a long time together vigorously and violently, made little or no difference.' Two days earlier Byron recorded eating a copious dinner. He blamed it on his irritation that he had not received any mail: 'for when I am vexed, it makes me swallow quicker'. The next day, however, when he had dined before he knew it, he confessed he had 'added, lately, *eating* to my "family of vices"'.

Lord Byron, aet. 31, painted by Fagnani in 1860 from a miniature by Prepiani.

Teresa thought the miniature by Prepiani was the best likeness of Byron and allowed Joseph Fagnani to make a copy in Paris in 1860: from Emma Fagnani, The Art Life of a XIX Century Portrait Painter, Joseph Fagnani, 1819–1873 *(1930).*

One menu does survive from a Byron dinner, on 2 January 1822 in Pisa (the seventh anniversary of his wedding), with just three main courses, but eighteen dishes. All the dishes in each course would have been laid on the table at once for the guests to help themselves. The first course comprised a thick dark vegetable soup, or herb soup *à la santé*, served with fried sweetbreads or cream cheese; a salami of pork with lentils, spinach and ham; boiled capons; beef garnished with potatoes; and a fish stew. Once servants had removed that course they brought in the grand set pieces, which the host carved: veal, roast capons, roast woodcocks, baked fish, a fricassée of poultry, and another stew. The dessert comprised blanched and plain almonds with pears, oranges and chestnuts.

Byron was still overweight in July 1822, when Leigh Hunt saw him in Pisa and 'hardly knew him, he had grown so fat'. Arriving on 15 September, Hobhouse found Byron 'much changed, his face fatter and the expression of it injured'.

Within this period of copious eating, roughly from May 1817 to September 1822, Byron occasionally resumed his diet and then, briefly, he lost weight, for example after indulging himself in the Carnivals of 1819 and 1821. Meanwhile his habitual attitude towards the spirit's transcendence of the flesh tended to remain constant, even if he did not put it into practice. On 1 October 1821 he told Moore he was happy to feel a fever, an ague, coming on, because 'the agues do me rather good than harm. The feel after the *fit* is as if one had got rid of one's body for good and all.' Teresa Guiccioli, who lived close to Byron during the major part of his 'fat period', never mentioned it in her partial, heavily idealised record of their life together.

It may be easier to explain why Byron's attempt to remedy his obesity in 1809 turned into an eating disorder than to say why he put on weight some eight years later. Did he again revert to childhood in his relations with women, as he had in England? 'I feel with an Italian woman as if she was a full-grown child,' he told Lady Blessington, 'possessing the buoyancy and playfulness of infancy with the deep feeling of womanhood.' As we shall see, he certainly portrayed Juan's relationships with women in those terms. But that was in his fiction. Perhaps it's enough to say that Byron grew up? Given his starved metabolism, eating normally would induce corpulence. Perhaps health is a more complex, more mysterious phenomenon than sickness.

The change in his outward appearance followed in the wake of three different love affairs – as well as the more than 200 brief sexual encounters. At first it had no effect on his thinking or his poetry.

As Beautiful as Thought

Women are still bodiless in the art that he approved of. Shortly after he arrived in Venice in November 1816 Byron attended the salon of the Greek-born Contessa Albrizzi, where he admired the emphatically ideal beauty of Canova's sculpture of Helen of Troy. The marble bust was 'without exception to my mind the most perfectly beautiful of human conceptions – and far beyond my ideas of human execution'. It was 'Above the works and *thoughts* of Man'.

Antonio Canova, Helen (A Bust in Marble), *1812, which the sculptor gave to Contessa Albrizzi. She was 'particularly distinguished as the Illustrator of the works of Canova', Byron told Professor Pictet on 7 April 1817. Byron saw the bust in Palazzo Albrizzi in Venice in November 1816. According to the Countess, 'In this bust the genius of Canova has embodied those ardent but undefined ideas of Helen's beauty, which are raised in our minds by the reading of ancient story . . .a cap, resembling in form the half of an eggshell, the emblem of the offspring of Leda, covers the back part of her head; in the front, her beautiful tresses, divided at the middle of the forehead, lie back in undulations, and are gathered in a knot behind, while rich curls lie clustering down her cheeks, or wanton on her lovely neck. Her features, which are perfectly beautiful, and have all the fineness and delicacy of the Grecian face, are animated with a gentle and bewitching smile. Canova, whose genius can pourtray most refined and complicated affections, has united in this bust the dignity of a goddess, with the expression of human passions, which alone awaken human sympathies; while we gaze on it, respectful and voluptuous feelings contend within us, but beauty is finally triumphant.'*

Private collection

Guido Reni, The Massacre of the Innocents, *1611, Pinacoteca Nazionale, Bologna. Each of the five suffering women holds a baby.*

Su concessione dell MiBACT, Archivio fotografico Soprintendenza Bologna

Manfred and the Witch of the Torrent, from George Cruikshank's Forty Illustrations of Lord Byron, *dated 16 July 1826.*

In April 1817 Byron visited Bologna where, he told Hobhouse on 22 April, he admired 'a superb face in Guido's Innocents', commenting that it was 'the image of Lady Ponsonby – who is as beautiful as Thought'.

So Altered Since Last Year

The poetry that Byron first completed in Italy, such as *Manfred*, *The Lament of Tasso*, *Childe Harold* IV (begun on 26 June 1817), continues to celebrate bodiless women.

But by the summer of 1817 Byron recognised that his writing had changed. He attributed it to the sensuality of his new life in Venice:

> So altered since last year his pen is
> I think he's lost his wits at Venice –
> Or drained his brains away as Stallion
> To some dark-eyed & warm Italian

Byron wrote that verse letter when his quondam physician William Polidori sent Murray his new play and Murray asked Byron for help in rejecting it. With its opening lines Byron dares to credit poetry with physical effects:

> Dear Doctor – I have read your play
> Which is a good one in its way
> Purges the eyes and moves the bowels
> And drenches handkerchiefs like towels

Byron's attitude to the discrepancies between flesh and spirit softens: tragic consternation yields to comic quizzicality. His poetry gradually encompasses more of life; it approaches the openness of his prose letters. Corpulence was the outward and visible sign of an inner change. At last women can take physical form in his poetry. The masterpieces of his Italian years, *Beppo* and *Don Juan*, rejoice in three-dimensional women of flesh and blood.

In August 1817 he met Margarita Cogni, a baker's wife. He had many other mistresses but Margarita's ascendancy over her rivals was 'often disputed & never impaired', he told Murray on 1 August 1819, explaining that he was attracted by her ferocity:

> Wild as a witch – and fierce as a demon . . . She was always in extremes either crying or laughing – and so fierce when angered that she was the terror of men women and children – for she had the strength of an Amazon with the temper of a Medea. She was a fine animal – but quite untameable. *I* was the only person that could at all keep her in any order – and when she saw me really angry – (which they tell me is rather a savage sight), she subsided.

His language is strikingly reminiscent of the way he talked about his other fine, untameable animals. And the reference to Medea recalls his first thrill on encountering that wild animal Lady Caroline Lamb.

Margarita Cogni in a portrait by G. Harlow, engraved by H. T. Ryall, 1836. She was 'one of those women who may be made any thing', Byron told Moore on 19 September 1818. 'I am sure if I put a poniard into the hand of this one, she would plunge it where I told her, – and into me, if I offended her. I like this kind of animal and am sure that I should have preferred Medea to any woman that ever breathed.' The 'pretty fiend' soon became his housekeeper. 'I know how to manage her', he boasted to Augusta Leigh on 21 September. Margarita Cogni's letter to Byron, dictated to a scribe in May 1819, reveals that Byron told her about his love for Augusta, and added, that she resembled his sister.

Better than Ideal Beauty

In 1817–18 Byron was on the brink of turning thirty and determined to make the most of his time for sex and for writing – the two activities were now closely linked in his mind. This period unleashes an unprecedentedly sensual indulgence of appetite, a feast of lust that appalled Shelley. 'There's a whore on my *right*,' Byron boasted to Murray in another verse letter that he sent on 8 January 1818, 'For I rhyme best at Night/When a C–t is tied close to *my Inkstand*.' His sex life went into promiscuous overdrive. He hired at least one 'casino' or pleasure-house, to facilitate his connections. Looking back on 8 September he told Wedderburn Webster that he had spent more than £2,500 on at least 200 women of one sort or another, perhaps more, for he had not 'lately kept the recount'. It's a lot of money and a remarkable score, given that he had lived in Venice for less than two years. According to Leporello's catalogue, Mozart and Da Ponte's Don Giovanni only 'loved' 640 women in Italy. Byron boasted to Hobhouse and Kinnaird on 19 January 1819 that he had 'run the Gauntlet' from countesses to cobblers' wives, which sounds rather like Don Giovanni's pursuit of 'women of every rank, shape and age', according to his servant Leporello in *Don Giovanni*. The extravagance of Byron's promiscuity may have attracted him to the topic of Don Juan.

In any case, Byron had formerly identified language as a spiritual medium; now he celebrates Italian's sensual capacity and revels in playful, almost Keatsian alliteration: 'I love the language, that soft bastard Latin,/ Which melts like kisses from a female mouth,/And sounds as if it should be writ on satin.' *Beppo* discusses food in Carnival and Lent and rhymes Harvey, a kind of sauce, with 'starve ye'. It anticipates the flesh tones of *Don Juan*, 'one continued painting of what is most sensual', as Hobhouse observed of Canto I.

On 22 January 1818, his thirtieth birthday, Byron again attended Contessa Albrizzi's salon. There he briefly met Contessa Teresa Guiccioli, who would become his last mistress. Teresa was nineteen and on her honeymoon, having recently married Alessandro, Count Guiccioli, who was fifty-seven. Byron gave her his arm when they went to look at the same sculpture by Canova that he had admired three months before. The encounter of the two busts, the ideal sculpture of Helen of Troy and Teresa's real, 'uncommonly good' bust, may have sparked Byron's imagination.

Byron did not mention Teresa until April 1819, but she surely left her mark on *Mazeppa*, which he wrote between 2 April 1817 and 26 September

Horace Vernet painted this copy of Mazeppa and the Wolves, *now in the Fondation Calvet, Avignon, in 1826, having damaged the original while fencing with a foil.*

1818. Mazeppa, a page to Jean Casimir, King of Poland, falls in love with a nobleman's wife, who is thirty years younger than her husband. Byron's source did not name the young, married noblewoman whom the hero loved; Byron calls her Theresa.

Mazeppa's plot foretold the way Byron would intervene in the Guiccioli marriage. It may also reflect how he anticipated that the notoriously vengeful Count Guiccioli was likely to react. Mazeppa is punished for adultery by being tied, naked, to the back of a wild horse that gallops for twenty-four hours and dies beneath him. The extraordinarily intense image may suggest that his crime was in some way particularly transgressive, possibly Oedipal in nature.

The poem also anticipates Byron's destiny: exiled from his homeland, Poland, Mazeppa then dedicates his life to liberating another country, the Ukraine.

Teresa Guiccioli, an engraving by H. Meyer from a sketch by Santo Panario, 1828.

On 29 August 1818 Byron heard an anecdote that would form the basis of *Beppo*, another, happier portrait of adultery, which he finished by 23 October. That poem allows him to praise a painting of a woman by Giorgione, 'such a woman! love in life!'

> Love in full life and length, not love ideal
> No, nor ideal beauty, that fine name,
> But something better still, so very real,
> That the sweet model must have been the same . . .

Originally, for the line 'Love in full life', he wrote: 'In the full bloom and/ of ripened womanhood'. According to Medwin, his description was meant for Teresa.

Giorgione's Tempesta, *c.1503–7. This was probably the painting that Byron mentioned in a letter to Murray on 14 April 1817 and referred to in* Beppo.

> *'Tis but a portrait of his Son, and Wife,*
> *And self; but* such *a Woman! love in life!*
>
> *Love in full life and length, not love ideal,*
> *No, nor ideal beauty, that fine name,*
> *But something better still, so very real,*
> *That the sweet model must have been the same*

25

ANOTHER WAR OF INDEPENDENCE, 1819–21

Early in April 1819, almost fourteen months after their first encounter, Byron met Teresa Guiccioli for the second time. On 6 April he announced that he had fallen in love with her.

She was three months pregnant – as Augusta Leigh had been, when he first fell in love with her. Teresa reminded him of his half-sister. And not simply because, as he told Augusta on 17 May, when he loved anyone, it was because she reminded him 'in some way or other' of her. Teresa 'has a good deal of *us* too', he explained, specifying that Teresa had the same 'turn for ridicule' as 'you and I & all the B's'. Teresa was 'pretty – a great Coquette – extremely vain – excessively affected – clever enough – without the smallest principle – with a good deal of imagination and some passion'. Byron relished the naive intensity of Teresa's feelings, delighted that she had been known for her furious temper at the convent school, which she had left only three years before. She was short, with hair 'the colour of flames – and the head under it, hotter than lava'. She was 'as fair as Sunrise – and warm as Noon'. The only day the lovers practised 'amatory abstinence', he told Douglas Kinnaird on 6 July 1819, was when her husband woke prematurely from his siesta.

Byron's long-term relationship with Teresa seems to combine features of both his previous, major Italian liaisons – the 'very tranquil' refuge with his landlady's wife, Marianna Segati, and his turbulent time with the fierce baker's wife, Margarita Cogni – which may explain why it lasted so long.

Bust of Teresa Guiccioli by Lorenzo Bartolini.
Ravenna, Biblioteca Classense. Photograph by Gabriele Pezzi

Teresa introduced a new element to Byron's love life: she was his social equal and returned several valuable presents that he gave her. Unlike his other, shorter-lived Italian loves (and Augusta), Teresa was a very cultivated young lady, with whom he could discuss Dante and other writers. Byron shared his life with her; he even allowed her to dominate it for a time – until he left Italy for Greece in July 1823. She was his longest-lasting (though not his last) love and he remained faithful to her, more or less, for over four years.

Servitude

The relationship soon made major new demands on him. Some ten days after they had fallen in love, Count Guiccioli announced that he and his wife would be returning to Ravenna. He invited Byron to visit them there. Byron intended to join Teresa in May, but he delayed leaving Venice. Moving to Ravenna represented a decisive step, one that would put his life at risk, since the notoriously jealous count was 'shrewdly suspected of two assassinations'. For Byron it also meant leaving a world that he had moulded to his taste and needs to enter unfamiliar moral territory: following someone else's initiative meant that he would risk compromising his independence. He had acted as *cavalier servente* to Marianna Segati and Margarita Cogni – but on his terms, since both women were his social inferiors. *Serventismo* to an equal meant that 'A man actually becomes a piece of female property', as he later complained.

He worried intensely about Teresa's health, his status and the future of their relationship. He resented it if she paid attention to another man, whether a stranger at the opera, or her husband. At one point he thought of leaving Italy; at another, he contemplated suicide. Such feelings would ultimately prompt the return of his anorexia. For four years he held it at bay with alternative, compensatory activities. He reasserted his independence as a writer on 20 May, only six weeks after his amorous '*servitude*' began. He repeated the assertion on two further occasions during the year. Increasingly he devoted time, energy and money to the cause of Italy's independence from papal and Austrian tyranny. Domestic claustrophobia seems to have fuelled his principled love of a people's freedom. He began to think about emigrating.

Byron did follow Teresa to Ravenna, but her husband soon took her away again. In August, only four months after their liaison had begun, solitude allowed regret to fester like heartburn: Byron felt it 'bitterly – that a man should not consume his life at the side and on the bosom – of a woman – and a stranger . . . But I have neither the strength of mind to break my chain, nor the insensibility which would deaden it's [sic] weight.'

Teresa learned tact. Byron could allow women to put on flesh in his poetry, but he could not entirely transcend his fear of their threatening physicality. In September 1819 the lovers travelled together from Ravenna back to Venice. On their way they made a pilgrimage to see Petrarch's home and tomb at Arqua. The poet was associated with platonic idealism. Teresa remembered that a servant offered her something to eat:

> but she declined all food except a peach, which she slipped from one hand to the other, admiring meanwhile its aroma and the beauty of its colours. At this point Byron expressed his admiration that she was so free from weakness and was not troubled by everyday needs and did not complain about anything. He was not certain whether her body was real or visionary; he desired that women should be like 'esprits de l'air', ethereal like the love they inspired. But when he saw how they ate and drank, she could not conceive, he said, the nausea that they infused in him.
>
> This feeling was stronger than his reason; Byron admitted that he did not find his antipathy in any way justifiable, even so little as the pretension that women 'should nourish themselves from the dew of heaven, the emanation of the spheres, or from sunbeams'.

Teresa and Byron then lived together in his villa outside Venice. Since his marriage he had never lived for long in settled, shared domestic intimacy. It soon palled; they were never to live on such close terms again: 'I am not tired of Italy,' Byron explained to Hobhouse on 3 October, '– but a man must be a cicisbeo and a singer in duets and a Connoisseur of operas – or nothing here . . . Better be a[n] unskilful planter – an awkward settler – better be a hunter – or anything than a flatterer of fiddlers – and a fan-carrier of a woman.' In November Byron persuaded Teresa, 'with the greatest difficulty', to return to married life in Ravenna. Traumatised by the experience of domesticated intimacy, he nearly left Italy for England.

At this point Teresa fell ill. When her father wrote and begged him to join her in Ravenna Byron acknowledged her as his 'Sovereign'. With the assurance that her husband acquiesced, Byron agreed on 10 December to 'return – and do – and be – what you wish'.

'Everything depends on you,' he told her on 16 June 1819, ' – my life – my honour – my love,' and this, he added in a letter probably written in June or July, 'having been a man known for the independence and force of his mind'. Byron hated feeling that he was being exploited by Guiccioli or treated as 'one of his dependents' ('un suo dependente'). 'For more than a year,' he told Teresa in an undated letter, probably written in May that year, 'I have done nothing but obey you in everything.' 'I don't want to degrade myself,' ('*Non voglio avvilirmi*') Byron warned Teresa on 10 January 1820. Five months later he had to accept that it had happened: he had indeed been very degraded ('*ben'avvilito*'). 'All these things degrade me,' ('*m'avviliscono*'), he told her in a letter probably from May 1820.

Byron was still overweight. He blamed the air of Ravenna for making him 'too fat' ('*troppo grasso*'). But he continued to indulge his appetite. He was 'eating flesh', he told William Bankes on 19 February, 'like yourself or any other cannibal, except it be upon Fridays'. His letters show that he ate goose, beef and duck at this time. He offered Moore 'a tureen of macaroni' on 24 May.

Eventually, the Guicciolis separated. The Pope ordered her to live with her family. Byron sent Teresa his cook and appointed a 'provisional vice-cook', who was particularly good at truffles or potatoes, ducks and '*baci di dama*', almond sweets, literally, 'lady's kisses'. The ducks were cooked without onions, according to Teresa's fastidious prescription, though Byron was not sure whether she meant it seriously. On 17 July he reassured

Teresa: such dishes demonstrated that he was not trying to get thin (‘*non faccio magro*’).

Sardanapalus, the play he wrote between 13 January and 28 May 1821, marks the apex of Byron’s Italian sensualism, his relish for the material life. At the same time it anticipates reality – he would revert to a compulsive diet in 1822.

Byron’s Sardanapalus, an Assyrian leader dedicated to pleasure rather than conquest, recalls the portrait of its author that Leigh Hunt sketched

Illustration to Sardanapalus *from* The Byron Gallery, *1833.*

in the summer of 1822, 'metamorphosed, round-looking, and jacketed . . . with . . . an air of voluptuous indolence'. A pragmatic sceptic (like the Narrator of *Don Juan*), the Assyrian king laughs at conventional heroics – his attitude may have been partly inspired by Shelley. Sardanapalus complains that his weapons and armour are 'too heavy'. A general assumes that the king experienced battle as 'The brightest and most glorious' hour of his life, only to hear that it was 'the most tiresome'. The king's Greek slave/lover Myrrha is there to speak for spirit: she persuades Sardanapalus to purify himself 'from some/Of the gross stains of too material being' by burning himself to death. Fire will redeem him, since it is 'that absorbing element,/Which most personifies the soul as leaving/The least of matter unconsumed'. She assures him that death is 'A shore, where mind survives . . . as mind,/All unincorporate'. Byron first called her Byblis, after Ovid's character in the *Metamorphoses*, who was in love with her brother. Myrrha, also from Ovid, has an incestuous passion for her father.

The Self-Destruction of Sardanapalus.

Myrrha lights the funeral pyre for Sardanapalus. From George Cruikshank's Forty Illustrations of Lord Byron, *1826*

Byron could only dream of such disembodiment. In reality he experienced its opposite – mindless physical prostration. He ended his Ravenna Journal on 27 February 1822 with a *Don Juan*-esque account of self-indulgence, in which he 'suffered horribly': Teresa persuaded him to eat supper, 'a quantity of boiled cockles, and to dilute them, *not* reluctantly, with some Imola wine'. At home, apprehensive of the consequences, he swallowed four glasses of spirits and went to bed. Feeling 'somewhat swollen and considerably vertiginous', he got up again, mixed some soda-powders, and drank them. The relief was temporary, so he drank more soda water. Meanwhile he remarked 'the complete inertion, inaction, and destruction of my chief mental faculties'. He 'could not rouse them – and this is the *Soul*!!! I should believe it was married to the body, if they did not sympathise so much with each other. If the one rose, when the other fell, it would be a sign that they longed for the natural state of divorce. But as it is, they seem to draw together like post-horses. Let us hope for the best – it is the grand possession.'

Gradually Byron accepted that the Italians would never achieve independence. His attention turned to Greece, where, in March 1821, after more than three centuries of oppression, the Greeks began to fight for liberty and sporadically slaughtered their Turkish masters. Byron considered joining the Greeks' campaign for independence, together with Teresa's idealistic younger brother, Pietro Gamba. But, for the moment, he yielded to her pleas. She also persuaded him by 6 July 1821 to stop writing *Don Juan*, because it was so immoral.

When the papal authorities banished her father and brother from Ravenna in the summer of 1821, Teresa followed them into exile in Florence. Byron remained in Ravenna, alone, for more than three months. The lovers had never been apart for so long. 'I was dreadfully in love,' Byron told Augusta on 5 October, 'and have not the least wish – nor prospect of separation from her. – She herself – . . . is still more decided.' The past tense betrays his reservations. Teresa complained bitterly of his dilatoriness, but Byron knew that in leaving Ravenna to return to her side would entail sacrificing his independence. That was surely why he suffered from a 'growing depression of my spirits, without sufficient cause.

I ride – I am not intemperate in eating or drinking – and my general health is as usual, except a slight ague, which rather does good than not'. Byron's 'not intemperate' suggests his diet may have been as severe as the '*very temperate*', which is how he described his starving regime. The clearest signs that his eating was disordered are his pleasure in an ague and his ominous resorting to purgatives: 'The thing that gives me the highest spirits (it seems absurd, but true) is a dose of *salts* – I mean in the afternoon, after their effect.' A week later he mentioned a 'great depression of spirits' to Hobhouse.

PART XI

DON JUAN: LOVE AND GLORY, 1818–22

'The Separation, a Sketch from the private life of Lord Iron who Panegyrized his Wife, but Satirized her Confidante!!' *A caricature of Byron after the separation in 1816, when his Don Juanism had become public knowledge.*

26

OH LOVE!

Oh Love! Oh Glory! What are ye who fly
Around us ever, rarely to alight?

Don Juan, VII, I

Ostensibly *Don Juan*'s great themes are love and war – 'Oh Love! Oh Glory!' and Byron said that he planned to alternate between them. They are not so easily separated, but it may help to follow his schema, looking first at *Don Juan*'s women and then at the men, using our knowledge of his private concerns to see the epic through his eyes.

'I could not shut it sooner for the soul of me,': the poet of *Don Juan* relishes the aerial, disembodied abstraction inherent in narration. At the same time narrating *Don Juan* allows Byron to create three-dimensional portraits of dominant, sensual women. The new relation between the Narrator and his hero licenses this freedom. Childe Harold remained a nominal presence within *Childe Harold*, a pale and fading projection of its author; Juan is at once Byron and not-Byron, his partner, his double, with whom he plays – perhaps rather in the way a child plays with a toy, a blanket or other transitional object. Byron defines his 'poesy' in *Don Juan* as 'a bubble, not blown up for praise/But just to play with, as an infant plays'. The space between the disembodied Narrator and his fleshy hero allows the poem to tolerate reality, to allow for mortal practice alongside theoretic idealism. Byron can afford to compromise his old, exclusively spiritual, heroic ideals and accept that man is compounded of 'fiery dust'. 'I can give my whole soul up to mind,' he writes in Canto VI, 22; 'Though what *is* soul or mind, their birth or growth,/Is more than I know – the deuce take them both.'

The new alignment is evident on the smallest linguistic scale in puns (on 'goût/gout' or 'sage') and structurally, in the way the poem delights in both incongruity and continuity. Byron was writing Canto V of *Don Juan* on 9 December 1820, when a soldier was assassinated in the street outside. It prompted a 'digression' that apparently had nothing to do with what he had been saying and what he would go on to say. But all passages share a concern for the apt and crucially Byronic topic of soul subdued by matter.

'If that man had respected his dinner, he never would have written *Don Juan*.' Thackeray was wrong: Byron conceived and wrote nearly all of *Don Juan* when his eating was not disordered; not-dieting coloured its conception, rather in the way that the Corsair's ascetic, teetotal, vegetarian diet generated his powers of leadership. *Don Juan*'s motto is inclusiveness, and it starts from the stanza form. Ottava rima is only one line longer than the Spenserian stanza Byron revived in *Childe Harold*, but eight lines allow for thesis and antithesis over three couplets, which can then be synthesised (or refuted) in the final couplet. The form licenses free-ranging prolixity. Over six years, *Don Juan* grew to seventeen cantos and some 1,950 stanzas.

The poem celebrates Byron's reconciliation with physicality, even though it explores the conflict between flesh and spirit.

Juan and his Women

At ease in an affair with Teresa that suited his needs, Byron felt free to explore relationships with women at arm's length. Yet his female characters become more and more overpowering. The sequence echoes the changing course of Byron's relationship with Teresa. In July 1821 she asked him to stop writing *Don Juan*. When he went back to it – on 14 April 1822 – the women that he created became still more threatening.

Byron had met Teresa and her husband only once when he wrote Canto I – long before he mentioned that he had fallen in love with her. And yet Juan's first affair recreates aspects of their triangular situation, which he

Don Juan, Julia and her husband, Don Alonso in an engraving by S. S. Smith, after E. T. Parris, The Byron Gallery.

had already sketched in *Mazeppa*: Julia is twenty-three and married to Don Alfonso, a man of fifty, when she falls in love with Juan. He is seven years younger than her and the Narrator emphasises the lovers' different maturities, focusing on her complexity, her 'conscious heart' and lack of self-knowledge. Juan is seen through her eyes: 'Juan she saw, and, as a pretty child,/Caressed him often'. He has a 'half-girlish face'. Dominated by his mother, his most salient feature is his immaturity. When Don Alonso bursts in on his wife, Juan is as effectively concealed from the reader's, as he is from the husband's, attention: 'Young, slender and packed easily, he lay/

Don Alfonso finds a man's shoe in his wife's bedroom, illustration by Richard Westall. Byron said that Westall's illustrations to Don Juan *were 'superb – the brush has beat the poetry'.*

Private collection

No doubt, in little compass, round or square'. What other Don Juan was ever 'packed'? The passive mood suits this Juan.

After a long sequence devoted to Julia, the Narrator turns back to the hero, only to snub him: 'But as for Juan, he had no more notion/Than he who never saw the sea or ocean'. The image is not fortuitous; in the course of the poem women are repeatcdly identified with the sea or ocean to suggest the overwhelming, inexhaustible nature of their sexuality. And again, after exploring Julia's emotional depths at length the Narrator snubs Juan: 'So much for Julia; now we'll turn to Juan./Poor little fellow, he had no idea/Of his own case and never hit the true one'.

Juan's mother follows the advice of some old ladies: 'She sent her son to be shipp'd off from Cadiz.' Julia's long letter to Juan extends over six stanzas. We hear nothing whatsoever of Juan's reaction, until seasickness sabotages his attempt to make a farewell speech. That episode establishes Juan's immaturity; his passiveness, while his women are active; his subsidiarity: we hear less of him and therefore assume that he feels and matters less than 'his' women. The pattern remains constant throughout the work. In Canto II Juan plays a still more restricted, submissive role. The Greek idyll focuses on Haidee: most of the time 'she' alternates with 'they' and only occasionally with 'he'. Haidee dominates in terms of her physique, too. We hear repeatedly that she is tall; her stature was 'Even of the highest for a female mould . . . And in her air/There was a something which bespoke command'. 'Her overpowering presence made you feel/It would not be idolatry to kneel'. Juan, on the other hand, is faint, emaciated and stark; he resembles 'a young flower snapped from the stalk,/Drooping and dewy', 'a withered lily'. He's unconscious and wakes only to go back to sleep. Repetitions throughout the canto build up a hypnotic, oneiric effect: 'Juan slept'; 'Young Juan slept all dreamless'; 'He slumbered'; 'Juan slumbering still'; 'lone repose'; 'His rest'; 'he might sleep his fill/And need he had of slumber yet'; 'That sleep which seemed as it would ne'er awake'; 'Lulled like the depth of ocean when at rest'; 'He woke and gazed and would have slept again'; 'weariness and pain/Had further sleep a further pleasure made'; 'Juan, who was somewhat fond of rest'; 'her yet slumbering guest'; 'his lulled head'. Even after his long convalescence Juan remains 'somewhat fond of rest'.

In striking contrast to the 'languid Juan' Haidee stays awake. We hear on three occasions that her pleasure was to watch Juan sleeping.

Canto III begins:

Hail Muse! *et cetera*— We left Juan sleeping,
    Pillow'd upon a fair and happy breast,
And watch'd by eyes that never yet knew weeping

Don Juan discovered by Haidee.

Illustration, by George Cruikshank, from George Clinton, Memoirs of the Life and Writings of Lord Byron, *1825.*

Juan is the passive object of love, 'So gentle, stirless, helpless, and unmoved', which inevitably hints at his infancy and Byron heightens that inference: 'like an infant Juan sweetly slept'.

> And she bent oer him, and he lay beneath,
> Hushed as the babe upon its mother's breast,
> Drooped as the willow when no winds can breathe.

Juan, like Byron, recovers from starvation in the arms of a motherly woman:

> He ate, and he was well supplied, and she,
> Who watched him like a mother, would have fed
> Him past all bounds, because she smiled to see
> Such appetite in one she had deemed dead.

Juan and Haidee, an illustration from The Byron Gallery, *1833.*

Inevitably, this Oedipal idyll cannot last. When Lambro, Haidee's father, cuts it short he intervenes like a cuckolded husband – he is compared to Ulysses, returning to his wife Penelope.

Typically, the lovers' final scene together is a siesta. While we hear only of Juan's physical reaction – 'ever and anon a something shook/Juan, and shuddering o'er his frame would creep' – Haidee's intense dream occupies five successive stanzas.

Haidee saving Don Juan from her Father's Wrath.

Illustration, by George Cruikshank, from George Clinton, Memoirs of the Life and Writings of Lord Byron, *1825.*

Finally, Juan is, once again, 'suddenly to sea *sent*,/Wounded and chained, so that he cannot move'.

In Canto IV Juan is purchased at a slave market, and then passed around like a package, from a eunuch to Gulbeyaz, to the Sultan, to the Matron and then to Lolah, Katinka and Dudu. With no insight into Juan's feelings he seems vacuous, rather than enigmatic. His 'somewhat manly majesty of stride' is only apparent when he is humiliated, unmanned – forced to wear women's clothing, under the threat of castration.

Like her predecessor Gulbeyaz dominates the relationship: her beauty is 'of that overpowering kind'; in 'her large eyes wrought/A mixture of sensations might be scanned,/Of half voluptuousness and half command'. 'Something imperial or imperious threw/A chain o'er all she did'; her 'small feet . . . trod as upon necks'. Her 'despotism' and 'tyranny', her

'Passion and power' contrast with Juan's vulnerability. He resists her command to love, but the Narrator's deflating simile denies him heroic status: 'He stood like Atlas, with a world of words/About his ears, and nathless would not bend'. Byron refers to Milton's Satan who, 'alarm'd,/Collecting all his might, dilated stood,/Like Teneriffe, or Atlas, unremoved'. A 'world of words' carries a ticking charge of bathos but Juan cannot even sustain that mock-heroic pose. Thirteen stanzas later 'These words went through his soul like Arab-spears,/So that he spoke not, but burst into tears'.

The other women in the harem ooze sensuality. Lolah is 'dusk as India and as warm'; Katinka seems ethereal at first: her feet were 'so small they scarce seemed made to tread,/But rather skim the earth'. Later, however, the stanza's concluding couplet dares to fuse sentiment and sex: 'But here Katinka interfered and said/She also had compassion and a bed'. Meanwhile Dudu, that 'sleepy Venus . . . Looked more adapted to be put to bed,/Being somewhat large and languishing and lazy'. 'She was a soft landscape of mild earth'.

Centre stage, twenty-nine stanzas evoke Gulbeyaz's 'anguish', 'convulsion', 'brief agony' and 'deep emotion' (87–116), while Juan stays in the wings. Summoned to see her, all we hear for some sixty stanzas is that he looked 'silly'.

Having put *Don Juan* aside at Teresa's behest, some ten days later Byron began *Cain*, a still more 'offensive' piece of writing. When he returned to *Don Juan*, he portrayed his most potent female character, Catherine the Great, whose love nearly kills Juan.

After the Siege of Ismail, Juan is yet again 'sent off'. The epic has alternated between the themes of love and war but in Canto IX Byron combines love and glory in one woman, the Empress Catherine, whom he describes as 'the grand epitome/Of that great cause of war or peace or what/You please', meaning sex, i.e. her sexual organ, 'thou nondescript!/Whence is our exit and our entrance'. She looked on war 'Between these nations as a main of cocks,/Wherein she liked her own to stand as rocks'. The pun on cocks is reinforced by 'stand' and followed

The Sultana Gulbeyaz despairs, in George Cruikshank's Forty Illustrations of Byron, *1826*

by many more ('falls and rises'; 'With or without thee all things at a stand/Are or would be'; 'this great whole'; 'the standing army who stood by'; young people should be able 'To come off handsomely'.

Catherine the Great is the poem's most powerful woman, while Juan is at his most vulnerable. He has clearly shrunk, since in Canto I he was 'Tall, handsome, slender, but well knit'. The discrepancy between young man and older woman is also intensified. She seems at first to be in 'Her prime of life, just now in juicy vigour'. But by Canto X, 10 she is one of the 'Middle-aged ladies' and by stanza 29, an 'old woman'.

The empress falls in love, as Juan kneels at her feet. Byron's imagery hints that her voracity will challenge Juan's sexual stamina, 'for the eye/In love drinks all life's fountains (save tears) dry'. Now the image becomes invasive to reflect female sexuality's major difference from male

A caricature of Catherine the Great, dated 12 April 1791. The empress's colossal stride stretches from Russia to Constantinople. Seven 'European Powers' gaze awestruck up her skirts, highlighting her reputation for prodigious sexual and political appetites. The sultan remarks, 'The whole Turkish Army wouldn't satisfy her.'

© The Trustees of the British Museum

potency, its inexhaustibility – a 'perennial fountain', the 'sea of life's dry land!'

Byron compares the empress's joy at hearing of the Russians' victory at Ismail, her 'Glory and triumph', to

> . . . an East Indian Sunrise on the main.
> These quenched a moment her Ambition's thirst;
> So Arab Deserts drink in Summer's rain.
> In vain! As fall the dews on quenchless sands,
> Blood only serves to wash Ambition's hands!

The metaphor extends to the whole court, which, relieved at her delight in Juan, is 'Like flowers well watered after a long drouth'.

> What a strange thing is man, and what a stranger
> Is woman! What a whirlwind is her head,
> And what a whirlpool full of depth and danger
> Is all the rest about her!

The process by which they fall in love is another liquid event:

> for Cupid's cup
> With the first draught intoxicates apace,
> A quintessential laudanum or 'black drop',
> Which makes one drunk at once, without the base
> Expedient of full bumpers, for the eye . . .

Juan's love or lust has the urgency of youth, now with a penetrative character, 'As bold as Daniel's in the Lion's den':

> So that we can our native Sun assuage
> In the next Ocean, which may flow just then
> To make a twilight in, just as Sol's heat is
> Quenched in the lap of the salt Sea or Thetis.

So sighs subside and tears shrink 'Like Arno in the summer'.

Motivated by 'Self-love' and lust, here Juan appears to be behaving like a traditional Don Juan. But 'he grew sick'. His decline re-establishes him as a passive victim of circumstances: Catherine no sooner saw his 'dropping' eye but 'She then resolved to send him on a mission'.

For the fourth time Juan is 'sent' somewhere – all those incidents stand in ironic distance to the legendary Don Juan's fate, proclaimed in the poem's first stanza: 'Sent to the devil, somewhat ere his time.'

One-third of the poem is set in England, yet Juan only has one more love adventure there. He does not pursue the intensely physical Duchess of Fitz-Fulke, 'whose mind,/If she had any, was upon her face' and the last stanza suggests that his encounter with her exhausted him. We will return to this theme after considering *Don Juan*'s other major focus.

27

OH GLORY!

I Want a Hero

Byron's idiosyncratic concept of heroism evolved during the fifteen months before he began to write *Don Juan* on 3 July 1818.

In April 1817 he visited Ferrara and saw the cell where Torquato Tasso was confined. The idea of a poet incarcerated unfairly for madness interested Byron as intensely as it did Shelley. The hero of Byron's *The Lament of Tasso* insists, like Manfred, that 'in the innate force/Of my own spirit shall be found resource'. But, unlike Manfred, he is saved by words. Writing poetry enables Tasso to make himself 'wings wherewith to overfly/ The narrow circus of my dungeon wall'.

Byron's heroic impulse, undeterred by Napoleon's failure, his desire and determination to 'do something or other', as he put it in a letter to Moore of 28 February 1817, gradually gathered like a storm cloud around his head. He described the process in *The Lament of Tasso*:

> But all unquenched is still my better part,
> Dwelling deep in my shut and silent heart
> As dwells the gathered lightning in its cloud,
> Encompassed with its dark and rolling shroud,
> Till struck, – forth flies the all-etherial dart!

James Barry's etching, Tasso in Prison Crowned by Urania and Attended by the Three Graces, *c.1792.*
Image © Ashmolean Museum, University of Oxford

Byron expressed his 'better part' in prophecy, in curses or in appeals to Nemesis, the ancient Greek personification of vengeance. He cursed his wife explicitly in a letter of 25 March 1817 that he never sent. Other victims included the Tory Poet Laureate Robert Southey, Byron's cousin George Anson Byron and the lawyer Sir Samuel Romilly. Such actions presuppose confidence in the power of words. In his *Prophecy of Dante* Byron looked back to a time 'When words were things which came to pass', but that was in 'Days of old'.

Byron celebrated verbal power in the fourth canto of *Childe Harold*, which he wrote between 26 June 1817 and January 1818. 'I stood in Venice on the Bridge of Sighs': from that opening line onwards a newly authoritative voice soars above its surroundings. As for the poem's nominal subject, Childe Harold first surfaces in stanza 164 (of 186). Canto IV describes Rome's Pantheon, its shrine to the memory of heroes; it also effectively recreates it in verse. Byron's heroes, however, 'Spirits which soar from ruin', are now nearly all writers. Napoleon appears as a 'vain man . . . vanquish'd by himself, to his own slaves a slave', a merely 'bastard Caesar'. Crucially Byron stakes his own (unspoken) claim to Napoleonic and Satanic status in the context of ancient Rome, when he asks his soul to 'meditate amongst decay, and stand/A ruin amidst ruins'. Once again the verb 'stand' trails the independent glory associated with Milton's Satan.

Hopes of freedom have been disappointed so far, but Byron refuses to be dispirited:

> Yet let us ponder boldly – 'tis a base
> Abandonment of reason to resign
> Our right of thought – our last and only place
> Of refuge . . .

'Pondering boldly' takes the form of another appeal to Nemesis. Byron is confident that 'The deep prophetic fulness of this verse' will 'pile on human heads the mountain of my curse'. He found the perfect vehicle for his prophetic impulse and his Satanic/Napoleonic ambition in *Don Juan*.

To Laugh at All Things

That may sound unlikely. In general readers no longer take *Don Juan* seriously. Byron led the way, saying that he went 'rattling on exactly as I

Byron, contemplating the ruins of the Coliseum in Rome, Finden

talk'. That prompted W. H. Auden to salute him as 'the master of the airy manner'. This viewpoint aligns *Don Juan* with *Beppo*. Byron indeed promised that *Don Juan* would be 'in the Beppo style' but he also told Murray on 19 September 1819 that it would be 'a little quietly facetious upon everything'. The two remarks are incompatible, since that laconic disclaimer makes vast claims: 'facetious upon everything' means that nothing is sacrosanct; his epic will respect no taboos. Byron cultivates an airy, casual pose ('a little', 'quietly') to demonstrate his gentlemanly ease, his '*sprezzatura*'.

His publisher was well aware of the difference between the two poems. 'Do let us have your good humour again,' Murray begged Byron on 29 October 1822, 'and put Juan in the tone of Beppo.' Byron did not oblige. Soon, Murray refused to publish it.

Canto I establishes *Don Juan*'s dangerous remit. There is nothing in *Beppo* as outrageous as the blasphemous parody of the Ten Commandments, 'Thou shalt believe in Milton, Dryden, Pope'. It represented a kick in his readers' teeth. It was 'surely inadmissable', Hobhouse told Byron on 5 January 1819. 'I can hardly think you meant it should stand.' Only three months previously, on 28 September, Hobhouse had assured his friend that, as an author, 'you might positively do what you pleased'. Hobhouse and their Cambridge contemporary, the dandy and gambler Scrope Berdmore Davies read the manuscript of Canto I together. The scarcely veiled portrait of Lady Byron as Donna Inez offended against every canon of good taste. 'Every now and then . . . both the one and the other exclaimed, "*it will be impossible to publish this*".' Hobhouse felt bound to warn Byron: in 'taking advantage of your great command of all readers . . . you will find in a short time that a rebellion will be excited, and with some pretext, against your supremacy.' At least Hobhouse's martial imagery acknowledged Byron's aggressive, heroic intentions in *Don Juan*.

The poem's 'real qualities are not on the surface –', Byron told Douglas Kinnaird on 4 November 1821, 'but still if people will dive a little – I think it will reward them for their trouble.' The epic's 'real qualities' include a serious, even a Napoleonic thrust. Napoleon is indeed central to *Don Juan*'s purpose, which is why it matters that he does not appear in two major studies of Byron's treatment of the Don Juan theme.

His Want of All Community of Feeling

> what he most likes in [Napoleon's] character
> was his want of sympathy
>
> *Lady Blessington's Conversations of Lord Byron*, 82

Byron's heroic ideal remains consistent, from the early fantasies to the late comic epic. In his oriental tales Byron described the actions and character of a heroic male, a renegade, pirate or other outsider. Now the poet moved from description to performance. Having observed the phenomenon of Napoleon and analysed heroism explicitly, implicitly and by analogy in oriental tales and plays, Byron launched his own exercise in Napoleonic heroism in the narration of *Don Juan*.

As John Clubbe has pointed out, when Byron began to write his *Memoirs* and *Don Juan* on 3 July 1818, both were inspired by Napoleon's example. William Warden, a surgeon on board the *Northumberland*, the ship that carried the emperor to St. Helena, published *Letters . . . in which the Conduct and Conversation of Napoleon Buonaparte are Faithfully Described and Related* (1816) and reported that Napoleon 'was seriously and laboriously engaged in writing the Annals of his Life'. The emperor himself corrected Warden's errors in *Letters from the Cape of Good Hope in reply to Mr. Warden* (1817). Byron owned both of these books, along with *Memoirs of . . . Count de Las Cases . . . Giving a Faithful Account of the Voyage of Napoleon to St. Helena, His Residence, Manner of Living, and Treatment on that Island* (1818).

Byron followed in Napoleon's footsteps when he set out in his *Memoirs* and in *Don Juan* to rewrite history, to give his side of the story of his life.

But I think Napoleon inspired more than the epic's autobiographical slant.

Don Juan's mental soarings, the Narrator's disembodied flight as 'a versified Aurora Borealis', enable him to survey everything from a great height. In consequence, his 'bird's eye view' exposes our earthbound illusions, conventions and prejudices, to reveal 'Glory's dream/Unriddled'. The Narrator's 'true Muse' recognises no received truth at all:

> When we know what all are, we must bewail us,
> But, ne'ertheless, I hope it is no crime
> To laugh at *all* things – for I wish to know
> *What* after *all*, are *all* things – but a *Show*?

Elevated, indifferent, the Narrator displays 'That just habitual scorn which could condemn/Men and their thoughts', which was characteristic of other Byronic heroes and which Byron projected on to Napoleon. Byron blamed the emperor's failure on his scornful attitude to humanity: 'For sceptred Cynics Earth were far too wide a den'. *Don Juan*, however, offered Byron the ideal space for his 'tendency to under-rate and scoff/At human power and virtue, and all that'. His attitude in *Don Juan* is the one he allows Napoleon in *The Age of Bronze*, written in 1822–3:

> How, if that soaring Spirit still retain,
> A conscious twilight of his blazing reign,
> How must he smile on looking down, to see
> The little that he was and sought to be!

In the same way, the world that the Narrator surveys becomes his risible Lilliput.

Compare the Narrator's attitude with Napoleon's as seen by Madame de Staël: 'He turned everything, however glorious, into ridicule, except force; *shame to the vanquished* was the declared maxim of his reign.'

Crucially, *Don Juan*'s Narrator can supersede the emperor, in that only Byron can afford to demonstrate his independence from his 'people', his 'subjects', who are his readers and his characters. Refusing to empathise with his hero's plight; insisting that readers distance themselves from Juan's rare moments of feeling or of action; the Narrator's use of direct snubs and partial irony, his biased presentation of his hero recreate and even surpass Napoleon's distance from his followers.

The Narrator can afford to be *more* Napoleonic than Napoleon – the Corsair's Corsair. Byron demonstrates this as early as Canto II. Nowadays the shipwreck scene tends to be read as a black comedy. While the humour of Canto II reflects the 'terrible jocundity' and 'sportive ferocity' of Kean's acting, which we explored in Chapter 15, it also expresses Byron's serious, indeed heroic intentions.

Byron believed that Napoleon's 'great error' in practical terms was his 'continued obtrusion on mankind of his want of all community of feeling for or with them'. Napoleon exemplified this habit in the remark, which he 'is said to have used on returning to Paris after the Russian winter had destroyed his army, rubbing his hands over a fire, "This is pleasanter than Moscow"'. According to Byron, this 'would probably

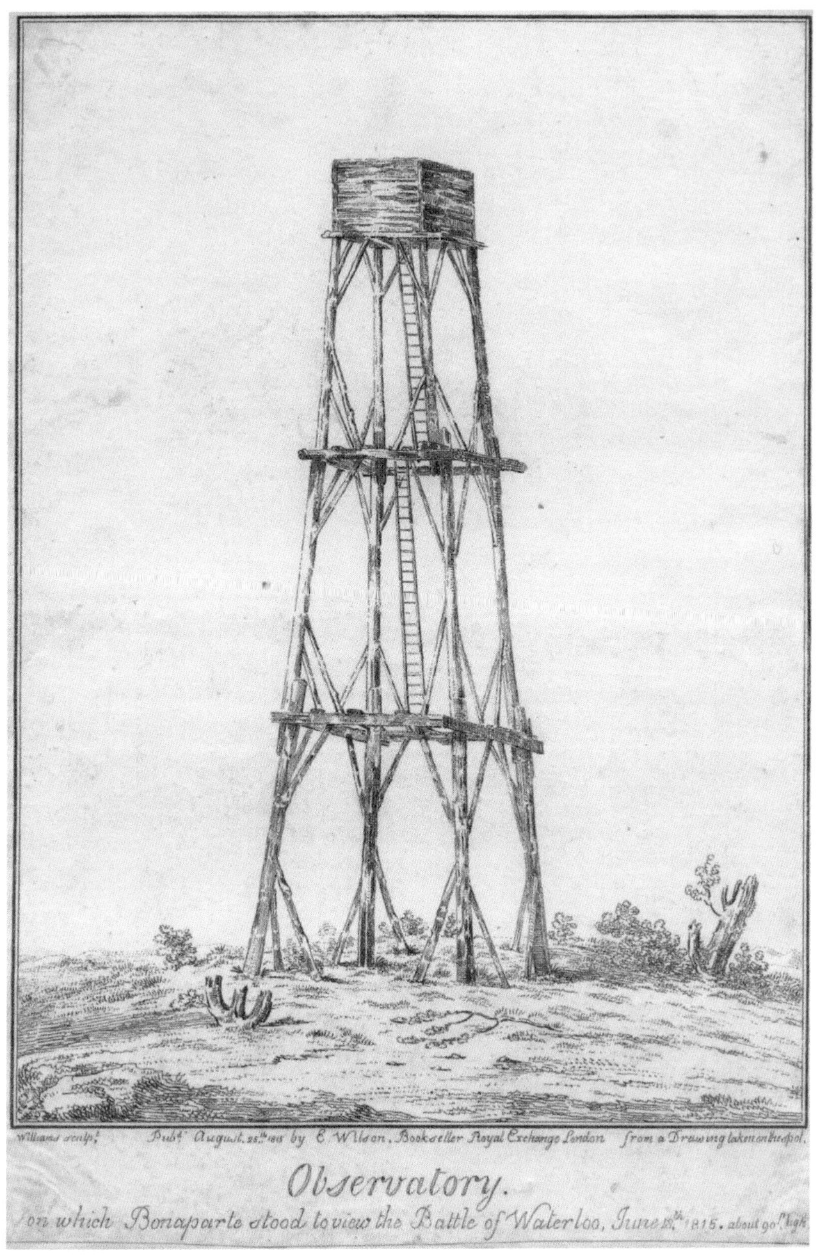

Napoleon had a tower constructed on the battlefield of Waterloo, 'about 90' high', to enable him to see into the distance. This engraving of his 'Observatory' was made by Williams 'from a drawing taken on the spot' on 18 June 1815.

Private collection

alienate more favour from his cause than the destruction and reverses which led to the remark'. Napoleon's grandly bathetic remark was monstrous, 'perhaps more offensive to human vanity than the active cruelty of a more trembling and suspicious tyranny', but Byron felt that its titanic lack of 'bonhomie' represented not a moral weakness but a tactical error. Blaming any offence it caused on 'human vanity' suggests that Byron felt it was, in fact, admirable.

In Canto II, outrageously, the Narrator refuses to allow the shipwreck any 'community of feeling'. Byron imitates Napoleon's use of litotes, the rhetorical device of understatement to achieve maximum effect – as he did when he threatened that *Don Juan* was meant to be 'a little quietly facetious'. The waves that oozed through Pedrillo's porthole made 'His birth a little damp'. Some landsmen would have 'looked a little pale' as 'The water rush'd through in a way quite puzzling'. Byron insists on using inappropriate, minimal epithets and grotesquely irrelevant commonplaces:

Illustration by George Cruikshank, dated 7 May 1825

> But still t'is best to struggle to the last,
> 'Tis never too late to be wholly wreck'd:
> And though 'tis true that man can only die once,
> 'Tis not so pleasant in the Gulf of Lyons.

Byron surely used the word 'pleasant' deliberately, in homage to Napoleon's usage 'on returning to Paris after the Russian winter had destroyed his army, rubbing his hands over a fire'. The word returns in a related context to evoke the slave market in Constantinople: ''Tis pleasant purchasing our fellow creatures'. Byron used it once again when he evokes the assault on Ismail, conscious that the episode was 'like the storm in Canto Second': 'Also to have the sacking of a town,/A pleasant thing to young men at their years'.

Of all *Don Juan*'s scenes, the shipwreck most appalled his contemporaries – exactly as the author hoped, since that demonstrated his independence: it proved his claim to Napoleonic/Satanic status. *Blackwood's Edinburgh Magazine* called Byron 'a cool unconcerned fiend, laughing with a detestable glee over the whole of the better and worse elements of which human life is composed'. In the shipwreck scene, 'the demon of depravity does not desert him'; it manifests the author's 'demoniacal laugh'. Goethe paid tribute too: 'The technical handling of the verse is quite in harmony with the strange, wild, ruthless content; the poet spares his language as little as he spares humanity.'

Its style is consistent with Napoleon's character, as outlined by Madame de Staël in her *Considérations sur la Révolution Française*, first published posthumously in French and in English. Murray promised to send it to Byron in a letter of 7 July 1818. She may well have shown the manuscript to those who were interested and who visited her at Coppet, as Byron did in 1816. 'Such a being,' she wrote of Napoleon, 'having no parallel, could neither feel nor arouse any sympathy: he was either less or more than a man . . . He regards a human being as a fact or as a thing, but not as a fellow-creature . . . I felt in his soul a cold sharp-edged sword, which froze the wound that it inflicted; I perceived in his mind a profound irony, from which nothing great or beautiful, not even his own glory, could escape . . . his contempt of the human race had quite dried up his soul, and he believed that there was no depth but in the region of evil.'

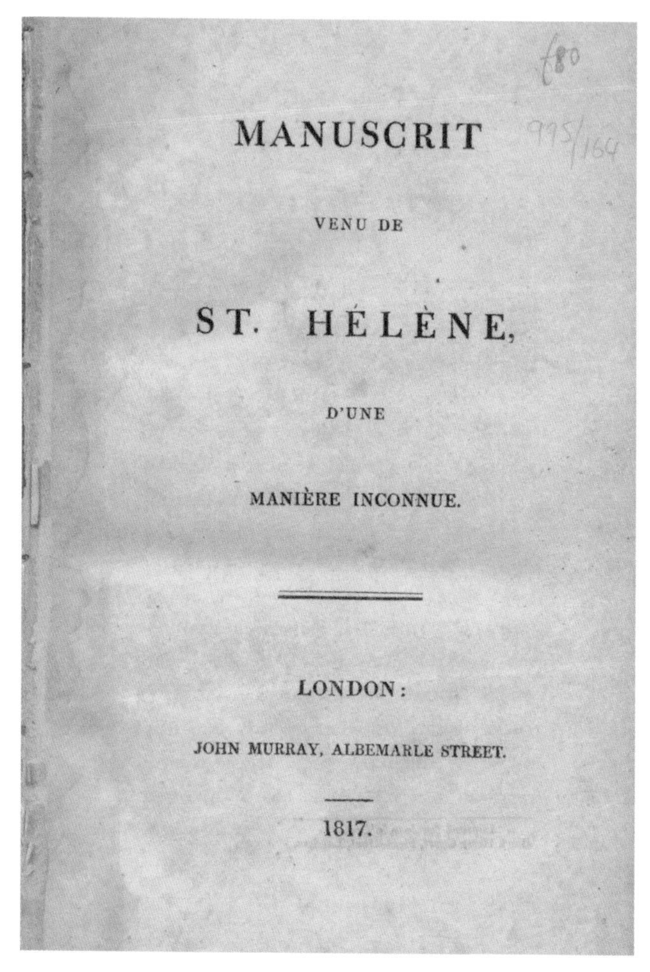

MANUSCRIT

VENU DE

ST. HÉLÈNE,

D'UNE

MANIÈRE INCONNUE.

LONDON:

JOHN MURRAY, ALBEMARLE STREET.

1817.

Title page of the Manuscrit venu de St Hélène, *which John Murray published in French and English and sent to Byron in 1817. The* Manuscrit *was anonymous, but Hortense, the ex-Queen of Holland, Napoleon's stepdaughter and sister-in-law, believed it was authentic – according to Byron's friends the Kinnairds. 'Never was a little book so interesting,' Haydon commented in his diary on 28 March 1817, '. . . it does one's mind good to read it, and gives one a higher idea of Buonaparte's intellect than all the battles he has fought.' Haydon declared it authentic in the* Examiner *on 27 April and 1 May 1817. According to Barry O'Meara's* Napoleon in Exile, *published in 1822 (and read by Byron), the Emperor himself conceded that 'it must have been written by a person who had heard him reason, and was acquainted with his ideas'. Byron certainly believed it was authentic, as a letter to Hobhouse of 11 September 1823 shows.*

Private collection

In this way Byron chose to fulfil and even exceed expectations of his work that had been nurtured by his cult of the Satanic hero. Lady Byron recognised the model for her husband's writing when she read *Childe Harold* III in 1816: 'He is the absolute monarch of words, and uses them, as Bonaparte did lives, without more regard to their intrinsic value.'

Byron owned an apparently objective, authentic (but neglected) source for his idea of the way Napoleon would express himself. The anonymous *Manuscrit venu de St Hélène* was part of lot 147 in the catalogue of his library when it was sold on 6 July 1827, along with twelve other works related to Napoleon.

Napoleonic Style

'I have just received in a way perfectly unaccountable, a MS. from St Helena – with not a word,' Murray told Byron on 20 March 1817. 'I suppose it to be originally written by Buonaparte or his agents. – It is very curious his life, in which each event is given in almost a word – a battle described in a short sentence.'

Murray published the *Manuscrit* in French and English. 'I think you will like my MSS. de St Helena,' he told Byron on 5 August 1817, immediately after recommending Coleridge's 'Life & Opinions', *Biographia Literaria*, 'wch will I think interest you'. Byron was intrigued and, even before he read it he referred to the *Manuscrit* as 'A smart Critique on St. Helena' in his letter to John Murray of 21 August. Kinnaird brought both works to Byron in October.

Their conjunction could not have been more apt.

The *Manuscrit*'s substance so perfectly fits with Madame de Staël's analysis of Napoleon's character that it is tempting to attribute it to her, rather than to her friend Lullin de Châteauvieux, to whom it has been credited. He was an agronomist whose other works display none of its style. Napoleon was tempted to imagine she wrote it, but thought that it had too many vulgar errors to be by her. Instead, he concluded, 'The sentences expressed in it are such as Madame de Staël would talk.' 'Bonaparte, when

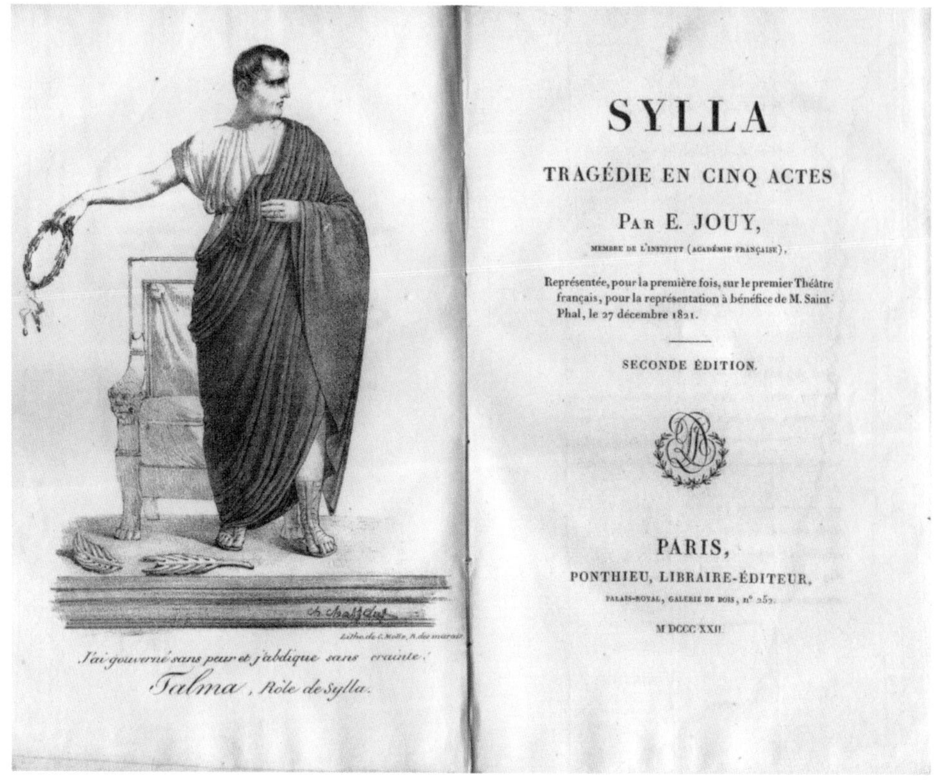

SYLLA

TRAGÉDIE EN CINQ ACTES

PAR E. JOUY,

MEMBRE DE L'INSTITUT (ACADÉMIE FRANÇAISE),

Représentée, pour la première fois, sur le premier Théâtre français, pour la représentation à bénéfice de M. Saint-Phal, le 27 décembre 1821.

SECONDE ÉDITION.

PARIS,

PONTHIEU, LIBRAIRE-ÉDITEUR,

PALAIS-ROYAL, GALERIE DE BOIS, n° 252.

M DCCC XXII

The French actor François Joseph Talma (1763–1826) as the Roman dictator Sulla. When Talma read the Manuscrit, *Murray told Byron on 5 August, he felt 'that he conversed with Buonaparte', who was the actor's friend and admirer. The engraving shows that Talma's performance made obvious reference to Napoleon.*

Private collection

he had a million armed men at his disposal, did not on that account attach less importance to the art of guiding the public mind by the newspapers; he himself often dictated articles for the journals, which might be recognized by the violent jolts of style: one can see that he would have wished to put blows instead of words in what he wrote.'

The *Manuscrit* demonstrates Napoleon's fiendish rationalism by supplying evidence for it. The speaker remarks of his youth: 'My understanding led me to detest impositions. I always discerned truth at once, and, for that reason, I always saw better than others to the bottom of things.' He writes of his first experience of battle: 'I felt no kind of emotion; it was not worthwhile; I attended to the action.'

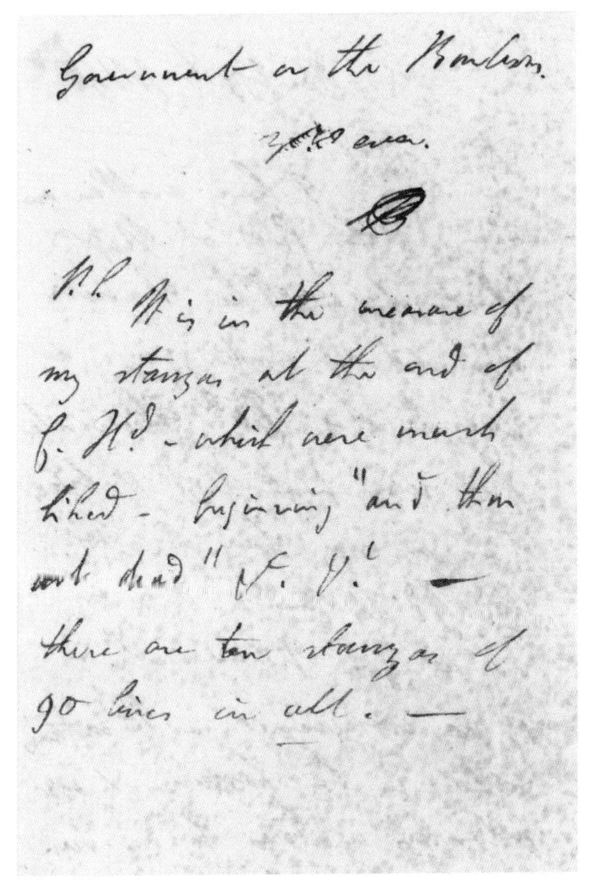
Government on the Bourbons.

NB

P.S. It is in the measure of
my stanzas at the end of
C. Hd – which were much
liked – beginning "and thou
art dead" —
there are ten stanzas of
90 lines in all. —

When Byron's mother-in-law Lady Noel died in January 1822, Byron had to add 'Noel' to his name, in order to inherit his share in her estate. According to Leigh Hunt, 'he delighted, when he took the additional name of Noel . . . to sign himself N.B.; "because," said he, "Bonaparte and I are the only public persons whose initials are the same."' Byron signed NB in a letter to Hobhouse of 12 October 1821.
© John Murray Archive, National Library of Scotland

Napoleon's politics in the *Manuscrit* realise his literary style and vice versa: 'The time is past for finessing in politics: the people are too well informed: the gazettes disclose too much. There is but one secret for governing the world; it is, Be strong: in strength there can be neither error nor deception: it is truth naked.'

An abstracted, remote observer tabulates events and facts without giving any weight to assumptions or associations. The mind behind such remarks rejects all conventions and illusions and is consequently capable of a skeletal wit, a ruthless, aggressive irony.

Poetic War

At more than one point in *Don Juan* the Narrator explicitly confronts his own Napoleonism. The references have been read as ironic and as mock-heroic. But are they? In Canto XI Juan enters English society and encounters 'the eighty "greatest living poets"':

> Even I – albeit I'm sure I did not know it,
> Nor sought of foolscap subjects to be king, –
> Was reckoned a considerable time,
> The grand Napoleon of the realms of rhyme.

The next stanza, which Byron inserted later, continues: 'But Juan was my Moscow, and Faliero/My Leipsic, and my Mont Saint Jean seems Cain'.

'But' seems to suggest that Byron's controversial works cost him his Napoleonic status; in reality, however, all Byron lost was the undisputed primacy he enjoyed during his 'reign' in the spring of 1812. Reliving Moscow, Leipzig and Waterloo with his publications *confirms* Byron's claim to Napoleonic status or identity – under attack, alone against the world, like his father. Later in Canto XI the Narrator reaffirms his actively Napoleonic ambition: 'Now that the Lion's fall'n . . ./. . . I will fall at least as fell my hero;/Nor reign at all, or as a monarch reign'. He alludes to his own behaviour as Narrator: in *Don Juan*, as Narrator he can still function as a 'monarch', i.e. as an autocrat. He also surely alludes to Napoleon: in his diary for 29 December 1815 Hobhouse recorded Napoleon's remark to General Sebastiani 'during his last reign: ". . . it is very well talking of the English Constitution, but I would rather not reign at all than reign as King of England."' Byron's mock-heroic self-coronation contained a determinedly serious, even heroic intent.

As Stendhal saw, 'it was not at all the despotic and odious part of Napoleon's character that displeased the English peer.' Napoleon's 'monarchism' led to his downfall: he lost power, once his followers felt that he despised them. Here Byron knew that he could prove more heroic, more

An unrepentantly positive portrait of 'An Island Exile' (Napoleon), probably by George Cruikshank, from A Political Lecture on Heads by the Black Dwarf *[William Hone], 1820:*

> *Here's the head of an Exile, a Hero, a Chief –*
> *Whose misplac'd reliance now causes his grief;*
> *Whose name shall exist when its foes' are forgot,*
> *And the present Legitimates gloriously rot –*
> *Whose talents eclipse all the talents on earth,*
> *As far as relates to monarchical worth . . .*

Napoleonic than Napoleon. At one point he asks his readers to cooperate with him, to class 'My faults even with your own! which meaneth, Put/A kind construction upon them and me'. But that would risk compromising his independence from his subjects/readers, so he recants in the next line: 'But *that* you won't – then don't – I am not less free'.

If he seems to retreat, it is for strategic reasons, so as to launch another attack. In Canto IV, for instance, he claims that he 'once had great alacrity in wielding/My pen, and liked poetic war to wage'. Five cantos later he changes past to future tense, promising, 'And I will war, at least in words (and should/My chance so happen – deeds) with all who war/With Thought'. When he pauses, he does so in martial fashion, 'as doth a crew/ Before they give their broadside'. Digressions carry an imperial charge, as 'addresses from the throne,/Which put off business to the ensuing session'. The Narrator may condescend to address his readers *ad hominem*, but the congruence of 'my people' and 'throne' confirms that in the world of his poem, he is king. 'I may stand alone,' he comments disingenuously at the end of Canto XI, 'But would not change my free thoughts for a throne'. Byron's 'free thoughts' in the narration constitute a greater throne than any monarch's, since its authority remains independent of its subjects' approval. Byron promised Murray on 1 August 1819 that 'the public opinion – never led nor ever shall lead me. – I will not sit on "a degraded throne".'

In 1817 a Venetian newspaper asserted that Napoleon was 'the protagonist' of *Childe Harold* III 'under a fictitious name'. Byron wrote to correct the mistake, but it may have inspired him to make Napoleon the protagonist and Narrator of his new poem, *Don Juan*, which he began that autumn.

He insisted on publishing *Don Juan* in the teeth of advice from his friends in London: 'I will battle my way against them all,' he announced to Murray on 6 April 1819, having sent off Canto II, '– like a Porcupine.' His tone harks back to spring 1814 when he 'battled his way' against public opinion, rather as Napoleon fought against the snows of Russia.

No wonder that, at the very start of *Don Juan*, at his first mention of Buonaparte, Byron notes that his friend Douglas Kinnaird reported how 'one of the nearest family connections of Napoleon (Eugène Beauharnais)' authorised him to say that 'the delineation of Napoleon' in *Childe Harold* III 'was complete – or words to this effect'.

From this admittedly partial point of view, *Don Juan* is Byron's *Eroica*. Beethoven named his Third Symphony 'Bonaparte', but then tore off the title page from the score. Instead, it became the *Eroica*, the Heroic Symphony, 'in memory of a great man'. He still wrote on the title page '*Geschrieben auf Bonaparte*', written on or about Bonaparte.

Napoleon seemed to embody the revolution: the power that had erupted in the mass storming of the Bastille was apparently reborn in one man's headlong leading of the attack at Lodi, the liberation of Italy and other campaigns: he was, as Hölderlin said in his poem 'Buonaparte', '*der schnelle*', the fast one.

The *Eroica* reflects and embodies Beethoven's own harnessing of revolutionary energy. He restaged the storming of the Bastille in the original version of his only opera *Leonore* (later recast and renamed *Fidelio*): a mob breaks down the prison wall, in a riotous, anarchic moment that at first causes fear, rather than relief. Beethoven later recreated that irresistible flood of energy in the overture, *Leonore No. 3*, in his Fifth Symphony and again in his Ninth Symphony. The composer takes over from Napoleon-as-liberator, incorporating into his music French revolutionary themes and referring to his ballet *The Creatures of Prometheus* and to an English *contredanse* in order to incite listeners to rise up, to swear allegiance to the cause of liberty.

28

NARRATOR versus HERO

Odd Couples: Comparative Heroics

Don Juan's Narrator and hero frequently become rivals, when the Narrator offsets the actions of the 'young fellow' with his own scornful reactions. Intrusive, digressive asides and explicit snubs inhibit any sympathy with 'our little friend'. Byron reinforces this comparative habit by staging Juan's encounters with other, older male partners.

When he first meets Haidee's father Juan 'sprung', 'caught', 'snatched', but Lambro rebukes his childish impetuosity: '"put up, young man, put up your silly sword."' The pirate-father shows up Juan's inadequacies. In Juan's cheek 'the blood/Oft came and went', whereas 'You never could divine his [Lambro's] real thought'. 'High and inscrutable the old man stood,/Calm in his voice, and calm within his eye –/Not always signs with him of calmest mood'. A 'man of savage temperament,/Of mild demeanour though of savage mood', 'mildest manner'd' Lambro displays the qualities Byron admired in Ali Pacha and in his boxing coach John Jackson.

In the fight that follows Juan faces an unnamed 'wary, cool old sworder' and is soon 'floored and helpless', 'o'ermastered and cut down'. Aptly, geography serves to reinforce the imbalance: when he returns to consciousness and slavery Juan gazes on the sea 'O'ershadowed by many a hero's grave', namely the heroic landscape of ancient Troy.

In the fifth canto Juan meets John Johnson. His name betrays his comparative role. 'John Johnson' and 'Don Juan' share assonance, alliteration and, indeed, meaning. Byron himself was 'John's son'. The fictional couple of John and Juan recreate the missing relationship that Byron longed for, of novice with initiate, of juvenile, 'page' or protégé, with an older man, his patron, mentor or protector.

In John Johnson Byron pays a generous, explicit tribute to his mentor John Jackson. On sale at the slave market, 'Juan was juvenile . . . he looked a little dull,/And now and then a tear stole down by stealth'. Just two stanzas later 'A man of thirty, rather stout and hale,/With resolution in his dark gray eye,/Next Juan stood'. The Englishman's 'sang froid' is clearly contrasted with the 'mere lad's' moment of sensibility: Juan weeps, whereas Johnson only cried when his first wife died; when his second wife ran away; and when he ran away from his third wife. His prosaic common sense puts Juan's misery into perspective: '"'Tis bad and may be better – all men's lot"'. Juan boldly suggests, '"If we should strike a stroke to set us free"'. Johnson pragmatically rebuffs the initiative: he needs food. Having eaten, he will consider Baba's offer of circumcision, which Juan rejected with an intemperate, tactless display of histrionics.

The odd couple next appear together at the Siege of Ismail. Warfare might seem likely to bring out Juan's latent virility. But as soon as he is pervaded with the 'thirst Of Glory', the Narrator reminds us in the couplet that he was 'a generous creature/As warm in heart as feminine in feature'. Juan 'fought He knew not why', 'For he was dizzy, busy'. Johnson, on the other hand, that 'clever fellow', 'Knew when and how "to cut and come again:"'

> Seldom he varied feature, hue, or muscle,
> And could be very busy without bustle;
>
> And therefore, when he ran away, he did so
> Upon reflection . . .

The Siege of Ismail presents Johnson as a Byronic hero, a leader whose 'soul' inspires his body of men.

The name Johnson may also allude to another champion boxer, who made his debut in the ring in 1783 and died at forty-seven in 1797.

Whether inspired by Tom Johnson and/or by John Jackson, boxing itself provides a model for Johnson and Juan's relationship and for the parental bond that the poem celebrates elsewhere, both explicitly and implicitly.

Sparring

> SPARRING is absolutely necessary to form a complete pugilist. It is, certainly, a mock encounter; but, at the same time, a representation, and, in most cases, an exact one, of real fighting.
>
> Pierce Egan, *Boxiana*, II, 16

As we saw, boxing matches confront a hero with his doppelgänger. *Don Juan* consists of multiple sparring matches. The principal bout between John Johnson and Don Juan reflects that between Narrator and hero. Indeed, Johnson's remark to Juan serves as an epigraph to this book, because it could stand as a motto for the entire poem:

> you will allow,
> By setting things in their right point of view,
> Knowledge, at least, is gained . . .

But Lambro, Suwarrow and Potemkin all double the Narrator's comparative role.

In Canto VII the Russian Field Marshal Suwarrow turns out to be another 'spirit leader' who inspires his 'body' of men, shining over them like 'a dancing Light,/Which all who saw it followed, wrong or right'. ''Tis thus the spirit of a single mind/Makes that of multitudes take one direction'.

As a 'philosopher' Suwarrow echoes the Narrator's scoffing tendency:

> . . . drilling,
> Exclaiming, fooling, swearing at the inert,

> And lecturing on the noble art of killing, –
> For deeming human clay but common dirt,
> This great philosopher was thus instilling
> His maxims . . .

At least four of Suwarrow's activities listed above apply to the Narrator, who participates in five more: 'Surveying, drilling, ordering, jesting, pondering'. Suwarrow sums up the Siege of Ismail with a ruthless brevity that recalls

Gillray's portrait of Suwarrow, 23 May 1799. The etching claims to be 'after the Original Drawing taken from Life by Lieutenant Swarts, of the Imperial Regiment of Barco Hussars': 'This extraordinary Man is now in the prime of life, – Six Feet, Ten Inches in height; – never "tastes either Wine or Spirits; takes but one Meal a day; & every morning plunges into an Ice Bath; – his Wardrobe consists of a plain Shirt, a White Waistcoat & Breeches, short Boots, & a Russian Cloak; he wears no covering on his head either by day or night – when tired, he wraps himself up in a Blanket & sleeps in the open air; – he has fought 29 pitched Battles, & been in 75 Engagements" – See Vienna Gazzette'.

Private collection

Souvaroff teaching his Recruits to use the Bayonet.

Illustration by George Cruikshank, from George Clinton, Memoirs of the Life and Writings of Lord Byron, *1825.*

Napoleon's style. In the original Russian it was 'A kind of couplet; for he was a poet'.

After sixty stanzas away from the hero we are reintroduced to Juan in a roundabout, doubly oblique manner. The point of view the reader shares is that of General Suwarrow, the centre of attention over twelve previous stanzas. Johnson himself is 'put up against' Suwarrow. Their encounter takes up twenty densely dramatic lines and boasts an unexpectedly poignant quality. It makes Johnson authentically heroic.

Don Juan constructs a ladder of heroism: at its top, Suwarrow looks up to Prince Potemkin, as Johnson does to Suwarrow, and as Juan looks up to Lambro, Johnson and the Narrator. This 'young fellow', as Suwarrow calls Juan, echoing the Narrator, behaves like 'an ass', or like 'a mere novice', whose 'Mere virgin valour never dreamt of flying,/From ignorance of danger'. Byron pairs the characters to show up the inadequacies in his hero that he exposes elsewhere, directly.

Lambro, Johnson and Suwarrow share in the Narrator's Napoleonic

Byron loved masquerades, ever since he attended one as a child visiting Bath with his mother in the autumn of 1802. He appeared in the character of a Turkish boy, which, as Moore pointed out, anticipated his own orientalist fiction. 'On his entering into the house, some person in the crowd attempted to snatch the diamond crescent from his turban, but was prevented by the prompt intervention of one of the party.' On 1 July 1814 he attended a masquerade at Burlington House in honour of Lord Wellington. Hobhouse noted in his diary, 'Byron as a monk looked very well'. Byron used this mask at the Ravenna Carnival in February 1820.

Keats-Shelley Memorial Association, all rights reserved

heroism. He refers to Johnson as Jack and Jack was, as Byron knew, one of the English nicknames for Napoleon.

We may deprecate the horrified reaction of Byron's original readers, but at least they appreciated what he was up to. The anonymous *Apology for Don Juan Cantos I–II* (by John Wesley Thomas, 1824) identifies the author with such authentically, Byronically, heroic figures as Lucifer, Prometheus and Cromwell. Byron would have been delighted.

Byron attacked the Restoration of the Bourbons as a 'damned, insipid medium'. As we have seen, extremism was one of the crucial traits of his heroic ideal, exemplified by Lara, who opted for 'no tame, trite medium'.

'Donny Johnny will either succeed greatly – or tumble flatly,' Byron predicted to Hobhouse on 30 July 1819, '– there will be no medium – at least I think not.' By 'Donny Johnny' he means of course the poem *Don Juan*, not the wimpy eponym Don Juan.

The distance between Narrator and hero is not found elsewhere in Byron's poems. It may be analogous to the relationship of spirit to flesh; it certainly corresponds to the Byronic hero leading his body of men. The Narrator's bias against his hero, the way he intrudes his self-reflecting comments and partial irony, the way he insists on comparing his experiences and achievements with Juan's, offer Byron an ideal opportunity to display the Corsair's 'power of Thought – the magic of the Mind!. . ./That moulds another's weakness to its will'.

But why associate the idea of Don Juan with Napoleon? Coleridge linked the two in the book that Kinnaird brought Byron, along with the supposed Napoleonic memoirs.

Byron's friend, banker and 'very effective "hit-man"', the Honourable Douglas James William Kinnaird muses in open-collared Byronic style in a painting attributed to J. R. Smith. It is a study in hero-worship: Kinnaird holds a copy of Byron's Parisina *while he contemplates a bust of Napoleon and engravings of Clint's portrait of Edmund Kean as Sir Giles Overreach and of Westall's portrait of Byron. Kinnaird was briefly MP for Bishop's Castle, Shropshire.*

Photo: Bishop's Castle Town Council

29

INTELLECTUAL LORDSHIP

Coleridge and the Byronic Hero

In 1809 Coleridge cannot have enjoyed being the butt of Byron's patronising laughter in *English Bards*: 'Shall gentle COLERIDGE pass unnoticed here?/To turgid ode, and tumid stanza dear?/Though themes of innocence amuse him best,/Yet still obscurity's a welcome guest.' Byron regretted his attack, which was, he told Coleridge on 31 March 1815, 'pert, and petulant, and shallow enough'. Coleridge already envied Byron's success as the handsome, younger, noble and newly fashionable poet. From what he heard of *Childe Harold*, Coleridge commented in 1812, it was 'exactly on the plan that I myself not only conceived six years ago, but have the whole Scheme drawn out in one of my old Memorandum Books'. Resentment festered, even before Byron offered him practical help and financial support. On the other hand Coleridge was dazzled when he first met Byron: 'so beautiful a countenance I scarcely ever saw – his teeth so many stationary smiles – his eyes the open portals of the sun – things of light, and for light'.

Adulation followed by disappointment: the sequence is common to Coleridge's relationships with Byron and with Napoleon.

Milton's Satan linked them, viewed through the perspective of contemporary politics.

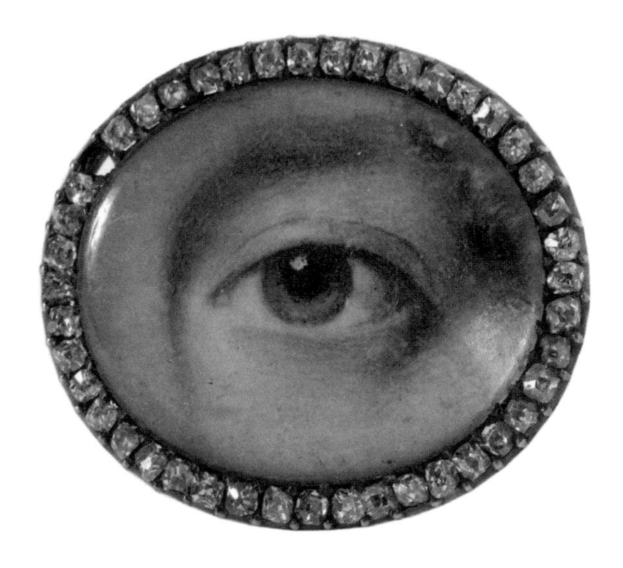

Byron's left eye in a miniature now in the Musée Carnavalet, Paris. Its case has engraved on the back, 'LORD BYRON'. The eye's colour is not the blue that Byron expected to see in his daughter Allegra's eyes, but witnesses disagree: his eyes were described as grey, light blue, brown, azure, even greenish.
© Roger-Viollet/Topfoto

Byron and Coleridge

Byron admired Coleridge's poetry. He persuaded John Murray to publish *Christabel* and other poems, and to raise the fee he had offered. When Sotheby asked Byron to help Coleridge, Byron sent him a cheque for £100, at a time when he was 'under siege from bailiffs'. Having joined the Drury Lane Theatre's Sub-Committee of Management, Byron encouraged Coleridge to write a play for the reopening of the theatre, '*not* disinterestly [*sic*] but as a *Committee* man'. Coleridge failed to deliver the promised play in time. To his fury the theatre reopened in May 1816 with Maturin's *Bertram*, which Byron and Scott endorsed. Coleridge assumed it had been preferred to his makeshift *Zapolya*, which he submitted late, on 10 April. *Bertram* proved a success.

Unfortunately, as though to rub salt into the wound, when the *British Review* discussed Coleridge's *Christabel* that August it felt 'obliged' to draw attention to 'the great disparity between' it and, of all works, *Bertram*,

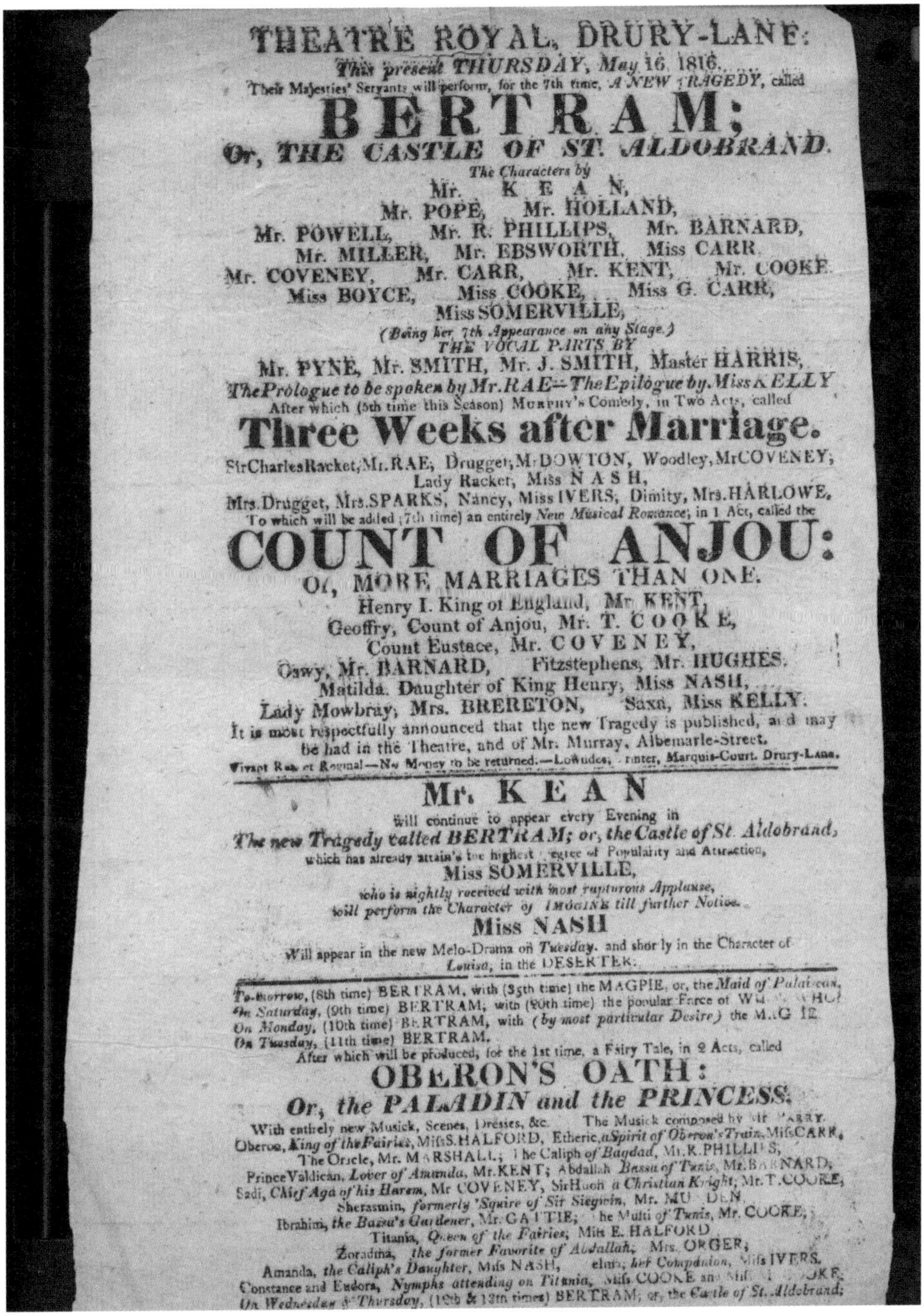

THEATRE ROYAL, DRURY-LANE:
This present THURSDAY, *May* 16, 1816,
Their Majesties' Servants will perform, for the 7th time, *A NEW TRAGEDY*, called

BERTRAM;

Or, THE CASTLE OF ST. ALDOBRAND.

The Characters by
Mr. KEAN,
Mr. POPE, Mr. HOLLAND,
Mr. POWELL, Mr. R. PHILLIPS, Mr. BARNARD,
Mr. MILLER, Mr. EBSWORTH, Miss CARR,
Mr. COVENEY, Mr. CARR, Mr. KENT, Mr. COOKE,
Miss BOYCE, Miss COOKE, Miss G. CARR,
Miss SOMERVILLE,
(Being her 7th Appearance on any Stage.)
THE VOCAL PARTS BY
Mr. PYNE, Mr. SMITH, Mr. J. SMITH, Master HARRIS,
The Prologue to be spoken by Mr. RAE—The Epilogue by Miss KELLY
After which (5th time this Season) MURPHY'S Comedy, in Two Acts, called

Three Weeks after Marriage.

Sir Charles Racket, Mr. RAE; Drugget, Mr. DOWTON, Woodley, Mr. COVENEY;
Lady Racket, Miss NASH,
Mrs. Drugget, Mrs. SPARKS, Nancy, Miss IVERS, Dimity, Mrs. HARLOWE,
To which will be added (7th time) an entirely *New Musical Romance*, in 1 Act, called the

COUNT OF ANJOU:

Or, MORE MARRIAGES THAN ONE.
Henry I. King of England, Mr. KENT,
Geoffry, Count of Anjou, Mr. T. COOKE,
Count Eustace, Mr. COVENEY,
Oswy, Mr. BARNARD, Fitzstephens, Mr. HUGHES.
Matilda, Daughter of King Henry, Miss NASH,
Lady Mowbray, Mrs. BRERETON, Saxa, Miss KELLY.
It is most respectfully announced that the new Tragedy is published, and may be had in the Theatre, and of Mr. Murray, Albemarle-Street.
Vivant Rex et Regina!—No Money to be returned.—Lowndes, Printer, Marquis-Court, Drury-Lane.

Mr. KEAN

Will continue to appear every Evening in
The new Tragedy called BERTRAM; or, the Castle of St. Aldobrand,
which has already attain'd the highest degree of Popularity and Attraction,
Miss SOMERVILLE,
who is nightly received with most rapturous Applause,
will perform the Character of IMOGINE *till further Notice.*
Miss NASH
Will appear in the new Melo-Drama on *Tuesday*, and shortly in the Character of
Louisa, in the DESERTER.

To-morrow, (8th time) BERTRAM, with (35th time) the MAGPIE, or, the *Maid of Palaiseau*,
On Saturday, (9th time) BERTRAM, with (20th time) the popular Farce of WHO [illegible]
On Monday, (10th time) BERTRAM, with *(by most particular Desire)* the MAGPIE
On Tuesday, (11th time) BERTRAM.
After which will be produced, for the 1st time, a Fairy Tale, in 2 Acts, called

OBERON'S OATH:

Or, the PALADIN and the PRINCESS.

With entirely new Musick, Scenes, Dresses, &c. The Musick composed by Mr. PARRY.
Oberon, *King of the Fairies*, Miss S. HALFORD, Etheric, *a Spirit of Oberon's Train*, Miss CARR,
The Oracle, Mr. MARSHALL; The Caliph *of Bagdad*, Mr. R. PHILLIPS,
Prince Valdican, *Lover of Amanda*, Mr. KENT; Abdallah *Bassa of Tunis*, Mr. BARNARD,
Sadi, *Chief Aga of his Harem*, Mr COVENEY, Sir Huon *a Christian Knight*, Mr. T. COOKE,
Sherasmin, *formerly 'Squire of Sir Siegwin*, Mr. MUNDEN,
Ibrahim, *the Bassa's Gardener*, Mr. GATTIE; The Mufti *of Tunis*, Mr. COOKE,
Titania, *Queen of the Fairies*; Miss E. HALFORD
Zoradina, *the former Favorite of Abdallah*, Mrs. ORGER,
Amanda, *the Caliph's Daughter*, Miss NASH, [illegible], *her Companion*, Miss IVERS.
Constance and Eudora, *Nymphs attending on Titania*, Miss COOKE and Miss [illegible]
On Wednesday & Thursday, (12th & 13th times) BERTRAM; or, the *Castle of St. Aldobrand;*

Playbill for Maturin's *Bertram; Or, The Castle of St Aldobrand*, 'which has already attain'd the highest degree of Popularity and Attraction', 16 May 1816, with Edmund Kean in the title role.

Private collection

'in the merits of the compositions': Coleridge's volume was 'a weak and singularly nonsensical and affected performance, but the play of Bertram is a production of undoubted genius'.

George Cruikshank's undated portrait of Kean as the 'Byronic hero' of Maturin's play, Bertram, *first performed in May 1816.*

Private collection

Coleridge responded by savaging *Bertram* in five letters that were published in the *Courier* between 29 August and 11 September 1816. He then reprinted them as Chapter 23 of *Biographia Literaria*, in order to help bulk it out to two volumes. Maturin invested his anti-hero Bertram with a routine, second-hand, Satanic, Byronic aura. Coleridge pointedly denies Bertram any glamour, calling him a 'thief-captain, this loathsome and leprous confluence of robbery, adultery, murder, and cowardly assassination'. He claims that Maturin took the 'substance' of *Bertram* from Shadwell's Don Juan play *The Libertine* (1675). Coleridge then wilfully lavishes a Byronic, Satanic glamour on Shadwell's one-dimensional villain Don John. Coleridge calls him 'Don Juan'. From now on in this book inverted commas distinguish Coleridge's figure from Byron's. By changing Don John to 'Don Juan' Coleridge tries to substantiate his claim that he is not dealing merely with Shadwell's (inadequate) text, but rather with the archetypal legend. He claims that 'the *Don Juan*', as he calls *The Libertine*, 'is capable of interesting without poetry, nay, even without words, as in our pantomime of that name'.

Shadwell's version of the Don Juan legend is, according to Coleridge, 'throughout imaginative . . . The comic parts, equally with the tragic; the living, equally with the defunct characters, are . . . as little amenable to the rules of ordinary probability, as the *Satan* of *Paradise Lost*, or the *Caliban* of the *Tempest*, and therefore to be understood and judged of as impersonated *abstractions*.' He adds a page later that 'Don Juan is . . . an intelligible character so much so as the Satan of Milton.'

Coleridge further defines the character's 'abstraction' as 'the union of every thing desirable to human nature, as means . . . which therefore . . . become at length desirable on their own account. On their own account, and in their own dignity they are here displayed, as being employed to ends so unhuman, that in the effect, they appear almost as means without an end.' Inevitably, this sounds reminiscent of Napoleon: 'He was not sanguinary but indifferent respecting the lives of men, considering them but as a means of attaining his end or as an obstacle to be removed out of his way. He was even less irascible than he often seemed to be: he wished to terrify by

Frontispiece to Thomas Shadwell, Don John: or, The Libertine Destroy'd (1675), *1736. The Libertine, 'a rash fearless Man, guilty of all Vice', as the cast list calls him, invites the statue of Don Pedro, Governor of Seville, to dinner. Don John, guilty of parricide, multiple rapes and murders, killed Don Pedro, because he 'kept his sister from' him.*

his words, in order to spare himself the act by the threat. Everything with him was means or end; nothing involuntary was to be found either in good or evil.'

To protect himself, Coleridge claimed in a letter of 15 April 1817 that his essay on 'Don Juan' comprised 'Thoughts, that had been collected from my conversation years before the Bertram was in existence'. He has a point: these 'Thoughts' echo his reactions to politics over twenty years. Back in

1794, Coleridge thought that Robespierre was a heroically Satanic figure, 'whose great bad actions have cast a dangerous lustre on his name', and who (like 'Don Juan') 'possessed a glowing ardor that still remembered the *end*, and a cool ferocity that never either overlooked, or scrupled, the *means*'. Robespierre therefore anticipated Napoleon, whose

> early education must have given him a predilection for a Theory conducted throughout with mathematical precision . . . REASON is the sole Sovereign, the only rightful Legislator; but Reason to act on Man must be impersonated. The Providence which had so marvellously raised and supported him, had marked HIM out for the Representative of Reason, and had armed him with irresistible force, in order to realize its Laws. In Him therefore MIGHT becomes RIGHT . . .

By 1816 Coleridge's references in Chapter 23 of *Biographia Literaria* to Milton's Satan make 'Don Juan' sound like a Byronic hero. As Byron surely appreciated, Coleridge's portrait of 'Don Juan' strongly resembles Byron himself, as seen by contemporary reviewers and readers. This was not a coincidence. In the same chapter Coleridge hints that Byron had much in common with the legendary villain-hero when he analyses the paradoxical characters of 'Don Juan' and of the Supreme Committee of Management of Drury Lane Theatre – whose foremost representative was that self-confessed '*Committee* man' Lord Byron:

> Rank, fortune, wit, talent, acquired knowledge, and liberal accomplishments, with beauty of person, vigorous health, and constitutional hardihood, – all these advantages, elevated by the habits and sympathies of noble birth and national character, are supposed to have combined in Don Juan . . .

Whereas:

> Rank, fortune, liberal education, and (their natural accompaniments, or consequences) critical discernment, delicate tact, disinterestedness,

> unsuspected morals, notorious patriotism, and tried Maecenasship, these were the recommendations that influenced the votes of the proprietary subscribers of Drury Lane Theatre, these the motives that occasioned the election of its Supreme Committee of Management.

A month later, on 3 October 1816, Coleridge attacked the Drury Lane Committee in an unsigned essay published in the *Courier*. He focused on Lord Byron.

Byron insulted Coleridge in *Don Juan* I, calling him 'drunk'. Coleridge answered him ironically in a letter dated 4 September 1819, calling the insult 'flattery' and correcting 'the extravagance of [his] praise'.

But three years later, on 29 December 1822, Coleridge still seethed. He implicitly identified Byron as another Robespierre/Napoleon/Satan/'Don Juan', asking, 'Is it not unnatural to be always connecting very great intellectual power with utter depravity? Does such a combination often really exist in rerum natura?'

Critics have tried to apply Coleridge's insights in Chapter 23 to Byron's Juan. This takes considerable effort, since Juan hardly displays 'intellectual superiority' or 'entire wickedness', let alone both. Most recently *Don Juan: Variations on a Theme* (1990) surveyed the way the legend has been treated from its beginning until the late twentieth century. In the chapter devoted to Byron it argued that 'Superficially . . . Byron's hero is not much like a Don Juan at all. What links him to the type is that, for him too, nature is the only guide.' The difference is that traditional Don Juans justify their behaviour by reference to nature; Byron's Juan feels no need to justify anything. Typically, his Narrator offers the specious argument on his behalf.

No, Coleridge's ideas inspired the poem itself, rather than its hero's character. Byron saw what Coleridge was up to and retaliated by using 'the idea of Don Juan' in the way that Coleridge himself proposed: Coleridge identifies 'abstraction' as 'Don Juan's 'charm and universal interest'; Byron turns him into a disembodied voice, the Narrator, who relishes his abstraction. Coleridge compares 'Don Juan' to 'the idealized figures of the

Apollo Belvedere, and the Farnese Hercules. What the Hercules is to the eye in corporeal strength, Don Juan is to the mind in strength of character.' Coleridge adds that, 'of all power, that of the mind is, on every account, the grand desideratum of human ambition. We shall be as gods in knowledge, was and must have been the first temptation.' Furthermore, 'the co-existence of great intellectual lordship with guilt' allows us to 'contemplate the intellect of man more exclusively as a separate self-subsistence, than in its proper state of subordination to his own conscience, or to the will of an infinitely superior being'.

The narration of *Don Juan* indeed displays 'the intellect of man . . . as a separate self-subsistence'.

To sum up: Coleridge relates 'Don Juan' to Napoleon, Satan and Byron. Byron appropriates these ideas and realises them in *Don Juan*, not in his eponymous 'hero', but in the character and actions of the Narrator, the latest avatar of the real 'Byronic hero'.

At the same time Byron reduces 'Don Juan', whom Coleridge identifies as the ultimate hero, to Juan, a 'mere lad'.

As Ronald Paulson pointed out, 'Byron has also retained the active Don Juan, though years older, in his narrator . . . a literary Napoleon who has lived through the experience of revolution, been defeated, driven into exile, and now comments on the whole process, writing an equivalent of Napoleon's memoirs on St. Helena.'

'Mefistocles'

In Canto XIII the Narrator draws attention to his offensiveness, his indiscriminating objectivity: 'For my part, I am but a mere spectator,/And gaze where'er the palace or the hovel is,/Much in the mode of Goethe's Mephistopheles'. Given the author's well-established Satanic reputation, and the increasing infamy of *Don Juan*, it was outrageous of Byron to draw attention to his devilishness – especially in such a casual manner. The joke, like the daring rhyme, screws home the point. Goethe's Mephistopheles may now seem a wit, rather than anything more formidable. There is 'nothing titanic about this devil', according to the only full-length study of *The Byronic Hero*. But Byron called Goethe's Mephistopheles 'one of the finest and most sublime specimens of human conception'. Mephistopheles, like Milton's Satan, surely gained resonance in the early nineteenth century from a (probably) fortuitous topicality. Madame de Staël's comment on Mephistopheles' 'infernal irony' recalls her portrait of Napoleon: 'I felt in his soul a cold sharp-edged sword, which froze the wound that it inflicted; I perceived in his mind a profound irony, from which nothing great or beautiful, not even his own glory, could escape; for he despised the nation whose votes he wished, and no spark of enthusiasm was mingled with his desire of astonishing the human race.' (Incidentally, Goethe met Napoleon in 1808 and later said that he was 'daemonic by nature'.) 'Farewell, Mefistocles', Lady Caroline Lamb wrote to Byron on 3 June 1814, when she also addressed him as Richard III, Valmont (the villain of *Les liaisons dangereuses*), Machiavelli, Napoleon '& Kean in Othello'. She knew what she meant when she referred to Mephistopheles since she corrected the proofs of her husband's edition of the English translation of Madame de Staël's *De L'Allemagne*.

If *Don Juan*'s Narrator 'is' Mephistopheles, then could Juan perhaps be a version of Faust? Not the titanic intellectual that we know, but Faust as seen through the severe eyes of Madame de Staël: 'a perfect example of someone fickle and mobile, whose feelings are still more ephemeral than the short life of which he complains'. That does correspond to aspects of Byron's Juan, the dizzy victim of circumstances, the adolescent 'tossed, he scarce knew whither'. Byron even refers to de Staël's discussion of Goethe in *Don Juan*, in the context of the poet at Haidee and Juan's feast, a trimmer.

Byron's Juan is nothing like the traditional Don Juan Tenorio of Tirso de Molina, Molière's Dom Juan or Mozart and Da Ponte's Don Giovanni. He is more like Mozart's adolescent pageboy Cherubino in *Le nozze di Figaro*, another 'curly-headed, good-for-nothing,/And mischief-making monkey . . . the most unquiet imp upon earth'. Byron compares Juan to a page and even presents him as 'Love turned a Lieutenant of Artillery', a cupid dressed for war, echoing Figaro's restyling of Cherubino in the Act

I finale, 'Non più andrai'. Cherubino 'has none of Don Giovanni's active and deliberate character, and not a touch of Don Giovanni's brazenness. Intellectual self-justification in the enlightenment manner would never enter his head.' Cherubino and Juan are repeatedly compared to their masters, Count Almaviva and the Narrator. The androgynous, adolescent eroticism of Byron's Juan is passive, like Cherubino's; whereas the Narrator and Count Almaviva's adult sexuality is aggressive, rakish, compulsive, Don Juan-esque.

'Young Juan . . . seemed/Active though not so sprightly as a page'. Byron only named one other character in his work Juan, and that was the Corsair's page. Composing *Don Juan* allowed Byron to fill the gap in his life between the departure of his English page Robert Rushton and the arrival of his Greek protégé, Luka Chalandritsanos.

Juan as a Don Juan

When he takes 'our old friend' Don Juan as his hero Byron reminds his readers that the legendary figure was an active, heartless, adult libertine. He then inverts the tradition to record a passive, sensitive, adolescent idealist's series of affairs with older, more experienced women. Byron's version shows how 'the advances always come from the females', as he told Medwin. The poem celebrates female sensuality at the expense of the nominal hero's standing. This raises a question that is as obvious as it has been neglected: why take an archetype and then deny it its identifying traits? Has anyone bothered to portray a stupid Faust, a stay-at-home Ulysses or a pacific Cain?

Byron's epic stages a series of encounters between doubles, between the nominal and the real Don Juan – the Narrator – both in the terms that Coleridge establishes in Chapter 23, as another Byronic hero, and in the conventional, traditional terms that the Narrator outlines in Canto I. 'I love the sex, and sometimes . . . wish . . ./That Womankind had but one rosy mouth/To kiss them all at once from North to South'. The Narrator adds that he had such a wish 'not now, but only while a lad', which emphasises how inadequate his Juan is, another 'lad', who never had that wish. The

Narrator presents himself as an improviser who, like Kierkegaard's Don Juan, can go on indefinitely. Byron's impulse towards literary promiscuity is even fuelled (as, perhaps, it often is with Casanovas) by a fear of impending (intellectual) impotence: 'In youth I wrote, because my mind was full,/And now because I feel it growing dull'.

The relation of Narrator and hero in *Don Juan* offers Byron the opportunity to play light-hearted and serious games with heroism. In his epic's arena Byron can stage a battle of titans, a *King Kong Meets Godzilla*, setting 'Napoleon' versus 'Don Juan'. His epic allows him to furnish the emperor with the worthy 'adversary', which Byron felt he never found.

Coleridge's unwitting contribution to *Don Juan* comes into clearer focus, when it is seen in the light of Byron's last, unfinished play, *The Deformed Transformed.*

The nominal hero Arnold knows that his beloved Olimpia neither loves nor feels gratitude towards him. The devil Caesar asks him, 'would you owe/To thankfulness what you desire from Passion?'

> No – No – you would be *loved* – what you call loved –
> *Self-loved* – loved for *yourself* – for neither health
> Nor wealth – nor youth – nor power – nor rank – nor beauty –
> For these you may be stript of – but *beloved*
> As an Abstraction – for – you know not what –

'It is so sweet to be loved for oneself!' Beaumarchais's Count Almaviva sighs. But Byron expands the idea from his source in Chapter 23 of Coleridge's *Biographia Literaria*:

> There is no danger (thinks the spectator or reader) of *my* becoming such a monster of iniquity as *Don Juan*! *I* never shall be an atheist! *I* have not the least inclination to be so outrageous a drawcansir in my love affairs! But to possess such a power of captivating and enchanting the affections of the other sex! . . . To be so loved for my *own self*, that even with a distinct knowledge of my character, she yet died to save me! this, sir, takes hold

The portrait of Coleridge in old age that John Murray commissioned.
Private collection

> of two sides of our nature, the better and the worse . . . it is among the mysteries, and abides in the dark ground-work of our nature, to crave an outward confirmation of that *something* within us, which is our *very self*, that something not *made up* of our qualities and relations, but itself the supporter and substantial basis of all these. Love *me*, and not my qualities, may be a vicious and an insane wish, but it is not a wish wholly without meaning.

In particular, Coleridge uses the word 'abstraction' several times in that chapter:

> It is not the wickedness of Don Juan, therefore, which constitutes the character an abstraction, and removes it from the rules of probability; but the rapid succession of the correspondent acts and incidents, his intellectual superiority, and the splendid accumulation of his gifts and desirable qualities, as co-existent with entire wickedness in one and the same person . . . [Don Juan's] abstraction [is] the union of every thing desirable to human nature, as means . . . which therefore . . . become at length desirable on their own account. On their own account, and in their own dignity they are here displayed, as being employed to ends so unhuman, that in the effect, they appear almost as means without an end.

Byron's epic poem and his last play are indeed closely linked. The play's central image of the heroic cripple is buried in *Don Juan*, in a detail Byron added to his source for the Siege of Ismail. It retells the familiar Byronic story of a son rejected by his father who remains loyal to him. A brave Tartar Khan's sons defend him before they all die. His fifth son, though 'by a Christian mother nourished,/Had been neglected, ill-used, and what not,/Because deformed, yet died all game and bottom,/To save a sire who blushed that he begot him'. Originally, Byron specified that the boy was 'a Hunchback', like Arnold and then Caesar.

Both the epic and the play mock the Byronic hero.

Aside and Laughing

The devil/Caesar in *The Deformed Transformed*, like the Narrator in *Don Juan*, is an unsympathetic, remote scoffer, another 'mere spectator', whose 'sport' is 'just now to gaze'. Caesar's 'fiendish sarcasm' presupposes the unsympathetic, Napoleonic distance that the Narrator maintains from his 'subjects', mocking his victim/hero, as he 'can mock the mightiest'. The name Caesar alludes to Napoleon, 'His country's Caesar', as Byron said in *The Age of Bronze*, as well as to his own ambition to be Caesar or nothing. Caesar speaks with the Narrator's voice: 'Well! I must play with these poor puppets: 'tis/The Spirit's pastime in his idler hours'.

Arnold is another 'puppet' who begins as a 'Soaring spirit', a classic Byronic hero, but is snubbed as often as Byron's Juan. By the second scene of Part 2 he has lost any distinction. The stage direction reads, '*The City. – Combats between the Besiegers and Besieged in the streets. Inhabitants flying in confusion.*' 'I cannot find my hero;' Caesar complains, 'he is mixed/With the heroic crowd. . .' In effect he rewrites *Don Juan*'s opening line, 'I want a hero.'

Byron never completed Part III of *The Deformed Transformed*, but a note marked 'Mem.' (memorandum) hints that he intended the deformed, intellectual Caesar to triumph at the expense of the handsome, 'heroic' Arnold, rather as the disembodied Narrator triumphs over Juan:

> Jealous – <of>
> Arnold of Caesar
> Olimpia at first not
> Liking Caesar – thus
> Arnold jealous of
> himself under his
> former figure, owing
> to the Power of
> Intellect &c. &c. &c.

Caesar's 'power of Intellect' identifies the Corsair's 'power of Thought' with the 'power . . . of the mind' and 'intellectual superiority' that Coleridge discovered in the legendary 'Don Juan' and that Byron manifested as the Narrator of his *Don Juan*.

PART XII

THE LAST WAR OF INDEPENDENCE, 1822–4

Count D'Orsay's sketch of Byron in Genoa in 1823. At thirty-five Byron rationalised his dietary behaviour as vanity, an attempt to recreate his youthful appearance, but extreme thinness aged him, as the sketch shows. According to Medwin, Byron 'reduced himself . . . to a perfect shadow, a mere skeleton . . . He was become, in fact, the thinnest man I ever remember. The Guiccioli used to put her finger in her cheek to intimate that the hollowness of his visage kept pace with his general emaciation; she did not by any means approve of his Pythagoreanism – his ascetic diet.'

Private collection

30

THIN, THINNER, THINNEST, 1822–3

I have hopes that the cause will triumph;
but, whether it does or no, still
'Honour must be minded as strictly as a milk diet.'
I trust to observe both.

Byron to Moore, 27 December 1823

Byron officiated at the cremation of Shelley's body on the beach near Viareggio on 16 August 1822, an extraordinary procedure that may have been Byron's idea, inspired by ancient Greek funeral ceremonies, and prefigured in his play *Sardanapalus*. After that traumatic experience Byron went for a 'stupid long swim' out to his schooner the *Bolivar* and back 'in the heat of the sun', some three miles 'or better, in all'. As a result, he told Kinnaird on 20 August 1822, his skin '*peeled off in blisters*'. He was now 'as glossy as a snake in its new suit', he told Moore a week later, perhaps thinking of his nickname for Shelley. The experience caused him 'acute pain', Teresa remembered. She kept among her Byronic relics a piece of blistered skin. She had no doubt: 'His loss of weight, which became very marked, dated from that <day> episode. Madame Guiccioli always said that his health received a sharp shock that day.' She blamed 'the luckless Shelley, [who] alive or dead, still brought him misfortune.'

But that experience may not have triggered Byron's weight loss, any more than high-minded economy did: he boasted to Kinnaird on 12 September that his '*table*' did not 'cost four shillings a day' and he explained that he spent so little on food because he wanted to 'get a sum together to go amongst the Greeks or Americans – and do some good'. No, once again, as in 1807, claustrophobia prompted starvation and that was not something Teresa would accept. Byron admitted to Hobhouse a week later, for the first time, that he did not wish to continue his liaison.

Byron had stopped eating by the time he reached Genoa, around 3 October. 'Nothing gratifies him so much as being told that he grows thin,' Lady Blessington observed. 'This fancy of his is pushed to an almost childish extent; and he frequently asks – "Don't you think I get thinner?" or "Did you ever see any person so thin as I am, who was not ill?".'

Matter – Soul – and body

In his poetry, however, he did not immediately lose his new tolerance of matter. In Canto XI of *Don Juan*, which he wrote during his first month in Genoa, the Narrator longs to believe in Berkleyan idealism, but indigestion won't let him.

> And that which after all my spirit vexes,
> Is, that I find no spot where man can rest eye on,
> Without confusion of the sorts and sexes,
> Of being, stars and this unriddled wonder,
> The World, which at the worst's a glorious blunder—

A cancelled, variant line specifies that the 'sorts' are composed 'Of Worlds and Species – Matters – Souls/Matter – Soul – and body.' The disparity has lost its tragic edge; now it merely 'vexes' his spirit.

Byron's principal concern remained, as always, independence. He explained to Kinnaird on 28 November that he cared so much about financial matters, writing him 'a long tirade upon business', because it was 'time to mind it – at least for me to mind it – for without some method in it where or what is independence? the power of doing good to others or yourself.'

By December he had 'subsided into [his] former more meagre outline'; indeed he was 'Thinner even than in 1813'. He convinced himself that he was obliged to be 'very abstinent by medical advice – on account of liver & what not'. Whatever was wrong with his liver, starvation would not help. At best, he could claim that his health was 'not quite wrong', because he was '*very temperate now* as once in my youth'. The word 'temperate' always had a special meaning for Byron.

The few lapses in his diet over his eight months in Genoa highlight its habitual rigour. He celebrated his daughter Ada's birthday on 10 December

Count D'Orsay's drawing of Byron in 1823. On 6 May 1823 Byron asked the artist (through Lady Blessington) to add his cap, 'it would complete the costume – & smooth his brow which is somewhat too inveterate a likeness of the original, God help me!'

Harry Ransom Center, The University of Texas at Austin

with a mutton chop and a bottle of ale. And in January he feasted on mince pies given by an English couple (the first time he had tasted them in seven years).

Abstinence once again expresses his need to escape from smothering domesticity. By 12 January he admitted to his friend Henry Edward Fox that he wished to 'go either to Greece or England in order to regain his liberty'. On 27 February 1823 Byron corrected Augusta's misapprehension that he had put on weight, exactly as he had done eighteen years before: 'so far from being fatter – at *present* I [am] much thinner than when I left England, when I was not very stout . . . Hobhouse can tell you all particulars – though I am much reduced since he saw me – and more than *you* would like.' 'I am as thin as a Skeleton,' he boasted to Hoppner on the same day, 27 February, ' – thinner than you saw me at my first arrival in Venice.' But, he added ruefully, innocently, he was 'far from well'. Starvation destroys the stomach's capacity to digest food; Byron interpreted this to mean that he *needed* to diet. He told Moore on 2 April that he had been ill and was now 'thin, – perhaps thinner than you saw me, when I was nearly transparent, in 1812, – and am obliged to be moderate of my mouth'.

That Voluptuous State and the Ripe Banana

Byron was on the point of transforming himself, about to act, rather than write heroically. At that point he looked back on his old literary heroism and contemplated an alternative course of action – passive submission. He wrote *The Island*, his last large-scale work apart from *Don Juan*, between 11 January and 10 February 1823. It portrays different types of heroes among the mutineers from the *Bounty*. Byron hints that the chief rebel Fletcher Christian is a novice to Captain Bligh's initiate, while the syntax manifests mutual incompatibility: 'Then forward stepped the bold and froward boy/His Chief had cherished only to destroy'. Christian exhibits traditional Byronic heroic traits, with several references to the Miltonic Satan's 'standing' such as 'Fast by the rock, all menacing, but mute,/He stood'. He dies, throwing himself down on to another rock.

His antagonist, Torquil, is potentially another Byronic hero: 'A soaring spirit ever in the van,/A patriot hero or despotic chief,/To form a nation's glory or its grief'. But Torquil yields to 'that voluptuous state,/At once Elysian and effeminate', to femininity and its element, water. Torquil escapes death by diving after the Tahitian girl Neuha, into the sea. He regresses to childhood, thanks to her, 'the infant of an infant's world', who blushes 'Like coral reddening through the darken'd wave/Which draws the driver to the crimson cave,/Herself a billow in her energies'. The lovers surface in a cave paradise, where they feast on 'the cocoa-nut, the yam, the bread/Borne of the fruit . . . The gourd with water recent from the rill,/The ripe banana from the mellow hill'.

The Tahitian Neuha introduces the British sailor Torquil to her hidden, underwater cave in H. Richter's illustration to The Island*: engraved by H. C. Shenton, from* The Byron Gallery*, 1833.*

The Island is a very Shelleyan, utopian idyll and may indeed represent Byron's memorial elegy to Shelley, whose own golden age idyll, 'Epipsychidion' of 1821, was inspired by *Don Juan*, Canto II. But Byron could not sustain its borrowed, visionary/sentimental optimism, any more than he could stay with Teresa. On 5 April Byron received a representative of the London Greek Committee and agreed to visit Greece. On 10 April Mary Shelley told John Williams that 'The Guiccioli and he are as ill together as may be' and that Byron was going to Greece partly because 'he hates Genoa'.

On 23 April Byron refused Lord Blessington's invitation to dinner 'tomorrow – nor indeed any day this week – for *three* days of dinners during the last seven days – have made me so head-achy and sulky – that it will take me a whole Lent to subside again into anything like independence of Sensation from the pressure of materialism.' Teresa Guiccioli underlined this passage (from 'subside') in her copy of Lady Blessington's *Conversations of Lord Byron*. 'I belong to *no* party,' Byron asserted to John Hunt on 5 May, '– and claim the independence of saying what I please of *any* according to their acts.' Once again he is as concerned for his soul's, as for his literary and political, independence.

Later that month Byron admitted that he was 'tired of this place, the shore, and all the people on it'. On 10 June in a letter to Lady Hardy he explicitly equated his 'long foreign liaison of *five* [actually four] years' with 'being exceedingly governed and kept tight in hand', adding:

> I am very much reduced – partly by uncertain health in the winter and partly by the rigorous abstinence necessary to preserve it. – But it is far better – that it makes me more like what I used to be ten years ago – in part at least. – Kinnaird – who had not seen me for two years and a half – was as much struck with the *re-alteration* at present – as he had been with the *former* alteration in the fourth or fifth year since I left England.

'It is not good for your Body or Mind to starve –' Lord Blessington wrote fruitlessly to Byron on 23 April 1823, 'think of Liberty & Live.'

Engrossed by Matter

This background helps us understand why Byron stopped writing *Don Juan* at this particular point. He contemplated several different conclusions but he ends it with the return of his anorexic nightmare, the soul oppressed by the body. Juan is overwhelmed by matter on five different occasions: at a dinner, a banquet, a breakfast, and in two encounters with a powerful, sensual woman.

The dinner in Canto XV (written between 8 and 25 March 1823) features three different soups, turbot, turkey, John Dory, pork, fowls, salmon, venison, ham, wines, champagne, partridge, along with game and game stew, salmi, purée, fruits, ices. As the Narrator comments, 'The mind is lost in mighty contemplation/Of intellect expended on two courses'. It leaves Juan feeling 'restless, and perplexed, and compromised'.

Canto XVI (written between 29 March and 6 May) divides into two halves, each containing a supernatural visitation and a meal.

When he first introduced his hero the Narrator defined him by his traditional fate: Don Juan was 'Sent to the devil, somewhat ere his time'. In a sense Byron re-stages and inverts the traditional ending to the Don Juan legend, in which the hero confronts a ghost, in the form of a statue. The legendary stone statue was solid and nearly immobile. In Byron's *Don Juan*, however, 'Once, twice, thrice passed, repassed – the thing of air'. Adeline's aria stresses the monk's immateriality: 'he did not seem formed of clay'. Whereas Juan is, by contrast, 'petrified'; he 'could not speak or move; but, on its base/As stands a statue, stood'. Byron redistributes the traditional parts and sexes – as he reverses expectations throughout the poem.

Traditionally 'Don Juan' reacts bravely, when the ghost of the man he murdered comes to dinner. But here, instead of offering a Promethean resistance and daring, Byron's Juan is 'powerless', 'shorn of half his strength'. Even Shadwell's limp Don John dared to ridicule the ghost; this Juan is afraid of ridicule and intellectually challenged: 'The more he thought, the more his mind was posed'. The next morning at breakfast

Don Juan surprised by a midnight Visitor.

Illustration by George Cruikshank. Again, Don Juan is made to resemble Lord Byron.

he occupies the centre of our attention, since two of the principal women 'looked' at and one 'surveyed' him. He is negligent in his toilette, distrait and put out by his hot tea. He rallies his spirits, but by dinner his 'nervous feelings' have got the better of him.

The reversals that Byron inflicts on his hero represent tricks, which have been associated with the 'Don Juan' figure ever since his first literary incarnation as Tirso de Molina's Don Juan Tenorio, 'El Burlador de Sevilla' (1630). This first, Spanish Don Juan uses 'burlas' as lethal levelling weapons: his 'tricks' are iconoclastic and laugh at all that is held sacred. Byron's appropriation reinforces the Narrator's Don Juanism at his hero's expense.

At Lord Henry's 'great banquet', Juan's soul fails to cope 'With the substantial company engrossed/By Matter, and so much materialised'. Byron used Ude's book on cooking to supply dishes served at the Amundevilles' dinner:

There was a goodly *'soupe à la bonne femme'*,
Though God knows whence it came from; there was too
A turbot for relief of those who cram,
Relieved with dindon à la Perigueux;
There was also—the sinner that I am!
How shall I get this gourmand stanza through?—
Soupe à la Beauveau, whose relief was Dory,
Relieved itself by pork, for greater glory.

Byron details 'Fowls *à la Condé*, slices eke of salmon,/With sauces Genevoises and haunch of venison'.

315. *Fowl à la Condé.*

Procure a nice fowl, singe and truss it up as above; slit the breast, and introduce small slices of truffles cut into the following shape into the slits that you have made: cover the whole with slices of bacon, and let it be stewed as above. Care must be taken, however, when you pour out the bacon, not to derange the symmetry.

This dish requires to be garnished in imitation of a chambord (No. 77), with larded sweetbread, cockscombs, pigeons à la gautier, large quenelles à la cuillière, and financier's sauce (No. 75).

316. *Fowl à la Turque—(Turkish Fowls.)*

Empty a fine fowl, and be particular in washing the inside of it with very hot water; if you leave any blood in it, the rice will be full of scum. Your rice having boiled sufficient time in rich consommé (stock-broth), season it with salt, and introduce some into the body of the fowl,

The original recipe from Louis Eustache Ude, The French Cook, *1813.*

Then there was God knows what 'à l'Allemande',
'À l'Espagnole,' 'timballe' and 'Salpicon'—
With things I can't withstand or understand,
Though swallow'd with much zest upon the whole;
And 'entremets' to piddle with at hand,
Gently to lull down the subsiding soul,
While great Lucullus' *robe triumphal* muffles—
(There's fame)—young Partridge' fillets, deck'd with truffles.

Those truffles too are no bad accessories,
  Followed by 'Petits puits d'Amour'—a dish
Of which perhaps the cookery rather varies,
  So every one may dress it to his wish,
According to the best of dictionaries,
  Which encyclopedize both flesh and fish.
But even sans 'confitures', it no less true is,
There's pretty picking in those 'petits puits'.

After the banquet Byron emphasises Juan's spiritual capacities but only so as to ridicule them. When Juan meets the apparition again, his 'internal ghost' begins to 'quell his corporal quaking'. His moment of dynamic heroism makes him look still more ludicrous, as spiritual resources prove irrelevant to a purely fleshly encounter. Juan dares to touch the ghost, only to discover it is a woman: his arm 'pressed upon a hard but glowing bust'. The next morning he looks 'wan and worn'. Sumptuous alliteration highlights Juan's obtuseness in mistaking the Duchess for a spirit: 'In full, voluptuous, but *not o'er*grown bulk,/The phantom of her frolic Grace – Fitz-Fulke!' This sequence aptly concludes the story of Byron's reconciliation with femininity and flesh, which began when he encountered both a marble and a mortal bust in 1818.

Juan once more stands in 'his' woman's shadow, subordinated once again to her. Before Canto XVII breaks off it spells out the Duchess's effect on Juan, whose exhaustion recreates his former limpness at the hands of Catherine the Great. No wonder the canto stops after fourteen stanzas. The poem's finale dramatises Byron's state of mind, as his eating disorder returned, his soul subsiding, his independence vanishing.

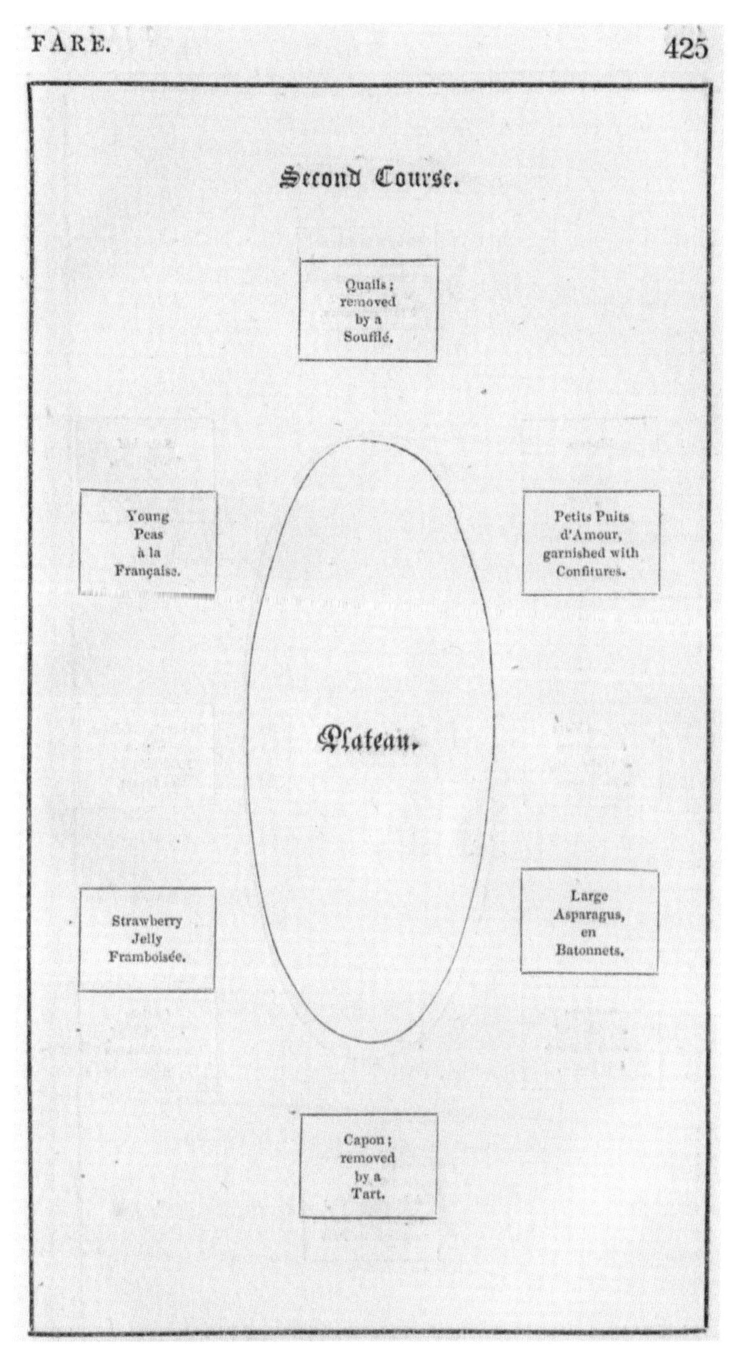
FARE. 425

Second Course.

Quails; removed by a Soufflé.

Young Peas à la Française.

Petits Puits d'Amour, garnished with Confitures.

Plateau.

Strawberry Jelly Framboisée.

Large Asparagus, en Batonnets.

Capon; removed by a Tart.

A suggestion for how the table should be laid from Ude's The French Cook, *1813, one of the sources of* Don Juan *XV, 53ff. Byron redefines Ude's 'Petits puits d'amour garnis des confitures' as 'a classical and well-known dish for part of the flank of the second course'.*

31

STARVED TO DEATH

Genoa, July 1823–Missolonghi, 24 April 1824

What can a son or man do more?

Ulric to his father, *Werner*, IV, i, 411

'I cannot bear to have him unjustly spoken of.' Byron leaped to defend the reputation of his father, Captain Jack Byron at the beginning of July 1823, just as he was about to embark from Genoa in order to devote his energies, his money and his life to the Greeks' fight for independence from the Ottoman empire. A new, French edition of his works included an inaccurate, slanderous attack on Byron's 'genius and character'. Nothing remarkable in that. He only objected, because his great-uncle, the 5th Baron, and, 'more especially', his father, were 'cruelly calumniated'.

Byron looked back, as he had all his life. The poem he chose to head his first book of verse, 'On Leaving Newstead Abbey', dated 1803 when he was fifteen, summons up his 'fathers', the 'Shades of heroes'. Byron traced his ancestry to Ralph de Burun, whose surname suggests he came from Beuron, a village in Normandy. He may have come over to England with William the Conqueror. Later Byrons went on the crusades, fought at Crécy and at Agincourt, in the Wars of the Roses and at Bosworth Field. Henry VII knighted John Byron and, when the monasteries were sold off, Sir John Byron bought the former Augustinian priory at Newstead, along with more land, for £180.

Seven Byron brothers became notable defendants of the Royalist cause in the Civil War. The barony dates back to 1643, when King Charles I granted a peerage to the fifth Sir John, who chose the title Baron Byron of Rochdale.

A fortune-teller once predicted to Mrs Byron that her son would die before he was thirty-six years old. Byron was now thirty-five, the age at which his father died in 1791, and he knew he was facing a pivotal moment in his life. Having established himself as the most important poet of his generation, he chose to abandon writing for action, to risk his life, as well as spend all his energy and his money to fight for the Greeks' independence. In a sense he would at last follow his father's example: Captain Byron had proved himself 'a good officer . . . in the Guards, in America'. Now Byron would fight in another war of independence – in support of rebellion, however, rather than to defend the colonial power. He was about to leave a woman, as his father had left his mother. Both relationships lasted five years.

The Greek expedition represented Byron's last attempt to realise the dream of heroic action, modelled on Napoleon, that he had depicted in his tales and plays and manifested metaphorically in the narration of *Don Juan*.

N.B. in Greece

. . . after all it is better playing at Nations than gaming at Almacks or Newmarket or in piecing and dinnering

Byron to Kinnaird, 23 December 1823

'The Greeks will, sooner or later, rise against them [the Turks];' he predicted in 1810, 'but if they do not make haste, I hope Buonaparte will come and drive the useless rascals away.' Buonaparte never came; Byron did and he ensured that Napoleonic associations haloed his enterprise.

Shortly before she left Genoa, the Countess of Blessington gave Byron one of her rings as a memento. In return he gave her a pin with a small

'A rich chased gold Snuff Box with fine Enamel paintings of Napoleon Maria Louisa & the King of Rome': John Murray bought it for £105 from Love, the jeweller, on 7 November 1818 and gave it to Byron. The bill of sale is in the John Murray Archive at the National Library of Scotland. This was probably the box that Lord Blessington tried to buy from Byron for fifty guineas. Byron eventually sold it to raise funds for the Greek expedition. It was on the London art market in 1982.

cameo of Napoleon. The next day, 2 June 1823, he wrote to ask for it back, explaining that he was 'superstitious, and [had] recollected that memorials with a *point* are of less fortunate augury'. He asked her 'to accept, instead of the *pin* – the enclosed chain – which is of so slight a value, you need not hesitate . . . You will perhaps have the goodness to acknowledge the receipt of this note – and to send back the pin (for good luck's sake).' In Greece he carried a cameo with the head of Napoleon in his waistcoat pocket.

A portrait drawing 'from life' of Byron in uniform in Genoa, dated 2 June 1823.
Private collection

Before he embarked from Genoa Byron persuaded Trelawny to let him have his servant, Benjamin Lewis, a twenty-six-year-old black American. Napoleon was attended by just such a figure on St Helena. Byron insisted that Lewis always addressed him as 'Massa'.

As for his Napoleonic carriage, Byron could not take it with him to Greece but he wrote to his banker Charles Barry on 24 July to 'particularly recommend' it to his care, adding that he 'would not part with [it] for any consideration'. On 27 October he reminded Barry to keep it 'in good order'. Later Byron instructed him to sell off everything he had left behind, apart from a few books and prints (unless they were portraits of him). He also excepted his Napoleonic carriage. Ten days before he died he was still determined to keep it.

During the voyage Byron read the first volume of Las Cases's *Mémorial de Ste Hélène*, 'just out', Swift's life and letters and about South America's war of independence, according to Trelawny. Byron ate 'a considerable quantity of decayed Cheshire cheese, with pickled cucumbers or red

In 1823, anticipating military action, Byron commissioned magnificent helmets in Genoa for himself, Pietro Gamba and Trelawny to wear in Greece. Homer inspired their form. 'I go forth to be recognized,' Byron's Sardanapalus explained of his distinctive helmet, 'and thus/Shall be so sooner'. Byron never saw military action so he may never have worn his crested, plumed helmet. As Mary Shelley told Leigh Hunt on 13 September 1823, 'Helmets so fine were never made to hack.'

Courtesy of Nottingham City Museums and Galleries

cabbage, which he quaffed down by drinking at the same time either a bottle of cider or Burton ale'. He boxed with Trelawny and fenced with Pietro.

Cephalonia, where Byron lived for five months, was one of the Ionian Islands, a British Protectorate that observed neutrality in the war between Greeks and Turks. Byron contributed 20,000 Spanish dollars, so that the Greek navy could relieve the Turkish blockade of Missolonghi. As a sum, he noted in his Journal on 17 October, it was 'not very large – but double that with which Napoleon the Emperor of Emperors – began his campaign in Italy'.

The ship carrying Byron and his entourage moored at Argostoli. The next morning, a group of wild-looking Albanian tribesmen came on board, exiles from their homeland of Suli. On his first visit to Greece Suliotes looked after Byron in shipwreck and in illness, and he celebrated their hospitality and heroism in *Childe Harold*. Byron 'bounded on deck, evidently very much affected', a witness, James Hamilton Brown recorded, 'his expressive countenance radiant with gladness to receive them'. Here surely was the body of men that he longed to lead. Trelawny, a less sympathetic witness recorded, however, that 'a flock of ravenous Zuliote refugees alighted on our decks, attracted by Byron's dollars'. Byron was unwilling to accept that they were out to exploit him. He proposed to pay forty Suliotes a dollar a day more than the Greek government offered. They wanted even more and insisted on being paid a month in advance. Disappointed, Byron gave them another month's pay and sent them away.

To Byron's surprise, the British welcomed him, the Resident, Colonel Napier, who was sympathetic to the Greek cause, as well as his regiment. Soon Byron found their hospitality 'rather oppressive – for dinners kill a weakly stomached Gentleman', as he told Hobhouse on 11 September.

I Cannot Abstain

He wrote only rarely to Teresa and then briefly. On Christmas Eve he asked his banker to tell her that he and Pietro were leaving for the Greek mainland, the war zone. He did not write to her again for a month.

A view of Cephalonia in an engraving by Finden.

Byron had regained his independence. There is some evidence to suggest that once he was away from Teresa he no longer suffered from anorexia. He continued to diet sporadically, however, *on principle*, believing that he needed to punish his body to free his soul – to generate his capacity to lead his men. Certainly, he now found it harder to starve himself. He achieved it through sheer willpower.

He displayed the way his dietary behaviour now vacillated on an excursion he had proposed to the nearby island of Ithaca. He ordered his servant Tita Falcieri to provide 'l'Hippocrena!' The Classical Hippocrene spring's water was supposed to bring inspiration. Thomas Smith remembered:

> This brought from the bows of the boat a huge Venetian gondolier, with a musket slung diagonally across his back, a stone jar of two gallons of what turned out to be English gin, another porous one of water, and a quart pitcher, into which the gondolier poured the spirit, and laid the whole, with two or three large tumblers, at the feet of his expectant lord, who quickly uncorked the jar, and began to pour its contents into the smaller vessel.

> 'Now, gentlemen, drink deep, or taste not the Pierian spring; it is the true poetic source. I'm a rogue if I have drunk to-day. Come' (handing tumblers round to us), 'this is the way;' and he nearly half-filled a tumbler, and then poured from the height of his arm out of the water-jar, till the tumbler sparkled in the sun like soda-water, and drunk it off while effervescing, glorious gin-swizzle, a most tempting beverage, of which everyone on board took his share, munching after it a biscuit out of a huge tin-case of them.

The island's native ruler provided a substantial lunch, with beef, fowls and ham. Byron preferred the cold fish and salad that were served to the Greeks, because they were observing a fast day. At breakfast the next day Byron insisted on eating 'fresh-gathered grapes', though the regimental doctor advised against them and 'riper and safer figs and nectarines' were available. Byron explained that he ate the only 'just ripened' grapes, 'as I take other prohibited things – in order to accustom myself to any and all things that a man may be compelled to take where I am going – in the same way that I abstain from all superfluities, even salt to my eggs, or butter to my bread; and I take tea,' he told the Resident's wife, Mrs Knox, 'without sugar or cream. But tea itself is, really, the most superfluous of superfluities, though I am never without it.' On their way back Byron ensured that they enjoyed another 'round of the immortal swizzle'. '"Verily," said his lordship, "I cannot abstain."'

It wasn't just drink: on Cephalonia Hancock observed that 'although he invariably set out with professing a system of diet and abstemious living, he never adhered strictly to it when he had his friends about him – he had a soul for conviviality.' The regimental physician Dr Millingen confirmed that Byron ate meat only once a month: 'Soup, a few vegetables, a considerable portion of English cheese, with some fried crusts of bread, and fruit, constituted his daily fare. He eat [*sic*] with great rapidity, and drank freely.'

George Finlay also dined with Byron, who finished his 'scanty dinner of soup, potatoes, and cheese, and boasted of the short time he took to his dinner, and called in Fletcher's concurrent testimony'. But when Finlay praised 'some fish . . . he commenced again with fish, made a very tolerable dinner, finished with soup, and drank a few glasses of hock'.

On 4 September Byron moved to Metaxata while he waited for news from the Greeks' provisional government. For a time he doubted whether he would 'be of use' and he told Teresa on 11 September 1823 that he contemplated returning to Italy. But he stayed and refused to rush into dramatic, premature action, sustained by his heroic ideal, his hope of leading. His model remained Napoleon: he compared his situation to the emperor on Elba, waiting for the 'March of Events'. The Suliotes wanted Byron to become their chief; he reckoned he could afford to maintain 'a respectable clan or Sept or tribe or horde – for some time'.

Prince Mavrocordato, who had the command of western Greece, persuaded Byron that he needed to 'exert his influence' on the mainland of Greece, where his presence would '*electrify* the troops'. Byron was duly inspired, telling Hobhouse on 27 December 1823: '"En avant", or as the Suliotes shout in their war cry – "Derrah! Derrah!" which being interpreted, means "On – On – On!"'

Byron arrived in Missolonghi on 3 January 1824 and disembarked the next day, enthusiastically welcomed by a large crowd of local people and soldiers who had assembled on the beach. He probably wore his striking, scarlet military uniform.

Missolonghi was 'indeed nothing but mud and mire', as the British volunteer Leicester Stanhope commented.

The Mental Being

But by the beginning of February Byron 'seemed almost to despair of success . . . There was then a pallidness in his face, and knitting of his brows, that indicated both weakness and vexation.' That was William Parry's impression when he first met Byron. Parry was another British volunteer, a professional soldier, a fire-master, 'a fine fellow – extremely active – and of strong – sound – practical talent', according to Byron. Parry became

Byron in a tartan cloak as 'The Advocate and Supporter of the Greek Nation', engraved by R. Martain after a drawing by T. Fairland, 1827. Fletcher's inventory of Byron's wardrobe specified 'Braided Plaid Jackets'. Byron wore tartan to demonstrate 'his love of Scotland', telling George Finlay, 'we are all Scotchmen here; and I wish to do every thing to wipe out the remembrance of my old quarrel [with the 'Scotch Reviewers'].''' At Metaxata he sat on his balcony 'wrapt in his Stewart tartan cloak, with a cap on his head, which he affected to wear as the Scotch bonnet'. His language now often refers to Scott's novels, which celebrated Scottish heroism.

Private collection

Lord Byron's Residence at Missolonghi.

Illustration by George Cruikshank, from George Clinton, Memoirs of the Life and Writings of Lord Byron, *1825.*

an important ally: Byron appointed him major in his 'artillery-brigade' (which offended all the other officers) and soon made him responsible for allocating his funds.

Byron rationalised his eating disorder in the belief that leadership depended on mental power, which a hero strengthened by punishing the flesh. Under stress and in a real military context, as opposed to in imagination or in lyrical metaphor, Byron tried to observe his most ascetic diet. He maintained his weight, his wrist and waist size 'by taking a large dose of Epsom salts, besides the usual pills'. While Byron devoted his money and his energy to the cause of Greek independence and lived in discomfort in marshy, malarial Missolonghi he undermined his digestive system with laxatives.

'The respect I had for him, with his condescension and kindness to me, gave him immediately something of that power over my mind which the late emperor Napoleon is said to have had over his soldiers.' Byron would have liked the testimony of Parry, who added that Byron 'was more a mental being, if I may use this phrase, than any man I ever saw. He lived on thought more than on food.' Byron seemed about to realise his Corsair's fictional ideal as a leader, as 'an immaterial being' in Teresa's words. But leadership proved elusive and, in the event, his 'heroic' diet contributed to his early death.

My Boys

Bouwah! Bouwah!

A Suliot war cry

The reality of his life in Greece combined public display and private disillusionment. In principle, Byron was welcomed as 'the father of all the Greeks': he 'relieved the distress of so many unfortunate persons, that every one looked upon him as a father and public benefactor'. 'We did not mourn the loss of the great genius,' Gamba wrote after Byron's death, ' – no, nor that of the supporter of Greece – our first tears were for our father, our patron, our friend.'

Byron agreed to maintain a troop of 500 Suliotes for a year, expecting that the government would pay for another hundred. They didn't. The Suliotes occupied a large outer room of his house 'and their carbines were suspended along the walls, along with swords, pistols, Turkish sabres, dirks, rifles, guns, blunderbusses, bayonets, helmets and trumpets, fantastically suspended, so as to form various figures'. When Byron rode out, his Suliot bodyguard ran ahead of him, carrying their carbines, and 'were always able to keep up with the horses'. Count Gamba and his Greek interpreter rode on either side of Byron. Two servants rode behind him – generally his black groom Benjamin Lewis and Tita, 'both dressed like the *chasseurs* usually seen behind the carriages of ambassadors, and another division of his guard closed the cavalcade'. Tita's immense stature, bushy beard and livery were offset by 'silver epaulettes'.

Byron 'burns with military ardour and chivalry', Stanhope wrote carefully on 14 January.

Byron focused his military ambitions on one glorious object: taking the fort at Lepanto, which commanded the Gulf of Corinth. It had a major historical and symbolic as well as a tactical value: the Battle of Lepanto in 1571 marked the Turks' first significant defeat. Byron knew the site from his first visit to Greece fifteen years before. In *Childe Harold*, he called Lepanto and Candia (modern Crete) 'names no time nor tyranny can blight'.

The assault offered Byron his chance to lead the Suliotes into battle. It would be his show: as 'these fellows do mind me a little', he told Hancock diffidently on 5 February, '– it is the opinion that I should go'. Byron 'joked a good deal about his post of "*Archistrategos*," or commander-in-chief' but, as Pietro saw, 'the romance and the peril of the undertaking were great allurements to him'.

For once, poetry could also play a public role. Byron seized the opportunity to act as Tyrtæus, the ancient Athenian poet, 'lame of one leg', whose oratory 'reanimated the drooping minds of the Spartan people', as William Mitford said in his *History of Greece*, which began publishing in 1808. That was the year Byron first performed this bardic role, when his poetry inspired revolting schoolboys at Harrow. On his first visit to Greece Byron learned the patriotic war songs of Constantine Riga, 'who perished in the attempt to revolutionize Greece' in 1798. Byron translated one into English, 'Sons of the Greeks, arise!' and published it with *Childe Harold*. Now, the same impulse inspired one of his last, worst poems, his 'Song of the Suliotes', which begins,

> Up to battle! Sons of Suli –
> Up, and do your duty duly –
> There the wall – and there the Moat is
> Bouwah! Bouwah! Suliotes!
> There is booty, there is Beauty –
> Up my boys and do your duty. –

An anonymous caricature of Count Pietro Gamba, mentioned by Harold Nicolson in Byron: The Last Journey *(1924), and recently identified in the Duke of Devonshire's library, reproduced here for the first time.*
© Devonshire Collection, Chatsworth
Reproduced by permission of Chatsworth Settlement Trustees

In reality, the fort at Lepanto did not present much of a challenge: the Albanian garrison 'had not been paid for sixteen months, was discontented, and would willingly surrender', as long as they were presented with a show of force, paid off and guaranteed a safe retreat. But the Suliotes did not want to be led. They united only to extort more money from Byron and to agree that they 'had no mind to march against "stone walls"'.

Of all his difficult children, none proved as refractory as the Suliotes. Byron had encountered them on his first visit to the Levant, when he saluted their dogged resistance to Ali Pacha in a note to *Childe Harold*: 'Five thousand Suliotes, among the rocks and in the castle of Suli, withstood 30,000 Albanians for eighteen years: the castle was at last taken by bribery. In this contest there were several acts performed not unworthy of the better days of Greece.'

But Byron's idea of 'a respectable clan or Sept or tribe or horde' of Suliotes proved a romantic illusion. The Suliotes split into at least five different clans, who hated each other 'and the house of Lord Byron was daily the theatre of their animosities'. On 14 February, the day the expedition was to start against Lepanto, the men demanded 'that out of three or four hundred actual Suliotes, there should be about one hundred and fifty above the rank of common soldiers', distinguished by increased pay and dignity. Byron was 'exceedingly vexed': he renounced all agreements with the 'untractable mercenaries', though he promised to look after their families.

'Nothing, during his residence at Missolonghi, distressed him more than the conduct of the Suliots whom he had taken into his pay,' the historian George Finlay recorded. 'He saw that he had degraded himself into the chief of a band of personal followers, who thought of nothing but extorting money from their foreign leader.'

(In)temperance

On 15 February, in a moment of bitter disillusionment, when he saw he had failed as a leader, he fell ill. He had a fit, which he described as 'a strong shock of a Convulsive description' but his doctors could not decide 'whether Epilectic – Paralytic – or Apoplectic'. For about ten painful minutes his features were distorted, 'his mouth being drawn down on one side', he could not speak, became unconscious and went into convulsions. He recovered, but the stroke left him excessively weak.

It seems obvious now that Byron's starvation contributed to his vulnerability. It was as obvious then, to some observers, such as Pietro Gamba. Parry saw that Byron was already 'half-starved' and advocated

'Oh! who is more brave than a dark Suliote,/In his snowy camese and his shaggy capote?' An illustration by William Haygarth: Dervishi an Albanian Soldier Athens Dec. 1810, *now in the Gennadius Library, Athens. When Byron and his entourage were forced to land on the coast of Suli in 1809, they were rescued, fed and lodged by an Albanian chief, who refused to accept any money in recompense, assuring Byron, 'I wish you to love me, not to pay me.' How bitter that memory must have tasted in 1823.*
Private collection

'a more nourishing and generous diet'. But Byron remained 'quite sure he ought to live low'; and his physician Dr Bruno agreed.

Dr Bruno blamed Byron's attack of 'epilepsy' on his 'incessant mental vexations and his increased addiction to spirits', and he held Parry responsible. He insisted on bleeding Byron. When the flow of blood could not be quenched, Byron fainted. Millingen applied 'lunar caustic', which produced 'acute pain', as he admitted, but it staunched the blood. The doctors' clumsiness infuriated Parry, who reproved them violently. Once he had recovered, Byron defended them, to Parry's rage: 'Thus did he, by his kindness, in a manner, court his own fate. Had he turned them out of doors, and returned to the habits of an English gentleman, as to his diet, he would, probably, have survived many years, to have vindicated with his sword the wrongs of his beloved Greece.'

Bruno claimed that he had cured Byron's 'attack of epilepsy' by drawing off 'four pounds of blood', half the total in his body. He then dosed his patient with laxatives 'in the form of English salts and magnesia'; he prescribed 'complete abstinence from spirituous liquors or wine and moderation in all mental exertions' as well as dieting.

Byron himself blamed factors such as lack of exercise; violent agitation 'with more than one passion'; political and private worries. He refused to admit that his diet made things worse. On the contrary, he told Augusta on 23 February, it had been 'perhaps not so temperate as I may generally affirm that I was wont to be'. The fit had shaken him but he determined on 'fighting it off with abstinence and exercise'. So he reduced his diet even further, drank only water and cut out meat completely. Byron resolved to starve himself out of his epilepsy. His 'nervous system was in fact in a continued state of erethism [irritation],' Millingen recognised, 'which could only be augmented by the low debilitating diet, enjoined him by his physician'. Byron could not be persuaded to adopt 'a tonic plan'. Feeling that he was already 'a young old man', he did not care to live for a long time. All he cared about was avoiding either 'a bed of torture', or ending his days like Swift, 'a grinning idiot!'

From that moment on, Millingen thought, Byron's nervous system was broken. He 'fell into a state of melancholy, from which none of our reasonings could relieve him. He felt assured that his constitution had been irretrievably ruined by intemperance; that he was a worn-out man; and that his muscular power was gone. Flashes before his eyes, palpitations and anxieties, hourly afflicted him.'

R. Seymour's drawing engraved by I. Clark, 1825, shows Byron out riding, attended by his Suliote guards, 'their special skill being a running pace by which they kept up with the horses'.
Private collection

And All Obey

Among the greatest disillusionments of Byron's last months must have been the realisation that, even though he observed his Corsair's diet, it did not yield him his hero's power of leadership:

> But while he shuns the grosser joys of sense,
> His mind seems nourished by that abstinence.
> 'Steer to that shore!' – they sail. 'Do this!' – 'tis done:
> 'Now form and follow me!' – the spoil is won.
> Thus prompt his accents and his actions still,
> And all obey . . .

Parry saw that 'The last of [Byron's] exertions and the last of his orders for the good of Greece, were directed to forming an effective body of soldiers, who he knew would, if well disciplined, be the most useful present he could make to his favourite cause.' On 17 February Byron made a final attempt to subject 'his' wild tribesmen to decent, English notions of military discipline. Parry wrote out and Byron corrected his 'General Orders to the Suliotes'. It ended wearily and with some pathos:

IT IS EXPECTED THAT EVERY OFFICER,
NON-COMMISSIONED OFFICER,
SOLDIER, & CIVILIAN,
WILL OBEY ALL ORDERS GIVEN
WITH
PROMPTITUDE & ALACRITY –
GENERALE NOEL BYRON
COL. OF THE 1ST REGT. OF SULIOTES
&
COMMANDER IN CHIEF
OF WESTERN GREECE

The manuscript of the whole of this order, which Byron dictated to William Parry and then amended by hand, was in the Gennadius Library, Athens, when Marchand included a transcription in his edition of Byron's letters and journals. The original has since disappeared.

That day news arrived that a Turkish brig of war had run aground near Missolonghi. Byron was too weak to 'rise from his sofa' but he urged Parry to lead the attack, inspiring him with the words, 'Onward, death or victory!' And to forestall a massacre he offered 'two dollars a head for every prisoner saved'. But the Turks fired the ship. The Greek and Albanian soldiers' accumulated energy issued in a riot. Byron remained calm and sent for the Suliote chiefs or captains. Colonel Stanhope witnessed the operatic scene that followed:

> Soon after this dreadful paroxysm, when Lord Byron, faint with over-bleeding, was lying on his sick bed, with his whole nervous system completely shaken, the mutinous Suliots, covered with dirt and splendid attires, broke into his apartment, brandishing their costly arms, and loudly demanding their wild rights, Lord Byron, electrified by this unexpected act,

> seemed to recover from his sickness; and the more the Suliots raged, the more his calm courage triumphed. The scene was truly sublime.

Byron paid off most of the Suliotes, on condition that they left Missolonghi, but he continued to maintain a bodyguard of fifty-six men.

The weather improved and Byron could go riding again. 'We feared, however,' Gamba recorded in his diary for 23 to 28 February, 'that he had adopted too abstemious a mode of living . . . He was always inclined to follow extremes.' Byron assured James Kennedy on 10 March, 'I adhere to your regimen, and more, for I do not eat any meat, even fish.' Touchingly, that day Byron also sent 'a thousand thanks to Muir for his Cauliflower – the finest I ever saw or tasted – and I believe the largest that ever grew out of Paradise – or Scotland'.

Moore recorded that:

> From the period of his attack in February [Byron] had been, from time to time, indisposed; and, more than once, had complained of vertigos, which made him feel, he said, as if intoxicated. He was also frequently affected with nervous sensations, with shiverings and tremors, which, though apparently the effects of excessive debility, he himself attributed to fulness of habit. Proceeding upon this notion, he had, ever since his arrival in Greece, abstained almost wholly from animal food, and ate of little else but dry toast, vegetables, and cheese. With the same fear of becoming fat, which had in his young days haunted him, he almost every morning measured himself round the wrist and waist, and whenever he found these parts, as he thought, enlarged, took a strong dose of medicine.

In March Byron 'frequently complained of slight pains in the head, shivering fits, confusion of thoughts, and visionary fears, all of which indicated to [Parry] increased debility'. So he 'endeavoured to persuade him to live a little better, to eat more meat, and drink more wine'. But Byron believed in Dr Bruno, who insisted that 'his disorders all arose from too much blood, and that his system required to be still further reduced.'

Starved to Death

On 9 April Byron stayed out late riding. He was 'caught in a shower, and remaining exposed to it for more than an hour, he complained in the evening of shooting pains in his hips and loins'. The next day he 'felt himself perpetually shuddering'. 'He could eat nothing,' Parry noted, 'and in fact took no nourishment whatever.' Pietro and Parry recognised that Byron's soaking 'affected him the more readily on account of his over-abstemious mode of life'.

Bruno 'administered a purgative' on 12 April, 'and kept up its effects by a solution of cream of tartar, which the Italians call "Imperial lemonade"'. On 13 April Byron 'had not been able to sleep since his attack, and he could take no other nourishment than a little broth, and a spoonful or two of arrow-root'. Byron assumed that his condition was improving. His fever increased, but he refused to be bled, until he was warned that 'the disease might . . . entirely . . . deprive him of reason'. He was also 'dreadfully distressed by want of sleep', knowing that 'without sleep, a man must die or go mad'. His 'fever became stronger than it had been hitherto. The

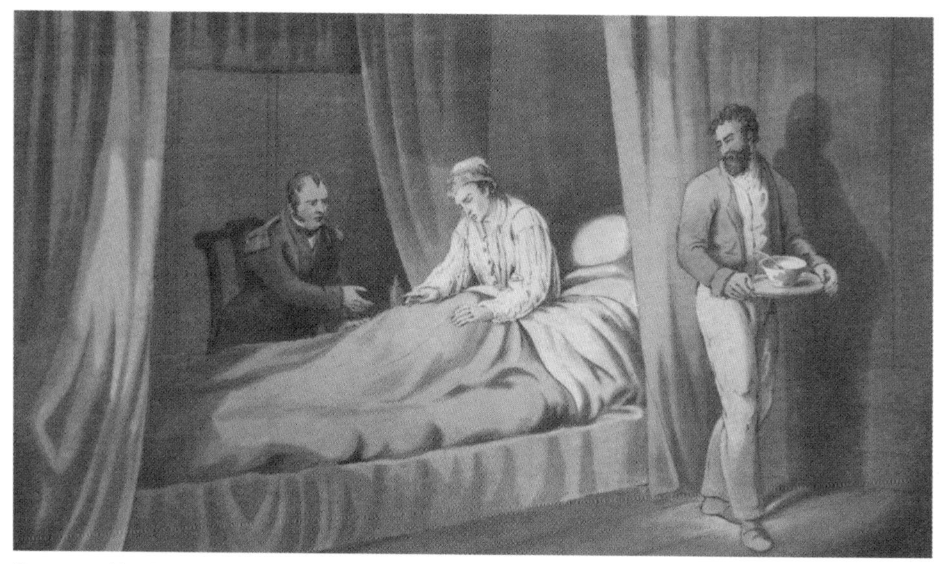

Byron on his deathbed, attended by Captain William Parry and by Byron's valet William Fletcher, frontispiece to William Parry's The Last Days of Lord Byron, *1825.*

restlessness and agitation increased, and the patient spoke several times in an incoherent manner.' For Parry, Byron's delirium was 'that alienation of the mind, which is so frequently the consequence of excessive debility'. 'He was, before the fever attacked him, reduced to a mere shadow . . . However learnedly the doctors may talk and write on the subject, it is plain and palpable to common observation, that Lord Byron was worried and starved to death.' William Fletcher testified that 'The whole nourishment taken by my master, for the last eight days, consisted of a small quantity of broth, at two or three different times, and two spoonsfull of arrow-root on the 18th, the day before his death.' Recent research has attributed Byron's terminal illness to malaria and/or neurosyphilis. But in any case Byron's starvation diet contributed fatally to lower his resistance.

'His diet was dictated by his own will,' Parry recorded, 'and for that he is responsible.'

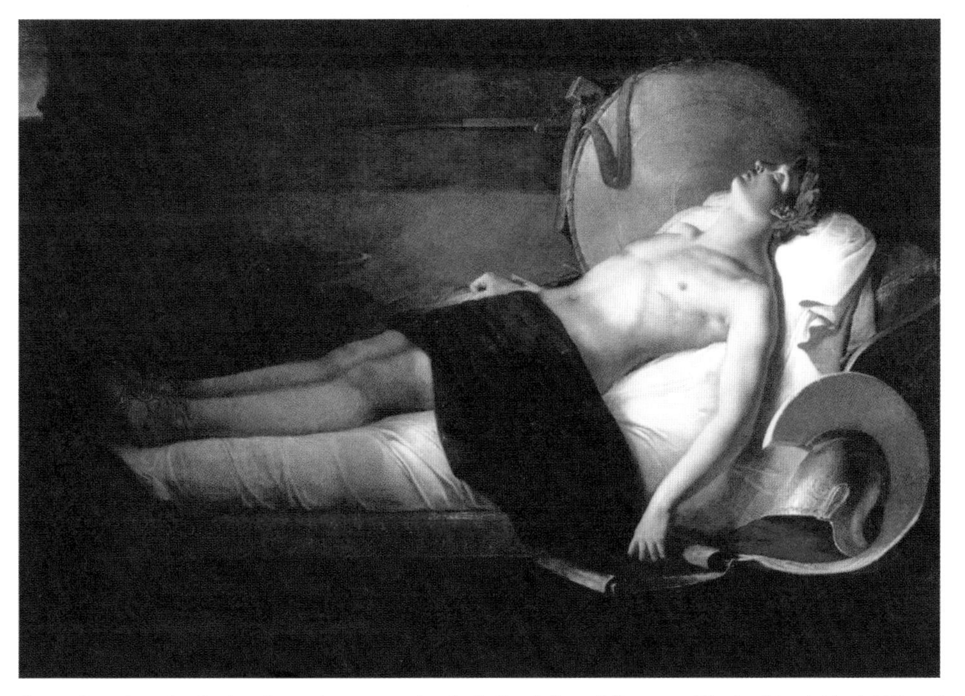

An unsigned, early nineteenth century, neo-classical oil painting of Byron on his deathbed: his right hand grips a sword; his left hand, a scroll of verse, while a new day heralds the dawn of freedom for Greece.
Private collection, London

Byron behaved with heroic courage and dignity, as Millingen testified. 'At one moment I heard him say: "Shall I sue for mercy?" After a long pause he added: "Come, come, no weakness! Let's be a man to the last."' Millingen's 'infinite regret', that Byron did not repent or appeal to God, makes his testimony all the more convincing.

On Easter Day, 18 April 1824, Byron received a letter from Hobhouse, who assured him that his 'present endeavour' was 'certainly the most glorious ever undertaken by man'. Byron tried to give Fletcher messages for his sister and his wife, but he could not make himself understood. At some point, 'a fit of delirium ensued; and he began to talk wildly, as if he were mounting a breach in an assault, calling out, half in English, half in Italian, "Forwards – forwards – courage – follow my example," &c. &c.'

Byron probably remembered the Suliot war cry, which he had recounted to Hobhouse in a letter of 27 December 1823. To the very end, Byron was trying to lead and inspire those who followed him.

He died at a quarter past six in the evening of 19 April 1824, at the age of thirty-six.

APPENDICES

Appendix 1

DINNER WITH LORD BYRON, 1811

all human history attests,
That happiness for Man – the hungry sinner!—
Since Eve ate apples, much depends on dinner.

Don Juan, XIII, 99

What Byron did and did not eat expressed his private needs, but his diet also reflected contemporary prejudice and knowledge. If it's seen in context, does it make more sense?

The dinner that Thomas Moore attended, and which he recorded, took place on 4 November 1811. It provides an opportunity to look in more detail at Byron's diet, to establish what he ate and why.

Reading about Diet

Books on diet that Byron owned throw some light on his behaviour at this dinner and throughout his life, though they do not explain it. Take his most recent purchase, *Cursory Remarks on Corpulence*, whose title page reveals that its author, Dr Wadd, was based in Park Place, St James's Street, very near Byron's lodgings at 8 St James's Street. For those wanting to lose weight Wadd advocates 'mild diuretics, particularly soap'. He means 'the inward use of soap': by drinking 'at bed-time, a quarter of an ounce of home-made castile soap, dissolved in a quarter of a pint of soft water' one of his patients lost two stone in two years.

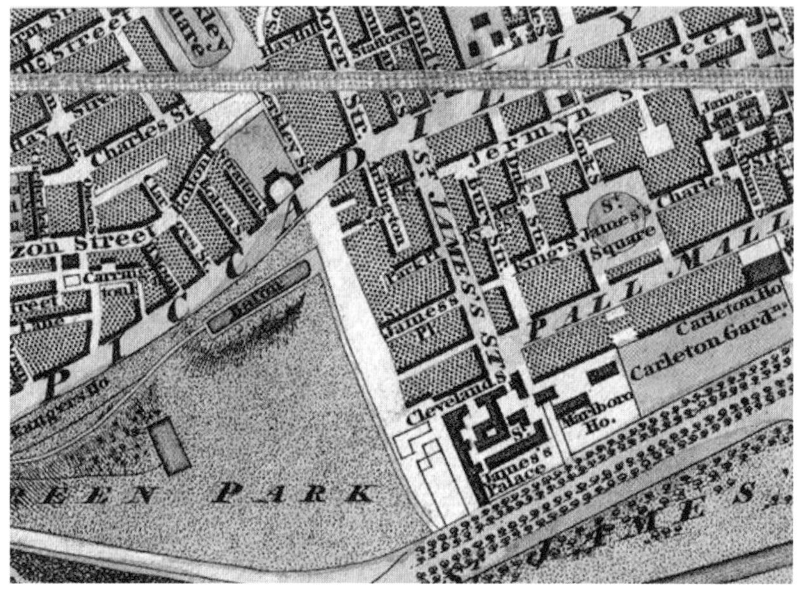

Detail from Mogg's Pocket or Case Map of London, 1806.

James Makittrick [Adair], the earliest authority that Byron owned, boasted in *An Essay on Diet and Regimen for the Preservation of Health, especially of the Indolent, Studious, Delicate and Invalid* (1799), that by following his own prescriptions he had reached the age of seventy-three.

Sir John Sinclair's *Code of Health and Longevity* was published in four volumes in 1807, the year Byron first acted on his hatred of 'even *moderate* fat'. The catalogue of the 1816 auction of his books shows that Byron possessed *two* copies. Sinclair's eldest son George was one of Byron's friends at Harrow, 'The prodigy of our School-days', who did his friends' exercises for them. Furthermore, one of the authorities Sir John Sinclair consulted was John Jackson, Byron's boxing coach, friend and mentor. Sir John cites his opinion several times and he also published an interview with Jackson, which is reprinted below in Appendix 2.

Sir John's eclectic, often inconsistent *Code of Health and Longevity* suggests that its author was a man of wide reading and little discrimination. As 'an individual, unconnected with the medical profession', when Sir John finds two experts who disagree, he tends to report both opinions with impartial enthusiasm. Occasionally he speaks out definitively. For example,

THE

CODE

OF

HEALTH AND LONGEVITY;

OR,

A CONCISE VIEW,

OF THE PRINCIPLES

CALCULATED FOR

THE PRESERVATION OF HEALTH,

AND

THE ATTAINMENT OF LONG LIFE.

BEING AN ATTEMPT TO PROVE THE PRACTICABILITY, OF CONDENSING, WITHIN A NARROW COMPASS, THE MOST MATERIAL INFORMATION HITHERTO ACCUMULATED, REGARDING THE DIFFERENT ARTS AND SCIENCES, OR ANY PARTICULAR BRANCH THEREOF.

BY

SIR JOHN SINCLAIR, BART.

VOL. I.

Neque enim ulla alia re homines propius ad Deos accedunt, quam salutem *hominibus dando.*—CICERO, PRO LIGARIO, C. 38.

EDINBURGH:

Title page of Sir John Sinclair's Code of Health and Longevity. *Sir John Sinclair, MP for Caithness from 1780 to 1811, compiled* The Statistical Account of Scotland *(twenty-one volumes, 1799). He also published accounts, addresses, circulars, dissertations, essays, hints, histories, letters, lucubrations, maxims, observations, plans, proposals, remarks, reports, reviews, sketches and thoughts on topics as diverse as experiments to promote the improvement of fruit trees, British wool, a history of the public revenue of the British Empire, the Scottish dialect, the approaching crisis, currency, the poems of Ossian and cattle. He had six daughters, all of whom attained at least six feet in height.*

'there is no better mode of preserving the stomach in good order, than to keep the feet perfectly clean, washing them daily, or at least very frequently, in tepid, and afterwards, if possible, in cold water'. Byron's trainer Jackson believed that the same procedure prevented colds.

No one authority provides a key to unlock all the mysteries of Byron's diet. Furthermore, he prided himself on his 'natural love of contradiction and paradox' and claimed that he only ever ate meat in Lent.

Samuel Rogers's Account of Dinner with Lord Byron

'When we sat down to dinner, I asked Byron if he would take soup? "No; he never took soup."'

Soup formed part of Byron's first diet in 1807. He later agreed with Lady Adelaide Forbes about 'the excellence of white soup and plovers eggs for a light supper' in 1814. When he ate 'mutton broth for dinner' in January 1816 it was newsworthy enough for his sister to record the fact. There were later soups in Italy.

'Presently I asked if he would eat some mutton? "No, he never ate mutton."'

Byron did eat mutton. Meat featured in his diet sporadically throughout his life. He ate woodcock 'every day' in Athens in January 1811, though he had given up meat by March. In 1816, when his eating was generally disordered, his sister saw him eat 'a stewed knuckle of Veal with broth & rice'. Byron recommended 'beef-steak' as a remedy against seasickness in *Don Juan*. 'But man is a carnivorous production,' he insisted later in the same canto, 'Although his anatomical construction/Bears vegetables, in a grumbling way/Your labouring people think beyond all question/Beef, veal, and mutton, better for digestion.' He served 'a very English joint of roast beef' to English visitors during the summer of 1817. And he continued to eat meat regularly. In Ravenna on 24 January 1821 he complained that the beef was tough. He thanked John Hay for a gift of wild boar in February 1822. Superstitiously, he felt he needed to eat goose on Michaelmas Day, otherwise the year would be fatal but he still allowed them to live, so as '"to test the theory of their longevity"'. The ones he carried from Pisa to Genoa 'became such pets that he caressed them constantly'. On the other hand, he conformed to local, i.e. Catholic custom and, even when he was eating meat, his valet Fletcher recorded that he 'always left [Fridays] . . . apart for a day of abstinence'. In general, Byron preferred a vegetarian diet.

Abstinence

Abstinence meant abstaining from meat. The word vegetarian did not exist until 1842. The other popular term was Pythagoreanism, after the ancient Greek, vegetarian philosopher Pythagoras. It was not an English habit.

Eccentrically, Sir John Sinclair recommends a vegetarian diet. His grounds may have made particular sense to Byron: 'As animal food fills the blood-vessels fuller with blood than vegetable, it naturally increases our muscular strength; but then it loads the brain at the same time, which occasions heaviness and stupor; whereas vegetable food, from not loading the system with blood, rather diminishes muscular strength, but enables the blood to act with greater force. Vegetable food, therefore, is fitter to give clearness of ideas, and animal food is best adapted to labour.'

Sinclair reported that 'Indulging in animal food, renders men dull', whereas vegetable food 'is considered to have a particular influence on the powers of the mind; and tends to preserve a delicacy of feeling, a liveliness of imagination and an acuteness of judgment'.

Byron agreed and this belief allied them both with radical vegetarian philosophers, such as Joseph Ritson. Shelley blamed most of man's evil habits on eating meat, for it

> Kindled all putrid humours in his frame,
> All evil passions, and all vain belief,
> Hatred, despair, and loathing in his mind,
> The germs of misery, death, disease, and crime.

Utopia will be realised, if man stops eating meat: 'All things are void of terror: Man has lost/His terrible prerogative, and stands/An equal amidst equals'. In an appendix Shelley boasted of 'The improvements of health and temper' that followed, when he and his wife 'lived on vegetables for eight months'.

Jackson also subscribed to the doctrine of sympathy: 'The legs of fowls, being very sinewy, are much approved of.'

Samuel Rogers: 'Would he take some fish? "No, he never took fish."'

Surprising, this, since Byron 'could live on nothing but fish & two grooms were constantly looking for it', according to Mrs Clermont, who may have been exaggerating. In Athens he claimed to have eaten red mullet 'every day'. He said he never forgave Sir Godfrey Webster for stealing his 'fav'rite lobster claw' in 1811. Dining with Lord Holland on 28 November 1813, Byron 'Stuffed [himself] with sturgeon'. Moore records a dinner with Byron at Watier's club on 19 May 1814, 'as it may convey some idea of his irregular mode of diet, and thus account, in part, for the frequent derangement of his health'. Knowing that for two days, Byron had only eaten 'a few biscuits and (to appease appetite) [chewed] mastic', Moore ensured that there would be 'a good supply of at least two kinds of fish. My companion, however, confined himself to lobsters.' Byron ate 'two or three', but he interposed mouthfuls alternately with up to six small liqueur glasses of 'strong white brandy' and sometimes a 'tumbler of very hot water', without which 'he appeared to think the lobster could not be digested.' He probably remembered Sinclair's advice that 'spiritous liquors are often requisite' to assist the digestion of fish. Byron and Moore then 'despatched two bottles' of claret, before parting at about four o'clock in the morning.

After seeing Edmund Kean as Richard III on 16 July 1814 Byron and Hobhouse 'supped or dined . . . at the Cocoa-Tree [club], on fish and champagne'. When Leigh Hunt invited Byron and Moore to dine, the latter 'only stipulated, that there should be "plenty of fish and vegetables for the noble bard," his Lordship at that time being Brahminical in his eating.' That year Byron fished at Newstead Abbey, having run out of books to read, and caught 'a great many perch and some carp'. Three years later he 'got some famous trout out of the river Clitumnus'. Later, however, he equated the 'solitary vice' of fishing with murder in cold blood – unlike hunting: 'No angler,' he wrote in a note to *Don Juan*, 'can be a good man.' One Friday in 1821 he avoided inviting someone to dinner, 'because there was a small *turbot* . . . which I wanted to eat all

Anecdotes of Byron . . . or a touch of the Marvellous, *a caricature from 12 November 1824: 'Taste – He had a strong antipathy to pork when under done or stale & nothing could induce him to partake of fish which had been caught more than ten days; indeed he had a singular dislike even to the smell.'*
Private collection

myself. Ate it.' According to Trelawny, Byron ate 'salad and sardines' in Genoa.

Fish appealed to Byron not just as a palatable alternative to meat but also on its own account. Lady Blessington teased him by affecting 'to think that his excellence in, and fondness of, swimming, arose from his continually living on fish, and he appeared disposed to admit the possibility, until, being no longer able to support my gravity, I laughed aloud, which for the first minute discomposed him.'

Samuel Rogers: 'I then asked if he would take a glass of wine? "No, he never tasted wine."'

After reading the *Edinburgh Review*'s savage review of *Hours of Idleness* in 1808 he needed 'three bottles of claret' (shared with Scrope Davies) to raise his spirits.

At Newstead Abbey in 1809 'a human skull filled with burgundy' was handed round after dinner. Clearly, on 4 November 1811 Byron was on his best behaviour, at his most extreme point of teetotal asceticism. His behaviour at Lady Jersey's in his social heyday, around 1812, prompted Chester '(the fox hunter)' to exclaim, 'by G–d he *drinks like a Man*!'. Byron did 'very well for a "holiday drinker"', according to the rakish

The dining room at Newstead Abbey, 1874, showing the antique mantelpiece.
Photo: Richard Allen

Scrope Davies (who favoured the Burgundy, Clos Vougeot). In 1813 Byron emptied the skull cup, 'which holds rather better than a bottle of Claret[,] at *one draught*'. He claimed in 1814 that neither champagne nor claret ever affected him. He drank 'stiff *rum punch*' in Venice and recommends 'hock and soda-water' in *Don Juan*, which, according to Terese Guiccioli, he wrote 'with repeated glasses of gin-punch by his side'. On the island of Cephalonia in 1822 the Governor, Colonel Napier, offered him local wines, 'which his Lordship, who liked claret, could not abide'. Byron 'frequently hazarded a conjecture whether Napier would indulge him with a bottle of his favourite beverage, adding, that [a] man's society must be deucedly attractive, when it made him forgo Bordeaux wine'.

Samuel Rogers: 'It was now necessary to inquire what he *did* eat and drink; and the answer was, "Nothing but hard biscuits and soda-water."'

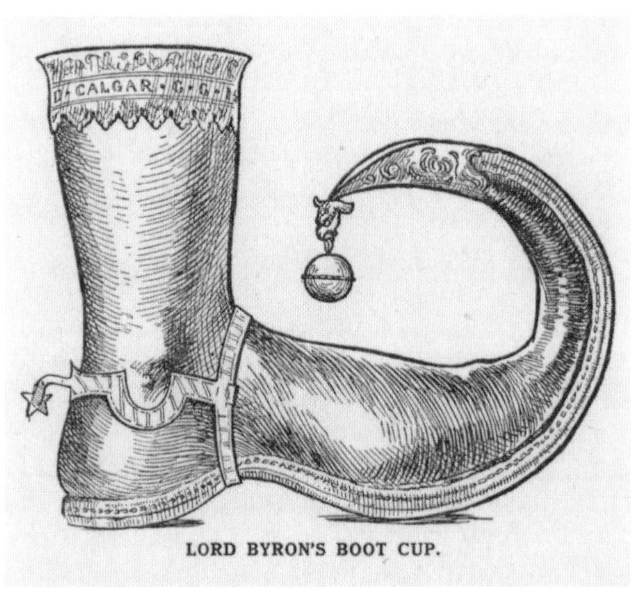

'Lord Byron, with his love of the bizarre, was also the possessor of a black leather boot which he used as a drinking vessel . . . It was silver-mounted round the top, bearing the inscription on the rim: "VT. QVID. CVRRENTI. CALCAR. G. G. G 1599." A silver spur adorned the heel of the boot, whilst the forepart was similar to that of a fourteenth century shoe, the pointed toe being turned up to form a handle . . . and from the extreme end of it hung a silver ball. The history of this boot-cup can be traced to it being presented in 1599 to George Gordon, created Marquis of Huntly in that year; Byron's mother was descended from this peer and it was on this account that it was purchased by the poet from a member of the family.'

Both items had been prescribed by his doctor in 1807, though only as part of a temporary, reducing diet. Biscuits and soda water represent an epicure's or rich man's version of that standard starvation diet, bread and water – 'which by the way', Byron remarked in 1823, '– are very nourishing – and sufficient – if good of their kind'.

There was a general prejudice against fresh bread, on the grounds that it was unhealthy. 'Well fermented whited brown bread is preferable to white, and biscuit to either,' according to Dr James Adair, who recommended (in note form), 'Different sorts of wheaten bread, without butter, the second day of baking. The crust more digestible than the crumb.' Perhaps that explains the 'peculiarity', which struck Isaac Nathan: Byron 'was particularly fond of eating the crusty part of a loaf, which he always cut himself'.

John Jackson was firm on this point: 'Soft bread, or new bread is never eaten, being of a spongy nature, and expanding in the stomach; stale bread is wholesome, but probably biscuit might be as good. Several people prefer biscuit.'

Sir John Sinclair agreed: 'Bread should be kept till it is stale; or, if it is consumed when fresh, it should either be thoroughly baked or toasted.' 'Of all the unleavened sorts of bread, biscuit is by far the best, and in all cases where leavened bread does not agree, it cannot be too strongly recommended. In equal quantities, it is more nutritive than fermented bread; it is also lighter, and less liable to create acidity and flatulence.' When he was starving himself in 1813 Byron limited his intake of food to six biscuits a day.

He was about to leave London in April 1816, when Isaac Nathan sent him 'some Passover Cakes' or unleavened bread, 'denominated by the Nazarenes *Motzas*' for his journey, knowing that 'he was particularly fond of biscuits'. Byron was delighted.

In Pisa biscuits 'appear regularly in the housekeeping bills as *ciambelletti biscottati*' and were probably 'very small ring-shaped rolls, like crisp doughnuts, but unsweetened, of which no fewer than four hundred were supplied every week.'

As for soda water, Byron was partial to it at Cambridge, even before he went on his diet, probably because, as Hobhouse noted, it counteracted the magnesia he indulged in. Byron's bill for soda water (due to R. Shipwash, of 27 St. Albans Street) from October to December 1814 was £6 *1s 0d*, which means he ordered twenty-two dozen bottles. Hobhouse visited Byron in 1816 and reported back to Augusta on 9 September that her brother's health was greatly improved: '– no brandy – no very late hours – no quarts of magnesia nor deluge of Soda Water – neither passion nor perverseness – even the scream has died away'.

Byron's letters from Italy frequently request pounds of soda-powder. He noted in his Ravenna Journal for 2 February: 'In England, five years ago, I had the same kind of hypochondria, but accompanied with so violent a thirst that I have drunk as many as fifteen bottles of soda-water in one night, after going to bed, and been still thirsty – calculating, however, some lost from the bursting out and effervescence and overflowing of the soda-water, in drawing the corks, or striking off the necks of the bottles from mere thirsty impatience.' He added that 'Le Man (the apothecary) cured me of the thirst in three days, and it has lasted as many years. I suppose that it is all hypochondria.' On 26 February he resorted to 'mixing some soda-powders' when suffering from indigestion after eating 'a quantity of boiled cockles' at supper. And he asked for 'some more pounds weight of Soda powders' to be sent to him on 21 April, because he drank them 'in Summer by dozens'. When he left for Greece in 1823, three dozen 'Soda powder' cost him more than the fifty bottles of Cognac.

Apart from its supposed medical property, soda water had associations that Byron valued highly: its bubbles were metaphorical equivalents for the body's redeeming spirit. So, the evaporation of a joyous day is 'like a soda bottle when its spray/Has sparkled and let half its spirit out'.

Artificial mineral waters had been manufactured in Britain since 1781, using Priestley and Lavoisier's method of carbonating water and chemists' analyses of the chief British and continental spa waters, such as those at Cheltenham, Bath, Seltzer, Pyrmont and Spa. Jacob Schweppe moved from Geneva to London in January 1792 and set up a factory at 141 Drury Lane. By 1795 he was based in Margaret Street, Cavendish Square. Dr Erasmus

Darwin recommended Schweppe's 'factitious Seltzer water' to treat a 'Stone of the bladder' in his *Zoonomia*. Byron drank 'some Seltzer-water' on 8 January 1821. Matthew Boulton, like Dr Darwin a member of the Lunar Society of Birmingham, reported that Schweppe had impregnated water 'so highly with fixable air as to exceed in appearance Champaign and all other Bottled Liquors. He prepares it of 3 sorts. No. 1 is for common drinking with your dinner, No. 2 is for Nephritick patients, and No. 3 contains the most alkali and is given only in more violent cases, but I know not the quantity of alkali in either. It is contained in Strong Stone Bottles and sold for 6s 6d per doz. including the Bottles.' The term soda water was probably first used in association with Schweppe's products and in advertisements for them. The earliest containers were glass or earthenware ovate, corked bottles.

Sinclair's comprehensive *Code* contains a section 'Of Artificial Mineral Waters', where he cites 'that respectable physician Dr Pearson, of Leicester-Square in London'. Dr Pearson concludes that 'both as a *medicine*, and as an article of salutory luxury, [soda water] *may be justly reckoned the greatest improvement in diet of the present age*.' His 'hints respecting water impregnated with fixed air, or the carbonic acid, as manufactured by J. Schweppes, late of Geneva' recommend Acidulous Soda Water for 'complaints of the kidneys, ureters, or bladder, when these organs are either obstructed or irritated by calculous matter, or are in an irritable or corroded and ulcerated state'. A few months after this dinner, Byron suffered 'an attack of the *Stone* in the *kidney*'. Soda water was prescribed by the Brighton physician, whom Byron consulted in 1812. Byron later considered himself liable to some nephritic disorder. He had also experienced the effect of an ulcerated urethra by 1819.

In his *Treatise on Corpulence* Wadd cited one authority, who recommended his patients 'to drink as little as possible of any fluid, but aerated alkaline water, which he recommend from an idea of its rendering fat more fluid'. This expert counselled 'that the eating of much salt, or salted meat, is more efficacious than soap, as it increases perspiration, and produces thirst, by which, if the patient can bear it, the absorption of his fat will be greatly increased, as in fever'.

'No salt meat is given,' Jackson insisted in his advice on training, 'nor any thing that can create thirst. The less one drinks the better. Drinking certainly encourages soft unhealthy flesh.' Restricting his intake of fluids to a few bottles of soda water may have damaged Byron's kidneys.

Samuel Rogers: 'Unfortunately neither hard biscuits nor soda-water were at hand; and he dined upon potatoes bruised down on his plate and drenched with vinegar.'

According to Sinclair, potatoes are 'the most valuable of all the articles of subsistence produced under the surface', because they are the most 'farinaceous'; they are therefore nearest to biscuit.

Vinegar has traditionally been used as an aid in slimming. Perversely but, as always, authoritatively, Jackson prescribes 'some vinegar with food, which prevents thirst and is good to promote leanness'. 'While at Athens, [Byron] took the hot bath . . . three times a week, – his usual drink being vinegar and water, and his food seldom more than a little rice.' Most people knew, however, that vinegar could ruin the digestion, as Wadd confirms. Byron had been reminded of its 'baneful effects' a month before Rogers's dinner.

Rogers ends his account by claiming that **'Byron, after leaving my house, had gone to a Club in St. James's Street and eaten a hearty meat-supper.'**

Rogers's canard is unlikely to be true. Byron asked him in 1813 to be allowed to 'come in *after* dinner', as the '*light* supper – the other night – half killed' him, since he had 'so bedevilled [his] digestion'.

Appendix 2

JOHN JACKSON: VIVA VOCE

While Sinclair's book *A Collection of Papers, on the Subject of Athletic Exercises, &c.*, 1806, is available in a digital version, his later 'Observations' were omitted, which is why they are reprinted here.

Reprinted from Sir John Sinclair,
The Code of Health and Longevity, 4 Vol., 1807, Appendix IV,
'A Collection of Papers, on the Subject of Athletic Exercises, &c.', II, 90–103

The following Observations were taken by an Amanuensis from the viva voce *Answers made by* Mr J. Jackson, the celebrated Scientific Teacher of the Pugilistic Art, to the preceding Queries, as they were read to him.

1. *By what criterions or tests, they judge of the muscular strength, or wind, or other qualities of those who seek to put themselves under training? What is the earliest, and what is the latest age they would attempt to train?*

   In regard to size, that is immaterial, for those who are trained to running, may be from five feet to six feet hight; beyond that is too large, nor is there an instance of a very big man, being a first rate runner. As to form, long thighs and short legs are desirable. One of the most famous runners, West of Windsor, is only about five feet four, and he ran thirty-one miles in four hours and a quarter, at the age of forty-four. He beat the famous Powel. As to tests or qualities, they put men upon trial with short runs, sparring, &c.

A person trained to boxing ought to be of a good size and weight. The earliest age is eighteen, and thence to forty, but seldom beyond that age, though attention to diet and exercise, on the same system, would doubtless be of use to persons beyond that age.

2. *How they judge of the length of time that may be required for bringing a man into good plight, vigorous health, and free breathing; and what period of preparation is usually required for running a match?*

In general, they suppose that two months is sufficient to bring a man into good plight, either for boxing or for running a match, provided he is previously in tolerable good condition; but if the person is fleshy, it may require three months.

3. *What purges they use; and in what succession; and by what rules do they administer them; and how do they judge of their effects? Is the purging only preparatory, or is it regularly continued? Is it meant, by this process, to reduce the plethoric state of the system, (on the idea that there is too great a quantity of blood), or is it simply designed to put the bowels in the most favourable condition, for easy and good digestion? Is the reducing the actual size of the belly, necessary to more free and perfect breathing*.*

**The effects of taking up a running horse from idleness and soft pasture, to hard food and regular exercise, is attended with this peculiar effect, that while the animal becomes lank, sleek and glossy, while he gets fire in his eye, and a new vigour in his limbs, and wind and speed, his belly, (swollen with coarse indigestible food, eaten in great profusion), is drawn into half its size. May we not then presume from this analogy, that the state of the belly has a remarkable effect upon the wind?*

The training is begun with an emetic, and in about two days afterwards give them a dose of Glauber salts, from one to two ounces, and missing about two days another dose of physic, and then a third.

It is supposed that one emetic and three doses of physic will clear any man; and after the body is thus cleared of all noxious matter, it must be kept in good condition. It is necessary to give the emetic and physic at the commencement. The object is partly to get all the superfluities away, either of blood or any thing else, and also to promote good digestion afterwards. No man with a great belly can breathe freely.

4. *Is the diet rich or simple; of animal food, or of vegetable; in great quantity or sparing; is it increased gradually, or diminished gradually? What meals have they in the day; and at what hours; one or more; frequent feeding, in small and fixed portions, or full and substantial meals? What kinds of fish or meat is reckoned the best; whether beef, mutton, veal, pork, lamb, or fowl? Are any kinds of fish allowed? What quality of food is most conducive to strength? What quantity is necessary for maintaining the system in its most perfect state of vigour? Do they feed much in the intermediate days of the purges? Is abstinence required when they take their physic?*

The diet is simple; animal food alone: and it is recommended to take very little salt and some vinegar with the food, which prevents thirst, and is good to promote leanness. Vegetables are never given, as turnips, or carrots, which are difficult to digest, nor potatoes, which are watery. But bread is allowed, only it must be stale. They breakfast upon meat about eight o'clock, and dine at two. Suppers are not recommended, but they may taike a biscuit and a little cold meat, about eight o'clock, two hours before they go to bed. It is reckoned much against a man's wind to go to bed with a full stomach, and they in general take a walk after supper. Some people will have tea, but it is not recommended, nor is it strengthening, and no liquor is given warm. Full and substantial meals are given at breakfast and dinner. Beef and mutton are best. It is contended, that there is more nourishment in the lean of thc meat than the fat, which is fully proved by experiment, fat being of a greasy nature, causes bile, and fouls the stomach. The lean of fat meat is best. Veal and lamb are never given, nor is pork, which has a tendency to purge some people. The legs of fowls, being very sinewy, are much approved of. The yolk of a raw egg is reckoned the best thing in a morning, and is supposed to prevent bilious complaints.

Beef steaks are reckoned very good, and rather under done than otherwise, as all meat in general is: and it is better to have the meat broiled, than roasted or boiled, by which nutriment is lost. No fish whatever is allowed, because it is reckoned watery, and not to be compared with meat, in point of nutriment. The fat of meat is never given, but the lean of the best meat. No butter nor cheese on any account; cheese is indigestible. Meat must be dressed as plain as possible, without seasoning of any kind; no eggs are given excepting the yolk raw in the morning. Men will live longer on beef, without change, than any other kind of animal food, but mutton is reckoned most easily digested. The meat must always be fresh, and never salted. No quantity of meat is fixed; it depends upon the constitution and appetite. Little men will eat as much as large men, and very frequently more. Pies and puddings are never given, nor any kind of pastry. As to hard dumplings, people may as well take earthen ware into their stomach, they are so very indigestible.

In the intermediate days of the purges they feed as much as usual. No soups are given, nor any thing warm, excepting with their physic, which is worked off with gruel. After the physic is worked off, they get for their dinner a little boiled mutton and broth, with the fat taken off. The broth must be let cool, in order to take off the fat, and then it may be warmed again; or beef-tea, in the same way; but with little or no salt, as it occasions thirst.

5. *What kinds of liquors are reckoned best? Whether wine, ale, spirits, &c? Whether given hot or cold; in what quantities; and when ought they to be given?*

Malt liquor is best, and particularly home-brewed beer, old, and never bottled, that being windy. As to wine, a little red wine, which is much preferable to white; never more than half a pint of wine after dinner, and none after supper. The quantity of beer not to exceed three pints during the whole day, taken with breakfast and dinner, and a little after supper. Sometimes white wine and water is allowed to a man at breakfast, who does not like malt liquor. To much liquor is apt to swell the belly, and is bad for wind. The liquor should not be taken in great draughts, but by mouthfuls, which quenches the thirst better, and that is the only object required. No water is given alone. Malt liquor is almost never given, as it is apt to curdle upon the stomach, and has a fattening quality. Liquor is always given cold, but never before meals, unless in cases of extreme thirst, when a little wine and water may be taken. If a person is rather inclined to corpulency, and instead of taking large draughts and great quantities of liquor is satisfied with three pints a day, he will lose three or four pounds of his weight imperceptibly, in the course of two months. A gentleman in training, must follow exactly the same rules as others; but if he merely wishes to get into good condition, he may take wine and water, instead of malt liquor, if he prefer it. Much drinking promotes perspiration, which is very weakening.

6. *Are the very violent perspirations into which they throw their patients, designed to reduce the system, to extenuate the fat, to lessen the quantity of blood, the excess of which make us giddy or short breathed; or is it merely designed to produce a new condition of the skin, more favourable to health and muscular vigour; to produce a sharper appetite; a greater demand for food, and a quicker nourishment, or a greater nutrition from a more slender diet? Is the sweat at first produced by exercise, and only continued by the person, when trained, being put between two feather-beds, and encouraged by drinks; or is it produced by force of sweating drugs, or violent heats, or by continued friction? At what hours are the perspirations brought on? How is the pupil treated when the sweat is over? What becomes of the skin of a fat man, when by the process, he is reduced in size, and rendered lean? Does it hang loose, or is it tight? What if any effect upon that?*

The violent perspirations are intended to extenuate the fat, and also reduce the quantity of blood, and makes it thinner and lighter. Giddiness is much owing to foulness of stomach, as well as headaches and other complaints. Excess of blood also produces giddiness, but that is corrected in the course of training. The skin becomes much finer, but the pores closer. The skin is cleaner, and the veins distinctly seen through, and the skin also becomes elastic.

The appetite becomes much sharper by training. In training, the alvine evacuations are not very abundant, as so much matter goes off by perspiration. Perspiration is only intended to take off the superfluities of flesh and fat, which gives a person wind and strength. The exercise is always begun early in the morning, in summer at five, in winter at half past six, or as soon as it is light. We prefer rising early in the morning, indeed it is indispensable. Perspiration is usually produced by exercise, and no drugs are given for that purpose. The pupil is rubbed extremely dry with cold flannel, and has a change of clothes of course. Young people might wear calico next the skin, but older people wear flannel, which is more general. The skin of a fat man when he becomes lean, does not hang quite loose about him, but gets pretty tight and elastic. The bones get harder and tougher, and are less liable to injury by blows or exercise.

7. *What hours of exercise do they require of their pupils during the day? At what hours do they send them out in the morning? How long do they continue abroad? Are they loaded with clothes after the body is reduced, and becomes limber, and thin and muscular; or only while the sweating process continues? Are they fed before they go abroad, or when they return? What trials are made of their strength? When is a man known to be up to his full strength and breath in training? At what hours do they go to bed? What sleep are they allowed? What indispositions are they subject to during training? Are there any circumstances by which the process may be interrupted; or any circumstances, in consequence of which, it must sometimes by abandoned?*

They have an extra quantity of clothes to increase the perspiration, during the race, which may be continued for a mile or two in a morning. Their race is always in flannel; their walking exercise in their usual clothes; they come home, are rubbed dry gradually, generally are laid down on the bed and are rubbed in that situation, one limb after another, rubbed and clothed. They get their breakfast about eight o'clock, and after remaining at home about an hour, they take their regular exercise, either walking or cricket. The more they are in the open air, the firmer their flesh becomes, and they never mind the weather, only change their clothes if wet. Those who are trained to boxing, get a run in the morning, as those who are trained to running, and the same exercise, physic, &c. But they are not put between feather beds, or over-loaded with clothes, as those who run are. It is known when a man is up to his height, by the ease and speed with which he does his mile, and his condition at the end. They go to bed at ten, and are allowed from six to eight hours sleep.

They are sometimes a little feverish at first training, but are not liable to any other indisposition. If feverish, not quite so much exercise; exercise always creates a little thirst until they are in high condition.

8. *What is the state of the health, after they give up training? Are they subject to any complaints; and what are they? How long does the acquired excess of strength continue?*

The state of health after training is always good, and not subject to complaints. The acquired state of health would probably continue, if the system was persevered in.

9. *It is most interesting to learn, on which part of this process, the purging, the sweating, the exercise, or the feeding, they most depend; and whether it procures a permanent increase of vigour, easily maintained by suitable diet and exercises, or only a temporary excitement, calculated for the particular occasion? Also, whether persons have ever thought of undergoing this process, not for the purpose of running matches, but to*

recover health; with what success this has been done, and whether it is to be recommended for gout, corpulency, asthma, nervous disorder, or other maladies, as likely to be of service.

These are questions, of the importance of which, those who are best able to answer, may not be fully aware. But nothing which so suddenly changes the powers, and the very form and character of the body, from gross to lean, from weakness to vigorous health, from a breathless and bloated carcase, to one active and untiring, can ever be unimportant, either to the art of physic in general, or to that branch of it, more immediately connected with inquiries regarding health and longevity.

The purging and sweating are both of service, and necessary, but the exercise and feeding are the most essential. There is no instance as yet, of any person being positively put in training for the sole purpose of recovering health, but it certainly would be of great use in many disorders: and it is known, that a gentleman, after living hard in London, has gone to the country, and by living according to the above system, in some respects, has returned to London in perfect health.

Replies by Mr Jackson, *to some Additional Queries*[, which are not given]

1. Some boxers have lived long: Broughton to the age of eighty, Stevens, the nailer, above eighty; George Maggs, of Bristol, is about eighty, and a remarkably fine looking man. But many of the principal boxers have died young, owing to excesses of every sort, after the training was over; but were it not for that circumstance, and the injuries from blows on the body, they would live long enough: blows on the head are soon recovered.
2. A person in high life cannot be treated in exactly the same manner at first, from the indulgences to which he has been accustomed; nor is his frame in general so strong. They eat too much made dishes, and other improper food, and sit too long at table, and eat too great a variety of articles; also drink too much wine. No man should drink more than half a pint of wine. They also keep irregular hours, and lie too long in bed.

3. I am convinced that the gout might be prevented by following a regular system, and it is probably owing to their greater temperance that women have it so seldom. Even after having had the gout, by living very plainly and taking regular exercise, the disease has been prevented from recurring; keeping the shoes easy is of great use when gout attacks the feet.
4. A course of training would be an effectual remedy for bilious complaints.
5. Corpulent people, by the same system, could be brought into a proper condition.
6. It would prevent the rheumatism, by taking great care to keep the clothes dry. With regard to the stone and gravel, exercise is materially useful in these complaints, as it makes the urine pass off quickly.
7. As to consumption, the frame of such persons is in general too delicate to carry the training to any extent, but being much in the open air is certainly of great service.
8. Bathing is of great use. To prevent colds, bathing the feet in cold water every morning is of great advantage to men.

   Bathing in salt water three days a week is salutary, but the shorter time a person remains in the water the better. Fresh water is good, if salt cannot be had. The tepid bath was never tried.
9. Electricity has a greater effect upon muscular and healthy men than upon others; and more upon them than even upon children, and gives them a greater shock, probably owing to the greater resistance.

   West of Windsor could have gone over a hundred miles, running it in eighteen hours; and other people, properly trained, could do the same, if naturally formed for running. West could run forty miles in five hours and a half, which is near eight miles an hour. Mr Fozzard of Parklane's head hostler, known by the name of Fozzard's Joe, made ten miles in fifty-seven minutes, at forty years of age. He was however beat on Sunbury Common, by a Warwickshire man, who walked the last 500 yards in at the race, which was ten miles an hour. Joe was in a second within the time. It was a most sultry day, and the runners must have been very much exposed to the dust of 500 horsemen, who were present. Forty miles have been run at York, two years ago, in twenty minutes and nineteen seconds. They are famous in Yorkshire for running, but the Lancashire men are the best short-racers, being continually in practice. A curious fact is, that in racing, for the first 200 or 300 yards one feels very much distressed, after that a *second wind* comes, which lasts until one is spent with bodily fatigue. A quarter of a mile may be run about a second or two under the minute, and the half mile in two minutes; one mile a quarter of a minute under the five. Two miles have been done under ten minutes. 100 yards has been done under ten seconds.

Common emetics are given, such as ipacacuanha.

Persons trained, are generally costive. To keep clear of griping pains, no vegetables are given, which are of an opening quality: for the same reason pork and veal are avoided. The skin always becomes quite clean in training, even although formerly subject to eruptions.

Additional Queries suggested by a Friend.

1. *Why do you prefer early rising? Is not the morning air raw, cold, and moist, often accompanied with thick fogs, and consequently unwholesome?*

Answered by Mr Jackson.

The air is always cooler in the morning, therefore exercise can be easier taken. Men should be able to bear every kind of weather, only their feet must be kept dry; they never sit down without changing their clothes, whilst they are training, for fear of the rheumatism.

2. *Would not biscuit do better than bread, as any thing fermented is not reckoned strengthening?*

Soft bread, or new bread, is never eaten, being of a spongy nature, and expanding in the stomach; stale bread is wholesome, but probably biscuit might be as good. Several people prefer biscuit. No salt meat is given, nor any thing that can create thirst. The less one drinks the better. Drinking certainly encourages soft unhealthy flesh.

3. *The ancients thought that water was the best drink instead of fermented liquors. Has it ever been tried in any training in England?*

   I have never known a person drink water alone during training. Malt liquor, good and old, without bottling, is best. If any person accustomed to drink wine would try malt liquor for a month, he would find himself much the better for it.

4. *What is reckoned the proper quantity of sleep?*

   Eight hours a day is necessary, though much depends upon habit. People who take a good deal of exercise must have rest.

5. *What would be the effect of training persons who have nervous disorders?*

   Any gentleman during training, may occasionally read; but in general, boxers, &c. are employed in cricket, and other active amusements. In Broughton's time they were used to have music, which is very proper, and dancing, if they like. The mind is diverted from intense employment. They play quoits, which is a fine exercise.

   If a muscular man in training gets much thinner, his exercise must be reduced, but if he gets fatter, it is a proof it agrees with him.

6. *Would it have a tendency to prevent palsy and apoplexy?*

   Nervous disorders are always prevented; I have never seen an instance of nervous disorders in trained persons.

7. *The ancients reckoned pork the most nourishing diet.*

   Palsy prevented by the same means. There never was an instance of a trained person paralytic, which is supposed to proceed from want of exercise. The blood is so fine and thin that disorders of this nature are obviated.

   Perspiration is particularly good, which improves the wind. Perspiration from exercise never weakens.

   Boxing is the best exercise of any, from exercising all the members of the body. Fencing occupies only one side. Most people are right-handed, and the exercise is partial, but boxing calls both arms into action; and both hands must be equally employed both in hitting and parrying. In this species of exercise, the mind also must necessarily be more occupied.

8. [Sinclair only lists seven queries, though he prints fourteen answers.]

   By training, the mental faculties are also improved. The attention is more ready and the perceptions more acute, probably owing to the clearness of the stomach and the better digestion.

9. The use of animal food seems absolutely requisite to produce bodily strength; vegetables do not appear to contain so much nourishment.

10. Training always appears to improve the state of the lungs; one of the most striking effects of it is to improve the wind, that is, it enables a man to draw a larger inspiration, and to hold his breath longer.

11. Clearness of the skin is the best proof of a man being in good condition. The state of the skin is the criterion by which amateurs judge of a person being fit for exercise. During a course of training, the skin always becomes clear, smooth, well coloured and elastic.

12. A man properly trained, feels himself light and *corky*, as the technical phrase is.

13. Persons who are regularly and constantly exercised, as fencing-masters, &c. retain their appearance, carriage, and shape to the last.

14. A head proportionately small is supposed to betoken corporeal strength; and a person so formed is reckoned peculiarly fit for training.

Appendix 3

THE NAMING OF ADA, 1816

Byron hoped and expected that his first legitimate child would be a boy. A daughter was born at 1 p.m. on 10 December 1815 and christened Augusta Ada. With her first name Byron paid tribute to his half-sister who was also, until he married, his lover. For a time the child was known as 'Augusta Junior'. Ada, the name buried at first in secondary obscurity, told other, related tales. It was only from the summer of 1816 that Lady Byron called her daughter by her second name, in order to highlight her alienation from her sister-in-law.

Where did that name come from?

Byron was fascinated by what he called 'The Glory and the Nothing of a Name', by the tension between identity, inherited status and hard-won fame. He uses the word 'name' seventeen times in *English Bards and Scotch Reviewers*; twelve times in the first two cantos of *Childe Harold*; fourteen times in *The Giaour*; eight times in *The Corsair*; fifty-two times in *Werner*. He tended to call his fictional characters by names that resonated with borrowed meanings (Conrad, Medora, John Johnson).

Ada is another of the names he used that recreated the frame of 'A's around Augusta's name. He paid her this homage long before Annabella's presence made this habit seem uxorious. *Lara*, for example, alludes repeatedly to a secret that cannot be disclosed. In the 'Opening Lines to *Lara*', which Byron began in May 1814, he even referred to his beloved as 'Azora dearest'. Byron loved to hint at the dark secret of his incestuous love and went on to call his illegitimate daughter Allegra. 'Great is their love,' Anah insists in *Heaven and Earth*, 'who love in sin and fear'.

Byron could have called his legitimate daughter Agatha, Amelia, or Ava. Why did he choose Ada?

The name certainly had 'a private, probably sexual, significance' for her parents. 'I won't grow melancholy,' Annabella promised, when husband and wife parted in the summer of 1815, and she signed herself 'A—da'. Byron ended his letter to her of 1 September 1815 'yrs alway most conjugally B', adding 'A—da—' underneath. This gave Lady Byron a private reason for the name.

Byron claimed that Ada was a 'very antique family name, – I believe not used since the reign of King John'. Violet M. Walker, the historian of the Byron family, noted in 1988 that 'the name does not appear in the annals of the Byrons'. And yet biographers have repeated this story ever since.

But perhaps Byron was referring to the other side of his family, to the Gordons, who descended from Scottish kings?

There was an important Ada in the Scottish royal family during the life of the English King John (1167–1216). Ada de Warenne was born in 1120 and married Henry, Earl of Huntingdon, the son and heir to David I, 91st King of Scotland. Widowed in 1152, Ada saw her eldest son succeed his grandfather the following year, as Malcolm IV, 92nd King of Scotland. He was known as 'the Maiden', from his youth, the gentleness of his disposition and his insistence on celibacy. According to an English chronicler of the next generation, his mother tried (unsuccessfully) to seduce him.

On Malcolm's death in 1165 another of Ada's sons succeeded him, as 93rd King of Scotland. William 'the Lion' reigned for forty-nine years. His nickname comes from his standard of a rampant red lion, which has since been incorporated into Scotland's coat of arms.

Calling his daughter Ada therefore meant that Byron could anticipate her giving birth to two sons, who would both become kings.

Byron wrote to his estranged wife on 14 April 1814, asking her to ensure that a ring that had 'no lapidary value' should be given to their daughter, because 'it contains the hair of a king and an ancestor'.

But there was more to the name. Two Adas from the worlds of biblical and classical history, in sources that were well known to Byron, suggest that he intended to mark out a more definitively Byronic destiny for his daughter – in terms of heroic motherhood, kinship with Cain, bigamy and incest.

Byron had read the Old Testament 'through and through' and 'as a pleasure', before he was eight. He need not have read far in the first book, Genesis, to reach Chapter 4, verses 19 and 20, where he would encounter Ada, variously spelled as Adah. She was only the second woman to be named in the Bible. 'It is in an early chapter of Genesis as the name of the wife of Lameth,' he told Murray on 8 October 1820, adding, 'and I suppose Ada is the feminine of Adam.'

'Lamech took two wives: the name of the one was Ada, and the name of the other was Sella.

'And Ada brought forth Jabel: who was the father of such as dwell in tents, and of herdsmen.'

Lamech, the first man to commit bigamy, was Cain's great-great-great-grandson. Byron identified with Cain and had already associated Adam's elder son with two heroes, Childe Harold and Selim.

In *Cain*, the drama Byron wrote in 1821, he drew attention to the name Adah by reusing it for Cain's 'sister-bride'. According to Genesis Adah was Cain's great-great-great-granddaughter-in-law. Ada follows Thyrza: Byron used the latter name for his series of poems in memory of the boy he loved, John Edleston. Byron told his wife that he took the name Thyrza 'from Gessner – she was Abel's wife' in Gessner's *Death of Abel*. As a daughter of Adam, Thyrza was of course Abel's sister, as well as his wife.

And finally, Byron borrowed from ancient history to add a lurid, closely related colour to the biblical story.

Soon after he crossed the Hellespont in 334 BC Alexander the Great met Ada, Queen of Caria. She was 'sister-bride' to King Hildricus, from whom she inherited the throne. The royal family of Caria was a close one: Hildricus succeeded another sister, Artemisia, who inherited the throne from another brother, Mausolus, who was also her husband.

Byron read about Queen Ada in *The Campaigns of Alexander* by Arrian, 'the first historian of Alexander's actions', as Sir Richard Clayton put it in 1793, 'and the only one on whose authority any confidence is to be placed'. Byron included Arrian in the 'List of Historical Writers whose Works I have perused in different languages' that he compiled in 1807. 'Hildricus dying, left the administration of affairs in [Ada's] hands; for it had been an ancient custom among the Asiatics, ever since the time of Semiramis, that the widow should reign after her husband's decease.' Ada lost her throne to her usurping brother Pexodorus and was left with 'only one city in obedience, but that was the strongest in her territories, and named Alinda. She went forth to meet Alexander, who was marching with his army thither, and, delivering her city into his hands, adopted him as her son. Alexander, neither despising her liberality, nor disdaining the title of son, which she had conferred on him, left the city in her custody; and, after he had demolished Halicarnasssus, and reduced all Caria, honoured her with the government of the whole province.'

Byron relished the incestuous element in history or fiction wherever he found it. When he defended the original conception of *The Bride of Abydos* in 1813 he commented that 'the finest works of the Greeks, one of Schiller's and Alfieri's in modern times, besides several of our *old* (and best) dramatists, were founded on incidents of a similar cast'.

The essence of this Carian story was repeated by other, important historians of Alexander the Great, by Diodorus Siculus, and by Quintus Curtius Rufus, both of whose works were printed in new editions during the Napoleonic Wars. Hildricus may be spelled Hidreus or Idreus, but the satisfyingly simple geometry of Carian succession never varies.

Alexander the Great's career became newly topical in the early nineteenth century, as commentators struggled to find precedents for Napoleon's global conquests. As a historian pointed out in 1809:

> The middle-part of the narrative, and route, of the Macedonian expedition to the East, possesses new interest, on account of Buonaparte's designs on Persia; his proclaimed invasion of India, if any thing more than a machination to induce the Porte, as well as the Court of Tuhran, to permit his occupation of important possessions, is a distant object. Alexander

> subjugated as he went: we may calculate that Buonaparte will follow an example from which deviation would be unsafe, without expecting him to draw his catalogue of means from a magnanimous school.

Byron himself later rebuked Napoleon for not following Alexander's example.

There were other, less appropriate Adas to be found, in the annals of his family, the Bible and royal history. But to understand why Byron gave his daughter the second name of Ada, it surely helps to know that previous Adas were an English noblewoman who gave birth to two kings of Scotland; the bigamous wife of Cain's direct descendant; *and* the King of Caria's sister-bride, who adopted Alexander the Great as her son.

'I have always preferred my mother's family,' Byron told Douglas Kinnaird in 1821, '– for it's [*sic*] royalty.'

The name Ada was not popular in Britain until Byron summoned it from obscurity to garland his daughter, though Byron told Murray on 8 October 1820 that if he were to turn over the earlier pages of *The Huntingdon Peerage*, he would see 'how common a name Ada was in the early Plantagenet days'. In Henry Nugent Bell's *The Huntingdon Peerage* (1820), two thirteenth-century ancestresses of the Earl of Huntingdon bore the name Ada. In the same letter Byron added that 'It was also the name of Charlemagne's sister.'

Even before Ada, Countess of Lovelace, became a celebrity in her own right, as a pioneer of computing, Lady Caroline Lamb intervened with an alternately picturesque and tedious novel, *Ada Reis, A Tale*, which John Murray published in 1823. Several details suggest that she had Byron in her sights.

Lady Caroline justifies using the name Ada for her male hero by suggesting that as a boy he was adopted by a Genoese merchant, Adamo Remolo, 'who gave him the best education he could afford, placed him in an academy at Pisa, and, when he died, bequeathed him a small property and his name'.

Lady Caroline often crossed the gender line in her own life, so it is not surprising that she borrowed Byron's daughter's name to portray a patently

Byronic hero. The novel begins, 'Ada Reis appears to have been one of those daring characters which human nature produces now and then; one of those men who awe and overpower all the feeble and many of the stronger minded, by the success of their enterprises.'

At other points Lady Caroline goes out of her way to highlight those elements in Ada Reis's character and life that resonated with Byronic familiarity:

'"Arouse me – injure those I love – awaken the sleeping lion – and dread Ada Reis as a fiend, at once above and below mankind."'

'Ada Reis was superstitious, because he had long ceased to be religious.'

It may be relevant that all London knew of Byron's Memoirs, which he had begun writing in July 1818 and entrusted to Thomas Moore, who gave them to John Murray. Lady Caroline Lamb bases her novel around her hero's memoirs. She wrote it at a time when her friend John Murray was holding on to Byron's manuscript. He lent it to Lady Caroline. In 1823, a year before the Memoirs were burned in Murray's fireplace, it must have been tantalising to read in her novel that:

> Ada Reis, the once-famous Corsair, the merchant, the traveller, the Don Juan of his day, wrote his life, and left it as a legacy to his successors. His treasures he buried, his slaves he strangled, his wives he suffocated, but this MS. he left for the benefit of man-kind; I have not translated the part which related to his amours, not the confession of his crimes, not the catalogue of his wise sayings, but the simple narrative of what occurred to himself and his daughter, that those who read may place the awful record in their hearts and learn to worship God, and to be humble in themselves.

And the following:

> Whole pages [of his memoirs] are filled with description of his person. His clear auburn hair hanging in curls over his fair brow and white neck, his eyes beaming with love, his smile irresistible, his voice most melodious; he had only to speak to persuade, yet did he ever use but few words.

He acknowledges, however, that he delighted in low company, in throwing off all restraint, and in giving unbounded licence to his conversation, confesses more than once that he was a strange compound of every excellence and every vice.

"I love the way you weave together stories of your abused childhood with these delightful recipes for muffins and scones."

David Sipress's cartoon first appeared in Gastronomica, *Summer 2002, Vol. 2, No. 3, when it seemed a lot less edgy.*

David Sipress/The New Yorker Collection/The Cartoon Bank

Appendix 4

RECIPES

The Art of Cookery is a science appreciated only by very few individuals; and which requires, besides a great deal of studious application, no small share of intellect, and the strictest sobriety and punctuality, to be brought to perfection.

Louis Eustache Ude, *The French Cook*, 1813

Louis-Eustache Ude, the frontispiece to his book, The French Cook, *1826. Byron owned a copy of the 1815 edition.*

Much of the special vocabulary Byron employs to celebrate the Amundevilles' dinner in *Don Juan* appears on two of the Bills of Fare that Ude gives:

BILL OF FARE FOR NOVEMBER OR DECEMBER.

Six Entrées.

First Course.

2 Potages.

Le potage à la bonne femme, dit Flamande. White.
Le potage à la Beauveau. Brown.

2 Poissons.

Le turbot, sauce au homard.
Le dorey garni d'éperlans frits.

2 Relevés.

Le dindon à la Périgueux, purée de marons.
Le cuisseau de porc à demi sel, garni de choux.

6 Entrées.

Les côtelettes de mouton à la Soubise.
Le salmi de perdreaux à l'Espagnole.
Le vol au vent d'escalopes de cabilleau à la crême.
La casserole au ris d'un hachi de gibier au fumet.
Les escalopes de files to lapreaux à la conti au truffes.
Les cotelettes de filets de poulets gras en épigramme.

2 Plats de Rôt.

Les becasses.
Les perdreaux.

6 Entremets.

Les épinards au consommé, garnis de croutons.
Les cardons d'Espagne, à la moelle à l'essence.
Les truffes entières au vin de Champagne, dans une serviette.
La salade de homard dressée.
La gelée de vin de Madère gardie de gelée hachée.
Les gâteaux à la Polonaise.

BILL OF FARE FOR DECEMBER AND JANUARY

8 Entrées, and 4 relevés, or 10 entrées and 2 relevés.
The *potages* and fish, superseded by the 4 *relevés.*

2 Potages.

Le potage à la reine. La Brunoise au consommé clair.

2 Poissons.

Le turbot, garni d'éperlans. La matelotte de carpes à la royale.

2 Relevés des bouts.

Les poulardes à la Condé ragoût à l'Allemande. Le jambon de Westphalie à l'Espagnole.

8 Entrées.

Les filets de perdreaux sautés à la Lucullus.
Les petites timballes d'un salpicon à la Monglas.
Les croquettes de filet de volailles au velouté.
Les filets mignons de poulets gras à la Pompadour, Italienne blanchée liée.
Les perdreaux à la Barbarie, Italienne aux truffes. Three in number.
Les petits poulets à la reine. Aspic liée, pluches de persil. Two of these.
Les côtelettes de porc à la Mirepoix, Espagnole.
Le carré de veau à la Chalons, haricots vierges.

4 Plats de Rôt.

Les bécassines. Les sarcelles.
Le lièvre. Les poulets gras, un piqué.

8 Entremets.

Les salsifis à la sauce blanche.
Le maccaroni à l'Italienne, garni de croutons de patisserie.
Les oeufs brouillés aux truffes, garnis de croutons frits au beurre.
Les pommes de terre à la maître d'hôtel, coupée liards.
Les darioles à la crême.
Les canapés garnis de marmalade d'abricots.
La gelée de vin de Madère, décorée.
Le pain de framboises, à la glace.

4 Relevés de Rôt.

Les fondues au fromage de gruyère.
Les ramequins.
Les biscuits à la crême.
Le soufflé à la fleur d'orange.

Soupe à la Bonne-Femme.

Take two handfuls of sorrel; after having taken off the stalks put the leaves one above another and mince them. Take the hearts of two or three cabbage-lettuces, which mince likewise. Wash the whole well, then take about two ounces of fresh butter, and let your herbs melt as it were, in the butter. When so, moisten with a little broth, and let it boil for an hour. Skim off the grease, and throw in a little sugar, to take off the acidity of the sorrel. Then thicken your soup with the yolks of eight eggs, mixed with a little cream. Be mindful to keep a little broth for the bread to soak in, for this could not be accomplished in broth when thickened.

Potage à la Beaveau

Take some turnips, peel them, and use a cutter with which you cut out a few balls as round as possible, but very small. Blanch them, and boil them in some consommé, well clarified, with a little sugar. Serve up with bits of bread as above, soak singly, not to spoil the look of the soup, which must appear very bright, and put to it two spoon-fuls of *blond de veau*.

38. *The Genoese Sauce.*

This sauce is made by stewing fish, yet it is natural enough that it should find its place among the other sauces.—Make some marinade of various roots, such as carrots, roots of parsley, onions, and a few mushrooms, with a bay leaf, some thyme, a blade of mace, a few cloves, and some branches of sweet basil—fry the whole slowly, over a mitigated fire, in a stewpan, with butter, till the onions are quite melted. Pour in some Madeira or other white wine, according to the size of the fish you have to dress, and let the vegetables stew. When done enough, use it to stew your fish in, and take some of the liquor to make the sauce. Take a little brown thickening (No. 15), and mix it with some of the marinade, to which add two or three spoonsful of gravy of veal. Let these stew gently on the corner of the stove; skim off all the grease, season well, and pour the sauce through a tammy. Then add to it two spoonsful of essence of anchovies, and a quarter of a pound of butter kneaded with flour, and throw them into the sauce. When this is done, squeeze into it the juice of a lemon, work the sauce over the stove to make it very smooth, and cover the fish with the sauce, which must accordingly be made thick and mellow.

The original recipe for Genoese Sauce from Louis Eustache Ude, The French Cook, *1835.*

Dindon à la Périgueux

Take a nice fat turkey. The moment it has been killed, empty it, and put plenty of salt inside of the body. Then let it cool, and prepare some truffles in the following manner. Take a large quantity, peel them, and smell whether they be all of a good flavour. Then pick out the smallest, which chop very fine. Take some fat white bacon, and rasp it so as to procure the fat only without the nerves. When you have thus rasped a sufficient quantity to fill the body of the turkey, stuff the turkey with the chopped truffles and bacon seasoned with salt, spices, pepper, and cayenne-pepper, well mixed together. Sew the turkey up, and keep it in the larder for about a fortnight, so long as it retains a fine flavour. Then roast it well, wrapt up in layers of bacon and covered with paper, &c. Serve up with a *purée* of chestnuts *à brun*.

Puits d'Amour garnished with jam

Spread some puff-paste, a foot square, and three-eighths of an inch thick. Have a small cutter, cut about two dozen; brush a *plafond* over with a little *dorure* [beaten egg], and put those small pasties on it, pressing on each of them with your finger: then brush each of them over with the *dorure*; open the little mark in the centre with a knife, and bake them quickly in a hot oven. When done, sift some pounded sugar over them, and glaze very bright. Take out the crumb in the middle, and put the pasties on a clean sheet of paper, to draw off the butter. Garnish with different coloured sweetmeats, as cherry and apricot jam.

Appendix 5

JOHNSON THE BOXER

It is generally accepted that 'Gentleman' John Jackson inspired John Johnson in *Don Juan* but, as Byron's screen displayed a portrait of the pugilist Tom Johnson, it seems worthwhile looking into his character.

According to Pierce Egan, author of *Boxiana* and other works:

> JOHNSON was a hero among heroes, possessing all those requisites for pugilism, which rarely falls [*sic*] to the lot of an individual. NATURE had given him a form almost of Herculean strength, which rendered him either capable of resisting with ease, or in attacking with the utmost impetuosity; and he had improved these natural qualifications by a most minute attention to ART. His courage was of the finest order, well versed in the science, and possessed of a native coolness of disposition, that infused into his composition a superior degree of firmness over most of his competitors: and added to these great capabilities, JOHNSON had learned to subdue his passions – that, like the unrivalled BROUGHTON, when he mounted the stage, he was complete in his part, and proved himself a first-rate actor.
>
> JOHNSON was by no means a showy fighter, and his guard was generally considered as inelegant; his attitudes appeared more upon the defensive than otherwise; and in the fight was peculiarly steady, watching every movement of his antagonist, with a coolness unequalled; receiving the attack unappalled; and scarcely ever failing in the return of planting a most desperate hit. Jackson acted as Johnson's bottle-holder in the latter's second match against Bill Ryan.

Tom Johnson takes a prominent place at the top of the first fold of Byron's boxing screen. The screen's longest prose extract describes the match between Johnson and Big Ben Brian on 17 January 1791, illustrated above it. The 'hardest' round was the eighteenth of twenty-four: 'Both parties so desperate, and striking so furiously as to threaten each other with instantaneous death. Many of the [5,000] spectators were compelled by their feelings to turn away from the horror of the scene . . . both of them were bleeding so much, that it was almost a difficulty to distinguish the face from the hind part of the head.' The screen records two of Johnson's three fights; one account is handwritten.

Private collection

LIST OF ABBREVIATIONS

PEOPLE

AB:	The Hon. Augusta Byron 1783–1851
AL:	The Hon. Augusta Leigh 1783–1851
AM:	Annabella Milbanke, later Lady Byron, 1792–1860
EEW:	Edward Ellerker Williams 1793–1822
EJT:	Edward John Trelawny 1792–1881
ENL:	Edward Noel Long
EP:	Elizabeth Pigot 1783–1866
FH:	Francis Hodgson 1781–1852
Hoppner:	Richard Belgrave Hoppner 1786–1872
JCH:	John Cam Hobhouse (Lord Broughton) 1786–1869
JH:	John Hanson 1781–
JW:	Jane Williams 1798–1884
LCL:	Lady Caroline Lamb 1785–1828
LM:	Lady Melbourne 1751–1818
LyB:	Lady Byron 1792–1860
Mrs B:	Mrs Byron 1770–1811
MS:	Mary Shelley 1797–1851
PBS:	Percy Bysshe Shelley 1792–1822
SBD:	Scrope Berdmore Davies 1782–1852
TM:	Thomas Moore 1779–1852
WB:	William Bankes 1786–1855
WS:	Walter Scott 1771–1832

BYRON'S WORKS and SOURCES

Abeshouse:	Benjamin S. Abeshouse, *The Medical History of Lord Byron*, 1965
Ada Reis:	[Lady Caroline Lamb], *Ada Reis, A Tale*, 3 Vols, 1823
Allemagne:	Mme Anne Louise Germaine de Staël-Holstein, *De l'Allemagne*, 1810, 1813
Angeli:	Helen Rossetti Angeli, *Shelley and his Friends in Italy*, 1911
Angler:	Thomas Medwin, *The Angler in Wales, or Days and Nights of Sportsmen*, 2 Vols, 1834
AR:	Doris Langley Moore, *Lord Byron: Accounts Rendered*, 1974
Archer:	William Archer and Robert Lowe, *Hazlitt on Theatre*, 1957, 1971
Ashton:	John Ashton, *English Caricature and Satire on Napoleon I*, 2 Vols, 1884
Bainbridge:	Simon Bainbridge, *Napoleon and English Romanticism*, 1995
Barton:	Paul D. Barton, *Lord Byron's Religion: A Journey into Despair* (Mellen Studies in Literature. Romantic Reassessment, V. 160), 2003
Bate:	Jonathan Bate, *John Clare: A Biography*, 2003
Beaton:	Roderick Beaton, *Romantic Rebellion, Greek Revolution*, 2013
Beevers:	Robert Beevers, *The Byronic Image: The Poet Portrayed*, 2005

BG: *The Byron Gallery: A Series of Historical Embellishments to Illustrate the Poetical Works of Lord Byron*, 1832

BL: James Engell and W. Jackson Bate, ed., Samuel Taylor Coleridge, *Biographia Literaria, Collected Works*, Bollingen Series LXXV, 1983

Blessington: Ernest J. Lovell, Jr., ed., *Lady Blessington's Conversations of Lord Byron* (1834), 1969

Blumberg: Jane Blumberg, *Byron and the Shelleys*, 1982

Bodmer: Johann Jacob Bodmer, *Kritische Abhandlung von dem Wunderbaren in der Poesie und dessen Verbindung mit dem Wahrscheinlichen in einer Vertheidigung des Gedichtes Joh. Miltons von dem Verlohrnen Paradiese*, 1740

Bond: Geoffrey Bond, *Lord Byron's Best Friends from bulldogs to Boatswain and beyond, including a complete facsimile of Elizabeth Pigot's illustrated poem of 1807, "The Wonderful History of Lord Byron & His Dog"*, 2013

Boxiana: Pierce Egan, *Boxiana*, 1812

Boyd: Elizabeth French Boyd, *Byron's Don Juan: A Critical Study*, 1945

Boyes: Megan Boyes, *My Amiable Mama: The Biography of Mrs. Catherine Gordon, the Poet's Mother*, 1991

Brent: Peter Brent, *Lord Byron*, 1974

BRH:	John Jolliffe, ed., *Neglected Genius: The Diaries of Benjamin Robert Haydon, 1808–1846*, 1990
Brewer:	William Dean Brewer, *The Shelley-Byron Conversation*, 1994
Brophy:	Brigid Brophy, *Mozart the Dramatist* (1964), 1990
Browne:	J. H. Browne, 'Voyage from Leghorn to Cephalonia with Lord Byron, and a Narrative of a Visit, in 1823, to the Seat of War in Greece', *Blackwood's Magazine*, XXV (Jan 1834), 56–65, in Norman Page, ed., *Byron: Interviews and Recollections*, 1985, 125–137
Buchan:	Peter Buchan, ed., *Ancient Ballads and Songs of the North of Scotland, hitherto unpublished, with explanatory notes*, 2 Vols, 1828
Burke:	Conor Cruise O'Brien, ed., Edmund Burke, *Reflections on the Revolution in France, And on the Proceedings in Certain Societies in London Relative to that Event. In a Letter Intended to Have Been Sent to a Gentleman in Paris* (1790), 1968
Burns Letters:	James A Mackay, ed., *The Complete Letters of Robert Burns*, 1987
Butler:	Marilyn Butler, *Romantics, Rebels, and Reactionaries: English Literature and Its Background, 1760–1830*, 1982
Buxton:	John Buxton, *Byron and Shelley*, 1968

Cannon-Brookes:	Peter Cannon-Brookes, ed., *The Painted Word, British History Painting 1750–1836*, 1991
Canova:	Isabella Albrizzi, *The Works of Antonio Canova*, 1809
Champion:	*The Champion*, 20 February 1814
CH:	*Childe Harold*
Chesser:	Eustace Chesser, *Shelley and Zastrozzi: Self Revelation of a Neurotic*, 1965
Christiansen:	Rupert Christiansen, *Romantic Affinities: Portraits From an Age, 1780–1830*, 1987
Clark:	John Willis Clark, *Cambridge, Brief Historical and Descriptive Notes*, 1883
Cochran Burning:	Peter Cochran, *The Burning of Byron's Memoirs: New and Unpublished Essays and Papers*, 2014
Coleridge Essays:	*Essays on His Own Times, forming a Second Series of The Friend*, London: William Pickering, 1850; David V. Erdman, ed., *The Collected Works of Samuel Taylor Coleridge 3,* Essays on His Times *I–III in* The Morning Post *and* The Courier, Bollingen Series LXXV; 1978
Concordance:	Ione Dodson Young, ed., *A Concordance to the Poetry of Byron*, 1965
Connolly:	Cyril Connolly, *The Missing Diplomats,* 1952
Considerations:	Aurelian Craiutu, ed., Mme Anne-Louise Germaine de Staël-Holstein, *Considerations of the Principal Events of the French Revolution* , 2 Vol, 1818

Corbeau:	Jonathan David Gross, ed., *Byron's "Corbeau Blanc": The Life and Letters of Lady Melbourne, 1751–1818*, 1997
Cramond:	William Cramond, *Annals of Banff*, 1893
Crisp:	Arthur Crisp, 'Commentary: Ambivalence toward fatness and its origins', *British Medical Journal*, no. 7123, 20–27, December 1997, p. 1703; Hugh Baron and Arthur Crisp, 'Byron's Eating Disorders', *The Byron Journal*, No. 31, 2003, 91–100
Crompton:	Louis Crompton, *Byron and Greek Love: Homophobia in Nineteenth Century England*, 1985
Curran Wittreich:	Stuart Curran and Joseph Wittreich, 'The Dating of Shelley's "On the Devil, and Devils"', *Keats-Shelley Journal*, 21–22, 1972–3, 83–94
Dallas:	Robert Charles Dallas, *Memoir of the Life of Lord Byron*, 1824
DJ:	*Don Juan*
Douglass:	Paul Douglass, *Lady Caroline Lamb: A Biography*, 1994
DT:	*Detached Thoughts*, 1 May 1821 – 18 May 1822
EBSR:	*English Bards and Scotch Reviewers*
Eggert:	Gerhard Eggert, 'Lord Byron und Napoleon', *Palaestra*, CLXXXVI, 1933, 1–112
Eisler:	Benita Eisler, *Byron, Child of Passion, Fool of Fame*, 1999
Ellis:	David Ellis, *Byron in Geneva*, 2011
Elwin:	Malcolm Elwin, *Lord Byron's Wife*, 1962

Elwin Family:	Peter Thompson, ed., Malcolm Elwin, *Lord Byron's Family, Annabella, Ada and Augusta 1818–1824*, 1975
Falkner:	Nora Crook and Pamela Clemit, ed., Mary Shelley, *Falkner* (1837), 1996
Finlay:	George Finlay, *History of Greece*, 2 Vols, 1861
FitzSimons:	Raymund FitzSimons, *Edmund Kean, Fire from Heaven*, 1976
Frankenstein:	Marilyn Butler, ed., Mary Shelley, *Frankenstein*, (1818,1823), 2008
Freeman:	T. Freeman, 'Pregnancy as a precipitant of mental illness in men', *British Journal of Medical Psychology*, 1951, 24, 49–54
Galt:	John Galt, *The Life of Lord Byron*, 1830
Gamba:	Pietro Gamba, *A Narrative of Lord Byron's Last Journey to Greece*, 1825
Garlick:	Kenneth Garlick, *Sir Thomas Lawrence: A Complete Catalogue of The Oil Paintings*, 1989
Garnett:	Richard Garnett, ed., *Journal of Edward Ellerker Williams, Companion of Shelley and Byron in 1821 and 1822*, 1902
Gazette Littéraire:	'To the Editor of a Venice Newspaper', *Gazette Littéraire de Jéna*, 27 March 1817, April? 1817
Gisborne Williams:	F. L. Jones, ed., *Maria Gisborne and Edward E. Williams, Shelley's Friends*, 1951
Glenarvon:	Frances Wilson, ed., Lady Caroline Lamb, *Glenarvon* (1816), 1999
Glenbervie:	Walter Sichel, ed., *The Glenbervie Journals*, 1910

Godwin: William Godwin, *Enquiry Concerning Political Justice and its Influence on Morals and Happiness*, 1793

Goldring: Douglas Goldring, *Regency Portrait Painter, the Life of Sir Thomas Lawrence*, 1951

Gronow: John Raymond, ed., *The Reminiscences and Recollections of Captain Gronow, being Anecdotes of the Camp, Court, Clubs & Society, 1810–1860*, 1964

Guiccioli: Countess Guiccioli, *My recollections of Lord Byron: and those of eye-witnesses of his life*, 2 Vols, 1869

Harness: The Rev. J. G. L'Estrange, *The Literary Life of William Harness*, 1871

Haydon Diary: Willard Bissell Pope, ed., *The Diary of Benjamin Robert Haydon*, 5 Vols, (1863), 1960–3

Hayley: William Hayley, *Life of Milton*, 1796

H. C. Robinson: Thomas Sadler, ed., *Diary, Reminiscences, and Correspondence of Henry Crabb Robinson*, 3 Vols, 1869

Hewitt: Ben Hewitt, *Byron, Shelley, and Goethe's* Faust: *An Epic Connection*, 2015

Hobhouse: John Cam Hobhouse, *A Journey through Albania and Other Provinces of Turkey in Europe and Asia to Constantinople during the Years 1809 and 1810*, 1813

Hodgson: James Thomas Hodgson, *Memoir of the Rev. Francis Hodgson, B.D., Scholar, Poet, and Divine*, 1878

Hogg: Thomas Jefferson Hogg, *The Life of Percy Bysshe Shelley*, 2 Vols, 1858

Holmes Shelley:	Richard Holmes, *Shelley: The Pursuit*, 1974
Hunt:	Leigh Hunt, *Lord Byron and Some of his Contemporaries with Records of the Author's Life and of his Visit to Italy*, 1828
Hunt Correspondence:	Thornton Leigh Hunt, ed., *The Correspondence of Leigh Hunt*, 1862
Hunter:	P. D. Hunter, *The Harrow Collection*, 1994
HVSV:	Ernest J. Lovell, Jr., ed., *His Very Self and Voice: Collected Conversations of Lord Byron*, 1954
Jamison:	Kay Redfield Jamison, *Touched with Fire: Manic-Depressive Illness and the Artistic Temperament*, 1993
JCH *Recollections*:	Lady Dorchester, ed., Lord Broughton (John Cam Hobhouse), *Recollections of a Long Life*, 6 Vols, 1909–11
Jeaffreson:	John Cordy Jeaffreson, *The Real Lord Byron: the Story of the Poet's Life*, 1900
Johnson:	G. B. Hill, ed., Samuel Johnson, *Lives of the English Poets*, 3 Vols (1779), 1905
Kaplan and Kloss:	Morton Kaplan and Robert Kloss, 'Fantasy of Paternity and the Doppelgänger: Mary Shelley's *Frankenstein*,' in *The Unspoken Motive: A Guide to Psychoanalytic Literary Criticism*, 1973
Kennedy:	James Kennedy, *Conversations on Religion, with Lord Byron and Others: held in Cephalonia, a short time previous to his lordship's death*, 1830
Knowles:	John Knowles, *The Life and Writings of Henry Fuseli*, 3 Vols, 1831

Kraeger: Heinrich Kraeger, 'Der Byronsche Heldentypus', *Forschungen zur neueren Litteraturgeschichte*, 6, 1898

Kruitzner: 'The German's Tale. Kruitzner', in Sophia and Harriet Lee, *The Canterbury Tales*, 4 Vols, 1801, IV, 3–68

Lady Shelley: Richard Edgcumbe, ed., *The Diary of Frances Lady Shelley*, 1912–13

Lang: Cecil Y. Lang, 'Narcissus Jilted: Byron, Don Juan, and the Biographical Imperative', Jerome J. McGann, ed., *Historical Studies and Literary Criticism*, Madison, 1985, 143–79

Lasègue: Ernest-Charles Lasègue, 'De l'Anorexie Histérique', *Archives générales de Médecine*, 1, 1873, 385–403

Last Man: Mary Shelley, *The Last Man*, 1826

Lean: Edward Tangye Lean, *The Napoleonists, a study in political disaffection, 1760–1960*, 1970

Lectures Hazlitt: William Hazlitt, *Lectures on the English Poets*, 1818

Lockhart: John Gibson Lockhart, *Memoirs of the Life of Sir Walter Scott*, 7 Vols, 1837–8

Lovell: Ernest J. Lovell, Jr., 'Byron and Mary Shelley', *Keats-Shelley Journal*, 2 (Jan. 1953), 34–49

Lynch: Bohun Lynch, *The Prize Ring*, 1925

Manning: Peter J. Manning, *Byron and His Fictions*, 1978

Manning Kean: Peter J. Manning, 'Edmund Kean and Byron's Plays', *Keats-Shelley Journal*, 1 January 1972, Vol. 21/22, 188–206

Manning Kean:	Peter J. Manning, 'Edmund Kean and Byron's Plays', *Keats-Shelley Journal*, 1 January 1972, Vol. 21/22, 188–206
Marchand:	Leslie A. Marchand, *Byron: A Biography*, 3 Vols, 1957
Markham:	Sarah Markham, *A Testimony of Her Times: Based on Penelope Hind's Diaries and Correspondence, 1787–1838*, 1991
Mary Shelley Letters:	Betty T. Bennett, ed., *Selected Letters of Mary Wollstonecraft Shelley*, 1995
Mayne:	Ethel Colburn Mayne, *The Life and Letters of Anne Isabella, Lady Noel Byron*, 1929
Medwin:	Ernest J. Lovell, Jr., ed., *Medwin's Conversations of Lord Byron* (1824), 1966
Memorials of Gormandising:	Titmarch, M. A. (William Makepeace Thackeray), 'Memorials of Gormandising in a Letter to Oliver Yorke, Esq.', *Fraser's Magazine*, June 1841, 710–25
Millingen:	Julius Millingen, *Memoirs of the Affairs of Greece; Containing an Account of the Military and Political Events, which Occurred in 1823 and Following Years, with Various Anecdotes relating to Lord Byron and an Account of his Last Illness and Death*, 1831
Mitford:	John Mitford, *The Private Life of Lord Byron Comprising His Voluptuous Amours, Secret Intrigues and Close Connection with Various Ladies of Rank and Fame, in Scotland and London, at Eton, Harrow, Cambridge, Paris, Rome,*

Mitford:	*Venice, &c., &c, with a Particular Account of the Countess Guiaccoli and (never Before Published) Details of the Murder at Ravenna, which Caused His Lordship to Leave Italy, Various Singular Anecdotes of Persons and Families of the Highest Circles of Haut Ton*, 1828
Moore:	Thomas Moore, *Letters and Journals of Lord Byron: with Notices of His Life*, 2 Vols, 1830
Moore Memoirs:	Lord John Russell, ed., *Memoirs, Journal and Correspondence of Thomas Moore*, 8 Vols, 1853–6
Morton:	Timothy Morton, *Shelley, and the Revolution in Taste: The Body and the Natural World*, 1994
Murray Letters:	Andrew Nicolson, ed., *The Letters of John Murray to Lord Byron*, 2007
Nathan:	Isaac Nathan, *Fugitive pieces and reminiscences of Lord Byron, containing an entire new edition of the Hebrew melodies, with the addition of several never before published, the whole illustrated with critical, historical, theatrical, political, and theological remarks, notes, anecdotes, interesting conversations, and observations, made by that illustrious poet, together with His Lordship's autograph, also some original poetry, letters and recollections of Lady Caroline Lamb*, 1829
Newlyn:	Lucy Newlyn, *Paradise Lost and the Romantic Reader*, 1993

Nicolson:	Harold Nicolson, *Byron: The Last Journey, April 1823–April 1824*, 2nd ed., 1948
Newstead Abbey:	Rosalys Coope and Pete Smith, *Newstead Abbey, A Nottinghamshire Country House: Its Owners and Architectural History*, Thoroton Society Record Series, Vol. 48, 2014
Nicolson Prose:	Andrew Nicolson, ed., *Lord Byron: the Complete Miscellaneous Prose*, 1991
Normington:	Susan Normington, *Lady Caroline Lamb: This Infernal Woman*, 2001
Notebooks:	Kathleen Coburn, ed., *The Notebooks of Samuel Taylor Coleridge*, 5 Vols, Bollingen 50, 1958–2002
Oates:	Joyce Carol Oates, *On Boxing*, 2009
O'Meara:	Barry E. O'Meara, *Napoleon in Exile; or, A Voice from St. Helena. The Opinions and Reflections of Napoleon on the Most Important Events of his Life and Government, in his own words*, 2 Vols, 2nd ed. 1822
Origo:	Iris Origo, *The Last Attachment: The story of Byron and Teresa Guiccioli as told in their unpublished letters and other family papers*, 1949
Origo Allegra:	Iris Origo, *Allegra*, 1935
Parry:	William Parry, *The Last Days of Lord Byron: with his Lordship's Opinions on Various Subjects, Particularly on the State and Prospects of Greece*, London, 1825

Paulson:	Ronald Paulson, *Representations of Revolution, 1789–1820*, 1983
PL:	Philip Pullman, intr., John Milton, *Paradise Lost*, (1667), 2005
Polidori Diary:	William Michael Rossetti, ed., *The Diary of Dr John William Polidori, 1816, Relating to Byron, Shelley, etc*, 1911
Pratt:	Willis W. Pratt, *Byron at Southwell: The Making of a Poet*, 1948
Prothero Childhood:	Rowland E. Prothero, 'The Childhood and School Days of Byron', *Nineteenth Century Magazine*, Vol. XLIII, No. 251, Jan. 1898, 61–81
Prothero:	Rowland E. Prothero, ed., *The Works of Lord Byron: A New, Revised and Enlarged Edition, with illustrations. Letters and Journals*, 6 Vols, 1898–1901
Pushkin:	Tatiana Wolff, ed., *Pushkin on Literature*, 1998
RJ:	Ravenna Journal, 4 January to 27 February 1821, TM, II, 395–434 and I, 62–4
Read:	Herbert Read, *In Defence of Shelley and Other Essays*, 1936
Recollections:	Edward John Trelawny, *Recollections of the Last Days of Shelley and Byron*, 1858
Records:	Edward John Trelawny, *Records of Shelley, Byron, and the Author*, 1878
Retzsch:	Morris Retzsch, *Illustrations of Goethe's Faust*, 1819
Ritratti:	Ritratto XXIII, Isabella Teotochi Albrizzi, *Ritratti*, 4th ed., 1826, 93–103

Robinson:	Charles E. Robinson, *Shelley and Byron: The Snake and Eagle Wreathed in Flight*, 1976
Roe:	Nicholas Roe, *Wordsworth and Coleridge, The Radical Years*, 1988
Ross:	*Sermons by James Ross: with a Memoir of his Life*, 1825
Rutherford:	Andrew Rutherford, ed., *Byron: The Critical Heritage*, 1970
Sampson:	John Sampson, *The poems of William Blake*, 1921
Saveson:	J. E. Saveson, 'Shelley's Julian and Maddalo', *Keats–Shelley Journal*, Vol. 10 (Winter, 1961), 53–8
Schock:	Peter A. Schock, *Romantic Satanism: Myth and the Historical Moment in Blake, Shelley and Byron*, 2003
Schoina:	Maria Schoina, *Romantic 'Anglo-Italians': Configurations of Identity in Byron, the Shelleys, and the Pisan Circle*, 2009
Sebba:	Anne Sebba, *The Exiled Collector: William Bankes and the Making of an English Country House*, 2004
Semmel:	Stuart Semmel, *Napoleon and the British*, 2004
Seymour:	Miranda Seymour, *Mary Shelley* (2000), 2001
Shelley Prose Works:	Harry Buxton Forman, ed., *The Prose Works of Percy Bysshe Shelley*, 2 Vols, 1880

Shelley Prose:	Donald H. Reiman and Neil Fraistat, selected an ed., *Shelley's Poetry and Prose* (1977), 2nd ed., 2002
Sinclair:	Sir John Sinclair, *Code of Health and Longevity, or, A concise view, of the principles calculated for the preservation of health, and the attainment of long life*, 4 Vols, 1807
Smiles:	Thomas Mackay, ed., Sam Smiles, *A Publisher and His Friends, Memoir and Correspondence of the Late John Murray with an Account of the Origin and Progress of the House, 1768–1843*, 2 Vols, 1891
Sontag:	Susan Sontag, *Illness as Metaphor*, 1978
Southey:	Rev. Charles Cuthbert Southey, ed., *Life and Correspondence of the Late Robert Southey*, 6 Vols, 1850
Stanhope:	Colonel Leicester Stanhope, *Greece in 1823 and 1824, being a series of letters and other documents on the Greek Revolution written during a series of visits to that country*, 1825
Stendhal:	Geoffrey Strickland, ed., 'Lord Byron in Italy, An Eye-Witness Account 1816', *Selected Journalism from the English Reviews by Stendhal, with Translations of Other Critical Writings*, 1959
Stürzl:	Erwin A. Stürzl, ed., *A Love's Eye View: Teresa Guiccioli's* La Vie de Lord Byron en Italie, 1988
Symon:	J. D. Symon, *Byron in Perspective*, 1924

Thelwall:	Gregory Claeys, ed., *The Politics of English Jacobinism, Writings of John Thelwall*, 2001
Thornburg:	Mary K. Patterson Thornburg, *The Monster in the Mirror: Gender and the Sentimental/Gothic Myth in* Frankenstein, 1987
Thorslev:	Peter Thorslev, *The Byronic Hero, Types and Prototypes*, 1962
TLB:	George Paston and Peter Quennell, *'To Lord Byron', Feminine Profiles based upon unpublished letters, 1807–1824*, 1939
TM Memoirs:	Lord John Russell, ed., *Memoirs, Journal, and Correspondence of Thomas Moore*, 8 Vols, 1853–6
Towne:	R. D. Towne & J. Afterman, 'Psychosis in males related to parenthood', *Bulletin of the Menninger Clinic*, 1955, 19, 19–26
Tymms:	Ralph Tymms, *Doubles in Literary Psychology*, 1949
Ude:	Louis Eustache Ude, *The French Cook, or, The Art of Cookery Developed in All its Various Branches*, 1815
Valperga:	Mary Shelley, *Valperga, or the Life and Adventures of Castruccio, Prince of Lucca*, 1823
Veeder:	William Veeder, *Mary Shelley & Frankenstein: The Fate of Androgyny*, University of Chicago Press, 1986

Vessels: G. J. Monson-Fitzjohn, *Drinking Vessels of Bygone Days from the Neolithic Age to the Georgian Period*, 1927

Wadd: William Wadd, *Cursory Remarks on Corpulence*, London, 1810

Walker: Margaret J. Howell, rev., Violet W. Walker, *The House of Byron, A History of the Family from the Norman Conquest, 1066–1988*, 1988

Watkins: John Watkins, *Memoirs of the Life and Writings of the Right Honourable Lord Byron, with Anecdotes of some of his Contemporaries*, 1822

WLB: E. H. Coleridge, ed., *The Poetical Works of Lord Byron*, 7 Vols, 1898–1904

Zilboorg: G. Zilboorg, 'The Dynamics of Schizophrenic Reactions Related to Pregnancy and Childbirth', *The American Journal of Psychiatry*, Vol. 85, No. 4, 1 January, 1929, 733–67

NOTES

Preliminaries

Page ix

among my betters: Introduction to *Marmion*, 1830, in *Memoirs of the Life of Sir Walter Scott, Bart*, ed. John Gibson Lockhard, 3 Vols, 1837, I, 347.

respect and reverence: James Hamilton Browne, 'Narrative of a Visit, in 1823, to the Seat of War in Greece', *Blackwood's Edinburgh Magazine*, Vol. 36, No. 226 (September 1834), 394.

writer of the day: RJ, 12 January 1821.

in 1803: Cf. Youssef M. Choueiri, *Arab History and the Nation-State*, 1989, Appendix B, 'Muhammad Al-Alfi's Visit to London and the British Press', 207–19.

classical urn: see further, John Clubbe, 'Byron and Scott', *Texas Studies in Literature and Language*, Vol. 15, No. 1 (Spring 1973), 67–91.

gifts: TM, II, 165.

Introduction

Page xix

old man: Julius Millingen, *Memoirs of the Affairs of Greece*, 1831, 144.

formulating one: Marchand, Preface, ix.

partial portrait: Henry James, *Partial Portraits*, 1888. See also the wealth of scholarship on Napoleon and the British: Paul Holzhausen, *Byron, Bonaparte und die Briten*, 1904; F. J. Maccunn, *The Contemporary English View of Napoleon*, 1914; Edgar Munhall, 'Portraits of Napoleon' in *French Yale Studies 26: The Myth of Napoleon*, 1960, 3–20; David Calleo, 'Coleridge on Napoleon' in *French Yale Studies 26: The Myth of Napoleon*,

1960, 83–93; J. L. Talmon, *Romanticism and Revolt: Europe 1815–1848*, 1967; Simon Bainbridge, *Napoleon and English Romanticism*, 1995; John Clubbe, 'Between Emperor and Exile: Byron and Napoleon 1814–1816', *Napoleonic Scholarship: the Journal of the International Napoleon Society*, Vol. 1, No. 1, April 1997 at www.napoleon-series.org; John Clubbe, 'Napoleon's Last Campaign and the origins of *Don Juan*', *The Byron Journal*, No. 25, 1997, 12–22; Paul Stock, 'Imposing on Napoleon: the Romantic appropriation of Bonaparte', *Journal of European Studies*, 2006, 36 (3), 363–388.

in 1957: Marchand, Preface, vii.

recent studies: Andrew Elfenbein, *Byron and the Victorians*, 1995; James Soderholm, *Fantasy, Forgery and the Byron Legend*, 1996; Benita Eisler, *Byron: Child of Passion Fool of Fame*, 1999; Frances Wilson, *Byromania: Portraits of the Artist in Nineteenth- and Twentieth-Century Culture*, 1999; Fiona MacCarthy, *Byron: Life and Legend*, 2002; Tom Mole, *Byron's Romantic Celebrity: Industrial Culture and the Hermeneutic of Intimacy*, 2007; Ghislaine McDayter, *Byromania and the Birth of Celebrity Culture*, 2009; Caroline Franklin, *The Female Romantics: Nineteenth Century Female Novelists and Byronism*, 2012; Clara Tuite, *Lord Byron and Scandalous Celebrity*, 2015.

Page xx

that can: John Mitford, *The Private Life of Lord Byron*, 1826, 3.

Santa Mura: Ibid., 5.

very fond: Ibid., 191.

bisexuality: Bernard Grebanier, *The Uninhibited Byron: An Account of His Sexual Confusion*, 1970; Louis Crompton, *Byron and Greek Love: Homophobia in 19th-century England*, 1985; D. S. Neff, 'Bitches, Mollies, and Tommies: Byron, Masculinity, and the History of Sexualities', *Journal of the History of Sexuality*, 1 July 2002, Vol. 11 (3), 395–438; Peter Drucker, 'Byron & Ottoman Love: Orientalism, Europeanization and same-sex sexualities in the early nineteenth century Levant', *Journal of European Studies*, Vol. 42, No. 2, June 2012, 140–57.

Part 1

Page 1

The Wonderful History of Lord Byron & His Dog: reproduced complete in Geoffrey Bond,

Lord Byron's Best Friends from bulldogs to Boatswain and beyond, including a complete facsimile of Elizabeth Pigot's illustrated poem of 1807, "The Wonderful History of Lord Byron & His Dog", 2013, 57–65.

Chapter 1: Byron's First Diet, 1807

Page 3

91.63kg: To Edward Noel Young, 16 April 1807.

Page 4

so fat: In Moore, I, 76.

meant fat: To JM, 9 May 1817.

fortnight: To AB, 6 November 1805.

Page 5

forehead: Richard Cumberland, *The Wheel of Fortune*, 1795, III, i.

the versatility of my genius: John Till Allingham, *The Weathercock*, 1805, I, i .

gilt gorgets: AR, 200.

Fickle: To EP, 2 August 1807; Fickle: TLB, 7.

Page 6

singularly vibrated: Moore I, 65.

laughter: Pratt, 35.

Idleness: To William J. Bankes (March 1807).

Page 7

deemed necessary: John Murray Archive, National Library of Scotland, Ms 43549.

disease: Eisler, 121.

Page 8

broad: 'A Parody upon "The Little Grey Man" in Lewis' *Tales of Wonder*', 37.

effect: P. D. Hunter, *The Harrow Collection*, 1994, No. 47, 8.

Page 9

recognize him: To ENL, 29 June 1807.

alteration: To EP, 30 June 1807.

dissipation: To EP, 13 July 1807.

parties: Ibid.

training: Peter Cochran, ed., Michael Rees, trans., Teresa Guiccioli, *Lord Byron's Life in Italy*, 2005, 252.

Part Two

Page 11

Byron was seven: Hunter, No. 6, 2.

Chapter 2: Tender Parents

Page 13

madness: Jamison, 149–90.

Dilapidated state: Rosalys Coope and Pete Smith, 'Newstead Abbey, A Nottinghamshire Country House: its Owners and Architectural History', *Thoroton Society Record Series*, Vol. 48, 2014, 61–85; Dobson, 334.

Page 15

age: Galt, 10.

'Mad Jack': Watkins, 38.

arrived at: Medwin, 57n.

Page 16

1779: *Town and Country Magazine*, Vol. XI, Jan. 1779, X.

Page 17

o'Gight awa': 'Miss Gordon of Gight', 5ff, Buchan, I, 258.

Rascal: Walker, 166.

England: Millingen, 15n.

Lucifer: To JM, 16 October 1820.

obstinacy: JH to LB, 1 December 1805, AR, 97.

Page 18

provincial young woman: Hunter, 3.

Page 19

home again: Moore, I, 12.

John Cam Hobhouse: Hobhouse's notes (probably from Hanson), 1824, transcribed by Peter Cochran from BL Add.Mss. 56549: ff.157–66, in https://petercochran.files.wordpress.com/2009/12/32-1824-byron's-death-and-funeral.pdf

ached from it: JH to Mrs Byron, 1 September 1799, Rowland E. Prothero, 'The Childhood and Schooldays of Byron', *Nineteenth Century Magazine*, Vol. XLIII, No. 251, 76.

Page 20

his ruler: Moore, II, 133f.

abuse it: Blessington, 123.

beggared: Moore, I, 14.

Fanny: AR, 25.

Page 21

early loss, my own: 'Childish Recollections', 221ff.

no less: DJ XVII, 1.

considered repeatedly: CH IV, 695; *Sardanapalus*, IV, 381; *Marino Faliero* II, 298; DJ XVII, 16 etc.

Chapter 3: The Innocent Fault

Page 22

shoe: Symon, 38.

without seeing it again : Wendy Moore, *The Knife Man: Blood, Body-Snatching and the Birth of Modern Surgery,* 2006, 70.

in time: Symon, 38.

ground: Newton Hanson's Narrative, Murray MSS, in Marchand, I, 54.

Page 23

dysraphism: A. B. Morrison, 'Byron's Lameness', *The Byron Journal*, 3, 1975, 29.

it often hurt: TM Memoirs, V, 192.

1828: John Beckett, 'Byron and Rochdale', *Byron Journal*, 33, 2005, 33(1), 13–24.

Page 24

machine: James Lavender to JH, 6 April and 13 May 1802, Murray MSS.

signs of it in me: Moore, I, 127.

the shoe: William Swift, Byron's bootmaker, Hubert E. H. Jerningham, trans., Teresa Guiccioli, *My Recollection of Lord Byron and Those of Eye-Witnesses of his Life*, 2 Vol, (1878) 1879

rages: Prothero, 75.

pleasure: Moore, I, 76.

lame brat: Ibid., I, 25.

Page 25

in London: Gronow, I, 152.

Page 26

effected a cure: Timothy Sheldrake, *Animal Mechanisms*, 1832, 146

in body: Moore, I, 183.

at his birth: Medwin, 9 n.15.

spurned me from her: *DT* Pt. I, i, 341f.

defect: WLB, V, 474n.

Page 28

Mr Hobhouse: Galt, 24.

sounds bad: Markham, 99.

his person: Moore, II, 132.

walked astray: 'Epistle to Augusta', 26ff.

Chapter 4: The First War of Independence, 1807

Page 29

wounded him: Moore, I, 136.

lawyer, Hanson: Hanson to James Farquhar, 30 August 1798, in Alexander Larman, *Byron's Women*, 2016, 33.

Page 30

pleasing light: Prothero Childhood, 64.

peculiar style: Boyes, 100.

Page 31

vanity: Bailey, in Boyes, 62.

forehead: Moore, I, 98.

gait: Ibid., I, 25.

evade it: Lady Mildmay, Moore Memoirs, 2 July 1821, III, 293.

thunderbolts: HVSV, 294.

round game: EP, Moore, I, 55.

Box on the ear or Hands: Boyes, 70.

incomparable: DJ I, 17.

sixteen: Gronow, I, 152.

Page 32

extravagant: To Mrs Byron, 26 February 1806.

wrangling: AB to JH, 18 November 1804, in Prothero, I, 45n.

Page 33

bondage: To AB, 18 August 1805.

independent of her: To AB, 10 August 1805.

possible: To JH, 15 January 1809.

Indulgence: To JH, 13 December 1805.

Page 34

servants: Prothero I, 95n.

infant: To JH, 11 June 1807.

Mrs Byron: To EP, 26 October 1807.

bonds of clay: Epistle to Augusta, 30.

independence: in Danita Czyzewski and Melanie A. Suhr, eds, Hilde Bruch, *Conversations with Anorexics*, 1988, 19.

blond: To ENL, 14 May 1807.

look: Moore, II, 126f.

lit up within: DT, 15 October 1821.

Page 35

appreciated: Guiccioli II, 61.

Part Three

Chapter 5: The Reasonable Soul versus the Animal Body

Page 39

ten years of my life: to AM, 26 September, 1813.

Presbyterian: DJ XV, 91.

never moderate: Martin Procházka, ed., Bernard Beatty, 'Calvin in Islam: A Reading of Lara and The Giaour', in *Byron: East and West, Proceedings of the Twenty-Fourth International Byron Conference, Charles University, Prague*, (2000), 80; and cf. Gavid Hopps and Jane Stabler, ed., Christine Kenyon-Jones, 'I was bred a Moderate Presbyterian', *Byron, Thomas Chalmers and The Scottish Religious Heritage', Romanticism and Religion from William Cowper to Wallace Stevens*, 2006, 107–120.

young man: 'My Dictionary', 1 May 1821.

painstaking: Idem, 'Aberdeen', 1 May 1821.

Life: Paul D. Barton, 'Lord Byron's Religion – A Journey into Despair', *Mellen Studies in*

Literature. Romantic Reassessment, V. 160.

Page 40

passion: 'Sermon II, Religion an Ancient Path, and a Good Way', *Sermons by James Ross: with a Memoir of his Life*, 1825, 41.

his own ruin: Medwin, 1, 60.

Eve: Barton, 37.

damnation: Idem, 24.

Page 41

God: Idem, 43, n. 14.

in his mind: Elwin, 270.

aberrations: Ibid.

annoy her: Martin Procházka, ed., Bernard Beatty, 'Calvin in Islam: a reading of *Lara* and *The Giaour*' in *Byron: East and West, Proceedings of the Twenty-Fourth International Byron Conference*, 2000, 90.

below them: Moore, I, 76.

on my shoulders: *DT* Pt. I, i, 329ff.

Page 42

Tartar, win them: Ibid, 313–22.

his fellow-men: Introduction, 'The Black Dwarf', *Tales of My Landlord*, 1816, *The Waverley Novels*, 5 Vols, 1846, I, 1.

Byron's identity: To AL, [19?] February 1817 and n.

disabled: David Hewitt, ed., *Scott on Himself: A Selection of the Autobiographical Writings of Sir Walter Scott*, 1981, 1.

as Scott called it: Ibid, 21, 35.

exert himself physically: cf. David Hewitt, 'Scott, Sir Walter (1771–1832)', *Oxford Dictionary of National Biography*, 2004, 49, 491; Fiona Robertson, 'Disfigurement and Disability: Walter Scott's Bodies', Otranto 003 http://www.otranto.co.uk/index.php/publication/view/54

attached to him: Lockhart, 22.

Page 43

get drunk with him: RJ, 5 January 1821.

Page 44

literary father: To JM, 22 February 1824.

Chapter 6: Dinner with Lord Byron

Page 45

vegetables: Galt, 62.

orphan: Harold Nicolson, *Byron: The Last Journey, April 1823–April 1824*, 2nd edn, 1948, 40.

mentor: To Dallas, 20 January 1808.

Page 46

advocates of lust: EBSR, 290.

Moore's poems: To John Ridge, 11 November 1807.

Page 47

banker: To Bernard Barton, 1 June 1812.

good fellow: To JM, 20 February 1818.

Page 48

their host: *Catalogue of the Celebrated Collection of Works of Art and Vertû... the Property of the Late Samuel Rogers, Esq. Sold by Auction by Messrs. Christie and Manson, with the Purchasers' Names and Prices*, 1856, 15, lot no. 199.

all of his friends: Frances Wilson, ed., *Glenarvon* (1816), 1995, 95, 76; cf. DT, 23, Ravenna, October 1821.

Page 49

sarcastically: 'Question and Answer', 9 November 1820.

wistfully: To Bernard Barton, 1 June 1812.

existence: Journal, 22 November 1813.

Page 50

called him: CH II, stanza xiv

Neglected Genius: EBSR, 803n.

Page 51

4 November 1811: Ibid., 467n.

age or country: Galt, 166.

Page 52

features: Moore, I, 235.

a hearty supper: Ibid.

Chapter 7: He Would Rather Not Exist than Be Large

Page 53

sheer weakness: Markham, 98f.

again in 1813: To JCH, 1 October 1814.

vomiting: To JCH, 10 February 1812.

Page 54

passionate and stupid: Dallas, 198f.

Englishman: Paul Douglass, ed., *The Whole Disgraceful Truth, Selected Letters of Lady Caroline Lamb*, 2006, 80.

Page 56

regular action continues: Murray Ms. 43549.

use of the bowels: To JH, 1 October 1814.

a week without it: Edward John Trelawny to John Cam Hobhouse (but sent to Mary Shelley), after April 1824, Lady Shelley, ed., *Shelley and Mary*, 1882, 4 Vols, IV, 1006.

Boyish air: Blessington, 2.

fit him: Ibid., 3.

he is thin: Ibid., 139.

Page 57

exercising his mind: Ibid., 36.

pointed out in 1809: Hobhouse, 1809, 35.

eight Great Pieces: http://brightonmuseums.org.uk/royalpavilion/whattosee/the-great-kitchen/

two removes of rôt: Ude, Preface, ivf.

Page 59

merit to a dinner: Ibid., vii.

this grandure: text from the John Murray Archive at the National Library of Scotland, NLS Acc.12604 / 4247K transcr. Peter Cochran at

http://www.nottsheritagegateway.org.uk/people/byron/cochrane.pdf

Page 60

fight like devils: Shakespeare, *Henry V*, III, 7.

a pound of meat per meal: Ben Rogers, *Beef and Liberty: Roast Beef, John Bull and the English Nation*, 2004, 17.

public affairs: Tamara Hunt, *Defining John Bull: Political Caricature and National Identity in Late Georgian England*, 2003, 144.

a Royal John Bull: Leigh Hunt, 245.

what I am not accustomed to: Sedgwick, 77 in Tamara Hunt, 165.

Page 61

swinish multitude: Charles W. Eliot, ed., Edmund Burke, *Reflections on the French Revolution* (1790), The Harvard Classics, 1909–14, Vol. 24, Part 3, 133

Hog Trough found: Old Hubert qu. Titlepage, Daniel Eaton, *Politics for the People, No. 1 Hog's Wash, or A Salmagundy for Swine*, 4th ed., 1793.

Page 62

starve me: Robert L. Patten, Ge*orge Cruikshank's Life, Times and Art*, 1992, 2 Vols, II, 87.

Page 64

on Skiddaw: Southey, IV, 121f.

colours of absurdity: *The British Critic*, vol. xxxix, June 1812, ART. 23, 641.

Stendhal observed in 1816 and 1817: Strickland, 317.

makes you ferocious: Moore, I, 242 and cf. II, 133.

was to be patriotic: Blessington, 86 and cf. 192.

Chapter 8: Interpretations and Diagnoses

Page 65

Was Byron anorexic: World Medicine, Vol.17, No. 16, 15 May 1982, 35–38. Walter Vandereycken and Ron van Deth, *From Fasting Saints to Anorexic Girls: The History of Self-Starvation*, 1994, 227f; Jeremy Hugh Baron, 'Illness and Creativity: Byron's Appetites, James Joyce's gut, and Melba's meals and mesalliances', *British Medical Journal*, Vol. 315, No. 7123, 20–27 December 1997, 1697–1703; Arthur Crisp, 'Commentary: Ambivalence toward fatness and its origins', *British Medical Journal*, Vol. 315, No.7123, 20–27 December, 1997, p. 1703; Hugh Baron and Arthur Crisp, 'Byron's Eating Disorders', *The Byron Journal*, No. 31, 2003, 91–100.

this phenomenon: e.g. Michael Krasnow, *My Life as a Male Anorexic*, 1996; Anna Paterson, *Fit to Die: Men and Eating Disorders*, 2004; Jenny Langley, *Boys Get Anorexia Too*, 2005; John F. Morgan, *The Invisible Man*, 2008; K. Weintraub, 'Eating disorders are a guy thing, too', *The Boston Globe*, 14 November 2011, retrieved from http://bostonglobe.com/lifestyle/health-wellness/2011/11/14/eating-disorders-are-guy-thing-too/bzs6u8EZWWBHn7Xb80CQBK/story.html

almost amphibious: Medwin, 117.

3 miles: To EP, 11 August 1807.

Page 66

physical stamina: Lasègue, 148.

neurosis or psychosis: Idem, 254.

reduced to our labelling: Crisp, 1703.

Page 67

superb oarsman: Jeaffreson, 115.

impatient of his fat: Symon, 109.

his spartan regime: Marchand, I, 125.

slimming fad: AR, 390.

attributed it to vanity: Blumberg, 112.

consigned it to a footnote: Eisler, 308n.

cosmetic reasons: Morton, 78.

useful, longer footnote: Gilmour, 316.

Page 68

eating abstemiously: MacCarthy, 208.

delicate digestion: Ibid.

abstemiousness: Paul Douglass, 'Byron's life and his biographers' in Drummond Bone, ed., *The Cambridge Companion to Byron*, 2004, 27.

a tendency to corpulence: *The New York Review of Books*, 24 September 2009, 42.

Dr Lasègue in 1873: Lasègue, 141–55.

Antimatérialisme: Guiccioli, II, 1.

throughout his life: 'Unwriting His Body: Teresa Guiccioli's Transubstantiation of Lord Byron', in James Soderholm, *Fantasy, Forgery and the Byron Legend*, 1996, 102–30; cf. William Parry, Byron was 'a mental being', above, p. 425.

Page 69

the consumptive appearance: Sontag, 34.

he looks, in dying: Moore, I, 183.

pain in his foot: TM Memoirs, V, 192.

fevered and hurt it: Hunt, 88.

habitually occasioned him: Elwin Wife, 270.

spiritual man: Guiccioli, II, 57.

Page 70

prison of its flesh: in Kate Chisholm, *Hungry Hell, what it's really like to be anorexic: a personal story*, 2002, 39.

Part Four

Chapter 9: Mind versus Matter

Page 73

Byron's poetry: Concordance, vii.

Childe Harold: CH II, 4.

Page 75

Partiality for spirit: DT, 98.

on that plain: CH III, 63.

the quarter of a hero: Idem, 63n.

Page 76

which made me; *Manfred*, II, I, 34.

behind throws: DJ XIV, 7f.

masturbation: To PBS, 26 April 1821.

in their very conception: 'Letter to John Murray Esqre, 1821'.

Page 77

perhaps millions think: DJ III, 88.

ethereal nature: Gronow, I, 150.

Page 78

fleshy women: To JCH, 1 May 1816.

realm of fairy: DJ V, 4.

Mary Duff: Her great-grandfather's sister was Byron's maternal great-grandmother.

beauty and peace: DT, 79.

animation beam'd: 5f.

Page 79

curse of blood: 'The Duel', 42.

Newstead: Moore, I, 48.

Page 80

angelic: Medwin, 61.

Page 81

scarlet fever: To WS, 27 January 1822 P.S.

Stewart or Gordon tartan: 'Lachin y Gair', 10.

from its Effects: 'Song', 4n.

Page 82

the view: To JM, 26 May 1822.

by myself: Elwin, 286.

Page 83

in Manfred: III, i, 71ff (original version).

o'er the plain: John Milton, *Paradise Regained* (1671), IV, 541ff.

crushed feelings' dearth: CH III, 49ff.

Page 84

a sea of speculation:, DJ IX, 18.

abyss of thought: Ibid.

soul of me: Idem, VI, 56.

Part Five

Page 88

7 January 1820: Peter Cochran, ed., JCH Diary, 7 January 1820, https://petercochran.files.wordpress.com/2009/12/28newgate-and-westminster-18201.pdf

Chapter 10: Father Hunger

Page 89

father's care: 'Childish Recollections', 220.

mentor: To AB, 27 December 1805.

18 November 1804: Prothero, I, 45n.

Page 90

as you can: Ibid., 30; Boyes, 72.

rudder or compass: Thornton, 239.

in his eye: Moore, I, 35.

such figures: DT, 88; Recollections, 108.

as a father: 'An Extract from a Journal', 1821 and cf. CH IV, 674n.

Page 91

I expected: Moore, I, 35.

in 1803: Journal, 17 November 1813.

Page 92

government sponsored: Semmel, 44.

Vulture: CH I, 52.

Page 93

Portuguese: Eggert, 7–10.

Page 94

to the Thames: Diary, 16 April 1815; JCH Recollections, I, 256.

rejected by their country: Lean, 210. Could this phenomenon perhaps help explain President Trump's enthusiasm for President Putin? The President's father Fred Trump was investigated for wartime profiteering in 1954 and for civil rights violations in 1973.

Page 95

Father Found: Connolly, 20f.

that or tother: DT, 51.

excessive liking: Blessington, 120.

Page 96

in peace: F. M. Kircheisen, ed., E. M. Arndt, *Erinnerungen aus dem* äusseren *Leben*, 1913, 195, in Blumenberg, 485.

Chapter 11: From Self-Libel to Satanism

Page 97

than he really was: Rogers, HVSV, 287.

Walter Scott: Moore, II, 145; cf. I, 193, 227, 257n.; II, 506ff; Blessington, 75, 184.

led astray: EBSR, 689ff.

hypocrisy reversed: Richard Henry Stoddard, ed., *Personal reminiscences by Barham, Harness, & Hodder*, 1879, 192.

Virtue to Vice: Elwin, 323.

his enemies: Harness, 33.

Page 98

to his father: Ibid., 31f.

others just begin: 'Damaetas', 2–10.

Byron's son: Symon, 70.

her husband: To LM, 8 January 1814.

deigned to taste: CH I, 41ff.

Page 99

F. H.: Hodgson, I, 212; 'The Journal of Sir Walter Scott', 23 November 1825, at www.gutenberg.org/files/14860/14860-h/rol_i.html#NOVEMBER_1825

his memory: Works, VI, 232n.

funeral expenses: Prothero, 71.

Lady Holland :to Lady Holland, [12 February 1814]

as your father: Medwin, 57.

perfectly: Ibid., 55.

martial: *DT*, 34.

his foes: *Lara* II, 234f.

Deformed Transformed: DT, Pt I, ii, 175.

modelled definitively: PL, I, 125.

Page 100

the Devil: Nancy Moore Goslee, *Shelley's Visual Imagination*, 2014, 179.

against Temptation: *Sermons by James Ross: with a Memoir of his Life*, 1825, 318.

their merits: *Vison of Judgement,* st. 29, 225–32.

finest finished poem: Peter Cochran, note to his excellent edition of *The Vision of Judgement* at https://petercochran.files.wordpress.com/2009/03/3-the-vision-of-judgement-editions.pdf

sublimity: Burke, *A Philosophical Enquiry into Our Ideas of the Sublime and the Beautiful*, 1757, 67.

Page 101

Britain's best: *The Curse of Minerva*, 175f.

Page 103

burning Lake: William Hayley, 'An Essay on Painting in The Epistles to Mr Romney' in *Poems and Plays*, Vol 6, 1785, 1, Epistle 2, 50, 523.

companions: Johnson, i, 183.

his copy: Knowles, I, 199.

Page 104

Embellishments: Ian Haywood, *Romanticism and Caricature,* 2013, 15.

place or time: PL, I, 250–3; Burns Letters, I, 121.

Page 106

heroic energy: Philip Jacques de Loutherbourg opened the Eidophusikon on 26 February 1781, combining theatre and painting. In1782 he showed *Satan arraying his Troops on the Banks of the Fiery Lake, with the raising of the Place of Pandemonium*, from Milton; cf. Peter Cannon-Brookes, ed., *The Painted Word, British History Painting: 1750–1830*, 1991, 19.

fallen angel: Emil Palleske, ed., *Schiller's Life and Works*, transl. Lady Wallace, 2 Vols, 1860, I, 181.

have not recovered: Hazlitt, *Complete Works*, vi, 362, in Ben Hewitt, *Byron, Shelley and Goethe's* Faust*: An Epic connection*, 2015, n. 7, 71.

Page 107

pyramid of fire: PL, II, 1010.

Page 109

Schiller's robbers: Journal, 23 November 1813.

Chapter 12: Satan and Reality

Page 110

End of the eighteenth century: Napoleon is mentioned only once in Lucy Newlyn's *Paradise Lost and the Romantic Reader*, 1993, in a citation from Coleridge, 91. Napoleon's name does not appear in Jonathon Shears, *The Romantic Legacy of* Paradise Lost, 2009.

discussed elsewhere: Peter A. Schock, *Romantic Satanism: Myth and the Historical Moment in Blake, Shelley and Byron*, 2003; Simon Bainbridge, *Napoleon and English Romanticism*, 1995; Jonathon Shears, *The Romantic Legacy of* Paradise Lost, 2009.

in 1798: *Gebir*, ii.

Page 111

homage: Hayley, II, 130.

Spenser's Fairy Queen: Book i. Canto i. St. 37.

by Shakespeare: *Henry VIII*, II, 2.

Massinger: *A New Way to Pay Old Debts*, IV, 2.

speculations: *Lectures on the English Poets*, 1818, 66.

Page 112

Heaven itself: Burke, 92.

of 1796: referring to *Paradise Lost*, II, 625: Butler, 51.

Cruikshank: Schock, 21.

Politics for the People of 1793: Daniel Isaac Eaton, *Politics for the People*, I, No. 112, 1793, 172, in Schock, 22; cf. Hazlitt, who in defending Milton's Satan was defending Napoleon, Bainbridge, 185.

French Revolution: Knowles, I, 162.

general sympathy: *Analytical Review*, V, December 1789, 463f.

un-fiendish Satan: Though there are smaller versions in the Los Angeles County Museum of Art and the Bayerische Staatsgemäldesammlungen, Neue Pinakothek, Munich.

Page 113

without knowing it: *The Marriage of Heaven and Hell*, note, Sampson, 249.

as well as much else: Newlyn, 102, n. 38.

Page 114

assumed: Godwin, 261.

brute force: Ibid., 262.

in The Prelude: *The Prelude*, X, 458, alluding to PL VI, 370.

Mme de Staël recorded: Considerations, XIX, 553.

Page 115

opening speech: Roe, 206f.

on his name: CPW, II, 495.

the self denying Robespierre: in Kitson, 194.

Clarendon: Burke, 136.

of themselves: Roe, 210.

23 May 1795: Thelwall, 137.

commanded success: Ibid., 128, 132, 137.

and penetrating: *The Tribune* XXVIII, 3 June 1795, Thelwall, 303, 304;cf. Peter J. Kitson, 'Representations of Cromwell and the English Republic' in Timothy Morton and Nigel Smith, eds, *Radicalism in British Literary Culture, 1650–1830, From Revolution to Revolution*, 2002, 183–200.

god-like ambition: *Caleb Williams*, III, Postscript, 316.

Lalla Rookh (1817): Gregory Dart, *Rousseau, Robespierre and English Romanticism*, 1999, 75.

like a Demon: Nathan, 134.

Page 116

Bonaparte a worser: Harness, 5n. and cf. the pairing of Robertspier and Buonaparte in caricatures by Gillray in 1798, Bainbridge, 35.

Miltonic distinction: Bainbridge, 164ff.

a mean-minded villain: Southey, IV, 73.

Page 117

sublimity of mischief: Moore Memoirs 1, 355–6.

the Destroyer: Katherine C. Balderston, ed., *The Diary of Mrs Hester Lynch Thrale, 1776–1809*, 2nd edn, 2 Vols, 1951, II, 1003, in Schock, 23.

emperor: Stuart Semmel, *Napoleon and the British*, 2004, 141.

the fall: Bainbridge, 165.

his despicable actions: Heinrich Heine, Chapter XXIX, 'Die Reise von München nach Genua', *Reisebilder. Dritter Teil*, 1829.

Page 118

terrible hero: in *London und Paris*, Vol. 12, 1803, 298; and see 'Während der neuen Fehde. Die Invasionliteratur', Paul Holzhausen, *Bonaparte, Byron und die Briten*, 1904, 56–68.

by his name: Coleridge Essays, I, 208.

exploit: EoT1, 208.

made use of it: 21 April 1800, in Kathleen Coburn, ed., *Inquiring Spirit: A New Presentation Of Coleridge From His Published And Unpublished Prose Writings*, 1968, 282

the Mob: Lectures, 1795, 6.

Page 119

World-garden: Notebooks, I, 1166.

Page 120

increasingly apt: Coleridge Essays, II, 319.

Page 121

brute matter: *Courier*, 21 Dec 1809, referring to PL IV, 110.

to our children: Considerations, Ch XVIII, II 393/769.

Page 124

continual felicity: *Courier*, Essays, III, Appendix A, 102.

treacle: Goldring, 38.

Satan: Ibid., 115f.

life-size: Ibid., 110.

Evil be thou my good: George Somes Layard, ed., *Sir Thomas Lawrence's Letter-Bag*, 1906, 167

Chapter 13: Diabolism

Page 126

prodigies of valour: Moore, I, 76.

Corsair's helmet: *Giaour*, 469; *Corsair*, II, 756.

against mankind: *Werner*, II, i, 123ff.

Page 127

Transformed; *DT*, Pt. II, i, 65.

pale with fear: Ibid, Pt. I, i, 372ff.

received opinions: To LM, [July-Dec., 1812?].

associated with Satan: Harness, 33.

cloven foot of thine: *DT*, Pt. I, i, 103f.

as a stamp: H. C. Robinson III, 435.

rooted there: Elwin, 272.

to derangement: Ibid, 263.

the offspring of a demon: H. C. Robinson III, 123f.

first rebel: *Isaiah*, 14, 12–14.

Page 129

of the Devil: 'The Devil's Drive', st. 26.

quondam Aristocrat: Ibid., st. 17.

Hell-fire: To JM, 15 July 1817.

I am the devil: Gisborne Williams, 110.

6 May 1823: 'On the Countess of Blessington's expressing an intention to take the Genoese Villa called ('Il Paradiso') "the Paradise"', 6.

a sort of Satan: Stanhope, 537.

Lady Caroline Lamb and Harriet Wilson: TLB, 63.

his reputation: Strada, 'Portraits of Authors', VI, *The Champion*, 7 May 1813; Lady Shelley, I, 81, 236.

the moment you heard it: TLB, 191n.

Page 130

pleasing countenance: Kennedy, 318f.

of 1770: Mirosława Modrzewska, 'Byron's manipulation of authors and addressees in comical political poems', in Roderick Beaton and Christine Kenyon Jones, ed., *Byron: The Poetry of Politics and the Politics of Poetry*, 2017, 137f.

Devil's Thoughts: Wittreich, 161; cf. Darrel Sheraw, 'Coleridge, Shelley, Byron and the Devil', *Keats Shelley Memorial Bulletin*, XXIII, 1972, 6–9.

Part Six

Page 132

to Iceland: To AB, 10 August 1805.

Romantic Movement: AR, 106.

Chapter 14: Parental Feelings

Page 133

sent him: Moore, I, 32.

denied at home: 'Childish Recollections', 213–16.

obedient to command: Ibid., 99f

unblest by social ties: Ibid., cancelled line 227.

Page 134

protector: Moore I, 41.

those who succeed: 'To the Duke of D[orset]', 6n.

prosody: TM Memoirs, V, 303.

if I can: Harness, 4.

Page 135

sympathies: Ibid.

similar defects: Colonel Leicester Stanhope, HVSV, 543f.

in his profession: The Rev A.G. L'Estrange, *The Literary Life of the Rev William Harness*, 1871, 20.

Page 136

martial strife: 'The Episode of Nisus and Euryalus', 3, 38, 12.

partial mould: 'Childish Recollections', 309.

his boy: 'The Death of Calmar and Orla',13ff; 46f.

his play Werner: it was also Thomas De Quincey's favourite novel and see further, http://www.aphrabehn.org/ABO/recent-scholarship-harriet-sophia-lees-canterbury-tales-influence-gothic-beyond/

Page 137

assassin: 'The German's Tale. Kruitzner', Sophia and Harriet Lee, *The Canterbury Tales*, 4 Vol, 1801, IV, 330, 337, 331.

attention: Ibid., 216f.

equal mine: 'Epitaph on a Friend', 19f.

nurtured at Harrow: To JM, 19 November 1820.

Page 139

the humblest of your servants: To WB, 20 April 1812.

father of all mischief: To DK, 12 October 1820.

his iniquities to him: in Dorothy U. Seyler, *The Obelisk and the Englishman: The Pioneering Discoveries of Egyptologist William Bankes*, 2015, 233.

Page 140

connoisseur: To JCH, 4 August 1819.

to Venice on the second: Anne Sebba, *The Exiled Collector: William Bankes and the Making of an English Country House*, 2004, 157.

of my ferocities: to JM, 19 October 1820.

Page 141

of his rooms: in Sebba, 31.

singing boys: Wilfred S. Dowden, ed., *Journal of Thomas Moore*, 6 Vols, 1983–91, IV, 1540.

every day: J. W. Clark and T. M. Hughes, eds, *The Life and Letters of Rev. Adam Sedgwick*, 2 Vols, 1890, I, 259, in Sebba, 31.

Page 142

drowning: Pratt, 23.

hearing him sing: Moore, I, 53.

Page 143

devotion on the other: Idem, I, 53.

his protégé: To EP, 30 June and 5 July 1807.

light locks: To EP, 30 June 1807.

Page 144

parental kindness: AR, 90.

Chapter 15: Let a Person Depend on You

Page 145

merciful & just: TLB, 251.

Page 146

of course: To TM, 2 February 1816.

ecstasy: Stanhope, 533.

wood engravings: *The Gentleman's Magazine*, May 1825, vol. 137, 472.

Page 147

worse nerves: To JCH, 24 August 1819.

like her mother: HVSV, 252.

a native of Great Britain: Hunter, No. 69, 12.

his daughter Ada: HVSV, 390.

improper food: PBS to MS, 15 August 1821, qu. R Glynn Grylls, *Mary Shelley: A Biography*, 1969, 154

Page 148

trembled for his reason: Moore, II, 145.

little girls: Moore, I, 300.

better than sons: Journal, 1 December 1813.

pervading charm: Moore, I, 184.

Page 149

as Edleston had: AR, 441.

Houseless, helpless: DJ, VIII, 141

his protégée: Idem, 96.

therefore mine: Ibid., VIII, 100.

more tender: Ibid., X, 57.

in Don Juan: Ibid., III, 59.

nothing short of death: MS to JW, 7 March 1823.

an Englishman's care: Millingen, 99.

Page 150

educate her: To TG, [11 February 1824?].

a Companion for Ada: Millingen, 100.

adopted father: Kennedy, 384.

Page 151

friend and father: Introduction, HVSV, xxxvi.

who is to me a father: Nicolson, 239.

gifts on him: Parry, 16.

in his girdle: Medwin, II, 200.

that Byron appreciated: 'Byron's infatuation seems to have been fired rather than extinguished by the boy's disdain', Crompton, 328.

Page 152

where he pleases: To Lega Zambelli, 2 February 1824.

a disciple of mine: To CH, 5 February 1824.

Page 153

could not be disengaged: Moore, I, 63.

nearly ate me at twenty: To TM, 19 January 1815.

tomb for him: for further information on Byron's dogs, cf. Bond.

their portraits: To Hodgson, 13 October 1811.

Spa in 1765: Walker, 133.

Page 154

to his rescue: Moore, I, 75.

Page 155

breathes for him alone: 'Inscription on the Monument of a Favourite Dog', 7ff.

Page 156

his caresses on it: Nathan, 18.

mistook her aim: Ibid., 19.

owner's eyes and mine: Alpine Journal, 26 September 1816.

when he was told: To AL, 6 November 1816.

has been developed: Bond, 92.

accorded to eat it: To JCH, 19 December 1816.

Mocenigo in Venice: To JCH, 6 April 1819.

health and spirits: To AL [July 1819?].

British ones: To JM, 21 February 1820, in Bond, 87.

provisions: To AL, 18? October 1820.

the falcon's victuals: To RJ, 5 January and 16 February 1821.

Page 157

than their master: AR, 260.

a sort of affection: Origo VIII, 325, 344; Notes 513.

Page 158

security or repose: Parry, 27.

of his homage: Idem., 74f.

Page 159

longed to lead: 'Childish Recollections', 99f.

mere vermin: DJ, X, 50.

hostile, hazardous love: For an alternative view, that 'Byron's large dogs and Cambridge bear seem to have expressed the power and defiance of authority that the young lord would have liked to wield but was constrained from doing in reality', cf. Christine Kenyon-Jones, *Kindred Brutes: Animals in Romantic-Period Writing*, 2001, 34.

ferocity and combat: William Youatt, *The Dog*, 1852, in. Bond, 83.

bulldog for nothing: To LB, 9.

Don Juan in 1819: To JM, 1 August 1819, in Bond, 84.

suck his pipe: Lean, 344.

Page 160

threatened to do so: in Moore, II, 139.

advising his discharge: Walker, 127.

travelled abroad with him: Appendix 4, 'Old Joe Murray', AR, 471–4.

Page 161

pleas for mercy: AR, 85.

Page 162

boy reviled: CHI, 64–81.

red bedroom: To JCH, 16 January 1809.

disgust and fury: To Mrs B, 19 May 1809.

August 1811: AR, 106.

so kind to me: Moore, in Mayne, 188.

his master's death: Murray MS 43531, transcribed by Peter Cochran.

Page 163

Teresa remembered: Guiccioli, 332.

second father: Tita Falcieri to Hoppner, in Moore II, 494.

Chapter 16: 'Boxer Byron'

Page 164

retired to his room: Moore, I, 206.

Page 165

shadow: Oates, 12.

Murray: To Mrs B, 24 May 1810.

courage gives: DJ, II, 56.

enemies the French: *The Connoisseur*, No. XXX, 1754, in Julia Allen, *Swimming with Dr Johnson and Mrs Thrale: Sport, Health and Exercise in Eighteenth-century England*, 2012, 85.

Page 166

shipments from Lord Elgin: Byron refers to this scene in a note to *The Curse of Minerva* (179): 'Poor Crib was sadly puzzled when the marbles were first exhibited at Elgin House.' Professor McGann explains 'Crib: thieves' slang for a shop; hence, here, a shopman.' But Byron is referring to his 'old friend' the boxer Tom Cribb (1781–1848), champion of England in 1808, whose name he misspells in his Journal for November 1813. After 16 June 1807 Byron spent most of the summer in Brighton, but he doubtless heard about this event from fistic friends.

Sir William Beechey: Boxiana, II, 386.

firmness of mind: Sinclair, I, 618.

Page 167

1788: Lynch, 30; *The Sportsman's Magazine of Life in London and the Country*, I, 1845, 124.

Page 168

1821: Sawyer, 99.

Page 169

pass unnoticed: Boxiana, II, 13.

alternate days: Aylward, 157.

establishment; Moore, I, 61n.

bad form: Aylward, 164.

without reason: Boxiana, II, 18.

used his arms: Trelawny, 1973, 320.

a second: 'An Extract from a Journal', 1821.

hard hitter: Journal, 17 March 1814.

sparring: *DT*, 15 October 1821.

Page 170

youthful days: Cramond, I, 236.

violence … rage: Blessington, 80.

Page 171

defiance: Moore, I, 13.

Aberdeen: Ibid., 25.

Geordie Byron: Cramond, 237.

than take one: Moore, I, 16.

waistcoat pockets: Ibid., 26.

pastor and master: DJ, XI, 19n.

praise: Hunt, I.

Page 172

impossible, to replace: *Tom Crib's Memorial to Congress*, 1819, 13n.

Page 173

patron of boxing: Ford, 76.

scientific boxer: Boxiana, II, 29; Boxiana, 1812, 467.

and on the internet: *Pugilistica,* 185–9;

https://archive.org/stream/pugilisticahist02milegoog#page/n249/mode/2up/search/John+Gully

Childe Harold: Moore, I, 427.

Summer 1808: To JJ, 4 October 1808; 3 March 1817.

Page 174

high table: Clark, 40.

not strength: To JM, 12 November 1820.

Emperor of Pugilism: To TM, 9 April 1814.

since disappeared: To JM, 9 November 1820.

delayed to comply: Elwin, 288.

in his friend's life: To LM, 24 May 1813.

which he admitted: 'Farewell Petition to John Cam Hobhouse', 43.

Page 175

stunted invert: Peter Cochran, *The Burning of Byron's Memoirs: New and Unpublished Essays and Papers*, 2014, 40 and see further, Peter Cochran, *Byron and Hobby-O. The Relationship between Byron and John Cam Hobhouse*, 2010.

Page 176

better digestion: See below, Appendix 2

Page 177

fisty ring: DJ, XI, 55.

friendly circle: To Mr Falkner, undated.

Page 178

£250: *Pugilistica*, 496.

£5 16s: Elizabeth Stewart-Smith, *Lord Byron's Screen*, 1995, 8–16.

Mr Angelo: Pierce Egan, *Life in London and Sporting Guide*, 1825, 85.

Page 180

twelve thousand pounds: To JH, 18 November 1808.

Page 181

so I did: Journal, 22 November 1813.

stubborn foe: EBSR, 1051f.

book-shelves: Ibid., 726, 740n.

poetry of politics: Ravenna Journal, 18 February 1821.

Page 182

New York: *The London Chronicle*, 18 November 1788, in http://www.rarenewspapers.com/view/605429?acl=830045122&imagelist=1

fistic instinct: To JM (b), 23 March 1820.

boxing ring: Prose, 169f, 175.

a boxing-bout: 'Observations upon "Observations." A Second Letter to John Murray, Esq. on The Rev. W. L. Bowles's Strictures on the Life and Writings of Pope', 164.

parricide: Ibid., 183.

Page 183

gladiator front: Henry Downes Miles, *Pugilistica: Being One Hundred and Forty-Four Years of The History of British Boxing*, 3 Vols, 1906, I, 102.

Part Seven

Chapter 17: Fattening

Page 187

enthusiasm of love: Galt, 15, 16.

nothing much happened: Gronow, II, 196.

not at all in love: To LM, 15 September 1812.

Page 188

innocent and poetical: Galt, 119.

companions: Dallas, 61f.

Page 189

from a relative: To Dallas [11 March? 1812].

Page 190

not pursuing the author: *Lady Morgan's Memoirs*, 1863, II, 200.

dangerous to know: Ibid.

when misunderstood: Douglass, 264.

2000 years ago: To LCL [April 1812?].

Page 191

a young man: Douglas, 119

Page 192

untamed tigress: TLB, 61.

anything else: Douglass, 163.

Trojan War: To Hoppner, 20 October 1819.

that little maniac: To JCH, 17 January 1813.

that ever breathed: To TM, 19 September 1818.

and his nurse: To Henrietta D'Ussières, 8 June 1814.

in excess are female: *Sardanapalus* III, i, 380f.

Mrs Byron furiosa: To John Pigot, 9 August 1806.

less perfect: To LCL, 1 May 1812.

that she was saved: Hodgson, 59.

16 April 1812: in Elwin, 109.

Page 193

your principles: Elwin, 114.

revealing correspondence: To LM, 22 January 1815; To LM, 23 December 1812.

too much of it: Douglas, 113

any being on earth: To AM, 12 February 1814.

after her death: Blessington, 132.

Page 194

always in extremes: To LM, 15 September 1812.

becoming viands: To LM, 25 September 1812.
esteemed so much: To LM, 13 September 1812.
spit in his face: To LM, 28 September 1812.
never to meet: To LM, 18 October 1812.
hot suppers: To LM, 14 November 1812.
into an infant: To FH, 3 February [January?] 1813.
such like recreations: To LM, 18 November 1812.

Page 195

conversation with unnecessarily: The Rev A. G. L'Estrange, *The Literary Life of the Rev William Harness*, 1871, 23f.

Page 196

bad digestion: To LM, 12 January 1813.

Page 197

with the children: To LM, 5 April 1813; cf. To LM, 12 December 1814.
starving himself down: To LM, 10 [11?] November 1812.
bread & butter: To LM, April–2 May 1813.
ill fortune: To LM, 8 June 1813.
Bread and Butter: *Beppo*, stanza 39.
hysterics: To LM, 6 July 1813.
as laughs: in Burnett, 143.
approved of it: Elwin, 161f.

Page 198

after you: To AL, 17 May 1819.
affectionate brother: Moore I, 132.
of consequence: LyB to the Hon. Mrs George Villiers, 2 June 1816, in Ralph, Earl of Lovelace, *Astarte*, 1911, 220.
damnation: To LM, 11 January 1814.

Page 199

personal appearances: Lady Shelley, I, 53.
a thoughtless child: Ibid.
'baby' Byron: Hunt, 81.
as Child: To AL, 2 September 1811.
fattening: To LM, 1 October 1813.

spoiled all again: To LM, 28 September 1813.

Page 201

nephew of a Cain: *The Bride of Abydos*, I, 203.

pirate horde: Ibid., I, 321f.

every vein is boiling: Ibid., I, 207f.

Chapter 18: Wars of Independence

Page 203

company it contained: Lady Shelley, I, 52.

eating altogether: Journal, 10 December 1813.

December 1813: Smiles, I, 223.

correcting a line: Journal, 9 January 1822; Gisborne Williams, 124.

like a child: Elwin, 271; Lady Shelley, I, 52.

Page 204

generates anorexia: Manning, 46.

left Medora: *Corsair*, I, 532.

regimen: Ibid, 586.

Page 205

scarce deny: Ibid., 175ff.

the deed: Ibid., III, 1634.

Page 206

finished the poem: Ibid., III, 1820.

enormous dinner too: To LM, 8 April 1814.

Page 207

Medora was conceived: Elwin, 192, n.3.

crossed out: Corbeau, 171.

whom Byron knew: To LM, 10 June 1814.

Page 208

we have loved: *Manfred*, II, iv, 121ff.

sin and fear: *Heaven and Earth*, I, 67.

Page 210

to be governed: To Charles Barry, 25 October 1823.

in 1823: To Lady Hardy, 10 June 1823.

choose for myself: To LM, 26 November 1812.

playful: Mayne, 124.

in her words: Elwin, 234.

except my Lady: Moore, II, 223n.

Page 211

surely in hell: Elwin, 251.

even before the ceremony: To LyB, 31 December 1819.

divine mutton: Mayne, 243.

inclined to be greedy: Ibid., 23.

frightened the waiters: Ibid.

eating disorder: Michael and Melissa Bakewell, *Augusta Leigh, Byron's Half-Sister: A Biography*, 2000, 219.

Page 212

hot luncheons: To AM, 28 November 1814.

when he did so: Lady Byron's annotation of January 1851, Medwin, 42n.,105.

for B's dinner: LyB to FH, 15 February 1823.

on those points: Elwin, 282.

scrambling: Ibid., 286.

out of mischief: Mayne, II, 544.

to later years: qu. Mayne, 172

fool to wive: [Bout-rimés from Seaham][sic], 9ff.

Page 213

refused to sleep with him: To LyB, 17 May 1819.

almost ever seen him: Elwin, 299.

voracious stomach: Mayne, 184.

spirituous liquors: Elwin, 309.

expression of rage: Ibid., 326.

a labyrinth of difficulties: Mayne, 193.

a bed apart: Elwin, 317.

a Bad way: Mrs Clermont to AM, 5 February 1816, in Elwin Wife, 395.

vitiated stomach: in Mayne, 194.

extreme form of diet: Elwin, 323.

state of mind: *The Siege of Corinth*, 409–33.

paroxysms with his wife: JCH Journal, 12 March 1816, in Elwin Wife, 329.

Page 215

that Tale: Elwin, 303.

morose and abstracted: Kruitzner, 56.

into phrenzy: *Werner*, First Draft, I, ii, 256f.

phantasy and flame: CH, III, 55–60.

become pregnant: Zilboorg, 927–62 and cf. G. Zilboorg, 'Depressive reactions related to parent-hood', *American Journal of Psychiatry*, 1931, 10, 927–62; Freeman, 49–54; Towne, 19–26.

as a rival: JM to WS, 8 November 1815, Smiles, I, 286.

than her husband: Mayne, 191.

for the noise: Broughton, II, 279.

Part Eight

Page 217

from Waterloo: To JWW, 18 September 1818.

Correr in Venice: Origo, n. 29.

Chapter 19: How to be a Hero

Page 219

born for opposition: DJ, XV, 22.

weaker side: Ibid., XV, 23.

Ionian Islands: Peter Cochran, *Byron, Napoleon, J.C. Hobhouse, and the Hundred Days*, 2015, 11 and cf. Peter Cochran, 'Nature's Errors: Byron, Ali Pasha and the Ionian Islands', *Byron Journal*, 23, 1995, 12–35.

the Turks: Hobhouse, 119.

Page 220

follow him: Ibid., 53.

Page 221

a royal gift: Ibid., 112.

lead to consumption: Wadd, 18.

politically important: Muir, 10.

Page 222

Grand Tour in 1811: AR, 153.

mental energy: Wadd, 54.

Page 223

£4 8s: AR, 191f.

Page 224

weavers' suffering: Prothero, II, 97n.

declaiming a task: Dallas, 203.

Christian country: Dallas, 214f.

impudence: To FH, 5 March 1812.

6 and 7 March: Jeffrey Vail, 'Byron's "Impromptu on a Recent Incident": A New Text of a Regency Squib', *Keats-Shelley Journal*, Vol. 47, 1998, 29–31.

Page 225

parliamentary career: Moore, I, 263.

and mankind: DJ, IX, 10.

celebrated in songs: Beaton, 31ff.

unresting doom: CH, I, 826f.

Page 226

weighs twenty stone: DJ, VIII, 126.

Page 227

Austrians, Prussians, and Russians: Peter Cochran, *Byron, Napoleon, J.C. Hobhouse, and the Hundred Days*, 2015, 307, n.94.

Page 228

off his left shoulder: See further in Annette Peach, 'Portraits of Byron', *Walpole Society*, Vol. 62, 2000, 1–144

rolled impatiently: Diary, 25 March 1812, in Mayne, 36.

Shakespeare's Richard III: *Richard III*, IV, ii.

Page 229

mocks at misery: *Giaour*, 852.

curse and crime: Ibid., 912f, 203, 796, 1058.

Page 230

a father's name: Ibid., 769.

significant numbers: Muir, 288.

don't want him here: Journal, 17 November 1813.

Page 232

aught that he decides: *Corsair*, I, 169ff.

weakness to its will Ibid., I, 179ff.

the spoil is won: *Corsair*, I, 75.

Page 233

more terribly: William Hone, *Lord Byron's Corsair, Conrad, The Corsair; or, The Pirates' Isle, A Tale by Lord Byron Adapted as a Romance*, 1817, 10.

good to govern: DJ, III, 47.

Page 234

damned insipid medium: Journal, 19 April 1814.

perish or succeed: *Corsair*, I, 333f.

Napoleon's character: CH, III, 320ff.

Caesar or nothing: Journal, 23 November 1813.

very antithetical: To AM(a), 26 September 1814.

tame trite medium: *Lara*, 8, 119ff.

sought and feared: Ibid., 17, 1f.

to command: *Corsair*, I, 63.

deign reply: Ibid., I, 67–82

body of men: Ibid., I, 182.

Page 235

human race: JCH Recollections, I, 256.

contempt of mankind: Considerations, 764.

sa bonhomie: '*Vie de Napoléon*', in Christiane Benardeau, *Napoléon dans la littérature*, 2004, 41.

supreme contempt of mankind: Henri Martineau, ed., Stendhal, *Vie de Napoléon*, 1930, 170.

Miltonic tradition: Smiles, I, 313.

himself the censor: Mme Anne-Louise-Germaine de Staël-Holstein, *De l'Allemagne*, 2 Vols, 1814, II, 182.

evil pride: *Corsair*, I, 225; II, 768; II, 907.

with Napoleon: Hewitt, 48.

Page 237

self-esteem: Pushkin, 215.

a great measure relaxed: *Edinburgh Review*, dated April 1814, issued July 1814, Vol. XXIII, in Rutherford, 55.

new Napoleon: *Ode to Napoleon Buonaparte*, 11.

Chapter 20: Napoleon Falls

Page 240

gold balls: Newstead Abbey, 191.

Page 241

richly gilt: Ibid., 91.

ormolu: Ibid., 100.

on the chairs: William Michael Rossetti, ed., *The Diary of Dr William Polidori, 1816, relating to Byron, Shelley, etc*, 1911, 70.

narrow cage: *The Age of Bronze*, l. 55f.

exceeding light: *Julian and Maddalo*, 50ff.

Page 242

drinking cup: To JH, 17 January 1809; To LM, 17 October 1813.

Page 243

Portraits of Authors: No. VI, 7 May 1813.

the series: The poem was later attributed to Thomas Moore, which seems unlikely: 'To Lord Byron On Reading his Stanzas on the Silver Foot of a Skull Mounted as a Cup for Wine', 1ff, *The Poetical Works of Thomas Moore, Including his Melodies, Ballads etc*, 1829, 405.

glorious contempt: Journal, 19 April 1814.

paternal care: *Parisina*, 13, 288

abhorred control: Ibid., 285ff.

Page 244

round the room: Moore, I, 113.

my father still: Ibid., 309.

so erred the son: Ibid., 314.

and what not: To LH, 9 February 1814.

Page 245

heroic attitude: To LM, 11 February 1814.

Diabolism: To LH, 9 February 1814.

Page 246

regarded: Hunt, 27.

editions of his works: Medwin, 75, n.192.

Page 247

hatched in them: Journal, 6 March 1814.

at my expence: To Benjamin West, 19 September 1822.

the only one: To Benjamin West, 22 September 1822.

that territory: To LM 21 September 1812.

interested in buying them: Unpublished manuscript note from J. Tournier at 229 Piccadilly dated March 25th 1816, in John Murray Archive, National Libraries of Scotland, Ms. 43508.

Means and Ends: HCW, xvii, 22; Bainbridge, 131.

Page 248

suppressed it altogether: To W. E. West, 23 September 1822.

a world elsewhere: *Coriolanus*, III, iii.

place of resort: Moore, I, 394.

Page 249

1.7 metres: FitzSimons, 8.

GREAT SOUL: Ibid, 13.

the Drury family: *The Annual Biography and Obituary*, vol. XIX, 1835, 2.

the Kemble religion: Archer, 110.

a man in armour: Ibid., 122–30.

upon the bust of Tragedy: Archer, 91, in Peter J. Manning, 'Edmund Kean and Byron's Plays', *Keats-Shelley Journal*, 1972, Vol. 21/22, 191.

excelled in versatility: Ibid., 23.

fire and animation: Archer, 1.

Page 250

top left: Elizabeth Stewart-Smith, *Lord Byron's Screen*, 1995, 2–7.

Page 252

each new idea: 'Dramatic Review – Drury Lane – Mr Kean's Richard the Third', *The Champion*, 20 February 1814, 61.

good acting: To JM, 8? May 1814.

commented: Manning, 96.

in 1814: TLB, 63.

habit of chewing: Diary, 16 April 1815, in. Peter Cochran, *Byron, Napoleon, J.C. Hobhouse, and the Hundred Days*, 2015, 108.

the poetry of Byron: Manning Kean, 196.

following him everywhere: Ibid., 191.

a handsome snuffbox: Moore, I, 395.

Page 253

Sardanapalus: V, i, 24–39.

Kean's Richard III: Manning Kean, 95.

a sportive ferocity: Hobhouse Diary, I, 86.

particular passages: *New Monthly Magazine*, III, May 1815, 360ff, in Manning Kean, 200.

Chapter 21: Byron Rises

Page 254

four days: Journal, 10 April 1814.

this man's: Ibid., 9 April 1814.

for weeks: Haydon, I, 213; Lean, 259ff.

Page 255

so I told him: To TM, 9 April 1814.

yoke had borne: *Ode to Napoleon Buonaparte*, 59f.

Page 256

never to unite again: *Ode*, 225f.

ill-minded man: Ibid., 10.

Page 257

heart away: Ibid, 53f.

nameless thing: Ibid., 3.

starless night: Ibid., 95ff.

ethereal part: Journal, 10 April 1814.

a load of clay: 'On the Star of "The Legion of Honour"', 34f.

traumatic effect: Lean, 274ff.

19 January 1816: Elwin, 357.

broth & rice: Ibid., 368.

Page 258

except even him: Ibid. 369.

Page 259

name, Ada: Elwin, 1975, 45.

referred to as '—': JCH, Diary, 4 March 1816, in Marchand, II, 586 and cf. Andrew Elfinbein, 'The Shady Side of the Sword: Bulwer-Lytton, Disraeli and Byron's Homosexuality' in Jane Stabler, ed., *Byron*, 1998, 110–22.

Page 260

dining in it: Moore, I, 480.

tainted: 'Some Observations Upon an Article in *Blackwood's Edinburgh Magazine*', 1820, Nicolson Prose, 95.

from the Bible: Moore, I, 502.

Page 261

imperial eagle: TLB, 199, n.1. John Murray supplied the paper. Andrew Nicholson, ed., *The Letters of John Murray to Lord Byron*, 143.

Vesuvius: Blessington, 120.

Marengo: To TM, 6 November 1816.

non-completion: To AL, 13 October 1816.

rise as fall: CH, III, 320ff.

Page 262

upon him piled: Ibid., 350f.

weapon shone: Ibid., 361f.

Page 263

as much docility as men: Considerations, Ch. XV, 749.

Page 267

like a tower: PL, I, 589ff.

thee skill: *Paradise Regained*, IV, 551ff.

said and stood: Ibid., IV, 551f; 561

or forgot: CH, III, 1045ff.

the Rhine: Ibid., 413.

baser crowd: Ibid., 415f.

not their thoughts: Ibid., 1053ff.

a harmless wile: Ibid., 1040f.

words which are things: Ibid., 1054–61.

Part Nine

Chapter 22: Tête-à-Tête

Page 271

acknowledging the theft: Robinson, 14 and cf. Robinson, Appendix A, 'Some literary relations between Byron and Shelley from 1810 to 1816', 241–4.

in his diary: Polidori Diary, 101.

Page 272

in 1813: *A Vindication of Natural Diet, being One in a Series of Notes to Queen Mab, a Philosophical Poem*, 1813, 26.

vegetarianism: Timothy Morton, *Shelley and the Revolution in Taste: the Body and the Natural World*, 1994, 29.

never drank wine: Seymour, 269.

Page 273

chicken: Haydon Diary, 5 August 1822.

have I dined: Seymour, 250, 269.

smoking cigars: Moore, I, 498n.

asparagus: TLB, 218, 221; AR, 364.

Page 274

of good family: Preface, *Julian and Maddalo*.

indecorum: To Hoppner (b), 3 April 1821.

erase it: in Richard Holmes, *Shelley: the Pursuit* (1974), 1987, 342.

nudity on visitors: Angeli, 280.

Page 275

on principle: in TM, I, 616.

dreamed of revolution: Moore, I, 440.

scholar: Records, 100.

human nature: Guiccioli, 371.

out of the ground: Holmes Shelley, 172, citing the testimony of Thomas Jefferson Hogg (Beaton, 91, n.33).

from me: in Morton, 77f.

delineations of other minds: Robinson, 241f.

Byron's poems: Ibid., 244.

Fall of Bonaparte: Charles E. Robinson, 'Shelley to Byron in 1814: A New Letter', *Keats-Shelley Journal*, Vol. 35 (1986), 104–10.

Prometheus: probably inspired by Hobhouse, cf. John Clubbe, 'Between Emperor and Exile, Byron and Napoleon', http://www.napoleon-series.org/ins/scholarship97/c_byron.html

Page 277

kill pleasure: Seymour, 258.

cancelled the note: in Robinson, 66.

as demons: *De l'Allemagne*, 543.

rise up against me: Ibid., 527.

Page 278

Gothic fiction: Thornburg, 55.

thy foe: Stephen C. Behrendt, ed., *Zastrozzi, A Romance and St. Irvyne; or, The Rosicrucian, A Romance*, Appendix A, 'The Assassins', 2002, 265.

the double: Read, 53f; Chesser, 23.

almost like to twins: Seymour, 47.

purer mind: 'To Harriet *****', 9.

Page 279

in the garden: *Prometheus Unbound*, II, 191; cf. II, 193ff.

now disgusting: Guiccioli, 381.

did so too: Blumberg, 112.

and onwards: Robinson, 43.

like to mine: *Manfred*, II, ii, 105ff.

my own soul: *Alastor*, 153.

to nausea: Medwin, 194.

opinion or institution: Ibid., 38.

Page 280

literary heroism: 'Sonnet to Lake Leman', 1.

Page 281

new Napoleon: *Manfred*, II, ii, 34f; II, iv, 55ff.

breathing flesh: Ibid., II, ii, 57.

clay again: Ibid., II, ii, 78f.

called just: Ibid., 361.

enlightener of nations: Ibid., III, i, 121f.

tyrant-spell: Ibid., I, i, 43.

on St Helena: Ibid., II, iii, 16.

another's hell: Ibid., III, iv, 129ff; PL, I, 254f.

within our being: *The Prose Works of Percy Bysshe Shelley*, 2 Vols, 1888, II, 35.

words are breath: *Manfred*, II, ii, 128.

words are things: DJ, III, 88.

Promethean heat: *Monody on the Death of the Right Honourable R. B. Sheridan*, 23, 27, 30, 109, 44, 53f, 56.

Page 282

all eternity: *Queen Mab*, viii, 211n.

Page 283

1 December 1804: Moore, I, 20.

from Heaven: CH, IV, 163.

fire from Heaven: *The Prophecy of Dante*, IV,14.

his own mind: 'Prometheus', 35–8; Medwin, 156.

ghost story: *Frankenstein*, Introduction, 15 October 1831.

1819: Moore, I, 499n.

Intellectual Beauty: 'Hymn to Intellectual Beauty', 49–60.

overthrown by his son: Robinson, 113–37.

relationship: for more on Shelley's side, cf. Brewer; Robinson; James Bieri, *Percy Bysshe Shelley, A Biography: Exile of Unfulfilled Renown, 1816–1822*, 2005.

Page 285

attachment to Godwin: Mary Shelley Letters, II, 215.

Page 286

ugly: Marilyn Butler, ed., Mary Shelley, *Frankenstein* (1818), 2009, 46.

Frankenstein: Kaplan and Kloss, 134.

Page 287

Woodville: Ibid., 180, n.23.

husband of Mary: Ernest J. Lovell, Jr., 'Byron and the Byronic Hero in the Novels of Mary Shelley', *The University of Texas Studies in English*, XXX (1951), 175; cf. 'Byron and

Mary Shelley', *Keats-Shelley Journal*, 2 (January 1953), 35–49f; Lovell, 158–83.
Frankenstein does: cf. *Alastor*, II, 20–34.
terrible thunderstorm: *Frankenstein*, Vol. I, Ch. II, 40.
during a thunderstorm: Medwin Shelley, 72; Holmes Shelley, 17.
mockery and laughter: *Frankenstein*, Vol. 3, Ch. VII, 196.
half-hysteric laugh: Seymour, 88.
Catechism class: Hogg, 446, 451.
down the stairs: Medwin Shelley, 226.
bad teeth: Hogg, 191; AR, 335.

Page 288

Hogg and Teresa agreed: Hogg, 132, 134, 135; AR, 335; Stürzl, 246.
recollection: Nicolson, 20.
ear to ear: Hunt Correspondence, I, 189.
and a curse: Shelley Prose, I, 118
suggested: Holmes Shelley, 334.
Political Justice: Appendix I, 261.

Page 289

word for word: *Glenarvon*, III, 293, 366.
later novels: *Valperga*, 324; *The Last Man*, I, 125; *Falkner*, III, 65.
beautified Byron: Seymour, 354.
archangel: *Mathilda*, II, 31.
The Giaour: *Frankenstein*, Vol. I, Ch. VII, 74; *Giaour*, 755–86.
to his poem: Southey, *Poetical Works*, III, 265–6, cited in Beaton, 86, n.24.
silent listener: Introduction, *Frankenstein*, 8. LB = Lord Byron: MS Journal, 183f.
as by a spell: Hogg, 99; Preface, *Julian and Maddalo*.
as he did with Shelley: Hunt, 90.
discussion: *Last Man*, 65.

Page 291

in Italy: To DK, 13 January 1818.
position in life: Origo, *Allegra*, 34f

Page 292

a man is a man: To DK, 20 January 1817.

degree of friendship: 14 October 1814, AR, 294.

1817: Harold Bloom, *The Ringers in the Tower: Studies in Romantic Thinking*, 1971, 93.

to an eagle: 'Athanase', l.29f; Detached Passages (b) 22ff; 36f, in Kelvin Everest and Geoffrey Matthews, ed., *The Poems of Shelley*, 2 Vol., 2000, II, 311

Page 293

glee: *Julian and Maddalo*, 27, 29, 30.

yet pleasing: Ibid., 39f, 42, 41.

Paradise Lost: PL, II, 555–61.

know myself: *Julian and Maddalo*, 558ff.

pass over the centre: e.g. Blumberg, 86–102.

not revealing the truth: Mary Shelley's Journal, 38.

Shelleyan idealist: Robinson, 91; Saveson, 53–8.

assume, Shelley: 'Stanzas Written in Dejection', 25.

Page 295

unconscious homosexuality: Veeder, 245, n.7.

conversation: DJ, XIV, 9.

worldly-wise Narrator: John Buxton, *Byron and Shelley: the History of a Friendship*, 1968, 82f.

Chapter 23: The Sun versus the Glow-worm

Page 296

or Cain's: *Adonais*, stanza 34.

Page 297

1813: Journal, 17, 18 December 1813.

public neglect: PBS to LB, 16 July 1821.

Page 298

a Saracen's head: To JM, 15 February 1821.

August, 1820: To Hoppner, 10 September 1820.

Page 299

Shelley himself: Beaton, 168; Schock, 108.

Lucifer: *Cain*, I, i, 187ff, italics added.

doppelgänger: Kraeger, 94.

to sway: *Cain*, I, i, 213ff.

his imagination: *Edinburgh Review*, 36 (February 1822), 439; Henry Lytton Bulwer, *The Complete Works of Lord Byron, Reprinted from the Last London Edition, Containing Besides the Notes and Illustrations... to Which is Prefixed a Life*, 1841, 522, n.4.

mass of matter: *Cain*, II, i, 50f.

good and ill: *Lara*, I, 331ff.

inward feeling: *Cain*, II, ii, 460ff.

all things: Ibid., I, i, 14.

lov'st blood: Ibid., III, i, 255.

without gore: Ibid., 266f.

upon the earth: Ibid., III, I, 279.

thick with blood: Ibid., 285.

Page 300

empty of meaning: Barton, 58f.

poetry and prose: TM to LB, 19 February 1822; Robinson, 196.

with Cain: Robinson, 197.

no more: *Cain,* I, i, 223f, 192–246.

the serpent: *De l'Allemagne*, II, 518.

inventing Satan: Curran Wittreich, 83–94.

great modern poet: *Manfred*, I, I, 46; Shelley Prose, 273.

October 1820: 'Matter is eternal – always changing – but reproduced and as far as we can comprehend Eternity – Eternal – and why not Mind? – Why should not the Mind act with and upon the Universe? – as portions of it act upon and with the congregated dust – called Mankind? – See how one man acts upon himself and others – or upon multitudes? – The same Agency in a higher and purer degree may act upon the Stars &c. ad infinitum.'

According to Shelley's essay, 'the Greek philosophers abstained from introducing the Devil. They accounted for evil by supposing that what is called matter is eternal and that God in making the world made not the best that he, or even inferior intelligence, could conceive; but that he moulded the reluctant and stubborn materials ready to his hand into the nearest arrangement possible to the perfect archetype existing in his contemplation.' 'On the Devil and Devils', Shelley Prose

rhapsodies: Preface, Records, 52.

Page 302

material nature: Ibid., 179.

Page 303

captive: Records, 71.

subtle reasoner: HVSV, 273.

interested and amused: Ibid.

Page 304

ready to fly: 'The Blues' II, 129ff.

seen the joke: Incidentally Byron said in a note to *The Two Foscari* that he showed *Queen Mab* 'to Mr Sotheby as a poem of great power and imagination'.

Page 305

spirit of this place: EEW to EJT, 26 December 1821, Gisborne Williams, 160.

Page 306

Panmure Gordon: Hunter, No. 86, 14.

very weather: Ravenna Journal, 21 January 1821, referring to the period 1809–14.

Page 307

egotism: Gisborne Williams, 161.

Byron as God: Robinson, 206.

in Cain: *Cain*, I, 257f; cf. VI, 824–66.

himself as Faust: Holmes Shelley, 693.

tip of his tail: To TM [13? December 1821].

the comparison: Records, 105.

Page 308

a two-fold shape: Retzsch, 2.

swarthy Hungarian: Kruitzner, 333.

guardian angel: *Werner*, II, ii, 149; 219.

dared to think: Kruitzner, 354.

what you could think: *Werner*, V, i, 452f.

Page 310

personification: in Origo, 298.

what a poet should be: Preface, Records, March 1878.

thus disfigured: Shelley Letters, I, 139.

Page 312

Lady Noel: PBS to LH, 17 February 1821 [for 1822], Fredeerick L. James, ed., *The Letters of Percy Bysshe Shelley*, 6 Vol, 1964, 11, 389f.

Providence: *Julian and Maddalo*, 118f.

Page 313

another direction: TM Memoirs, V, 303.

stress on this: 'Mr Shelley's spectre had appeared to a lady, walking in a garden', Blessington, 91.

funeral rites: Millingen, 130.

like a demon: *DT*, Pt. I, i, 118f.

Shelleyan ideal: Beaton, 198.

in the suburbs: To TM, 25 October 1822.

Page 314

as much right as he: *DT*, Pt. II, iii, 73f.

Ha! Ha!: Ibid., Pt. I, ii, 324, 329.

great motives: Ibid., Pt. II, i, 167, 169.

Harlequin: PBS to John Taafe, 4 July 1821, James Bieri, *Percy Bysshe Shelley, A Biography: Exile of Unfulfilled Renown, 1816–1822*, 2005, Ch. 13, n.48.

took Jewry: *DT*, Pt. II, iii, 30ff.

Page 315

Master rather: Ibid., Pt. I, ii, 18f.

facetious nonsense: JM to LB, 12 August 1820.

public taste: To PBS, 20 May 1822.

Page 316

very muse of poetry: William Wanscher, *Artes*, tome 1, 1932, 308, in Beevers, 104, n.33.

Page 317

are you quoting: Gisborne Williams, 128.

de la pensée: *De l'Allemagne*, 508.

would not alter it: To John Hunt, 10 M[arch] 1823.

Part Ten

Chapter 24: Corpulence

Page 321

London in April: To JM, 25 March 1817

Page 322

seriously ill: Ibid.

usual dress: to AL, 25 March 1817.

hungry: Moore, II, 141f.

Page 323

peculiar to his head: Elwin Family, 177.

than ever yours was: Mayne, 277.

a different person: Smiles, I, 429.

lost in fat: Prothero, IV, 266–7n.

Page 324

musico: Moore, II, 127.

shabbily dressed: Glenbervie, II, 329.

Page 326

oranges and chestnuts: AR, 272f.

grown so fat: Hunt, 9.

injured: Hobhouse Diary, 15 September 1822, ed. Peter Cochran, https://petercochran.files.wordpress.com/2009/12/30-18221.pdf

1819 and 1821: To JM, 6 April 1819 and 26 April 1821.

feeling of womanhood: Blessington, 112f.

Page 327

human execution: To JM, 25 November 1816.

thoughts of man: 'On the Bust of Helen by Canova', 2, italics added.

finally triumphant: *The Works of Antonio Canova, in Sculpture and Modelling, Engraved in Outline by Henry Moses, with Descriptions from the Italian of the Countess Albrizzi, and a Biographical Memoir by Count Cicognara*, 2 Vols, 1824, II, n.p.

Page 329

warm Italian: To John Murray, 21 August 1817, 37ff.

Page 330

untameable animals: cf. 'Tame (but Not Tamed)', Ch. 15, 'Let a Person Depend on You'.

Page 332

writ on satin: *Beppo*, 44, 345ff.

of Canto I: JCH to LB, 5 January 1819, https://petercochran.files.wordpress.com/2009/02/08-venice-1818-1819.pdf

Byron's imagination: To JM [13–16? March 1821].

Page 334

been the same: *Beppo*, stanza 13.
meant for Teresa: Medwin, 21.

Page 335

been the same; *Beppo*, stanza XIIf.

Chapter 25: Another War of Independence

Page 338

two assassinations: To JCH, 17 May 1819.
as he later complained: To Hoppner, 31 May 1820.
servitude: To AL, 19 December 1816.

Page 339

it's weight: To JCH, 23 August 1819.
esprits de l'air: Stürzl, 3, 240.
sunbeams: Ibid., 3, 243.

Page 340

ben'avvilito: To TG [June? 1820].
troppo grasso: To TG [February 1820?].

Page 342

indolence; Hunt, I, 17.
inspired by Shelley: Brewer, 77–91.
too heavy: *Sardanapalus*, III, i, 100f, 128ff.
burning himself to death: Ibid., V, i, 424f.
unincorporate: Ibid., 433ff, IV, i, 58f.

Page 344

after their effect: to TM, 6 October 1821.

Part Eleven

Chapter 26: Oh Love!

Page 347

the soul of me: DJ, VI, 56.
as an infant plays: Ibid., XIV, 9.
fiery dust: Ibid., II, 212.

Page 348

goût/gout: Ibid., XV, 72.

sage: Ibid., 93.

continuity: Ibid., I, 132; VI, 47.

subdued by matter: Ibid., V, 32, 39, 49.

Don Juan, William Thackeray: 'Memorials of Gourmandising', *Fraser's Magazine*, June 1841, xxiii, 712f.

Page 349

conscious heart: DJ, I, 106.

caressed him often: Ibid., 69.

Page 350

beat the poetry: To JM, 31 August 1820; see further, John. R. Murray, *The Brush has Beat the Poetry! Illustrations to Lord Byron's Works*, 2016.

sea or ocean: DJ, I, 70.

Page 351

true one: Ibid., I, 8.

six stanzas: Ibid., 192–7.

she is tall: Ibid., 61; II, 15, 16.

bespoke command: Ibid., 116.

idolatry to kneel: Ibid., III, 74.

withered lily: Ibid., II, 106, 176, 110.

fond of rest: Ibid., 134, 135, 135, 137, 134, 137, 137, 146, 148, 149, 149, 168, 168, 134, 168.

languid Juan: Ibid., 157.

sleeping: Ibid., 168, 173, 195ff.

weeping: Ibid., III, I.

Page 352

and unmoved: Ibid., II, 197.

sweetly slept: Ibid., 143.

can breathe: Ibid., 148.

deemed dead: Ibid., 158.

Page 353

successive stanzas: Ibid., IV, 29, 30–4.

Page 354

cannot move: Ibid., 51, italics added.

majesty of stride: Ibid., V, 91.

overpowering kind: Ibid., 97.

half command: Ibid., 108.

all she did: Ibid., 110.

as upon necks: Ibid., 111.

despotism: Ibid., 110.

tyranny: Ibid., 113.

Page 355

passion and power: Ibid., 118.

would not bend: Ibid., 104.

Atlas unremoved: Ibid., PL, IV 985ff.

burst into tears: Ibid., VII, 7.

and as warm: Ibid., VI, 41.

skim the earth: Ibid., 41.

and a bed: Ibid., 47.

languishing and lazy: Ibid., 41.

mild earth: Ibid., 53.

in the wings: Ibid., 105, 106, 111.

looked 'silly': Ibid., 118.

sent off: Ibid., VIII, 139.

our entrance: Ibid., IX, 55.

as rocks: Ibid., 29.

Page 356

handsomely: Ibid., X, 55, 57, 78, 22.

most vulnerable: Ibid., IX, 47.

but well knit: Ibid., 47.

juicy vigour: Ibid., 72.

dry: Ibid., 67, 59.

Page 357

dry land: Ibid., 55, 56.

Ambition's hands: Ibid., 59.

Page 358

long drouth: Ibid., 61.

the rest about her: Ibid., 64.

for the eye: Ibid., 7.

lion's den: Ibid., 69.

sea or Thetis: Ibid.

self-love: Ibid., IX, 68.

grew sick: Ibid., X, 39.

on a mission: Ibid., 44.

Page 359

upon her face: Ibid., XVI, 49.

Page 360

I want a hero: DJ, I, 1.

dungeon wall: 'The Lament of Tasso', 22f.

all-etherial dart: Ibid,, 112ff and cf. CH, III, 905–13.

Page 361

Sir Samuel Romilly: To AL, 3 June 1817; To JCH, 12 December 1818; cf. to JM, 12 August, 1819.

Page 362

days of old: 'The Prophecy of Dante', II, 1–2.

nearly all writers: CH, IV, 492.

bastard Caesar: Ibid., 800f, 803.

a ruin amidst ruins: Ibid., 218f.

only place of refuge: Ibid., 1135ff.

mountain of my curse: Ibid., 1207f.

in *Don Juan*: DJ, III, 88 and cf. *Prophecy of Dante*, 1—2.

Page 363

exactly as I talk: DJ, XIV, 19.

airy manner: W. H. Auden, 'Letter to Lord Byron', III, 7.

no taboos: cf. DJ, VII, 2.

Dryden, Pope: Ibid., I, 205.

Page 364

against your supremacy: JCH to LB, 5 January 1819.

the Don Juan theme: Moyra Haslett, *Byron's Don Juan and the Don Juan Legend*, 1997; J.

W. Smeed, *Don Juan: Variations on a Theme*, 1990.

Page 365

Napoleon's example: John Clubbe, 'Napoleon's Last Campaign and the Origins of *Don Juan*', *Byron Journal*, No. 25, 1997, 12–22.

Annals of his Life: in Ibid., 14.

Aurora Borealis: DJ, VII, 2.

bird's eye view: Ibid., XIV,14.

true Muse: Ibid., VIII, 1.

but a Show: Ibid., VII, 2.

on to Napoleon: CH, III, 353f.

too wide a den: Ibid., 41.

Page 366

virtue, and all that: DJ, VII, 3.

and sought to be: *Age of Bronze*, 4, 89ff.

risible Lilliput: DJ, IV, 89.

maxim of his reign: Considerations, 656.

black comedy: e.g. Rupert Christiansen, *Romantic Affinities, Portraits from an Age, 1780–1830*, 1988, 199.

Page 368

the remark: CH, III, 41n.

a little damp: DJ, II, 25.

a little pale: Ibid., 26.

quite puzzling: Ibid., 28.

Page 369

Gulf of Lyons: Ibid., 39.

fellow-creature: Ibid., 599.

storm in Canto Second: To TM, 8 August 1822; DJ, VII, 18.

demoniacal laugh: *Blackwood's Edinburgh Magazine*, Vol. V, April–September 1819, 513.

spares humanity: in Butler, 49.

Page 370

could escape: Considerations, 600.

region of evil: Ibid., V, 27.

the Kinnairds: JCH Diary, 19 September 1817, https://petercochran.files.wordpress.

com/2009/12/26-venice-1817.pdf, 155

battles he has fought: BRH, 2, 106.

1823 shows: He compares himself in Metaxata to Napoleon on Elba, Manuscrit, 136.

Page 371

intrinsic value: LyB to Lady Anne Barnard, in Paulson, 275.

Madame de Staël would talk: O'Meara, II, 206.

Page 372

in what he wrote: Considerations, 655.

of things: Manuscrit,12.

to the action: Ibid., 5.

Page 373

initials are the same: Hunt, 73.

truth naked: Ibid., 18.

Page 374

mock-heroic: Bainbridge, 209f.

realms of rhyme: DJ, XI, 54.

as a monarch reign: Ibid., 56.

King of England: JCH Recollections, I, 330.

heroic intent: Bainbridge, 210.

English peer: Stendhal to Louise S. Belloc, 1824, in HVSV, 198.

Page 375

not less free: DJ, VI, 56.

Page 376

poetic war to wage: Ibid., IV, 88.

war with thought: Ibid., IX, 24.

broadside: Ibid., X, 84.

ensuing session: Ibid., III, 96.

free thoughts for a throne: Ibid., XI, 55.

that autumn: 'To the Editor of a Venice Newspaper'[? *Gazette Litéraire de Jéna*, 27 March 1817], [April? 1817].

words to this effect: DJ, I, 2n.

Page 377

revolutionary energy: Thomas Sipe, *Beethoven: Eroica Symphony*, 1998, *passim*; Rita

Steblin, 'Who Died? The Funeral March in Beethoven's "Eroica" Symphony', *The Musical Quarterly*, Vol. 89, No. 1 (Spring, 2006), 62–79.

the cause of liberty: Rhys Jones, 'Beethoven and the Sound of Revolution in Vienna, 1792–1814', *The Historical Journal*, 57, 2014, 947–71; 'Reviews of Beethoven also developed an unusual descriptive vocabulary, one that seemed to mirror the imagery of natural violence that so coloured the rhetorical experience of the French Revolution. Volcanic eruptions were depicted as expressions of popular will; thunderstorms became emanations of revolutionary justice: for Robespierre and his acolytes, little of the destructive, terrifying capacity of nature was beyond allegorical use. This vocabulary was thus pregnant with revolutionary meaning, and the "volcanic" and "thunderous" aspects of perceived Beethovenian rhetoric soon became entrenched in critical discourse. The result was a compelling portrait of revolutionary politics in music.' (351) Cf. John J. Haag, 'Beethoven, the revolution in music and the French Revolution: music and politics in Austria', in Kinley Brauer and William E. Wright, eds, *Austria in the age of the French Revolution*, 1990, 107–24.

Chapter 28: Narrator versus Hero

Page 378

our little friend: DJ, VIII, 52.

silly sword: Ibid., IV, 37.

real thought: Ibid., III, 41.

calmest mood: Ibid., IV, 39.

savage mood: Ibid., III, 53.

mildest manner'd Lambro: Ibid., 41.

cool old sworder: Ibid., IV, 49.

cut down: Ibid., 49, 58.

hero's grave: Ibid., 79.

Page 379

John Jackson: Cecil Y. Lang, 'Narcissus Jilted: Byron, Don Juan, and the Biographical Imperative', Jerome J. McGann, ed., *Historical Studies and Literary Criticism*, Madison, 1985, 143–79.

stealth: DJ, V, 8.

next Juan stood: Ibid., 10.

all men's lot: Ibid., 25.

feminine in feature: Ibid., VIII, 52

knew not why: Ibid., 29.

dizzy, busy: Ibid., 33.

cut and come again: Ibid., 35.

upon reflection: Ibid., VIII, 39.

body of men: Ibid., 38, 41.

Page 380

forty-seven in 1797: see Appendix 5, 'Johnson the Boxer'.

doppelgänger; cf. Ch. 14, 'Parental Feelings'.

knowledge, at least, is gained: DJ, V, 23.

wrong or right: Ibid., VII, 46.

one direction: Ibid., 48.

scoffing tendency: Ibid., 3.

Page 381

maxims: Ibid., 58.

jesting, pondering: Ibid., VII, 55.

Page 382

he was a poet: Ibid., VIII, 133n.

Prince Potemkin: Ibid., VII, 40.

as Suwarrow calls Juan: Ibid., 62.

like an ass: Ibid., VIII, 29.

ignorance of danger: Ibid., 36.

Page 383

one of the party: Moore, I, 25.

looked very well: Recollections, I, 157.

Johnson as Jack: Ibid., 41, 97.

nicknames for Napoleon: To James Cazenove, 23 July 1815.

insipid medium: Journal, 19 April 1814

trite medium: *Lara*, VIII

Page 384

to its will: *Corsair*, VIII, 182ff.

hit-man: Cochran Burning, 64. See further, 'Being Byron's Banker', Cochran Burning, 57–70.

a bust of Napoleon: Recollections, II, 176.

Chapter 29: Intellectual Lordship

Page 385

a welcome guest: EBSR, 255ff.

Memorandum Books: STC Letters, II, 583.

for light: STC to Unknown Correspondent, 10 April [May?] 1816, in Earl Leslie Griggs, ed., *Collected Letters of Samuel Taylor Coleridge*, 6 Vol, 1959, IV, 621.

Page 386

even greenish: Hanneke Grootenboer, *Treasuring the Gaze: Intimate Vision in Late Eighteenth-Century Eye Miniatures*, 2012, 160.

siege from bailiffs: AR, 225.

a Committee man: To STC, 18 October 1815.

Page 388

undoubted genius: *British Review*, viii, in STC Heritage, 226.

Page 389

cowardly assassination: BL, 233.

pantomime of that name: Ibid., 216.

impersonated abstractions: Ibid., 213.

the Satan of Milton: Ibid., 214.

means without an end: Ibid., 219.

Page 390

good or evil: Considerations, 766.

over twenty years: Cf. chapter 12, 'Satan and Reality'.

Page 391

reviewers and readers: Boyd, 36.

Lord Byron: To STC, 18 October 1815.

Page 392

on Lord Byron: Essays on His Times, 443.

calling him drunk: DJ, I, 205.

extravagance of [his] praise: Coleridge Letters, IV, 948, in Cochran Burning, 327.

in rerum natura: *Specimens of the Table Talk*, 1884, 16.

the only guide: Smeed, 37.

Page 393

superior being: BL, 217.

St Helena: Ronald Paulson, *Representations of Revolution (1789–1820)*, 1983, 280.

Goethe's Mephistopheles: DJ, XIII, 7.

Page 394

The Byronic Hero: Thorslev, 108.

human conception: HVSV, 440.

the human race: Considerations, Ch. XXVI, at http://oll.libertyfund.org/titles/l-considerations-on-the-principal-events-of-the-french-revolution-lf-ed?q=the+human+race#Stael_1459_57

daemonic by nature: *Conversations of Goethe with Eckermann and Soret*, trans. John Oxenford, 2 Vols, 1850, 2 March 1831, II, 359.

Kean in Othello: transcr. from the MS in Murray's archive at https://pastnow.wordpress.com/2014/06/03/june-3-1814-caroline-lamb-writes-to-lord-byron-again/

De L'Allemagne: Douglass, 63.

of which he complains: *De L'Allemagne*, 9.

he scarce knew whither: DJ, XII, 49.

a trimmer: Ibid., III, 86.

imp upon earth: Ibid., I, 25.

a page: Ibid., 54.

dressed for war: Ibid., IX, 44f.

Page 395

enter his head: Brophy, 108.

sprightly as a page: DJ, 1, 54.

as he told Medwin: Medwin, 165.

from North to South: DJ, VI, 27.

Page 396

growing dull: Ibid., IV, 10.

he never found: CH, IV, 181n.

you know not what: DT, Pt. III, Text of Fragment, 59ff.

Almaviva sighs: 'Il est si doux d'être aimé pour soi-même!', Pierre-Augustin de Beaumarchais, *Le barbier de Seville*, 1775, I, 2.

Page 397

without meaning: BL, 216f.

Page 398

means without an end: Ibid., 219.
blushed that he begot him: DJ, VIII, 110.
Arnold and then Caesar: Ibid., 110, variant l.879.
remote scoffer: Ibid., VII, 3.
mere spectator: DT, II, ii, 56; DJ, XIII, 7.
just now to gaze: Ibid., Pt. II, ii, 60ff; DJ, XIII, 7.
mock the mightiest: Ibid., Pt. I, i, 118, 129.
the Age of Bronze: Age of Bronze, V, 139.
Caesar or nothing: Journal, 23 November 1813.
idler hours: DT, Pt. I, ii, 320f.

Page 399

the heroic crowd: Ibid., Pt. II, ii, 1ff.

Part Twelve

Page 401

his ascetic diet: Angler, 197f.

Chapter 30: Thin, Thinner, Thinnest

Page 403

funeral ceremonies: Beaton, 217.
stupid long swim: To JCH, mid-December.
blistered skin: BLJ, 9, 197, n.3.
misfortune: Guiccioli, 482.

Page 404

his liaison: Hobhouse Diary, 19 September 1822, ed. Peter Cochran, https://petercochran.files.wordpress.com/2009/12/30-18221.pdf
who was not ill: Blessington, 86.
glorious blunder: DJ, XI, 3.

Page 405

liver & what not: To DK, 1 December 1822.
in my youth: To AL, 12 December 1822.

Page 406

a bottle of ale: To DK [9 December 1822?].

to regain his liberty: HVSV, 353.

only to destroy: *The Island*, I, viii.

He stood: Ibid,, III, iv and elsewhere I, iii; IV, xi.

Page 407

glory or its grief: Ibid., II, ix.

Elysian and effeminate: Ibid., xiii.

infant's world: Ibid., vii.

energies: Ibid.

mellow hill: Ibid., IV, viii.

Page 408

Don Juan, Canto II: Robinson, 13, 237–40.

all the people on it: HVSV, 375.

Liberty & Live: Introduction, Blessington, 35.

Page 409

two courses: DJ, XV, 69.

compromised: Ibid., XVI, 12.

ere his time: Ibid., I, 1.

thing of air: Ibid., 23.

formed of clay: Ibid., XVI, Song, 2.

petrified: Ibid., 22.

stood: Ibid., 23.

half his strength: Ibid., 25.

his mind was posed; Ibid., 28.

Page 410

surveyed him: Ibid., 30, 31.

the better of him: Ibid., 51.

great banquet: Ibid., XV, 78.

materialised: Ibid., 90.

Page 411

greater glory: Ibid., XV, 63.

haunch of venison: Ibid., 65.

truffles: Ibid., 66.

Page 412

petits puits: Ibid., 68.

ridicule them: Ibid., 107.

corporal quaking: Ibid., 118.

glowing bust: Ibid., 122.

wan and worn: Ibid., XVII, 14.

Fitz-Fulke: Ibid., 123.

Page 413

second course: Ibid., XV, 68n.

Chapter 31: Starved to Death

Page 414

cruelly calumniated: To J. J. Coulmann, [7?] July 1823.

Page 415

in America: Ibid.

useless rascals away: Moore, I, 177.

Page 416

fifty guineas: Introduction, Blessington, 37.

pocket: Kennedy, 316.

Page 417

addressed him as 'Massa': Parry, 157.

according to Trelawny: Records, 220.

Page 418

sooner: *Sardanapalus*, III, i, 143.

never made to hack: MWSL, I, 384–5; cf. Maud Howe Elliott, *Lord Byron's Helmet*, 1927.

Page 419

Burton ale: James Hamilton Browne, 'Voyage to Cephalonia from Leghorn with Lord Byron, and a Narrative of a Visit, in 1823, to the Seat of War in Greece', *Blackwood's Magazine*, Vol. 35, January 1834, 129.

in *Childe Harold*: CH, II, 67ff; 48 (l.4233)n.

to receive them: Browne, 66.

Byron's dollars: Trelawny, in HVSV, 402.

Page 421

a huge tin-case of them: HVSV, 418f.

never without it: Ibid., 417.

swizzle: Ibid., 420.

conviviality: BLJ, VI, 428.

drank freely: Millingen, 7.

Page 422

glasses of hock: Stanhope, 518.

March of Events: To JCH, 11 September 1823; Manuscrit, 136.

for some time: Journal, 17 October 1823.

electrify the troops: HVSV, 486.

Stanhope commented: Stanhope, 109.

vexation: Ibid., 21.

according to Byron: To Hancock, 7 February 1824.

Page 423

Plaid Jackets: Marchand III, 1098n.

Scotch bonnet: Millingen, 4.

Page 424

allocating his funds: Millingen, 94.

the usual pills: Ibid., 8.

Page 425

his soldiers: Parry, 24.

more than on food: Ibid., 88.

in Teresa's words: Guiccioli, II, 56.

the father of all the Greeks: AR, 400.

public benefactor: Millingen, 145.

our friend: Gamba, 267.

various figures: Millingen, 90.

cavalcade: Parry, 76.

silver epaulettes: Medwin, Angler, II, 200ff.

Page 426

14 January: Stanhope, 79.

nor tyranny can blight: CH, IV, 126.

allurements to him: Gamba, 111.

in 1808: William Mitford, *History of Greece*, 1808, I, 232.

at Harrow: To FH, 18 November 1808.

1798: Prothero, II, 330.

Page 427

safe retreat: Gamba, 94.

stone walls: To Samuel Barff, 26 March 1824.

Page 428

better days of Greece: CH, II, 47.

a romantic illusion; Journal, 17 October 1823.

animosities: Millingen, 91.

pay and dignity: Gamba, 165.

their families: Ibid., 168.

leader: George Finlay, *History of Greece*, 2 Vols, 1861, II, 24.

or Apoplectic: To Samuel Barff, 21 February 1824.

went into convulsions: Parry, 43.

such as Pietro: Gamba, 172.

Page 429

shaggy capote: CH, II, 253f.

Library, Athens: cf. Guy Evans, 'Byron's Albanians', *The Byron Journal*, vol. 5, 1977, 97f, cred. Dr Frank Walton, former dir.

not to pay me: To Mrs B, 12 November 1809.

generous diet: Parry, 45.

Dr Bruno agreed: Ibid., 44f.

held Parry responsible: Nicolson, 247f.

Page 430

staunched the blood: Millingen, 118.

beloved Greece: Parry, 46.

as well as dieting: Nicolson, 248.

out of epilepsy: Stanhope, 519.

a grinning idiot: Millingen, 120.

hourly afflicted him: Ibid., 119.

Page 431

kept up with the horses: AR, 414.

and all obey: *Corsair*, I, 75ff.

his favourite cause: Parry, 97.

Page 432

death or victory: Millingen, 121f.

every prisoner saved: Parry, 54.

Page 433

truly sublime: Stanhope, 537.

follow extremes: Gamba, 192.

or Scotland: To CH, 10 March 1824.

strong dose of medicine: Moore II, 481.

further reduced: Parry, 87.

Page 434

no nourishment whatever: Ibid., 118.

abstemious mode of life: Gamba, 245; Parry, 109f.

arrow-root: Gamba, 246.

or go mad: Ibid., 250.

Page 435

incoherent manner: Millingen, 132f.

excessive debility: Parry, 119n.

starved to death: Ibid., 132.

before his death: Blaquière, 118.

malaria: Costas Tsiamis, Evangelia-Theophano Piperaki, George Kalantzis, Effie Poulakou-Rebelakou, Nikolaos Tompros, Eleni Thalassinou, Chara Spiliopoulou, Athanassios Tsakris at https://www.researchgate.net publication /282185831_Lord_Byron's_death_A_case_of_late_malarial_relapse

neurosyphilis: D. Mellor, 'Was Byron's terminal illness a form of neurosyphilis?' *Byron Journal*, 34, 2006, 127–36.

he is responsible: Parry, 133.

Page 436

to the last: Millingen, 141.

undertaken by man: Graham, 352.

follow my example, etc etc: Moore, II, 191; Gamba, 255.

Appendices

Appendix 1

Page 439

particularly soap: Wadd, 21

two years: Ibid., 22

Page 440

reached the age of seventy-three: Byron asked Murray to send him a copy on 5 and on 14 September 1812.

even moderate fat: To TM, 7 July 1815.

exercises for them: DT, 89 [repeated].

impartial enthusiasm: Sir John Sinclair, Bart., *The Code of Health and Longevity: Or, A Concise View of the Principles Calculated for the Preservation of Health, and the Attainment of Long Life*, 2 Vols, 1807, I, 15.

Page 441

in cold water: Sinclair, I, 576.

prevented colds: See Appendix 3 and Sinclair, II, 99.

meat in Lent: To TM, 9 April 1814; to SBD, 25 March 1814.

Page 442

first diet in 1807: To EP, 5 July 1807.

light supper in 1814: To LM, 28 May 1814.

record the fact: AL to LyB, 19 January 1816, Wilma Paterson, *Lord Byron's Relish*, 1990, 26.

soups in Italy: AR, 272.

did eat mutton: To JM [9 December 1822].

January, 1811: To FH, 20 January 1811.

meat by March: To JCH, 5 March 1811.

broth & rice: AL to LyB, 21 January 1816, Wilma Paterson, *Lord Byron's Relish*, 1990, 65.

seasickness in Don Juan: DJ, II, 12.

in the same canto: Ibid., II, 17.

summer of 1817: Moore, II, 53.

eat meat regularly: See Chapter 12.

beef was tough: RJ, 24 January 1821.

in February 1822: To John Hay, 6 February 1822.

year would be fatal: Origo, 325.

a day of abstinence: William Fletcher to James Kennedy, 19 May 1824, Kennedy, 371.

Page 443

adapted to labour: Sir John also objected that 'the worst property in animal food, is its viscidity or glariness.' Sinclair I, 428.

acuteness of judgement: Ibid., I, 423.

Joseph Ritson: Colin Spencer, *The Heretic's Feast, A History of Vegetarianism*, 1993, 233; cf. William Nisbet, *A Practical Treatise on Diet, and on the Most Salutary and Agreeable Means of Supporting Life and Health, by Aliment and Regimen*, 1801, 11.

disease, and crime: *Queen Mab*, VIII, 215–18.

amidst equals: Ibid., VIIII, 225ff.

eight months: Ibid., Appendix, 27.

much approved of: Sir John Sinclair, Bart, M.P., *A Collection of Papers on the Subject of Athletic Exercises, etc*, 1806, 17.

Page 444

exaggerating: Elwin, 285.

red mullet every day: To FH, 20 January 1811.

lobster claw in 1811: 'Comments in Hobhouse's Imitations (1811)', Nicolson, 209.

sturgeon: Journal, 30 November 1813.

digestion of fish: Sinclair, I, 411.

in the morning: Moore, I, 398.

fish and champagne: JCH Recollections, V, 158.

Brahminical in his eating: Hunt, 2.

some carp: To JM, 7 September 1814.

Clitumnus: To JM, 4 June 1817.

solitary vice: DJ, XIII.

a good man: Ibid., 106n.

Page 445

Ate it: RJ, 26 January 1821.

sardines in Genoa: Records, 216.

discomposed him: Blessington, 86.

Page 446

raise his spirits: Journal, 22 November 1813.

after dinner: Charles Skinner Matthews to Miss I. M., 22 May 1809, Moore, I, 134.

drinks like a man: DT, 93.

Page 447

Clos Vougeot: To AM, 16 December 1814; T. A. J. Burnett, *The Rise and Fall of a Regency Dandy: The Life and Times of Scrope Berdmore Davies*, 1981, 55.

at one draught: To LM, 17 October 1813.

claret ever affected him: Journal, 28 March 1814.

rum punch in Venice: To TM, 24 December 1816.

soda-water in Don Juan: DJ, II,180.

gin-punch by his side: Malmesbury, Memoirs of an Ex-Minister, 2 Vol, 1884, I, 32.

Bordeaux wine: James Hamilton Browne, HVSV, 428f.

of the family: G. J. Monson-Fitzjohn, *Drinking Vessels of Bygone Days from the Neolithic Age to the Georgian Period*, 1927, 80.

Page 448

good of their kind: To DK, 18 January 1823.

it was unhealthy: cf. A.F.M.Willich, *Lectures on Diet and Regimen*, 4th edn, 1809, 216f; Alexander Thomson, M.D., *The Family Physician*, 1801, 46; Robert Thomas, M.D., *The Way to Preserve Good Health, Invigorate a Delicate Constitution, and Attain an Advanced Age*, 1822, 14.

the crumb: Dr James Adair, *Essay on Diet and Regimen*, 2nd edn, London 1812, and cf. Sinclair, I, 448.

always cut himself: Isaac Nathan, *Fugitive Pieces and Reminiscences of Lord Byron*, London, 1829, 94.

prefer biscuit: Sinclair, II, 101.

flatulence: Sinclair, I, 445f, 448.

six biscuits a day: Journal, 17 November 1813.

fond of biscuits: Nathan, 89.

delighted: Ibid., 90.

supplied every week: AR, 273f.

Page 449

on his diet: RJ, 12 January 1821.

magnesia he indulged in: JCH Recollections, II, 279.

twenty-two dozen bottles: Bohun Lynch, *The Prize Ring*, 1925, 33n.

scream has died away: JCH to AL, in https://petercochran.files.wordpress.com/2009/02/07-switzerland-18162.pdf

pounds of soda-powder: e.g. to JM, 18 June 1817 (specifying 'Burkitt's Soda-powders') and to JCH, 19 May 1818.

cockles at supper: RJ, 27 February 1821.

in Summer by the dozens: To JM, 21 April 1821.

fifty bottles of Cognac: AR, 376.

its spirit out: DJ, XVI, 10.

Page 450

Zoonomia: Erasmus Darwin, *Zoonomia, or The Laws of Organic Life*, 2 Vols, 1796, II, 32.

8 January 1821: RJ, 8 January 1821.

including the Bottles: Douglas A. Simmons, *Schweppes, The First 200 Years*, 1983, 26.

Leicester-Square in London: Sinclair I, Appendix II, 12.

the present age: Ibid., 14.

ulcerated state: Ibid., 12

Stone in the Kidney: To JCH, 10 February 1812.

nephritic disorder: Galt, 244.

urethra by 1819: To JM, 12 August 1819.

fat more fluid: Sinclair, I, 391.

Page 451

unhealthy flesh: in Sir John Sinclair, 'A Collection of Papers, on the Subject of Athletic Exercises etc. etc.', *A Code of Health and Longevity*, 4 Vols, 1806, II, 25.

nearest to biscuit: Ibid., 391, 430

aid in slimming: Wadd, 20.

a little rice: Moore, I, 184.

as Wadd confirms: Wadd, 30.

before Rogers's dinner: Markham, 98.

bedevilled [his] digestion: To Samuel Rogers [May, 1813?].

Appendix 3

Page 464

to be a boy: AL, 11 December 1815, Alexander Larman, *Byron's Women*, 2016, 322.

the Nothing of a Name: 'Churchill's Grave', 43.

sin and fear: *Heaven and Earth*, I, 3, 386. Cf. Astarte, *Manfred*, II, iv, 139ff; Angiolina, *Marino Faliero*; Aurora Raby, *Don Juan*.

Page 465

for her parents: Elwin Family, 9.

King John: To TM, 5 January 1816.

annals of the Byrons: Violet M. Walker, rev. and compl. Margaret J. Howell, *The House of Byron, A History of the Family from the Norman Conquest, 1066–1988*, 1988, 202.

story ever since: Fiona MacCarthy, *Byron Life and Legend*, 2002, 261.

Scottish kings: To Hanson, 4 August 1811: 'The Earl of Huntly & the Lady Jean Stewart daughter of James 1st of Scotland were the progenitors of Mrs Byron'. And cf. Marchand, 7, 196, n.7.

to seduce him: A. A. M. Duncan, 'Scotland, The Making of the Kingdom', *The Edinburgh History of Scotland*, ed. Gordon Donaldson, 4 Vols, 1975, I, 175.

Page 466

before he was eight: To JM, 9 October 1821.

Childe Harold: CH, I, 826f.

and Selim: *The Bride of Abydos*, 12, 686.

death of Abel: *Der tod Abels*, 1758, trans. Mary Collyer, 1761, in Elwin, 282.

Page 467

is to be placed: Sir Richard Clayton, *A Critical Inquiry into the Life of Alexander the Great, by the Ancient Historians: from the French of the Baron De St. Croix: with Notes and Observations*, 1793, 38.

compiled in 1807: Nicolson Prose, 3.

the whole province: Arrian, *History of the Expedition of Alexander the Great, and Conquest of Persia*, trans. John Rooke, 1812, Ch. XXIV, 28.

of a similar cast: To John Galt, 11 December 1813.

Diodorus Siculus: G. Booth, *The Historical Library of Diodorus the Sicilian, in Fifteen Books to which are added The Fragments of Diodorus*, 2 Vols, 1814, Vol. II, Book XVI, chapter XI, 137; Book XVII, Chapter II, 177.

Quintus Curtius Rufus: Quintus Curtius Rufus, *The History of The Life and Reign of Alexander the Great*, trans. Peter Pratt, 2 Vols, 1809, I, Bk II, Chapter VIII, 232ff.

Page 468

magnanimous school: Pratt, I, iii

Alexander's example: CH, III, 41.

royal history: Ada, Countess of Huntingdon, gave birth around 1146 to a daughter, Ada of Scotland, who married Floris (Florence) III, Count of Holland. Genesis also mentions that 'Esau took his wives from the daughters of Canaan: Adah the daughter of Elon the Hittite; Aholibamah the daughter of Anah, the daughter of Zibeon the Hivite; and Basemath, Ishmael's daughter, sister of Nebajoth' (Genesis 36: 1–3). According to the Tudor historian Raphael Holinshed, Ada, the eldest son of Ida, the Saxon who became king of Kent in 547, succeeded his father and reigned seven years. Another Ada was one of the sisters of Aurelius Ambrose, King of Britaine. She was 'maried unto Conranus, generall (as is said) of the Scotish armie. Howbeit she lived not past two yeares after, but died in trauell of child, which also died with the mother'. *Holinshed's Chronicles of England, Scotland, and Ireland*, 6 Vols, I–III, 1807; IV–VI, 1808; Vol. I, 583f; Vol. V, 149.

it's royalty: To Douglas Kinnaird, 2 February 1821.

the name of Ada: Henry Nugent Bell, The Huntingdon Peerage, 1820, 4–5; Andrew Nicolson, ed., *The Letters of John Murray to Lord Byron*, 2007, 358, n.16.

and his name: Ada Reis, I, 2.

Page 469

their enterprises: Ada Reis, I, 1.

below mankind: Ibid., I, 43.

ceased to be religious: Ibid., II, 40.

Lady Caroline: Mary O'Connell, *Byron and John Murray: A Poet and His Publisher*, 2014, 110.

humble in themselves: Ada Reis, I, Introduction, xvi.

Page 470

every vice: Ibid., II, 26.

ACKNOWLEDGEMENTS

Peter Conrad, Christopher Butler and John Buxton taught me to think about Byron while Dr and Mrs Croft enabled me to research the topic. I owe an immense professional and personal debt to Professor Marchand's work on Byron and also to the house of John Murray, Byron's original publishers, whose archives are now housed at the National Libraries of Scotland, where they are being catalogued. I am grateful to the archivists there, David McClay and Kirsty McHugh. I was fortunate to benefit from the knowledge and generous enthusiasm of John Murray VI and his wife Virginia, an exemplary archivist.

Peter Cochran (1944–2015) was a friend and colleague, who shared an encyclopedic knowledge of Byron in heated conversation and in twenty books on the subject. He earned nothing from his books and it is a pity his publisher makes them prohibitively expensive. I miss Peter's independence and caustic willingness to go against uncritical consensus. His well-maintained website https://petercochran.wordpress.com/ covers many topics apart from Byron and is as indispensable as it is entertaining.

My book crosses well-trodden territory, in terms of Byron, but also of Milton, Napoleon, Shelley and Coleridge. I hope I have acknowledged my debt to scholars in the notes: for the most part their names do not appear in the body of the book. As the credits piled up, reading the cluttered text felt like entering an awkward surprise party, to encounter all too many familiar faces. Perhaps because I am not looking for tenure, this book is about Byron, rather than 'Byron Studies'.

Subsidy from Howard Hodgkin's print *For Antony* has enabled illustrations to enhance points made in the text. I am very grateful to the owners of the copyright for allowing me to reproduce them, to those named in the text and anonymous collectors, and to Guy Robertson, Matthew Burdis, Christine Kenyon-Jones, Alex Alec-Smith and Tomasz Iżycki for help in researching them.

Libraries and their staff have played a major role in the creation of this book and I wish to pay tribute to the Bodleian and Christ Church Libraries, the British Library, the German Historical Institute, Keats House, the David Sassoon Library, Mumbai, and, above all, the London Library in St James's Square, which is privately funded and an excellent resource for anyone interested in reading. The fact that you can enter the stacks means that serendipity contributes to scholarship.

IN COMMEMORATION

Maria Bjornson
Wilfrid Blunt
Dr Luther Brady
William Brooker
Patrick Caulfield
Bruce Chatwin
Charles Correa
Gilbert de Botton
William Delafield
Clifford & Rosemary Ellis
Bunny & Philip Fellows
Margery Fry
Kadarijah Gardiner
Francis Golding
Max Gordon
Lawrence Gowing
Charles Handley-Read
Seamus Heaney
Ann Hodgkin
Eliot and Mimi Hodgkin
Gordon House
John Hoyland
Pat Kavanagh
Bhupen Khakhar
Barbara Lloyd
Colin McMordie
Sally Morphet
Foy Nissen
Alex Peattie
Jonathan Peattie
Mirza Peattie
Robert Rosenblum
Larry Rubin
John Russell and Rosamond Bernier
Keith Sachs
Michael Seifert
Colin Sharp
Andrea Signorello
Susan Sontag
David Sylvester
Bob Thomson
Dr Margret Tönnesmann
James Tower
Stuart Cary Welch
Henry Wimbourne
Theo Zinn
Diana Zvegintsov

Unbound is the world's first crowdfunding publisher, established in 2011.

We believe that wonderful things can happen when you clear a path for people who share a passion. That's why we've built a platform that brings together readers and authors to crowdfund books they believe in – and give fresh ideas that don't fit the traditional mould the chance they deserve.

This book is in your hands because readers made it possible. Everyone who pledged their support is listed below. Join them by visiting unbound.com and supporting a book today.

Geoff Adams
Alex Alec-Smith
Steve Allison
A. I. Amin & M. Spillane
Giti Amirani
Carina Andres Thalmann
Morgan Bale
Charles Barclay
Andy Barker
Julian Barnes
David Barrable
James Barron
Bath Spa University
Tracey Beresford-Brealey
Rosamond Bernier
Sara Bickley
Luther W. Brady
James Broomfield
Andrew Butler-Wheelhouse
Charles Butt
Tom Cairns
Vikrant/Claudio Chaudhery Koster
Marinus Christ
Marco Compagnoni
Philip Connor
Richard Connor
Caroline Conran
Philip Constantinidi
Jay & Elizabeth Cooper
Stephen Cooper
Beth Coventry
Sharon DeLano
Declan Donnellan
Kevin Donnellon
Marie Donnelly
Ivan Donovan

Jenny Doughty
Selina Fellows
James Fenton
Ted Few
Stephen Freiberg
Gagosian Gallery
Christopher Garratt
Susan Godfrey
Norman Goodman
Monica Greig
Paul Griffiths
Kit Grover
Tricia Guild
Jacqueline Hartnett
George Hayburn
Kevin Henson
Bruce Heyhoe
Simon Hopkinson
Jane E G Horovitch
Anabel Hudson
Penny Hull
Perdita Hunt
Elisabeth Ingles
Ri Iyovwaye
Jarndyce Books
Donald Johnston
Barbara Jones
Nikolas Byron Kashmen
Philip Katz
Christina Kennedy
Christine Kenyon Jones
Dan Kieran
Gyr King
Simon Kingston
Patrick Kinmonth
Doreen Knight
Nirmalya Kumar
William Lapthorn
Caroline Lever
Paul Levy
Robert Littman
Peter Liversidge
Fiona Maddocks
Peter and Helen Malone
Adam Mars-Jones
Jane Martineau
Edward McKirdy
Dee McQuillan
Sebastian A. Melmoth
James Meyer
Henry and Alison Meyric Hughes
Julian Mitchell
John Mitchinson
Susan Moore and David Ekserdjian
Richard Morphet
Milo F. S. Morris
David Moses
Carlo Navato
Nonie Niesewand
Satish Padiyar
Sarah Patmore
Nicholas and Linda Payne
Ralph Payne
Sebastian and Frances Payne
Sebastian Peattie
Jackie Peker

Claire Penhallurick
Carmen Perez-Seoane
Justin Pollard
Rhian Heulwen Price
Haydn Rees
Sandra Rennie
Jonathan Ressler
Frankie Rossi
Piers Russell-Cobb
Katherine and Keith Sachs
Dr. Robert and Malyne Sagerman
Teraza Salmon
Suhrid & Asha Sarabhai
Alex Sarll
Charles Saumarez Smith
Sabine Scharnagl
Karsten Schubert
Ruth Scurr
Michael Seifert & Caroline Conran
Praful Shah
Sara Stewart
John-Paul Stonard
Nina Stutler
Mahrukh Tarapor
Roger Thomas
Joanne Thomson
Sabine Tilly
Colin Tweedy
Robin Vousden
Nick Walker
Simone Warner
Sarah Whitfield
Oliver Wingate
Andrew Wyatt

INDEX

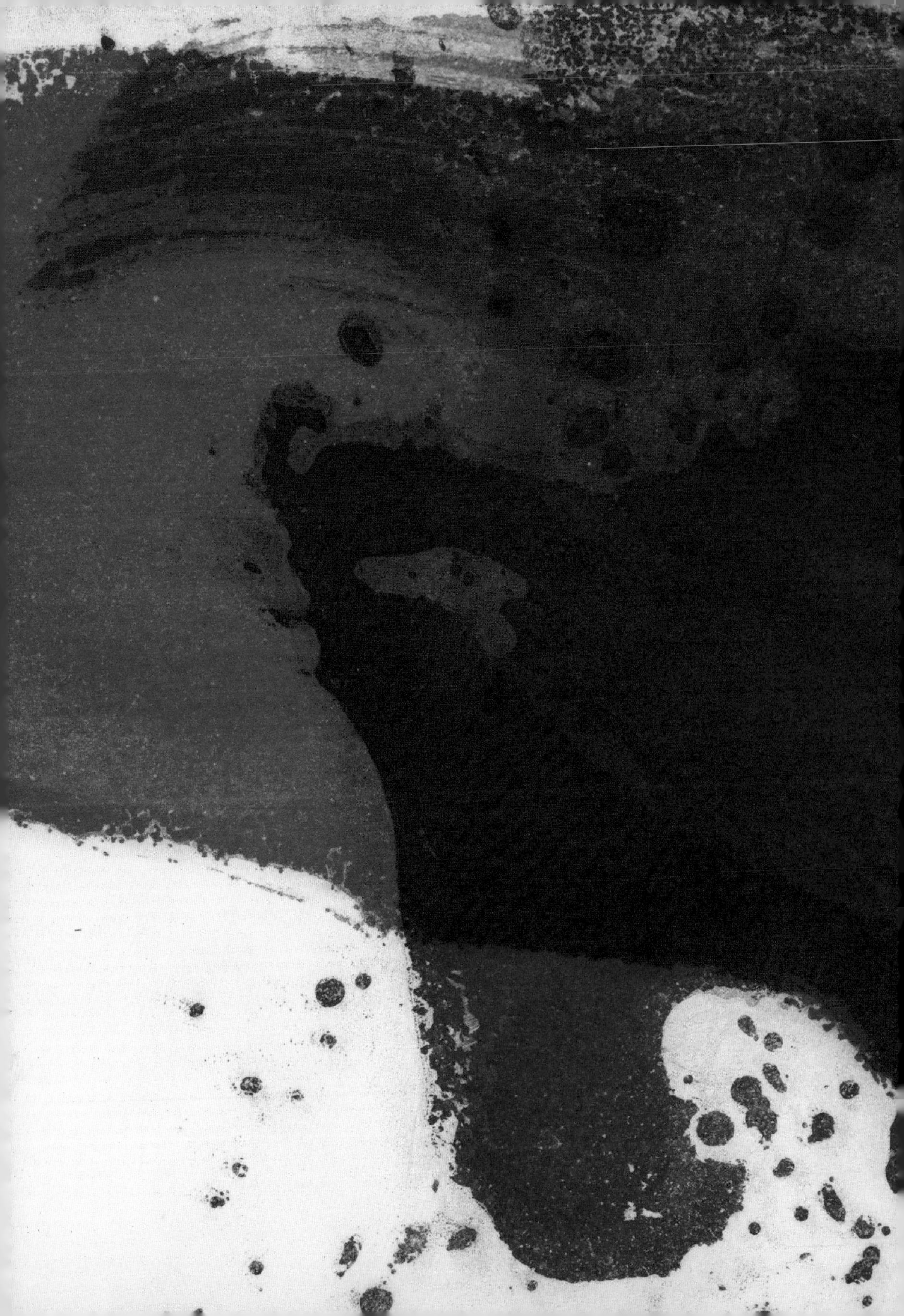